AF479238

RABBINIC NARRATIVE:
A DOCUMENTARY PERSPECTIVE
VOLUME III

THE BRILL REFERENCE LIBRARY OF JUDAISM

Editors

J. NEUSNER (*Bard College*) — H. BASSER (*Queens University*)

A.J. AVERY-PECK (*College of the Holy Cross*) — Wm.S. GREEN (*University of Rochester*) — G. STEMBERGER (*University of Vienna*) — I. GRUENWALD (*Tel Aviv University*) — M. GRUBER (*Ben-Gurion University of the Negev*)

G.G. PORTON (*University of Illinois*) — J. FAUR (*Bar Ilan University*)

VOLUME 16

RABBINIC NARRATIVE:
A DOCUMENTARY PERSPECTIVE

Volume Three:
Forms, Types and Distribution
of Narratives in Song of Songs Rabbah and
Lamentations Rabbah and a Reprise of Fathers
According to Rabbi Nathan Text A

BY

JACOB NEUSNER

BRILL
LEIDEN · BOSTON
2003

This book is printed on acid-free paper.

Library of Congress Cataloging-in-Publication Data

Neusner, Jacob, 1932-
Rabbinic narrative : a documentary perspective / by Jacob Neusner
        v. cm.—(The Brill reference library of Judaism, ISSN 1566-1237 ; v. 16)
        Includes bibliographical references and index.
        Contents: v. 1 Forms, types, and distribution of narratives in the Mishnah, Tractate
Abot, and the Tosefta—v. 2. Forms, types, and distribution of narratives in Sifra,
Sifré to Numbers, and Sifré to Deuteronomy. v. 3. Forms, Type, and Distribution of
Narratives in Song of Songs Rabbah and Lamentations rabbah and a Reprise of fathers
According to Rabbi Nathan Text A v. 4. The precedent and the parable in diachronic
view.
        ISBN 90-04-13023-3 (v. 1. alk. paper)— ISBN 90-04-13034-9 (v. 2. alk. paper)—
        ISBN 90-04-13035-7 (v. 3. alk. paper)— ISBN 90-04-13036-5 (v. 4. alk. paper)
        1. Mishnah—Criticism, Narrative. 2. Narration in rabbinical literature. 3. Rabbinical literature-
        History and criticism. 4. Midrash—History and criticism. 5. Parables in rabbinical literature.
        I. Title II. Series.
BM496.9 .N37 N48 2003
296.1/2066 dc21   2003050220
                                                                             CIP

ISSN   1566-1237
ISBN   90 04 13035 7

PRINTED IN THE NETHERLANDS

CONTENTS

PART ONE

NARRATIVES IN SONGS OF SONGS RABBAH
FORMS, TYPES AND DISTRIBUTION

PART TWO

NARRATIVES IN LAMENTATIONS RABBAH
FORMS, TYPES AND DISTRIBUTION

PART THREE

NARRATIVES IN THE FATHERS ACCORDING TO RABBI NATHAN
TEXT A: FORMS AND TYPES IN COMPARISON WITH THE FATHERS

PREFACE

Rabbinic documents encompass narratives along with expository, exegetical, and analytical writing, a fact established in volume one for the Mishnah and the Tosefta and in volume two for Sifra and the two Sifrés.[1] I demonstrate that same fact here for two important Rabbah-Midrash-compilations, Song of Songs Rabbah and Lamentations Rabbah, as well as for a systematic recapitulation of an early Rabbinic compilation, tractate Abot, the Fathers, by a later one, Abot deR. Natan, the Fathers According to Rabbi Nathan.[2] This completes the probe required to answer the question that precipitated the work: do narratives form part of the distinctive literary repertoire of particular documents in all their singularity, or do they qualify only as extra-documentary writing? For the documents treated in this study, the probe yields this result: *the fulcrum of interpretation and analysis, for narrative as much as for all other kinds of canonical writing in formative Judaism, is the document.*

To unpack this proposition: narratives constitute a coherent sector of Rabbinic documentary writing, with their own definitive traits, inductively discerned. These indicative traits of narrative moreover characterize one document, and not another, e.g. narratives in the Tosefta not in the Mishnah, or more commonly, those of one group of documents, and not those of some other group formed by shared documentary traits, e.g., the Mishnah and the Tosefta but not Sifra and the two Sifrés. Here we learn that Song of Songs Rabbah prefers the exegetical parable, Lamentations Rabbah lays a heavy burden on authentic narratives, and Fathers According to R. Nathan Text A lays stress on a particular type of narrative, with its own traits

---

[1] Continuing *Rabbinic Narrative: A Documentary Perspective.* volume one. *Forms, Types, and Distribution of Narratives in the Mishnah, Tractate Abot, and the Tosefta.* Leiden, 2003: Brill. THE BRILL REFERENCE LIBRARY OF JUDAISM; and *Rabbinic Narrative: A Documentary Perspective.* volume two. *Forms, Types, and Distribution of Narratives in Sifra, Sifré to Numbers, and Sifré to Deuteronomy.* Leiden, 2003: Brill. THE BRILL REFERENCE LIBRARY OF JUDAISM.

[2] A reprise of the findings in my *Judaism and Story: The Evidence of The Fathers According to Rabbi Nathan.* Chicago, 1992: University of Chicago Press. Reprint: Binghamton, 2002: Global Publications, CLASSICS IN JUDAIC STUDIES SERIES.

of rhetoric and topic, to deliver its message. These facts show that narrative types are chosen not arbitrarily but for reasons we can discern—reasons having to do with the task taken up by the compilers of a given document and the writers of its compositions and composites. So this research-report supplies these facts:

(1)   what in the document under examination are the preferred types and forms of Rabbinic narrative?

(2)   how are these classes of narrative distributed across the canonical documents of the formative age that have been examined to this point?

(3)   do the several canonical documents or groups of documents covered by this probe exhibit each its particular preferences for types and forms of narratives and if so, how come?

Why ask about the documentary standing of narratives in particular? An anomaly in the documentary program characteristic of the canonical writings explains why the answers matter. The well-established rule is that the respective Rabbinic compilations from the Mishnah through the Bavli form coherent documents, each distinguished from all others by its particular congeries of indicative traits of rhetoric, logic, and topic.[3] Consequently, if, possessed of a proper knowledge of complete canonical documents, we were handed a coherent piece of unattributed canonical writing of an exegetical, analytical, or expository character—indeed of any type of writing *but* narrative—we should have solid grounds on which to assign that writing to a particular document, whether the Mishnah,[4] whether Song of Songs Rabbah.

But narrative writing does not follow suit. Narratives do not respond to the otherwise prevailing documentary definitions of rhetoric, logic, and topic, respectively. In *Texts without Boundaries*[5] I demonstrate, for a sample of eight documents, that the writing roughly

---

[3] These traits are defined, document by document, in my *Introduction to Rabbinic Literature*. N.Y., 1994: Doubleday, which summarized twenty-five years of systematic research. The sole exception to the rule is Mekhilta attributed to R. Ishmael, where the sub-divisions of the document, the tractates, have to be differentiated from one another.

[4] With the qualification that the Tosefta and the Mishnah overlap.

[5] *Texts without Boundaries. Protocols of Non-Documentary Writing in the Rabbinic Canon*, Lanham MD, 2002: University Press of America. STUDIES IN JUDAISM SERIES. volume one. *The Mishnah, Tractate Abot, and the Tosefta;* volume two. *Sifra and Sifré to Numbers; Texts without Boundaries. Protocols of Non-Documentary Writing in the Rabbinic Canon*, volume three. *Sifré to Deuteronomy and Mekhilta Attributed to R. Ishmael.* volume four. *Leviticus Rabbah.*

classified as narrative ignores the conventional documentary indicators that operate in said documents. The unique congeries of rhetoric, logic, and topic that for the most part dictate the character of the writing in that document and in no other simply do not govern narrative writing located in that same document.[6] And whether or not the narrative writing serves a particular documentary purpose in its specific location(s), it ignores those indicative traits of rhetoric-logic-topic that govern there and nowhere else. Consequently, if we were handed a narrative without indication as to its source, we presently have only a limited[7] basis on which to assign it to one document and not to some other, e.g., to the Mishnah and not to Song of Songs Rabbah.

Now, in these three volumes covering the eight named documents, I ask the documents to reveal their preferences, respectively, as to narrative types and their functions. This we may find out by describing and classifying the narratives contained in each document in sequence. Do the documents provide a clear account of the kinds of narrative (1) they require to accomplish their goals—*and also* (2)

---

[6] That is not to ignore the appearance in more than a single document of some compositions and even composites. First, the volume of peripatetic writing in the aggregate is trivial, as I show in *Extra- and Non-Documentary Writing in the Canon of Formative Judaism. II. Paltry Parallels. The Negligible Proportion and Peripheral Role of Free-Standing Compositions in Rabbinic Documents.* Binghamton 2001: Global Publications. ACADEMIC STUDIES IN THE HISTORY OF JUDAISM SERIES. Second, and more important, in many, many instances in which a composition or composite or even entire chapter appears in two or more documents, we are able by appeal to the characteristic traits of each document to discern to which of the two documents the shared pericope is primary, and to which it is secondary. For example, a passage of the Mishnah cited in Leviticus Rabbah never conforms to the indicative traits of Leviticus Rabbah and always conforms to those of the rest of the Mishnah. More to the point (and more subtly), a protracted passage, an entire parashah, that occurs both in Leviticus Rabbah and Pesiqta deRab Kahana can be shown to be primary to Leviticus Rabbah (conforming to its paramount documentary traits) and secondary to Pesiqta deRab Kahana (not conforming to the otherwise-indicative traits of Pesiqta deRab Kahana). This I show in *From Tradition to Imitation. The Plan and Program of Pesiqta deRab Kahana and Pesiqta Rabbati.* Atlanta, 1987: Scholars Press for Brown Judaic Studies.

[7] Because of the results set forth in volume I, volume II, and here, we can now, in fact, define the narrative protocols that govern in the Mishnah and the Tosefta, Sifra and the two Sifrés, and, as I show in these pages, the two selected Rabbah-compilations of Midrash and The Fathers According to Rabbi Nathan text A. These protocols signal probabilities: a *ma'aseh*/case with certain attributes is very likely to derive from the Mishnah, not Sifré to Deuteronomy, and so on; so too for the *Mashal*/parable, and, most strikingly indeed, the type of narrative matches the documentary program where narratives figure at all as primary to that program.

those not required? This we may discover by comparing and contrasting the repertoire of types of narratives of one document with that of another document, whether kindred (Mishnah/Tosefta) or distinct (Mishnah, Song of Songs Rabbah).

Why do the answers matter for the study of Rabbinic Judaism? At this time we do not know how Rabbinic narratives correlate with the boundaries defined by a particular document—or whether in the Rabbinic canon narratives form a non-documentary corpus of writing altogether. And what is at stake in answering that question is how on the foundations of literary evidence and its traits we are to describe the Rabbinic structure and system. That is because a theory on the way in which the documentary evidence took shape and on how it accomplished its compilers' goals is required for that description. If we do not know whether or how narratives fit into the canonical constructions of Rabbinic Judaism in its formative age and normative statement, we cannot account for important data of that Judaism.[8]

Why then does the historical, literary, and religious study of that Judaism now require investigation of the order and regularity exhibited by narratives in the respective documents? Since narratives assuredly represent a distinct type of writing in the Rabbinic canon, we wonder whether they carry a distinctive message as well. Specifically, do they represent a separate component of the canonical documents in program as well as in form? Or do they cohere to the theological program of the document(s) in which they find their place? That is one way of dealing with the anomaly set forth by narratives in the canonical compilations, a way demanded by the interior logic of the documentary hypothesis.

That problem certainly leaves open a variety of illuminating matters, for example, problems of aesthetics simply are not dealt with here. Issues of "narrativity" and "poetics," important in the literary-theoretical context, do not pertain to the study of problems of religion, its history and theology.[9] To be sure, a definition of "nar-

---

[8] The outcome of lacking such a theory is illustrated in the aimless anthology by Jeffrey L. Rubenstein, *Rabbinic Stories.* Preface by Shaye J. D. Cohen. New York and Mahwah, NJ: Paulist Press, 2002.

[9] One current instance of the aesthetic reading of Rabbinic narrative is Jeffrey L. Rubenstein, *Talmudic Stories: Narrative Art, Composition, and Culture.* Baltimore, 1999: Johns Hopkins University Press. He "strives to recapture the meaning and literary impact that the stories would have had for their original authors and audiences,"

rative" in contrast to all other kinds of writing in the Rabbinic canon is required. But even there, the documentary hypothesis governs the kind of definition that is set forth. Specifically, in the Introduction to, and chapter one of, volume one, the latter devoted to what I call pseudo-narratives, I define what, for the present purpose, I mean by narrative. There I answer the two-sided question of inclusion and exclusion. In those two statements readers will find a full account of my analytical procedures: the questions I systematically raise, item by item, document by document, and how I find answers to them. For those who prefer a brief summary, I supply a precis in the Introduction to this volume, which follows.

What, then, do I claim in this project to prove? I state with heavy emphasis, starting once more from the opening lines of this Preface:

Narratives no less than expository, exegetical, and analytical writing, form part of the documentary self-definition of the Rabbinic canonical writings, a fact established in volume one for the Mishnah and the Tosefta, in volume two for Sifra and the two Sifrés, and here for Song of Songs Rabbah, Lamentations Rabbah, and The Fathers According to Rabbi Nathan Text A. The fulcrum of interpretation and analysis, for narrative as much as for all other kinds of canonical writing in formative Judaism, therefore is the document.[10]

What I show in these three volumes is that the repertoire of narrative forms and types in the documents treated in volumes one and two and here does serve the manifest documentary purposes of the

---

so Eliezer Segal, review, *Journal of American Academy of Religion* 2001, 69:954. Other instances are Yonah Frenkel, *Iyunim be'olamo haruhani shel sipur ha'agadah* (Tel Aviv, 1981), and Ofra Meir, *Hademuyot hapoalot besipure hatalmud vehamidrash* (Jerusalem 1977), and her *Sugyot bapoetikah shel sipure hazal* (Tel Aviv, 1993). My reading of David Stern, *Parables in Midrash. Narrative and Exegesis in Rabbinic Literature*, Catherine Hezser, *Form, Function, and Historical Significance of the Rabbinic Story in Yerushalmi Neziqin*, and Galit Hasan-Rokem, *Web of Life. Folklore and Midrash in Rabbinic Literature* is reproduced in the Appendix of volume one, and of the special problem of the parable in documentary context by Clemens Thoma and his co-workers, in volume two. These represent a vast literature of literary-critical analysis, both classical and contemporary. The answers to the documentary questions of a formal, form-analytical character that I raise in this exercise do not present themselves in that literature, with which I do not intersect.

[10] And that general judgment should not obscure the particular fact that compilations of Rabbinic stories find the majority of their candidates in the Talmud of Babylonia. The majority of the stories assembled by Rubenstein in his anthology (and Cohen in his preface) derive from the Talmud of Babylonia and only from that Talmud, a point of which Rubenstein does not take note. See Rubenstein, *Rabbinic Stories.*

respective compilers of those writings and does not ignore or disrupt them. The genre, the narrative, assumes a subordinated role within the programs of the several Rabbinic documents. And with what consequence for the study of the formative history of Judaism, which is the center of my enterprise? Again with emphasis:

It is analytically meaningless to talk about "the Rabbinic story" or "the Rabbinic narrative" or "the Rabbinic parable" or "the Aggadah" or "the Rabbinic folk-tale" or any comparable, generic category that ignores documentary boundaries. The principal, and primary, analytical initiative commences with the document—*the traits of* its *corpus of narratives. We may then speak of the narrative or parable (*Mashal*) or case/precedent (*Ma'aseh) in the Mishnah or the Tosefta or Sifra or one or another of the Midrash-compilations or of the Talmuds, and only then ask how the narrative or parable or* Ma'aseh *as represented by the one document compares or contrasts with that set forth in another. And that is the fact, even though a given narrative may serve the purposes of more than a single document.*[11]

In volume one I identified the documentary preferences as to narrative that characterize the Mishnah, tractate Abot, and the Tosefta,[12] and in volume two I did the same for the three Tannaite Halakhic Midrash-compilations, which carry forward the work of the Mishnah and the Tosefta and which cite both documents ver-

---

[11] I discuss the fact that some few compositions move from document to document in *Extra- and Non-Documentary Writing in the Canon of Formative Judaism*. I. *The Pointless Parallel: Hans-Jürgen Becker and the Myth of the Autonomous Tradition in Rabbinic Documents*. Binghamton 2001: Global Publications. ACADEMIC STUDIES IN THE HISTORY OF JUDAISM SERIES; *Extra- and Non-Documentary Writing in the Canon of Formative Judaism*. II. *Paltry Parallels. The Negligible Proportion and Peripheral Role of Free-Standing Compositions in Rabbinic Documents*. Binghamton 2001: Global Publications. ACADEMIC STUDIES IN THE HISTORY OF JUDAISM SERIES; *Extra- and Non-Documentary Writing in the Canon of Formative Judaism*. III. *Peripatetic Parallels*. Binghamton, 2001: Global Publications. ACADEMIC STUDIES IN THE HISTORY OF JUDAISM SERIES. Second edition, revised, of *The Peripatetic Saying: The Problem of the Thrice-Told Tale in Talmudic Literature*. Chico, 1985: Scholars Press for Brown Judaic Studies.

[12] Clearly, at this stage we can say nothing about the types of narrative viewed in abstraction from the documents, e.g., in a canonical framework: "*the* Rabbinic narrative," or "Talmudic stories" viewed without differentiation in their own framework or in documentary context, let alone "the Aggadic narrative," as though all "Aggadah" formed an undifferentiated composition. The conclusions of the Preface pertain. But once the types of narratives of each canonical document, viewed on its own, have been collected and classified rigorously—explaining not only inclusion but exclusion—then work on "the Rabbinic narrative" or "Talmudic stories" or "the Aggadic narrative" will become analytically possible. As matters now stand, the premise of inquiry—documentary lines mean nothing—is untested by Rabbinic narratologists.

batim. volume three now moves on to the characterization as to narrative preferences of two of the Rabbah-Midrash-compilations of the formative canon, as indicated. These yield readily-differentiated results of considerable interest. Further, for The Fathers According to Rabbi Nathan Text A I recapitulate findings published twenty years ago in *Judaism and Story*.[13] These cohere with the newer ones, particularly those for Lamentations Rabbah. The upshot is simple. Given an authentic narrative lacking all attribution, deriving from one or another of the documents analyzed here, we can, on the basis of the indicative traits of narrative in one or another of the compilations, accurately assign the composition to its rightful home.

Concrete results even now come into view. Just as the Mishnah-Tosefta prefer the *Ma'aseh*, the former in its stripped-down, economical version, the latter in that version and in developments thereof, so Sifra and the two Sifrés prefer the *Mashal*, some of the time, as the context requires, for Halakhic clarification or, still more commonly by far, for exegetical exposition. In both instances the *Mashal* derives from the exegetical or Halakhic context, particular to the case at hand, and only rarely from some corpus of free-floating stories adapted for the purpose at hand. Indeed, the *Mashal* and the *Ma'aseh* emerge even as affines in Sifra and the two Sifrés, differentiated by formal qualities, not by function at all. So too Lamentations Rabbah here proves to prefer the fully-articulated and protracted tale, the story with a beginning, middle, and end, with tension and resolution thereof, rather than the exegetical parable or the precedent. Song of Songs Rabbah follows its own, different course. And, as I showed for the Fathers According to Rabbi Nathan in *Judaism and Story*, the framers of that document showed a strong interest in what I called "the sage-story," biographical anecdotes of a highly particular character.

As is always the case, I conduct my research in conversation with many colleagues and through diverse media, reading and reviewing other peoples' publications not the least of them. From some writings and counselors I learn what to do, from other writings, what

---

[13] *Judaism and Story: The Evidence of The Fathers According to Rabbi Nathan*. Chicago, 1992: University of Chicago Press. Reprint: Binghamton, 2002: Global Publications, CLASSICS IN JUDAIC STUDIES SERIES.

not to do. I am especially thankful to those who, by telephone and
e-mail, comment as the work unfolds in its successive drafts and
changing results. In that context, as ever, Professor William Green
has been especially helpful—every day.

I am thankful in addition to Professor Ithamar Gruenwald, Tel
Aviv University, for his perpetual willingness to respond to propos-
als of ideas coming to him day by day by e-mail. The on-going con-
versation with him enriches. I express a special word of thanks to
English Professors Ben Lafarge, Bard College and David Gunby,
Canterbury University (New Zealand), and Folklore Professor Galit
Hasan-Rokem, Hebrew University of Jerusalem, for guiding me, in
questions of literary theory, to illuminating books and articles that
I should otherwise have missed.

Jacob Neusner
Bard College

INTRODUCTION

In volume one, introduction and chapter one, I define the project in detail. These accounts explain the program of volumes two and three. They are taken for granted in all that follows and would stand rereading. But for those readers who wish to proceed directly to the evidence and analytical problems addressed in these pages, a very brief précis of the main points follows.

I

What, Exactly, Do I Mean by "Narrative"?

A narrative piece of writing in the Rabbinic corpus of late antiquity is formed by a coherent statement governed by a teleological logic of coherent discourse, a matter defined presently, and all other kinds of writing in that same corpus cohere through an other-than-teleological logic of coherent discourse. That consideration affords a completely objective criterion for defining narrative both inclusively and exclusively. Where that logic functions, the composition qualifies as narrative, where not, not. But I hasten to qualify: the canon encompasses pseudo-narratives, meaning, writing that resembles a story but that coheres other than through teleological logic.

By "logic of coherent discourse" I mean, the logic by which the writer links two or more sentences into a statement deemed to cohere, to make sense, to form a whole that exceeds the sum of the parts as in syllogistic writing. The logic uniquely characteristic of narrative joins two or more facts to convey a proposition through the setting forth of happenings in a framework of inevitability, in a sequence such that the sequence itself makes the point. In Rabbinic narrative the order of the components of the completed construction (allegations, incidents, statements) establishes not merely the facts of what happens, but the teleology,—the purpose or goal of the facts in necessary order—that explains those facts. Then we speak not only of events but of their causal, consecutive relationships. This definition of matters takes on greater concreteness when we consider the alternative logics of coherent discourse that function in the Rabbinic canon.

Therein I discern four available logics of coherent discourse by which two or more sentences are deemed to constitute a statement of consequence and intelligibility.[1] These are as follows:

(1)   the teleological logic that imparts coherence to data to yield a coherence based on the teleology, or end-purpose, of all data, which is different from

(2)   the propositional, syllogistic logic that imparts coherence to data to yield a proposition and generate a syllogism, which is different from

(3)   the arbitrary logic that joins two or more statements together on purely formal grounds, and which also is different from

(4)   the paradigmatic logic that through the juxtaposition shows the structural coherence of two or more rules or cases, yielding a pattern, more concretely: producing (in context) jurisprudence out of laws, laws out of cases, exemplary cases out of random coincidences.

Of the four logics that in my survey I have found to define the media of establishing coherence within pericopes of the canonical documents, two require consideration here, teleological logic and by contrast syllogistic or propositional logic.

In the teleological mode of thought that signals narrative and only narrative we link fact to fact and also prove (ordinarily implicit) propositions by appeal to the goal or end—hence, *teleological*—a logic of coherence that is implicit in the purposive sequence of *facts*. The logic of narrative establishes coherence by the principle of much historical writing of facts deemed continuous and causative, *post hoc, ergo propter hoc:* because one matter preceded another, the prior matter has caused the posterior one—hence, history or story. It follows that only at the end of the composite do all the pieces fall into place. When the goal is realized, the consequences of the combination of *this* with *that* become apparent. Then the reason, first this, then that, emerges. So by invoking the word "teleology," I mean to stress that the pieces of data cohere not by reason of their own traits but by appeal to a goal beyond themselves.

---

[1] I have spelled these matters out in detail in *The Making of the Mind of Judaism.* Atlanta, 1987: Scholars Press for Brown Judaic Studies.

How come the goal is signaled by the very sequence of fact-bearing sentences? It is because the goal transcends, and imposes proportion, coherence, and order on, all the distinct parts of data. No datum is fixed and final until the end. Here the reader does not know what the message really is until the end of the story. In teleological discourse, therefore, the point is at the end, and not learned along the way. Stopping at any point before the end will demolish the construction and leave incoherent and senseless bits and pieces littering the path to nowhere. By contrast, in a propositional composition of a syllogistic character, each component is fully cogent in its own traits and terms, e.g., it may be constituted by an opinion that on its own bears a meaningful statement.

So what defines narrative and no other type of Rabbinic writing is a trait of mind that discerns purpose in the very order of facts, first this, then that, *therefore this led to that and explains it.* The "logic"[2] that makes sequence, movement, dialectics register so that "this" coheres to "that" as I said may be roughly characterized: *post hoc, ergo propter hoc:* that happened in sequence after this, it therefore happened because of this. In more abstract language, the logic particular to narrative joins a sequence of statements of action or thought in such a way as to yield a cogent statement. By reason of their order the parts cohere into a whole that exceeds the sum of the parts. That order is taken to bear meaning and exhibit purpose or intention, and that logic I therefore call "teleological," hence "the teleological logic characteristic of and, in Rabbinic context, unique to narrative."

Now contrast teleological with syllogistic or propositional logic. By far the most important logic of coherent discourse is the philosophical logic of proposition and syllogism. By it facts and reason cohere to yield syllogisms, e.g., two facts produce a third. A way of conducting philosophical argument is the demonstration we know in general as *Listenwissenschaft,* that is, a way to classify and so establish a set of probative facts. These compel us to reach a given conclusion, one that transcends any and all of the facts but is contained within each of them. These probative facts derive from the classification of data, all of which point in one direction and not in an-

---

[2] I put "logic" in quotation-marks here because of the dubious standing of the matter, as everyone recognizes. But then Aristotle produced natural philosophy but not the ordered history or intent and purpose that sustains unfolding stories.

other. Then the traits of the individual bits of data register on their own, and, seen in any order but only all together, they yield a pattern, produce a generalization, demonstrate a principle.

A catalogue of facts, for example, may be so composed that, through the regularities and indicative traits of the respective entries, the catalogue yields a proposition affecting more facts than are catalogued, thus producing a syllogism. In the Halakhah this may or may not be articulated, but it never has to be, that is the power and art of the Mishnah, the foundation-document of the Halakhah. In the Aggadah, in the main Rabbah-compilations, Leviticus Rabbah, for example, the besought proposition is ordinarily articulated, outset and end, in complex composites of a syllogistic character. Accordingly, items are interchangeable. Each exemplifies a trait common to them all; that is why the list works. Therefore the order of the items rarely registers the besought proposition; the traits common to the items, in whatever sequence, make all the difference.

A list of parallel or comparable items all together points to a simple conclusion; the conclusion may or may not be given at the end of the catalogue, but the catalogue—by definition—is focused. All of the catalogued facts are taken to bear self-evident connections to one another, established by those pertinent shared traits implicit in the composition of the list. These therefore bear meaning and point through the weight of evidence to an inescapable conclusion. The discrete facts then join together because of some trait common to them all. This is a mode of classification of facts to lead to an identification of what the facts have in common and—it goes without saying, an explanation of their meaning. These and other modes of philosophical argument are entirely familiar.

How do the two logics of coherent discourse compare and contrast? Philosophical logic of coherence differs from the teleological logic characteristic of narrative, for in philosophical logic, the sequencing of the facts in a philosophical construction bears no part of the burden; we can reproduce our cases in any order with the same result. By contrast, in teleological logic the manufactured sequence establishes a moral that by reason of the position of the data in some way, rather than in some other, is always blatant. Here too, it hardly matters whether or not the generalization is stated in so many words. That is because the power of well-crafted narrative is so to order the components of the construction as to make unnecessary explicitly announcing the moral. So narrative sees cogency in the necessary order of events understood as causative. Purpose, therefore cause, takes the form of a story of what happened—once upon a time, someone did something with such-and-such a consequence—because it had to happen.

Whatever the form, whether invested with the aura of story-telling or not, the presence of teleological logic marks a composition as narrative, and the absence of that logic denies it that status. If, as we shall now see in pseudo-narratives, we are told in the form of a story about what happens in the Temple on various occasions, the tale of how rites are performed, we can invoke the formal issue: does the outcome become clear only at the end, or is the sequence merely formal, a matter of a correct ordering of action, but not teleological—message-bearing, detail by detail when in fixed array.[3]

II

Pseudo-narrative

Let us return to the matter of verisimilitude as against authenticity: what about compositions that by the criterion of teleological logic do not qualify as narratives but that do convey a narrative "tone" or impression, e.g., a sequence of actions and their outcomes, or a setting for a story that is not actually told except through dialogue containing ideas, no action, e.g., "they were walking along the way and he said to him...," "he said to him..." "he said to him..."— with no action but only talk that is propositional, not ordered teleologically? I call "pseudo-narratives" those compositions that adopt what looks like a narrative tone but cohere on some foundation other than the logic of teleology. In that connection I identify three special problems, all involving a described action or event, none invoking teleological logic. These bear resemblance to stories, the rhetoric corresponding to what generally characterizes narratives in Rabbinic context. But their principal parts do not cohere through the required logic of coherent discourse. They are

(1)   "conversations"[4] ("he said to him... he said to him...");

---

[3] I follow Ithamar Gruenwald's definition of ritual in his *Rituals and Ritual Theory in Ancient Israel*. He sees ritual as action, fixed and autonomous, without reference to the story that accompanies the action (myth).

[4] Quotation-marks signify the distinction between verbatim reports of conversations and fabrications of "conversations" out of surmise or convention, such as

(2)   presentations of ritual conduct in the Temple (and in the court) ("he did this... he did that...");

(3)   the precedent or case, usually but not invariably marked *Ma'aseh*;[5] and

(4)   the parable, whether exegetical or Halakhic, which translates an abstract conception into a concrete story meant as a simile.

The "conversations" construct a setting for what are, in fact, merely exchanges of principles or arguments: scripted, artificial dialogue, a pseudo-narrative setting for an analytical presentation. An example would be an account of how one day, such-and-such happened, the rabbis ruled so-and-so, and Rabbi X argued... Rabbi Y argued... through several matched exchanges, followed by "they voted and ruled...." Here is an event that yields a rule, not a narrative.

The presentations of ritual conduct in the Temple represent a particular type of writing restricted to a particular topic. They imitate the preference of Scripture, e.g., Leviticus 16, for presenting rituals through described action, not "he should do thus and so" but "he did/does thus and so." Much scripted dialogue may accompany the presentation of cultic activities. But the details all register on their own, omit any one and the account fails. To make matters concrete, let me give a single example of such a pseudo-narrative cultic composition, one that sets forth the rite of reaping the barley sheaves used in the grain offering of the '*omer* on the opening day of Passover. Here we have a scripted language, a fixed exchange of formulas, each autonomous and bearing sense unto itself, not only at the end:

MISHNAH-TRACTATE MENAHOT 6:3

A.   How did they do it?

B.   Agents of the court go forth on the eve of [the afternoon before] the festival [of Passover].

---

characterize nearly the whole of the Rabbinic canonical record of things people supposedly said to one another. In that record literary convention and artifice govern; there is nothing that remotely qualifies as a verbatim report of things really said, as a conversation that really took place on some one day in some determinate situation.

[5] The distinction between a precedent and a unique case, lacking authority as a precedent, makes no difference in the contexts we survey, hence I avoid making a commitment as to how I classify the *ma'aseh* in the Mishnah. In the Tosefta the *ma'aseh* takes on further tasks in context, sometimes replicating the Mishnaic usage, some times going well beyond.

C. And they make it into sheaves while it is still attached to the ground, so that it will be easy to reap.

D. And all the villagers nearby gather together there [on the night after the first day of Passover], so that it will be reaped with great pomp.

E. Once it gets dark [on the night of the sixteenth of Nisan], he says to them, "Has the sun set?"

F. They say, "Yes."

G. "Has the sun set?"

H. They say, "Yes."

I. "[With] this sickle?"

J. They say, "Yes."

K. "[With] this sickle?"

L. They say, "Yes."

M. "[With] this basket?"

N. They say, "Yes."

O. "[With] this basket?"

P. They say, "Yes."

Q. On the Sabbath, he says to them, "[Shall I reap on] this Sabbath?"

R. They say, "Yes."

S. "[Shall I reap on] this Sabbath?"

T. They say, "Yes."

U. "Shall I reap?"

V. They say, "Reap."

W. "Shall I reap?"

X. They say, "Reap"-

Y. three times for each and every matter.

Z. And they say to him, "Yes, yes, yes."

AA. All of this [pomp] for what purpose?

BB. Because of the Boethusians, for they maintain, "The reaping of the [barley for] the offering of the first sheaf of barley is not [done] at the conclusion of the festival."

Here we have no one-time incident, recorded for its lesson to be sure. This account of the rite contains no prescriptive language of a Halakhic character. The upshot could readily be translated into the rhetoric of law, e.g., The agents of the court do thus and so…, without the colloquy that translates the law into a tale of how things were done. The effect is the same. The narrative is sustained by scripted language, fixed formulas that encase and encapsulate the activity. The tacked-on conclusion, AA-BB, does not serve to impose sense and meaning on the details, only on the rite overall; each detail is necessary in its own right. Do the components hold together only by reason of the goal of the narrative, or is there a principle of cogency deriving from sequence, so that each item on its own lays claim to its legitimate position in the whole? Do we have something akin

to the logic of proposition (if not syllogism) that generally characterizes the presentation of the Halakhah and of the theological constructions of the Aggadah? The answer presents itself when we realize
that the order of action in succession is everything. At stake is *the
sequencing of the rite*, and this is made explicit in every cultic pseudo-
narrative. Stop before the end and the account is incomplete, but
coherent to that point.

The indicative fact is, the pseudo-narrative of sequenced actions
that "he does... did... will do..." serves in the Halakhic documents,
particularly the Mishnah, only for ritual, and mainly for the Temple's
rituals. This well-documented preference for the use of the language
of description, in addition to the language of Halakhic prescription,
for the particular purpose of embodying ritual behavior, is best explained by Ithamar Gruenwald, in his *Rituals and Ritual Theory in
Ancient Israel*. Gruenwald addresses matters in this language, with what
is important for my argument in italics:

> The study of rituals mostly concerns the particulars of what is done,
> how it is done, and the reason and purpose of doing as embedded in
> the very act of doing... rituals are performative "signs"... Each ritual
> consists of several sub-acts that configure rituals as sequentially struc-
> tured events. They are spread out in time and in space. In other words,
> the doing of any rituals creates dynamics that turns complex struc-
> ture into a process.
>
> ... what makes the difference between a ritual and a non-ritual
> act.... The answer focussed on three factors: (1) the logic that shapes
> the internal structuring; (2) *the dynamics that emerges from the sequencing of
> ritual acts;* (3) and the mental process that activates intentionality. There
> is an inner logic that constitutes the structure of every ritual. Without
> that logic, the ritual statement becomes redundant. The specific manner
> in which the various parts become a coherent whole shows the man-
> ner in which every ritual becomes a compositional event. Whatever
> its shape, ritual always is a unique statement that exists in its own right.
> *In our understanding here, doing the ritual in the right manner means allocating
> to it, as well as its various components, processual coherence. In this respect, ritu-
> als are analogous to verbal arguments. Reverse or displace any part in a certain
> argument, or drop it altogether, and the whole argument changes, or loses its com-
> municative capacity.*[6]

What is important here is the stress on the sequencing of ritual acts,
the notion of ritual as process ("processual coherence"). He states

---

[6] Ithamar Gruenwald, *Rituals and Ritual Theory in Ancient Israel*. Leiden, 2002:
Brill. BRILL LIBRARY OF FORMATIVE JUDAISM series.

my point of emphasis in so many words: "rituals are analogous to verbal arguments..." That strikes at the heart of the matter and removes the tales of how things were or are done in the Temple from consideration within the definition of narrative as defined by the quality of logic of coherent discourse.

Indeed, Gruenwald captures the matter in the italicized portion of the cited passage. Within Gruenwald's theory of matters, which I find compelling, we are able to explain the traits of the narrative-Halakhic protocol, right alongside the philosophical-Halakhic protocol, serves in particular in the context of Temple rites and activities. There is no myth that accompanies the verbal realization of the rite; it does not belong, and if present, is tacked on and scarcely intersects in detail (as with the Boethusians of Mishnah-tractate Menahot). The logic is established in the gesture that establishes a series, that is, three times repeated. More to the point, everything rests on the sequencing of ritual acts, which is the point of emphasis that can be conveyed only in the narrative medium selected in the cases at hand. If the *sequence* is the key, how else to convey it than say, first he did this, then he did that? But, I repeat, the sequencing, step by step, violates the logic of teleology that signifies narrative and only narrative: not the sequence step by step but the goal and end of the whole impose coherence. That is precisely the opposite of the logic of ritual pseudo-narrative, by which every acted out component of the process belongs only where it is, takes on meaning and significance only in its proper position—and not from the *telos* of the whole.

Gruenwald's emphasis on ritual as process then provides us with the key to understanding the scripted exchanges that are portrayed in the Halakhah of the cult—alongside, I emphasize, the philosophical-expositional portrayal of that same Halakhic category-formation. Within the definition given in the Introduction for the logic that always signals the presence of narrative, the absence of which invariably marks a piece of writing as something other than narrative, Gruenwald's formulation of the traits of ritual discourse in the Halakhah validates treating the cited passages and their counterparts as other-than-narrative. Since in the Mishnah-Tosefta the use of descriptive language such as is cited above serves only Temple (and court) procedure, I am justified in omitting all such passages from my repertoire of candidates for analysis set forth in the Mishnah and the Tosefta.

As I showed in volume one, the *Ma'aseh* in the Mishnah follows a simple pattern: (1) in such and such a place, thus and so took place, and (2) Rabbi Y ruled in this wise—the whole stripped down to the essential facts. Each component is required in its place, and in context is clear; the conclusion resolves tension, it does not impose meaning on the antecedent components. The Tosefta invokes the marker, *Ma'aseh*, for both this and also other kinds of writing, some of which qualify as narrative. We pursued the *Ma'aseh* in the Tannaite Midrash-compilations and compare the data with those deriving from the Mishnah and the Tosefta. And here, in Song of Songs Rabbah but not Lamentations Rabbah, the exegetical parable, the *Mashal*, emerges as the paramount pseudo-narrative form, dependent for its coherence on exegetical (sometimes: Halakhic) context, not on its own internal sequential logic.

III

What Questions Do I Address to the Narrative Compositions?

What in documentary context do I wish to know about narratives (and pseudo-narratives)? Here is the set of questions, in the order that strikes me as logical and necessary, which, in the encounter with each authentic narrative in each document, I uniformly raise.[7] Then, at each point, in italics I underscore the particular aspects of special interest.

1.   We now realize that a piece of writing qualifies as a narrative because it attains coherence through the teleological logic of coherent discourse defined earlier. This commonly means that, at some point and in some articulated way, the narrative invokes a finite action, it records something that has happened, or it asks the reader to imagine a real-time, real-life event:

On what basis does the narrative attain coherence, e.g., what is the action or

---

[7] Obviously, a considerable range of questions bears on each pericope, and I select only those that advance the particular inquiry at hand. When it comes to the Mashal/proverb, for example, C. Thoma and his co-workers collect much information that my program does not require. In my review, I spell out why I think purposelessly collecting information yields facts but not knowledge. The same as to be said about collecting variant readings in the MSS evidence for a given document, let alone variant versions of a given composition spread over many documents. These represent interesting and occasionally useful collections of information, but on their own they lack self-evident pertinence to any given thesis or to the solution of a given problem.

event that precipitates the telling of the tale and how does the teleology assert itself?

The answer item by item is required to justify my classifying the composition as a narrative.

2. The sequence of data, I have argued, is not random but determinative. The sequence conveys the purpose, in context, that each component is meant to serve. A narrative thus coheres by reason of a tension that is precipitated and resolved, a point that is proved by the narrative: thus:

What point of conflict or intersection of wills accounts for the telling of the tale and how is the point of tension resolved?

3. The narratives fall into diverse categories, each with its own traits. These categories, defined by formal criteria, do not represent the outcome of taste and judgment and critical acumen, which I do not claim to possess, but only of a simple, material assessment of concrete features of the writing:

How, in light of other, comparable, pieces of writing and the data that they yield, is the narrative classified, and what are its indicative formal qualities, e.g., long or short, complex or simple?

But, I stress, these questions pertain to authentic narratives, not to inauthentic narratives, encompassing the *Ma'aseh* and the *mashal/* parable. There the question of narrative logic does not apply. With reference to the *Mashal,* I want to know whether the parable is particular to its exegetical context or adapted from a circulating, ready-made corpus of similes in the form of narratives. That is a key question for the study at hand, as is already clear. In many instances the simile/parable tracks the exegetical problem and is explicitly so characterized; in some instances the parable serves but not in all details and gives clear indication of adaptation. In due course we shall see that the *Ma'aseh* and the *Mashal* intersect in function, differing in formal aspects alone.

The larger question of documentary preferences as to narrative (or pseudo-narrative) is addressed at chapters nine, sixteen, and seventeen. There I ask whether the document contains compositions or composites that qualify as narrative, and, if so, whether these compositions and composites exhibit common traits or preferences. Then, in due course, I plan to compare and contrast the narratives characteristic of one document with those preferred by another: the forms of a narrative in Sifra as against those paramount in the two Sifrés, not to mention the Mishnah and Tosefta, on the one side,

Song of Songs Rabbah and Lamentations Rabbah, on the other. These studies only open the way to more encompassing comparisons and contrasts of documents' narrative preferences. For the entire canon has to be analyzed, though even now the outcome is perfectly clear.

What about the context in which narrative find their place? Through the use of diverse margins, broad for the narrative, indented for the context, I indicate my views on the form-analytical data of a given composition. In that way I preserve the narrative in its larger context while signaling its formal limits. The visual signal permits us to see very clearly the way in which authentic narratives are distinguished from their documentary context—if they are to be so distinguished.

IV

What Do I Mean by Distinguishing
Non-Documentary from Documentary Writing?

Clearly, I have pressed the question of whether a piece of writing conforms to the documentary program of the compilation in which it occurs. Before I explain why I deem the issue urgent, I have to clarify the distinction between documentary, extra-documentary, and non-documentary writing. With that distinction in hand, we turn to the difference that distinction makes.

Documentary writing conforms to the traits of a particular document so that, stripped bare of its reference-system (supplied in any case by modern scholarship) we should reliably assign the composition to the correct place within the canon. Extra-documentary writing exhibits the traits of documentary writing but belongs to no extant document. That is best illustrated by a composite devoted to the exposition of a passage of Proverbs or Chronicles, matching in rhetoric and logic of coherent discourse Rabbah-Midrash-compilations for Leviticus or Genesis or Song of Songs, but devoted to a topic, Proverbs or Chronicles, for which we have no document. That is extra- but not non-documentary writing.

Compositions and composites called "non-documentary," disregard the rules of documentary writing such as govern in any and all of the score of canonical compilations. They not only ignore the indicative traits of the documents in which they occur, but they in no way replicate for a fresh topic a known model of any extant docu-

ment. So while we have Midrash-compilations, if not for one scriptural book, then for another, we have no canonical compilation of
stories, e.g., lives of sages, on the one side,[8] histories of Israel, on
the other.[9] So too there are elaborate stories of the false Messiah
and the true one, and the like. But in the entire formative canon
there is nothing remotely recording the life of a Messiah, beginning
to end. Entire chapters in the lives of principal sages and their mas-
ter-disciple circles, sustained stories about paradigmatic events in
Israel's history—none of these types of writing coalesces into coherent
documents in the way in which the compositions and composites
located in the Mishnah or Genesis Rabbah or the Bavli (to name
three disparate cases) do. By that criterion the non-documentary
represent a kind of writing intended to stand on its own, not planned
for a larger composite.

That carries us to the perspective of the documentary hypothesis
on narrative: what difference, for the history of Rabbinic Judaism,
does the non-documentary status that completed research of mine[10]
has assigned to narrative make?

V

What Is at Stake?

Why does the status as to the documentary venue of narratives matter
in the formative history of Rabbinic Judaism? To specify the answers,
I track the unresolved questions, reproduced in italics, of religion,
literature, and history, that I spell out in *The Three Questions of Formative Judaism: History, Literature, and Religion.*[11]

1. RELIGION: *At stake for understanding the religious system of formative
Rabbinic Judaism: Do anomalous or asymmetric compositions or composites attest
to thought that takes place beyond the limits of the documents subject to the rules
and symmetry of the canon?*

---

[8] I deal with an aspect of this larger problem in *Why No Gospels in Talmudic
Judaism?* Atlanta, 1988: Scholars Press for Brown Judaic Studies. Now: Lanham
MD, 2001: University Press of America STUDIES IN JUDAISM series.

[9] I explain that fact in *The Presence of the Past, the Pastness of the Present. History,
Time, and Paradigm in Rabbinic Judaism.* Bethesda, 1996: CDL Press.

[10] All other inquiry into Rabbinic narrative ignores documentary lines and so
affirms the same premise as I did in the work that precipitated this project. Stern
on the Parable, treated in volume one, suffices to prove that point.

[11] Leiden, 2002: Brill. The Brill Reference Library of Judaism.

A corpus of extra-, including non-, documentary writing did find its way into the process of documentary composition and compilation. Of the three types of the identified extra-documentary writing—(1) exegesis of clumps of Scripture from books not accorded, by entire documents, systematic commentaries in the Rabbinic canon of late antiquity, (2) agglutination of topical miscellanies, and (3) narratives—the first two self-evidently cohere to the model of the canonical documents, though not to the particular program of any extant document. Hence they raise no questions of a documentary character, but rather confirm the definition of a conventional compilation. As large formal aggregates they cannot be differentiated from the documentary writing to which they correspond. I find no recurrent differences in the regnant conceptions of the anomalous writing that are asymmetrical or even jarring, let alone differences in contents.

What issue precipitates the inquiry? It is a debate that has flourished for nearly three decades, since the publication of my *Judaism: The Evidence of the Mishnah.*[12] In response, people posited a "Judaism beyond the texts." By that they mean to allege we have access to Judaic thought beyond the limits of the extant documents, knowledge that is a priori, on the one side, or that is represented in bits and pieces of writing that survive, out of context, in the Rabbinic documents. Here is a clear opportunity to investigate the qualities of normative-Judaic writings that originate outside of the documentary boundaries. So what about the "Judaism beyond the texts"— at least, that alleged Judaic structure and system to which the texts willy-nilly afford only occasional and fragmentary access?

2.   LITERATURE: *At stake for discerning the literary qualities of the Rabbinic canon: Does non-documentary writing exhibit readily-discernible patterns of form and meaning as does documentary writing? If so, what are these patterns and how are we to classify and to interpret them in documentary context?*

The question is readily unpacked. Extra-documentary writing is readily characterized within the limits of extant, documentary writing. For forms and patterns of the non-documentary writing, that is, the narrative compositions and composites, we do not know the answer. This part of the work supplies the beginnings of one.

3.   HISTORY: *What sort of historical data do narratives supply? What are the linkages between one narrative composition and another? Can we identify*

---

particular viewpoints or points of origin of one kind of story as against some other?

The answers to these questions yield points of regularity and order a given narrative contains to justify linking it with other items of a formally-comparable character: the taxonomic phenomenology of the narratives viewed as a whole. In the matter of Mishnah-Tosefta, that inquiry, independent of this study, concerned a narrative tradition deriving from the patriarchate, from Hillel through Judah the Patriarch's sons: a specific set of traits that differentiate that tradition from any and all other classifications of narratives.

So of the documents probed here I ask a uniform set of questions, thus imposing on the data a set of taxonomic considerations of a consistent order. In line with the important consideration just now introduced, I (1) establish my reason for regarding a pericope as "narrative" to begin with. I then (2) identify the source of the movement from one constitutive element of the tale to the next, indicating what imparts the dynamism and purpose ("teleology") to the composition. Finally, in line with the purpose of this survey, I finally (3) ask each item to tell how it is to be classified. The nature of the work—a piece by piece examination of the evidence—requires that the phenomenological outcome take shape cumulatively.

VI

A Special Problem in
Song of Songs Rabbah and Lamentations Rabbah

The Rabbah-compilations of Midrash contain a fair number of extensions of Scripture's own narratives. For the purpose of this study these are classified not as narratives or pseudo-narratives but as "exegetical amplifications" pure and simple. I therefore do not include these in this documentary probe of Rabbinic narrative. (In chapter seventeen, in the context of narrative in the Fathers According to Rabbi Nathan Text A, I refer to these as "Scripture-stories.") A single example suffices from each of the documents. Here is the one from Song of Songs Rabbah:

IX:ı

1.   A.   "I compare you, my love, to a mare of Pharaoh's chariots" (Song 1:9):

      B.   R. Pappias interpreted the verse, "'But he is at one with himself, and who can turn him' (Job 23:13):

C. "He judges on his own everyone who passes through the world, and none can answer the rulings of the One who spoke and brought the world into being."

D. Said to him R. Aqiba, "It would have been enough for you, Pappias, [not to claim that he rules all alone, which is not true, but only] to say that none can answer the rulings of the One who spoke and brought the world into being. For all is done in truth, and all is done in justice.

E. "For so it is written, 'I saw the Lord sitting upon a throne high and lifted up' (Isa. 6:1)."

F. Said R. Simon, "It is the throne that distinguishes between life and death."

G. [Continuing E:] "'And all the host of heaven were standing by him on his right hand and on his left' (1 Kgs. 22:19).

H. "Now is there such a thing as left on high? And is not everything on the right? 'Your right hand, O Lord, glorious in power, your right hand, O Lord, dashes in pieces the enemy' (Ex. 15:6).

I. "Why then does Scripture refer to 'his right hand and his left'?

J. "But these favor the right, those the left, meaning, these favor acquittal, those a verdict of guilty."

2. A. R. Yohanan in the name of R. Aha derived proof for the same proposition [that God does not judge all by himself] from the following: "And the word was true, even a great host' (Dan. 10:1).

B. "True is the ruling when a great host is formed."

3. A. That [same proposition, namely, that God does not judge all by himself] is in line with this verse: "But the Lord God is true" (Jer. 10:10).

B. What is the meaning of the word "true"?

C. Said R. Ibun, "It means that he is the living God and eternal king."

D. Said R. Eleazar, "Every passage in which it is said, 'and the Lord' refers to him and his court.

E. "And the generative analogy governing all of them is as follows: 'And the Lord has spoken evil concerning you' (1 Kgs. 22:23). [Here there is an explicit reference to the host of heaven standing by him, as at 1 Kgs. 22:19: 'And all the host of heaven were standing by him on his right hand and on his left.']

F. "That is the generative analogy governing all of them."

4. A. Now how does R. Eleazar interpret this verse of Scripture that is cited by R. Pappias, "But he is at one with himself, and who can turn him'" (Job 23:13)?

B. He alone seals the fate of all those who pass through the world, and no other creature seals the document with him.

5. A. What is the seal of the Holy One, blessed be He?

B. R. Bibi in the name of R. Reuben said, "It is truth: 'Howbeit I will declare to you that which is inscribed in the writing of truth' (Dan. 10:21).

C. "If 'truth' why then 'writing,' and if 'writing,' then why 'truth'? [Simon, p. 67, n. 4: (truth is) something written, but not necessarily decided upon].

D. "But until the document is sealed, it is merely written. When it has been sealed, then the decree is a judgment of truth."

6. A. Said R. Simeon b. Laqish, "And why is it 'truth'?

B. "Since the Hebrew word for truth consists of the letters A, M, and T, the word bears the A at the head of the alphabet, the M in the middle, and the T at the end.

C. "This then conveys the message, 'I am the first and I am the Last and besides me there is no god' (Isa. 44:6).

D. "'I am the first': 'I did not receive my dominion from anybody else.'

E. "'I am the last': 'I am not going to give it over to anybody else, there being no other.'

F. "'... and besides me there is no god': 'I have no second.'"

7. A. [=Genesis Rabbah XXI:V.1] [Concerning the verse, "Behold, the man has become like one of us" (Gen. 3:22),] R. Pappias interpreted the verse as follows: "'Behold, the man has become like one of us' means, like the unique one of the world."

B. Said to him R. Aqiba, "That is enough from you, Pappias."

C. He said to him, "Then how do you interpret the word, 'like one of us'?"

D.   He said to him, "Like one of the ministering angels."

E.   And sages say, "Not in accord with the position of this one, nor in accord with the position of that one. But it teaches the following:

F.   "The Holy One, blessed be He, set before him two paths, life and death, and he chose the 'other path,' [that of heresy, hence death] and he abandoned the path of life." [Freedman, Genesis Rabbah, p. 175, n. 1: That which God did not wish him to choose, that is, death. "Behold the man has become as one who knows good and evil of himself, of his own free will, and thereby has himself chosen the path of death."]

8.   A.   R. Pappias interpreted the verse, "'Thus they exchanged their glory for the likeness of an ox that eats grass' (Ps. 106:20).

B.   "Shall I infer that it speaks of the ox that is on high? Scripture says, 'that eats grass.'"

C.   Said to him R. Aqiba, "That's enough for you, Pappias."

D.   He said to him, "And how do you interpret the language, 'Thus they exchanged their glory for the likeness of an ox that eats grass' (Ps. 106:20)?

E.   "Might it mean, like an ordinary ox? Scripture says, 'that eats grass.'

F.   "Now as a matter of fact, you have nothing so degraded or disgusting as an ox when it is eating grass."

9.   A.   R. Yudan in the name of R. Aha said, "The magicians of Egypt did their enchantments, so that it appeared to be dancing before them.

B.   "That sense of the letters translated dancing occurs in this verse: 'Damascus has gotten weak, she turns around to flee, and trembling [using the same consonants] has seized her' (Jer. 49:24)."

10.   A.   R. Pappias interpreted the verse, "'I compare you, my love, to a mare of Pharaoh's chariots':

B.   "What is written is, 'at my rejoicing' [since the same letters translated 'to a mare' can be given vowels to make the word read, 'at my rejoicing].'

C.   "Said the Holy One, blessed be He, 'Just as I rejoiced at the fall of the Egyptians at the sea, so I would have rejoiced to destroy the Israelites. But what saved them?

D.   "'It was "at their right hand and at their left"' (Ex. 14:22: 'And the waters were a wall to them at their right hand and at their left').

E.   "That is, it was on account of the merit of the Torah, that they were destined to receive from the right hand of the Holy One, blessed be He, as it is said, 'At his right hand was a fiery law to them' (Dt. 33:2).

F. '"… and at their left': this refers to the mezuzah.

G. "Another explanation of 'at their right hand and at their left':

H. "'at their right hand': this is the recitation of the Shema.

I. '"… and at their left': this is the Prayer Said Standing."

J. Said to him R. Aqiba, "That is enough from you, Pappias! In every other passage in which the word 'rejoicing' appears, it is written with a sin, but here with a samekh [two different letters with an S-sound]."

K. He said to him, "And how do you interpret, 'I compare you, my love, to a mare of Pharaoh's chariots'?"

L. [Aqiba said to him,] "Pharaoh rode on a male horse, and, as it were, the Holy One, blessed be He, appeared to him on a male horse: 'And he rode upon a cherub and flew' (Ps. 18:11).

M. "Said Pharaoh, 'In a battle this male horse can kill its master. Now I'm going to ride on a female horse': "I compare you, my love, to a mare of Pharaoh's chariots.'

N. "Then Pharaoh went and mounted a red horse, a white horse, a black horse, so the Holy One, blessed be He, as it were, revealed himself on a red, white, and black horse too: 'You have trodden the sea with your horses' (Hab. 3:15), that is, horses of various kinds.

O. "The wicked Pharaoh came forth wearing a breastplate and helmet, so the Holy One, blessed be He, as it were, revealed himself wearing a breastplate and helmet: 'And he put on righteousness as a coat of mail' (Isa. 59:17).

P. "The former brought forth naphtha [for chemical warfare], so the Holy One, blessed be He, as it were, did the same: 'his thick clouds passed with hailstones and coals of fire' (Ps. 18:13).

Q. "He brought forth catapult stones, so the Holy One, blessed be He, as it were, did the same: 'And the Lord sent forth thunder and hail' (Ex. 19:23).

R. "He produced swords and lances, so the Holy One, blessed be He, as it were, did the same: 'He shot forth lightnings' (Ps. 18:15).

S. "He brought forth arrows, so the Holy One, blessed be He, as it were, did the same: 'And he sent out his arrows' (Ps. 18:15)."

> T. Said R. Levi, "'He sent out his arrows and scattered them' (Ps. 18:15): the arrows scattered them.
>
> U. '"… and he shot forth lightnings and discomfited them': this teaches that they threw them into confusion.
>
> V. "He confused them, frightened them, and took away their standards, so that they did not know what they were doing."

W. [Reverting to S and Aqiba's exposition:] "Pharaoh came forth in full armor, so the Holy One, blessed be He, as it were, did the same: 'The Lord will go forth as a mighty man' (Isa. 42:13).

X.   "He thundered with his voice, so the Holy One, blessed be He, as it were, did the same: 'The Lord thundered down from heaven' (2 Sam. 22:14).

Y.   "He made his voice loud, so the Holy One, blessed be He, as it were, did the same: 'And the Most High gave forth his voice' (2 Sam. 22:14).

Z.   "Pharaoh came forth in fury, so the Holy One, blessed be He, as it were, did the same: 'You march through the earth in indication' (Hab. 3:12).

AA.   "'... with a bow.' So, as it were: 'You uncover fully your bow' (Hab. 3:9).

BB.   "'... with shield and buckler.' So, as it were: 'Take hold of shield and buckler' (Hab. 3:9).

CC.   "'... with flashing spear.' So, as it were: 'at the shining of your glittering spear' (Hab. 3:11)."

11.   A.   R. Berekhiah in the name of R. Samuel b. R. Nahman: "When Pharaoh had used up all his weapons, the Holy One, blessed be He, began to exalt himself over him.

B.   "He said to him, 'Wicked one! Do you have the winds? Do you have the cherubim? Do you have wings?'

12.   A.   And whence did the Holy One, blessed be He, launch them?

B.   Said R. Yudan, "It was from between the wheels of his chariot.

C.   "The Holy One, blessed be He, loosened them and threw them onto the sea."

13.   A.   Said R. Hanina b. R. Papa, "A mortal who rides on his burden is on something tangible.

B.   "But the Holy One, blessed be He, is not that way.

C.   "He carries his chariot and rides on that which is ineffable: 'And he rode upon a cherub and did fly, yes, he swooped down on the wings of the wind' (Ps. 18:11)."

14.   A. [Supply: "And he rode upon a cherub and did fly, yes, he swooped down on the wings of the wind" (Ps. 18:11):]

B.   One version says, "he swooped," and another version reads, "he was seen" (2 Sam. 22:11) [both versions using some of the same consonants but exchanging the

> D and R, which are similar in appearance].
> C. How are the two versions to be reconciled?
> D. Said R. Aha, "On this basis we learn that the Holy One, blessed be He, had other worlds, and he went forth to make his appearance in them too."

This composite yields an implicit narrative but finds no place in the present probe, because the narrative is executed as an exegesis of the cited verses, not as a sustained exposition, such as we have found as the indicative trait of the narrative forms otherwise paramount in our documents. This entire composition has been parachuted down solely because of the appearance of Song 1:9 at No. 10. The focus for the conglomeration of the whole set of course lies with the formula in which Pappias's interpretation is rejected by Aqiba, who offers a better one of his own. There are various secondary accretions, and extensions, e.g., No. 2 for No. 1, No. 3 to No. 2, and so on, are self-evident. But the structure of the whole is visible to the naked eye, and it leaves no doubt that our compilers were perfectly contented to insert a passage with only the most superficial point of contact with the document at hand. Still, Aqiba's extensive comparison of Pharaoh with God, showing the enormous disparity between the earthly and the heavenly ruler, makes ample use of our base verse. But it would have served better without the accretions fore and aft. The upshot for this exercise is obvious: this represents a type of writing that is common in the Midrash-compilations and particular to them but that does not demand attention, at this time, in an account of the documentary preferences for narratives defined conventionally.

The counterpart Scripture-story in Lamentations Rabbah is as follows:

XXXV:IV.

1.   A.   Another matter concerning "[How] lonely sits [the city that was full of people]" [now with stress on "sits," in its sense of "sitting in mourning:"]

    B.   Said R. Nahman said Samuel in the name of R. Joshua b. Levi, "The Holy One, blessed be He, asked the ministering angels, 'A mortal king in mourning—what is fitting for him to do?'

    C.   "They said to him, 'He hangs sacking on his door.'

    D.   "He said to them, 'I too will do so:' 'I clothe the heavens with

> blackness, and I make sackcloth their covering' (Isa. 50:3).

E.   "'What else does a mortal king do?'

F.   "'He turns down the lamps.'

G.   "'I too will do so:' 'The sun and the moon are become black, the stars withdraw their shining' (Joel 4:15).

H.   "'What else?'

I.   "'He turns over the couch.'

J.   "'I too:' 'Until thrones were cast down, and One that was ancient of days did sit' (Dan. 7:9).

K.   "It is as though they were overturned [in mourning].

L.   "'What else?'

M.   "'He goes barefoot.'

N.   "'I too:' 'The Lord in the whirlwind and in the storm is his way, and clouds are the dust of his feet' (Nah. 1:5).

O.   "'What else?'

P.   "'He tears his purple clothing.'

Q.   "'I too:' 'The Lord has done that which he devised, he has performed his word' (Lam. 2:17)."

R.   What is the meaning of "that which he devised"?

S.   R. Jacob of Kefar Hanan said, "He tore his purple."

T.   [Continuing from Q:] "'What else?'

U.   "'He sits in silence.'

V.   "'I too:' 'He sits alone and keeps silent' (Lam. 3:28).

W.   "'What else?'

X.   "'He sits and weeps.'

Y.   "'I too:' 'How lonely sits....'"

Here is a weaving together of verses of Scripture to yield something comparable to a narrative, but there is no autonomous, free-standing story with a beginning, middle, and end; without the scriptural foundations, the story collapses. The Scripture-story represents a quite distinct type of writing and requires analysis in its own terms, which I cannot at this time define.

For those comparing the text with my selections, I have occasionally noted the omission of exegetical amplifications of Scripture's narratives and explained it.

PART ONE

NARRATIVES IN SONGS OF SONGS RABBAH
FORMS, TYPES AND DISTRIBUTION

CHAPTER ONE

SONG OF SONGS RABBAH
PARASHAH ONE

I:I

7.   A.   Another interpretation of the verse, "Do you see a man who is diligent in his business" (Prov. 22:29):

    B.   this refers to this is R. Hanina.

      8.   A.   They say:

        B.   One time he saw people of his village bringing whole-offerings and peace-offerings up [on a pilgrimage to the Temple].

        C.   He said, "All of them are bringing peace-offerings to Jerusalem, but I am not bringing up a thing! What shall I do?"

        D.   Forthwith he went out to the open fields of his town, the unoccupied area of his town, and there he found a stone. He went and plastered it and polished it and painted it and said, "Lo, I accept upon myself the vow to bring it up to Jerusalem."

        E.   He sought to hire day-workers, saying to them, "Will you bring this stone up to Jerusalem for me?"

        F.   They said to him, "Pay us our wage, a hundred gold pieces, and we'll be glad to carry your stone up to Jerusalem for you."

        G.   He said to them, "Where in the world will I get a hundred gold pieces, or even fifty, to give you?"

        H.   Since at the time he could not find the funds, they immediately went their way.

        I.   Immediately the Holy One, blessed be He, arranged for him for fifty angels in the form of men [to meet him]. They said to him, "My lord, give us five selas, and we shall bring your stone to Jerusalem, on condition that you help us with the work."

        J.   So he put his hand to the work with them, and they found themselves standing in Jerusalem. He wanted to pay them their wage, but he could not find them.

        K.   The case came to the Chamber of the Hewn Stone [where the high court was in session]. They said to him,

"It appears that in the case of our lord, ministering angels have brought the stone up to Jerusalem."
L.   Immediately he gave sages that wage for which he
had hired the angels.

1.   *On what basis does the narrative attain coherence, e.g., what is the action
or event that precipitates the telling of the tale?* The three units unfold
smoothly, A-D, E-H, I-K+L. The climax comes when the angels
disappear, and Hanina shows his honesty by turning to the high court
for a ruling. So the point of the story is at L: the scrupulosity of
Hanina, which imposes coherence on the first two units. First, he
has found for a peace-offering a stone, obviously unsuitable, but in
his sincerity he polishes and decorates the stone to bring to the
Temple. Second, he works with the laborers, J. Then he pays the
wage to sages. So the theme stated explicitly at the end runs through
each of the prior chapters, to be highlighted at the climax.
2.   *What point of conflict or intersection of wills accounts for the telling of the
tale and how is the point of tension resolved?* The contrast between the
peace-offerings of the others and that of Hanina, his poverty but his
sincerity, yields the tension that is resolved in the end.
3.   *How, in light of other, comparable, pieces of writing and the data that
they yield, is the narrative classified, and what are its indicative formal qualities, e.g., long or short, complex or simple?* This strikes me as an exemplary moral anecdote.

I:IV

1.   A.   Another interpretation of "The Song of Songs:"
      B.   This is in line with the following verse of Scripture: "And more
            so because Qohelet was wise; [he also taught the people knowl-
            edge, yes, he pondered and sought out and set in order many
            proverbs]" (Qoh. 12:9):
2.   A.   "And more so because Qohelet was wise; he also taught the
            people knowledge, yes, he pondered and sought out and set in
            order many proverbs" (Qoh. 12:9):
      B.   "He pondered" words of the Torah, and "he sought out" words
            of the Torah.
      C.   He made "handles" for the Torah. [This is spelled out at 4.A-
            C below.]
      D.   For you find that before Solomon came along, there was no
            parable [Hebrew: *dugma*, e.g., paradigm].
            3.   A.   R. Nahman said two things [in this connection].
                  B.   R. Nahman said, "[The matter may be compared]
                        to the case of a huge palace that had many doors, so who-
                        ever came in would wander from the path to the entry.

C.   "A smart fellow came along and took a skein of string and hung the string on the way to the entry, so everybody came and went following the path laid out by the skein.

D.   "So too, until Solomon came along, no person could comprehend the words of the Torah. But when Solomon came along, everyone began to make sense of the Torah."

E.   R. Nahman said the matter in yet another way: "[The matter may be compared] to the case of a reed marsh that no one could enter. A smart fellow came along and took a scythe and cut the reeds, so everybody began to go in and come out by chopping down the reeds.

F.   "So was Solomon."

4.   A.   Said R. Yosé, "[The matter may be compared] to the case of a basket full of produce but lacking a handle so no one could lift it up.

B.   "A smart fellow came along and made handles for it, so people began to carry it about holding on to the handles.

C.   "So too, until Solomon came along, no person could comprehend the words of the Torah. But when Solomon came along, everyone began to make sense of the Torah."

5.   A.   Said R. Shila, "[The matter may be compared] to the case of a big jug full of boiling water but lacking a handle so no one could lift it up.

B.   "A smart fellow came along and made handles for it, so people began to carry it about holding on to the handles.

C.   [Supply: "So too, until Solomon came along, no person could comprehend the words of the Torah. But when Solomon came along, everyone began to make sense of the Torah."]

6.   A.   Said R. Hanina, "[The matter may be compared] to the case of a deep well full of water, and the water was cold, sweet, and good, but no one could drink from it.

B.   "A smart fellow came along and provided a rope joined with another rope, a cord joined with another cord, sufficiently long so people could draw water from the well and drink it, and then everybody began to draw and drink.

C.   "So from one thing to the next, from one proverb to the next, Solomon penetrated into the secret of the Torah.

D.   "For it is written, 'The proverbs of Solomon, son of David, king of Israel, to know wisdom and instruction' (Prov. 1:1).

E.   "By means of the proverbs of Solomon, he mastered the words of the Torah."

7. A. And rabbis say, "Let a parable not be despised in your view, for it is through the parable that a person can master the words of the Torah.

B. "The matter may be compared to the case of a king who lost gold in his house or pearls. Is it not through a wick that is worth a penny that he finds it again?

C. "So let a parable not be despised in your view, for it is through the parable that a person can master the words of the Torah.

D. "You may know that that is so, for lo, Solomon through parables mastered the smallest details of the Torah."

The intersecting verse, Qoh. 12:9, stresses the wisdom of Solomon, and the task of the exegetical parables, 3B-D, E-F, 4.A-C, 5.A-C, 6.A-E, 7.A-D—six in all!—is to underscore the unique contribution of the wise man. The pattern in all cases involves an explicit statement of how the parable plays itself out: in what way does it apply to the case at hand? The variations among the parables is in imagery, not in purpose. Thus Nahman has someone hang a skein of thread or cut down reeds, and that is what Solomon did; Yose has someone invent handles, likewise Shila has the same image; Hanina has someone extend a rope to draw water. The sages praise parables, 7.A, then has wisdom compared to the wick that holds a flame for finding a treasure, repeating 7.A at 7.C. What marks the composite is its prolixity.

I:v

1. A. R. Phineas b. Yair commenced by citing this verse: "'If you seek it like silver [and search for it as for hidden treasures, then you will understand the fear of the Lord and find the knowledge of God]' (Prov. 2:4-5):

B. "If you seek words of the Torah like hidden treasures, the Holy One, blessed be He, will not withhold your reward.

C. "The matter may be compared to the case of a person, who, if he should lose a penny or a pin in his house, will light any number of candles, any number of wicks, until he finds them.

D. "Now the matter yields an argument *a fortiori:*

E. "If to find these, which are useful only in the here and now of this world, a person will light any number of candles, any number of wicks, until he finds them, as to words of Torah, which concern the life of the world to come as much as this world, do you not have to search for them like treasures?

F. "Thus: 'If you seek it like silver [and search for it as for

> hidden treasures, then you will understand the fear of the
> Lord and find the knowledge of God]' (Prov. 2:4-5)."

The exegetical parable illustrates the point that, to seek words of
Torah, one should search for them to receive the reward of eternal
life. This does not strike me as a very successful parable, because
the exposition of the parable shades over into an argument a fortiori, resting on the details of the parable, ignoring the power of the
parable in its own terms.

II.ii

    1. A.   Another interpretation of the verse, "O that you would
    kiss me with the kisses of your mouth:"

    9. A.   R. Yohanan interpreted the verse ["O that you would kiss
    me with the kisses of your mouth"] to speak of the Isra-
    elites when they went up to Mount Sinai:

    B.   "The matter may be compared to the case of a king who wanted
to marry a woman, daughter of good parents and noble family. He sent to her a messenger to speak with her. She said, 'I
am not worthy to be his serving girl. But I want to hear it from
his own mouth.'

    C.   "When that messenger got back to the king, his face was full of
smiles, but what he said was not grasped by the king.

    D.   "The king, who was astute, said, 'This one is full of smiles. It
would appear that she has agreed. But what he says is not to
be understood by me. It appears that she has said, 'I want to
hear it from his own mouth.'

    E.   "So the Israelites are the daughter of good parents. The mes-
senger is Moses. The king is the Holy One, blessed be He.

    F.   "At that time: 'And Moses reported the words of the people to
the Lord' (Ex. 19:8).

    G.   "Then why say, 'And Moses told the words of the people to
the Lord' (Ex. 19:9)?

    H.   "Since it says, 'Lo, I come to you in a thick cloud, so that the
people may hear when I speak to you, and may also believe
you forever' (Ex. 19:9), therefore, 'And Moses told the words
of the people to the Lord' (Ex. 19:9).

    I.   "He said to him, 'This is what they have asked for.'

    J.   "He said to him, 'They tell a child what he wants to hear.'"

The parable, B-D, is summarized at E and then tracks the exegetical problem laid out at F-H+I-J. Each detail of the parable matches the message of E, I-J. So here is a parable particular to its case.

II.ii

13. A.   R. Yudan in the name of R. Judah b. R. Simon, R. Judah, and
    R. Nehemiah:

B.   R. Judah says, "When the Israelites heard, 'I am the Lord your God' (Ex. 20:1), the study of the Torah was fixed in their hearts, and they would study and not forget.

C.   "They came to Moses saying, 'Our lord, Moses, you serve as intermediary, the messenger between us [and God]: "You speak with us, and we will hear" (Ex. 20:16), "... now therefore why should we die" (Dt. 5:22). Who gains if we perish?'

D.   "Then they would study and forget what they have learned.

E.   "They said, 'Just as Moses is mortal and passes on, so his learning passes away.'

F.   "Then they came again to Moses, saying to him, 'Our lord, Moses, would that he would reveal it to us a second time.' 'O that you would kiss me with the kisses of your mouth!' Would that the learning of Torah would be set in our hearts as it was before.'

G.   "He said to them, 'That cannot be now, but it will be in the age to come.'

H.   "For it is said, 'I will put my Torah in their inner part, and on their heart I shall write it' (Jer. 31:33)."

I.   R. Nehemiah said, "When the Israelites heard the word, 'You will not have other gods besides me,' the impulse to do evil was uprooted from their hearts.

J.   "They came to Moses and said to him, 'Our lord, Moses, you serve as intermediary, the messenger between us [and God]: "You speak with us, and we will hear" (Ex. 20:16), "... now therefore why should we die" (Dt. 5:22). Who gains if we perish?'

K.   "Forthwith the impulse to do evil came back.

L.   "Then they came again to Moses, saying to him, 'Our lord, Moses, would that he would reveal it to us a second time.' 'O that you would kiss me with the kisses of your mouth!'

M.   "He said to them, 'That cannot be now, but it will be in the age to come.'

N.   "For it is said, 'And I will take away the stony heart out of your flesh' (Ez. 36:26).'"

14.   A.   R. Azariah, and some say R. Eliezer and R. Yosé b. R. Hanina and rabbis:

B.   R. Eliezer says, "The matter may be compared to the case of a king who had a wine cellar.

C.   "The first guest came to him first, and he mixed a cup for him and gave it to him.

D.   "A second came and he mixed a cup for him and gave it to him.

E.   "When the son of the king came, he gave him the whole cellar.

F.   "So the First Man was commanded in respect to seven commandments.

G.   "That is in line with this verse: 'And the Lord God commanded the man, saying, You may freely eat of every tree of the garden, [but of the tree of the knowledge of good and evil you shall not eat, for in the day that you eat of it you shall die]' (Gen. 2:16)."

16.   A.   [Continuing Eliezer's statement, 14:G:] "As to Noah, a further commandment was assigned to him, not eating a limb cut from a living animal: 'Only flesh with the life thereof which is the blood thereof' (Gen. 9:4).

B.   "As to Abraham, a further commandment was assigned to him, circumcision.

C.   "Isaac devoted the eighth day to that rite.

D.   "As to Jacob, a further commandment was assigned to him, the prohibition of the sinew of the thigh-vein: 'Therefore the children of Israel do not eat the sinew of the thigh-vein' (Gen. 32:33).

E.   "As to Judah, a further commandment was assigned to him, levirate marriage: 'And Judah said to Onan, Go into your brother's wife and perform the duty of a husband's brother for her' (Gen. 38:8).

F.   "The Israelites, by contrast, made their own all of the religious duties, positive and negative alike."

17.   A.   R. Yosé b. R. Hanina and rabbis say, "The matter may be compared to the case of a king who was divvying up rations to his legions through his generals, officers, and commanders.

B.   "But when the turn of his son came, he gave him his rations with his own hand."

18.   A.   R. Isaac says, "The matter may be compared to a king who was eating sweetmeats,

B.   "And when the turn of his son came, he gave him his rations with his own hand."

19.   A.   Rabbis say, "The matter may be compared to the case of a king who was eating meat.

B.   "And when the turn of his son came, he gave him his rations with his own hand."

C.   And some say, "He took it out of his mouth and gave it to him: 'For the Lord gives wisdom, out of his mouth comes knowledge and discernment' (Prov. 2:6)."

The task of the exegetical parable, by reason of the location of No. 14, is to clarify the situation of Israel in the world to come, at which point they will retain the Torah that they have studied and not forget it. The point of the parable, however, does not intersect with that task, for its task is to distinguish between the first and the second guests, and the prince. The first two get a taste of wine, Adam and Noah in particular, but the prince, Israel, gets the whole wine cellar. Then what is clarified by the parable is the position of Adam, Noah, then Israel, but to achieve that outcome we have to regard 16.B-E as interpolated. In all, it is not a very successful composition, but the exegetical parable, not in its larger context, is very strong indeed: Adam/Noah/Israel as the first guest, the second guest, then the prince who gets it all. The second parable, No. 17, follows the pattern in more general terms, likewise No. 18 and No. 19. These look derivative. But the composition of a set of parables addressed to a single exegetical task clearly defines a preference for our document.

II.ɪɪ.

20. A.   R. Abbahu, and some say the following in the name of R. Judah, and R. Nehemiah:

  B.   R. Nehemiah said, "[The matter of 'O that you would kiss me with the kisses of your mouth!' may be compared to] two colleagues who were occupied with teachings of the law. This one states a general principle of law, and that one states a general principle of law.

  C.   "Said the Holy One, blessed be He, 'Their source is through my power.'" [Simon, p. 28: 'Their source comes from me.']

The simile is not fully exploited, let alone articulated.

IV:ɪ

1. A.   "Draw me after you, let us make haste. The king has brought me into his chambers. We will exult and rejoice in you; we will extol your love more than wine; rightly do they love you" (Song 1:4):

  B.   Said R. Meir, "When the Israelites stood before Mount Sinai to receive the Torah, said to them the Holy One, blessed be He, 'Shall I really give you the Torah? Bring me good sureties [Simon: guarantors] that you will keep it, and then I shall give it to you.'

  C.   "They said to him, 'Lord of the ages, our fathers are our sureties for us.'

  D.   "He said to them, 'Your fathers themselves require sureties.'

  E.   "To what is the matter comparable? To someone who went to borrow money from the king. He said to him, 'Bring me a surety, and I shall lend to you.'

  F.   "He went and brought him a surety. He said to him, 'Your surety has to have a surety.'

  G.   "He went and brought him another surety. He said to him, 'Your surety has to have a surety.'

H.   "When he had brought him yet a third surety, he said to him, 'You should know that it is on this one's account that I am lending to you.'

I.   "So when the Israelites stood to receive the Torah, he said to them, 'Shall I really give you my Torah? Bring me good sureties that you will keep it, and then I shall give it to you.'

J.   "They said to him, 'Lord of the ages, our fathers are our sureties for us.'

K.   "Said to them the Holy One, blessed be He, 'As to your fathers, I have my complaints with them.

L.   "'As to Abraham, I have my complaint against him, for he said, "How shall I know that I shall inherit it?" (Gen. 15:8).

M.   "'As to Isaac, I have my complaint against him, for he loved Esau, while I hated him: 'But Esau I hated' (Mal. 1:3).

N.   "'As to Jacob, I have my complaint against him, for he said, 'My way is hid from the Lord' (Isa. 40:27).

O.   "'Bring me good sureties, and then I shall give it to you.'

P.   "They said to him, 'Lord of the world, our prophets will be our sureties.

Q.   "He said to them, 'I have my complaints against them: 'And the shepherds transgressed against me' (Jer. 2:8); 'Your prophets have been like foxes in ruins' (Ez. 13:4).

R.   "'Bring me good sureties, and then I shall give it to you.'

S.   "They said to him, 'Lo, our children will be our sureties for us.'

T.   "Said to them the Holy One, blessed be He, 'Lo, these are certainly good sureties. On their account I shall give it to you.'

This stupendous construction announces its proposition, B-D, in exegetical context. God wants guarantors before giving the Torah to Israel. Then the parable, E-H, carefully constructs the counterpart to the case the exegete wishes to make, which is spelled out at I-T. The parable has three sureties, God dismisses Abraham, Isaac, and Jacob, and the prophets, finally accepting their children as guarantors. That is a very strong comparison, but it does not closely track the parable itself.

IV:iii

10. A.   R. Berekhiah in the name of R. Judah b. R. Ilai: "It is written, 'And Moses led Israel onward from the Red Sea' (Ex. 15:22):

B.   "He led them on from the sin committed at the sea.

C.   "They said to him, 'Moses, our lord, where are you leading us?'

> D. "He said to them, 'To Elim, from Elim to Alush, from Alush to Marah, from Marah to Rephidim, from Rephidim to Sinai.'
>
> E. "They said to him, 'Indeed, wherever you go and lead us, we are with you.'
>
> F. "The matter is comparable to the case of one who went and married a woman from a village. He said to her, 'Arise and come with me.'
>
> G. "She said to him, 'From here to where?'
>
> H. "He said to her, 'From here to Tiberias, from Tiberias to the Tannery, from the Tannery to the Upper Market, from the Upper Market to the Lower Market.'
>
> I. "She said to him, 'Wherever you go and take me, I shall go with you.'
>
> J. "So said the Israelites, 'My soul cleaves to you' (Ps. 63:9)."
>
> K. Said R. Yosé b. R. Iqa, "And lo, a verse of Scripture itself proclaims the same point: 'Draw me, after you let us make haste.'
>
> L. "If it is from one verse of Scripture to another verse of Scripture, if it is from one passage of the Mishnah to another passage of the Mishnah, if it is from one passage of the Talmud to another passage of the Talmud, if it is from one passage of the Tosefta to another passage of the Tosefta, if it is from one aspect of narrative to another aspect of narrative."

The exegetical parable compares Israel to the wife faithfully following her husband from point to point, and that is made explicit in the sequence of F-I to J. Once more the parable closely tracks it's the terms of the exegesis it is meant to clarify.

IV:v

1. A. "We will exult and rejoice in you:"

> 2. A. Another interpretation of the verse, "We will exult and rejoice in you:"
>
> B. There we have learned on Tannaite authority: If one has married a woman and lived with her for ten years and not produced offspring, he has not got the right to stop trying.
>
> > C. Said R. Idi, "There was the case of a woman in Sidon, who lived with her husband for ten years and did not produce offspring.
> >
> > D. They came before R. Simeon b. Yohai and wanted to be parted from one another.

E.   He said to them, "By your lives! Just as you were joined to one another with eating and drinking, so you will separate from one another only with eating and drinking."

F.   They followed his counsel and made themselves a festival and made a great banquet and drank too much.

G.   When his mind was at ease, he said to her, "My daughter, see anything good that I have in the house! Take it and go to your father's house!"

H.   What did she do? After he fell asleep, she made gestures to her servants and serving women and said to them, "Take him in the bed and pick him up and bring him to my father's house."

I.   Around midnight he woke up from his sleep. When the wine wore off, he said to her, "My daughter, where am I now?"

J.   She said to him, "In my father's house."

K.   He said to her, "What am I doing in your father's house?"

L.   She said to him, "Did you not say to me last night, 'See anything good that I have in the house! Take it and go to your father's house!' But I have nothing in the world so good as you!"

M.   They went to R. Simeon b. Yohai, and he stood and prayed for them, and they were answered [and given offspring].

N.   This serves to teach you that just as the Holy One, blessed be He, answers the prayers of barren women, so righteous persons have the power to answer the prayers of barren women.

O.   And does this not yield a proposition a fortiori: if a mortal person, on account of saying to another mortal, "I have nothing in the world so good as you!" has prayers answered, the Israelites, who ev-

> ery single day await the salva-
> tion of the Holy One, blessed
> be He, saying, "We have noth-
> ing in the world so good as
> you!"—how much the more so
> P.   Thus: "We will exult and
> rejoice in you."

1.   *On what basis does the narrative attain coherence, e.g., what is the action or event that precipitates the telling of the tale?* The climax of the story, L, puts into perspective all of the prior exposition. The story begins with the crisis represented by childlessness. But the couple asked for the wrong thing, not Simeon's prayer, but his approval of their separating. That makes possible his instruction, E-F. Then the next phase, G-H, has the wife take the husband home to her father's house, I-L. The story about the couple ends at that point. The climax then follows, M-N+O, which leaves the story behind.

2.   *What point of conflict or intersection of wills accounts for the telling of the tale and how is the point of tension resolved?* The conflict is between the law and the love of the couple, and it is resolved in the wife's solution to the problem of the separation.

3.   *How, in light of other, comparable, pieces of writing and the data that they yield, is the narrative classified, and what are its indicative formal qualities, e.g., long or short, complex or simple?* The anecdote is an authentic narrative, but not a very complex one. It is protracted because it carries its own message and that of the redactor, who wants N-O to be tacked on to link the whole to the exegetical setting.

3.   A.   [Supply: Another interpretation of the verse, "We will exult and rejoice in you:"] The matter [of the situation of the Israelites] may be compared to the case of a noble lady, whose husband, the king, and whose sons and sons-in-law went overseas. They came and told her, "Your sons are coming home."
B.   She said, "What difference does it make to me? Let my daughters-in-law rejoice."
C.   When her sons-in-law came home, they said to her, "Your sons-in-law are coming."
D.   So she said, "What difference does it make to me? Let my daughters rejoice."
E.   When they told her, "The king, your husband, is coming," she said, "This is the occasion for whole-hearted rejoicing, waves upon waves of joy!"
F.   So in the age to come the prophets will come

and say to Jerusalem, "Your sons come from afar" (Isa. 60:4), and she will say, "What difference does that make to me?"

G.   And when they say, "And your daughters are borne on the side" (Isa. 60:4), she will say, "What difference does that make to me?"

H.   But when they said to her, "Lo, your king comes to you, he is triumphant and victorious" Zech. 9:9), she will say, "This is the occasion for whole-hearted rejoicing!"

I.   For so it is written, "Rejoice greatly, O daughter of Zion" (Zech. 9:9); "Sing and rejoice, O daughter of Zion" (Zech. 2:14).

J.   Then she will say, "I will greatly rejoice in the Lord, my soul shall be joyful in my God" (Isa. 61:10).

The exegetical parable, continuing No. 2 preceding, now makes the point that only when the king comes home does the queen rejoice. Israel is the queen, God is the king. The parable then clarifies Israel's situation in the end of days.

VI:II

5.   A.   "[Do not gaze at me because I am swarthy, because the sun has scorched me" (Song 1:6):] And said R. Isaac, "There was the case [Ma'aseh] of a local noblewoman who had an Ethiopian slave-girl, who went down to draw water from the well with her friend.

B.   "She said to her friend, 'My friend, tomorrow my master is going to divorce his wife and take me as his wife.'

C.   "The other said to her, 'Why?'

D.   "'It is because he saw her hands dirty.'

E.   "She said to her, 'You big fool! Let your ears hear what your mouth is saying. Now if concerning his wife, who is most precious to him, you say that because he saw her hands dirty one time, he wants to divorce her, you, who are entirely dirty, scorched from the day of your birth, how much the more so!'

F.   "So too, since the nations of the world taunt the Israelites, saying, 'This nation has exchanged its glory [for naught],' as in the verse, 'They exchanged their glory for an ox that eats grass' (Ps. 106:20),

G.   "the Israelites reply to them, 'Now if we who are in that condition for an hour and have incurred liability on that account, as for you, how much the more so!'

H.   "And not only so, but the Israelites say to the nations of the world, 'We shall say to you to what we are to be compared:

I.   "It is [comparable] to a prince who went forth to the wilderness around the town, and the sun beat on his head so that his

	face was darkened. He came back to the town, and with a bit of water and a bit of bathing in the bath houses, his body turned white and regained its beauty, just as before.
J.	"'So it is with me [the Israelites continue]. If the worship of idols has scorched us, truly you are scorched from your mother's womb!
K.	"'While you are yet in your mother's womb, you served idols, for when a woman is pregnant, she goes into the house of her idol and bows down and worships the idol—both she and her child.'"

Here is a *Mashal* labeled a *Ma'aseh*! Once Isaac has announced the case, the exposition, F-G, leaves no doubt that the "case" yields an explicit lesson for Israel; and if we miss the parabolic character of the "case," H-K go over the same ground, now with explicit marker of the parable, prince and all. The first go-around, the case/parable, has Israel in the position of the wife to be divorced for transient reasons, as against the nations, who are permanently unworthy by reason of their idolatry. Then the second, now the parable, covers the same ground. In classification, then, the explicit parable classifies the falsely-labeled *Ma'aseh*.

IX:II

1.	A.	"I compare you, my love, [to a mare of Pharaoh's chariots]:"
	B.	Said R. Eliezer, "The matter may be compared to the case of a princess who was kidnapped, and her father was ready to redeem her.
	C.	"But she gave indications to the kidnappers, saying to them, 'I am yours, I belong to you, and I am going after you.'
	D.	"Said her father to her, 'What are you thinking? Is it that I do not have the power to redeem you? I would have you hold your peace [using the same word as 'compare you'], yes, be silent.'
	E.	"So when the Israelites were encamped at the sea, 'and the Egyptians pursued after them and overtook them in camp by the sea' (Ex. 14:9),
	F.	"the Israelites, fearful, gave indicates to the Egyptians, saying to them, 'We are yours, we belong to you, and we are going after you.'
	G.	"Said to them the Holy One, blessed be He, 'What are you thinking? Is it that I do not have the power to redeem you?
	H.	"For the word 'I have compared you' [bears consonants that yield the meaning,] 'I made you silent.'
	I.	"Thus: 'The Lord will fight for you, and you will hold your peace' (Ex. 14:14)."

The parable, B-D exactly matches the requirements of its exegetical context, E-G+H-I and has been constructed solely for exegetical purposes.

X:III

2. A. "... your neck with strings of jewels" (Song 1:11):

 B. R. Levi in the name of R. Hama b. R. Hanina said, "This refers to the lections of the Torah, which are connected to one another, lead on to one another, or leap from one to the other, or exhibit parallels to one another, or are related to one another."

  C. Said R. Menahema, "For example, the following:

  D. "'To these the land shall be divided for an inheritance' (Num. 26:53), followed by, 'Then the daughters of Zelophehad came near' (Num. 27:1); so too: 'The daughters of Zelophehad speak rightly' (Num. 27:7), followed by 'Get you up to this mountain of Abarim' (Num. 27:12).

  E. "What has one thing to do with the next?

  F. "Once the land had been divided, the daughters of Zelophehad came to take their share from Moses, and Moses recused himself from their case: 'And Moses brought their case before the Lord' (Num. 27:5).

  G. "Said to him the Holy One, blessed be He, 'Moses, from their case you recuse yourself, but from my presence you cannot recuse yourself: 'Get you up to this mountain of Abarim.'

  H. "He said before him, 'Lord of the world, since you remove me from the world, at least let me know what sort of leaders you are going to provide for the Israelites!'

  I. "Said to him the Holy One, blessed be He, 'Moses, concerning my children you have to have commandments, and concerning the work of my hands do you presume to command me? Instead of giving me instructions concerning my children, give instructions to my children concerning me!'

  J. "That is in line with this verse: 'Command the children of Israel and say to them' (Num. 28:2)."

   3. A. [Supply: "Command the children of Israel and say to them" (Num. 28:2):]

    B. The matter provokes a parable: to what may it be compared?

    C. To the case of a queen who was departing from this life. She said to him, "By the life of my lord, the king, I command you concerning my children!"

    D. He said to her, "Instead of giving me orders concerning my children, give my children orders concerning me!"

> E.   So when Moses said before the Holy One, blessed be He, "Lord of the world, since you remove me from the world, at least let me know what sort of leaders you are going to provide for the Israelites!"
>
> F.   [Supply:] Said to him the Holy One, blessed be He, "Moses, concerning my children you have to have commandments, and concerning the work of my hands do you presume to command me? Instead of giving me instructions concerning my children, give instructions to my children concerning me!" That is in line with this verse: "Command the children of Israel and say to them" (Num. 28:2).

The parable, X.iii.3, is tacked on because of the relevance of the base-verse of No. 3 to the antecedent composite. But the operative language, E-F, recapitulates the key-language of 2.I, and that marks the whole as an exegetical parable constructed to match the requirements of the verse subject to amplification and concretization. Then 3.E signals something out of phase, for the issue raised at that component is not the same as the issue of 3.F=2.I. What I gather, then, is that the parabolic materials, 3.C-D, are out of phase with 3.E. Since 3.F so closely fits those materials, the parable, 3.C-D, appears adapted to, not created out of the program of, the exegetical program.

XII:ii

1. A.   [Taking up Song 1:12,] R. Phineas in the name of R. Hoshaia said, "'While the king,' the King of kings of kings, the Holy One, blessed be He, 'was on his couch,' in the firmament, ['my nard gave forth its fragrance'], he had already anticipated [his descent on Mount Sinai] [Simon, p. 79, n. 4: by enveloping the mountain in flames and smoke],

   B.   "thus: 'And it came to pass on the third day, while it was yet morning, that there were thunders... upon the mount' (Ex. 19:16)."

2. A.   It may be compared to the case of a king who decreed, "On such and such a day, I shall enter town. The townsfolk slept all night, so when the king came and found them sleeping, he had the trumpets and horns sounded.

   B.   The prince of that town woke the people up and brought them forth to receive the king.

   C.   The king walked before them until he reached his palace.

   D.   Thus the Holy One, blessed be He, anticipated [his descent on Mount Sinai]: "And it came to pass on the third day, while it was yet morning, that there were thunders... upon the mount" (Ex. 19:16).

E. But prior: "For the third day the Lord will come down in the sight of all the people" (Ex. 19:11).

F. The Israelites had been sleeping all that night, for the sleep of Pentecost is very pleasant, and the night is brief.

G. R. Yudan said, "Not a flea bit them."

H. Came the Holy One, blessed be He, and found them sleeping. So he had the trumpets and horns sounded.

I. That is in line with this verse: "And it came to pass on the third day, while it was yet morning, that there were thunders... upon the mount" (Ex. 19:16).

J. Moses woke up the Israelites and brought them forth to receive the King of kings of kings, the Holy One, blessed be He: "And Moses brought the people forth to meet God" (Ex. 19:17).

K. The Holy One went before them until he came to Mount Sinai: "Now Mount Sinai was entirely in smoke" (Ex. 19:18).

God the King, Moses the prince, detail by detail, 2.D-K match the parabolic components, A-C, while amplifying them in a disciplined manner. Here is a parable that exactly matches the exegetical task assigned to it.

CHAPTER TWO

SONG OF SONGS RABBAH
PARASHAH TWO

XIX:ı

5. A. "[a lily of the valleys." (Song 2:1):] R. Azariah in the name of R. Judah in the name of R. Simon [interpreted the cited verse to speak of Israel before Mount Sinai].

B. ["'a lily among brambles':] The matter may be compared to a king who had an orchard. He planted in it rows upon rows of figs, grapevines, and pomegranates. After a while the king went down to his vineyard and found it filled with thorns and brambles. He brought woodcutters and cut it down. But he found in the orchard a single red rose. He took it and smelled it and regained his serenity and said, 'This rose is worthy that the entire orchard be saved on its account.'

C. "So too the entire world was created only on account of the Torah. For twenty-six generations the Holy One, blessed be He, looked down upon his world and saw it full of thorns and brambles, for example, the Generation of Enosh, the generation of the Flood, and the Sodomites.

D. "He planned to render the world useless and to destroy it: 'The Lord sat enthroned at the flood' (Ps. 29:10).

E. "But he found in the world a single red rose, Israel, that was destined to stand before Mount Sinai and to say before the Holy One, blessed be He, 'Whatever the Lord has said we shall do and we shall obey' (Ex. 24:7).

F. "Said the Holy One, blessed be He, [Lev. R.:] 'Israel is worthy that the entire world be saved on its account.'" [Song: "for the sake of the Torah and those who study it...."]

The exegetical parable precisely tracks C, E-F, matching the parable to its theological task. I see no marks of adaptation of a ready-made parable to the particular purpose at hand.

XIX:ı

6. A. R. Hanan of Sepphoris interpreted the verse to speak of acts of loving kindness [that one may do by helping others carry out their liturgical obligations]:

B. "Ten men entered a synagogue to say their prayers, but they did not know how to say the Shema and go before the ark to recite the Prayer. But there was among them one who did know how to say the Shema and to go before the ark.

C.   "Among them, he was 'like a lily among brambles.'

D.   "Ten men went in to greet the bride, but did not know how to say the blessings for the bride and groom. But there was among them one who knew how to say the blessing for bride and groom.

E.   "Among them, he was 'like a lily among brambles.'

F.   "Ten went into a house of mourning but did not know how to say the blessing for mourners. But among them one did know how to say the blessing for mourners.

G.   "Among them, he was 'like a lily among brambles.'"

The same model now governs secondary articulation, the exegetical parable delivering a message that serves other cases. But the primary message is at No. 5.

XIX:1

7.   A.   R. Eleazar Hisma went to a certain place. The people said to him, "Does my lord know how to recite the Shema's blessings?"

B.   He said to them, "No."

C.   They said to him, "Does my lord know how to come near to recite the prayer before the ark?"

D.   He said to them, "No."

E.   They said to him, "Is this R. Eleazar, the man for whom people make such a fuss? It is for nothing that people call you 'my lord!'"

F.   His face turned white. He went to R. Aqiba, and he looked sick. He said to him, "What's with you? You look sick."

G.   He told the story to him.

H.   He said to him, "Does my lord wish to learn?"

I.   He said to him, "Yes."

J.   After he had learned, he went to the same place. They said to him, "Does my lord know how to recite the Shema's blessings?"

K.   He said to them, "Yes."

L.   They said to him, "Does my lord know how to come near to recite the prayer before the ark?"

M.   He said to them, "Yes."

N.   They said to him, "Lo, Eleazar has regained the power of speech," and they called him R. Eleazar Hisma [=who can speak].

O.   R. Jonah would teach his disciples even the blessing for bride and groom and even the blessing for mourners, saying to them, "You should be masters in every detail."

1.   *On what basis does the narrative attain coherence, e.g., what is the action or event that precipitates the telling of the tale?* The story is attached because of the reference to nine men's not knowing various basic liturgical formulas. The point of the story is that with proper study, one may learn the liturgies, and the Rabbinical sage who did not know them with proper study succeeded in mastering them. The conclusion imparts purpose and coherence to all that has gone before: the play on the name of the master who is subject of the story.

2.   *What point of conflict or intersection of wills accounts for the telling of the tale and how is the point of tension resolved?* The conflict is between the peoples' expectation of the master and his actual knowledge, and it is resolved as indicated.

3.   *How, in light of other, comparable, pieces of writing and the data that they yield, is the narrative classified, and what are its indicative formal qualities, e.g., long or short, complex or simple?* The anecdote is simple and works itself out in the contrast between the two obvious units.

XX:1

6. A   "[As an apple tree among the trees of the wood so is my beloved among young men. With great delight I sat in his shadow, and his fruit was sweet to my taste" (Song 2:3):] R. Judah b. R. Simon made two statements:

    B.   "Just as an apple costs only a penny, but you can smell its fragrance any number of times,

    C.   "So said Moses to the Israelites, 'If you wish to be redeemed, you may be redeemed for a simple matter.'

    D.   "They may be compared to someone who had sore feet and he went to all the physicians for healing and was not healed. Then he came to one, who said to him, 'If you want to be healed, you can be healed in a simple way. Plaster your feet with bullshit.'

    E.   "So said Moses to the Israelites, 'If you wish to be redeemed, you may be redeemed for a simple matter.'

    F.   "'"And you shall take a bunch of hyssop and dip it"'" (Ex. 12:22).

    G.   "They said to him, 'Our lord, Moses, how much does this bundle of hyssop cost? Four or five cents?'

    H.   "He said to them, 'Even a penny. But it will make it possible for you to inherit the spoil of Egypt, the spoil at the Sea, the spoil of Sihon and Og, and the spoil of the thirty-one kings [of Canaan].'

    I.   "The palm-branch [for the Festival of Tabernacles], which costs someone a good dollar, and through which one carries out a variety of religious duties, all the more so!

  J. "Therefore Moses admonishes Israel, 'And you shall take for yourself on the first day' (Lev. 23:40)."

The exegetical parable, D, tracks the message of E-F+G-I, J, and is particular to its cases, which to be sure may be very many, all of them instantiating the same simple proposition.

XX:I.

7. A. ["As an apple tree among the trees of the wood so is my beloved among young men. With great delight I sat in his shadow, and his fruit was sweet to my taste" (Song 2:3):] R. Judah b. R. Simon made another statement:

  B. "The matter may be compared to the case of a king who had a precious stone and a pearl. His son came along and said to him, 'Give it to me.'

  C. "He said to him, 'It is yours, it belongs to you, and I give it over to you.'

  D. "So said the Israelites before the Holy One, blessed be He, "'The Lord is my strength and my song'" (Ex. 15:2).

  E. "Said to them the Holy One, blessed be He, 'It is yours, it belongs to you, and I give it over to you.'

  F. "For 'strength' refers only to the Torah: 'The Lord will give strength to his people' (Ps. 29:11). [Simon, p. 100, n. 3: So the Community of Israel said, "I longed for his shadow," i.e. "I longed for the Torah and the Divine protection it affords—and I did indeed sit there, God freely giving it to me, declaring it altogether mine."]

The Mashal simply translates into the king and the prince the transaction of God and Israel, an exact replication of the details—no adaptation here.

XXII:II

2.

  A. ["Sustain me with raisins refresh me with apples; for I am sick with love" (Song 2:3]): R. Simeon b. Yohai taught on Tannaite authority, "When the Israelites came forth from Egypt, what were they like?

  B. "They were comparable to a prince who recovered from an illness.

  C. "Said his tutor [to the king], 'Let your son go to school.'

  D. "Said the king to him, 'My son has not yet recovered his full color. For he has become pale because of his illness. Let my son take it easy and enjoy himself for three months with food and drink, and then he can go back to school.'

  E. "So when the Israelites went forth from Egypt, there

were among them those who had been deformed through the slave labor of mortar and bricks.

F. "The ministering angels said to him, 'Lo, the time has come. Give them the Torah.'

G. "Said to them the Holy One, blessed be He, 'My children have not yet recovered their full color on account of the slave labor of mortar and bricks.

H. "'But let my children take it easy for three months at the well and with the quail, and then I will give them the Torah.

I. "'And when is that? "In the third month"' (Ex. 19:1)." [Simon, *Song of Songs Rabbah* (London, 1948: Soncino), p. 106, n. 1: Hence now in the third month has the time come for you to 'Sustain me with raisins, refresh me with apples; for I am sick with love.']

The exegetical burden of the Mashal is to explain why God has to sustain Israel with raisins and apples. The comparison then invokes the recuperation of Israel in the wilderness before reaching Sinai. The king/prince analogy is all that is autonomous of the case. Simon's comment is required to complete the analogy: why the third month?

XXXI:i

6. A. "O my dove, in the clefts of the rock" (Song 2:14):] It was taught on Tannaite authority by the house of R. Ishmael, "When the Israelites went forth from Egypt, to what were they to be compared?

B. "To a dove that fled from a hawk and flew into the cleft of a rock and found a serpent hidden there.

C. "It went in but could not, because the snake was hidden there, and it tried to go backward but could not, because the hawk was standing outside.

D. "What did the dove do? It began to cry out and beat its wings, so that the owner of the dovecote should hear and come and save it.

E. "That is what the Israelites were like at the sea.

F. "Go down into the sea they could not, because the sea had not yet been split before them.

G. "Retreat they could not, because Pharaoh was already drawing near.

H. "So what did they do?

I. "'And they were afraid, and the children of Israel cried out to the Lord' (Ex. 14:10).

J. "Forthwith: 'Thus the Lord saved Israel that day' (Ex. 14:30)."

The exegetical parable is particular to the case, translating the situation of Israel at the Sea to the case of the trapped dove. Israel is the dove, God is the master of the dovecote, just as the base-verse requires.

XXXI:i

7. A. "O my dove, in the clefts of the rock" (Song 2:14)] R. Judah in the name of R. Hama of Kefar Tehumin: "The matter may be compared to the king who had an only daughter and wanted to listen to her converse.
B. "What did he do?
C. "He circulated an announcement and said, 'Let everybody assemble in the piazza.'
D. "When they had come forth, what did he do? He made a gesture to his servants, and they suddenly fell on her like thugs.
E. "She began to cry out, 'Father, father, save me.'
F. "He said, 'Had I not treated you in this way, you would not have cried out and said, "Father, save me."'
G. "So when the Israelites were in Egypt, the Egyptians enslaved them, and they begin to cry out and look upward to the Holy One, blessed be He: 'And it came to pass in the course of those many days that the king of Egypt died, and the children of Israel signed by reason of the bondage, and they cried' (Ex. 2:23).
H. "Forthwith: 'And God heard their groaning' (Ex. 2:24).
I. "The Holy One, blessed be He, heard their prayer and brought them out with am mighty and and with an outstretched arm.
J. "But the Holy One, blessed be He, wanted to listen to their voice, and they did not want it.
K. "What did the Holy One, blessed be He, do?
L. "He hardened Pharaoh's heart and he pursued after them: 'And the Lord hardened the heart of Pharaoh, king of Egypt, and he pursued' (Ex. 14:8); 'And Pharaoh brought near' (Ex. 14:10)."

9. A. [Continuing 7.L:] "When they saw them, they raised their eyes to the Holy One, blessed be He: 'The children of Israel lifted up their eyes, and behold, the Egyptians were marching after them, and they were much afraid, and the children of Israel cried out to the Lord' (Ex. 14:10).
B. "This was in the same way that they had cried out in Egypt.
C. "Now when the Holy One, blessed be He,

heard, he said to them, 'If I had not treated you in this way, I should not have heard your voice.

D.   "It is in connection with that moment that he said, 'O my dove, in the clefts of the rock.'

E.   "What is says is not 'let me hear a voice,' but 'let me hear your voice.'

F.   "For 'I have already heard it in Egypt.'

G.   "And when the children of Israel cried out before the Holy One, blessed be He, forthwith: 'thus the Lord saved Israel that day' (Ex. 14:30).

The exegetical parable completes its statement with G, and is then elaborated twice over. This secondary development amplifies the primary point but changes nothing. The Mashal itself invokes the persons of king and princess, but otherwise simply instantiates in the simile the course of the scriptural transaction as the exegete reads it.

XXXIII:ii

1.   A.   "... he pastures his flock among the lilies (Song 2:16):"

B.   R. Yohanan was punished with suffering from gallstones for three years and a half.

C.   R. Hanina came up to visit him. He said to him, "How're you doing?"

D.   He said to him, "I have more than I can bear."

E.   He said to him, "Don't say that. But say, 'The faithful God.'"

F.   When the pain got severe, he would say, "Faithful God," and when the pain became greater than he could bear, R. Hanina would come in to him and say something over him, and he restored his soul.

G.   After some time R. Hanina became ill, and R. Yohanan came up to visit him. He said to him, "How're you doing?"

H   He said to him, "How hard is suffering."

I.   He said to him, "Yes, but the reward is still greater."

J.   He said to him, "I don't want either them or their reward."

K.   He said to him, "Why don't you say that word that you said over me and restored my soul?"

L.   He said to him, "When I was up and about, I served as a pledge for others, but now that I am within, I don't need anybody else to serve as a pledge for me."

> M.   He said to him, "It is written, 'he pastures his flock among the lilies':
> N.   "the rod of the Holy One, blessed be He, draws near only to people whose hearts are as soft as lilies.'"

1.   *On what basis does the narrative attain coherence, e.g., what is the action or event that precipitates the telling of the tale?* The contrast between the two units, A-F, G-L, is resolved by M-N. That is, Hanina will heal others but does not want to burden others to heal himself, because God favors those who are full of mercy for others.

2.   *What point of conflict or intersection of wills accounts for the telling of the tale and how is the point of tension resolved?* The conflict is between Hanina's treatment of Yohanan and his failure to use the same measures to heal himself.

3.   *How, in light of other, comparable, pieces of writing and the data that they yield, is the narrative classified, and what are its indicative formal qualities, e.g., long or short, complex or simple?* This is a simple anecdote, which makes its point through the contrast as noted.

XXXIII:ii

> 2.   A.   Said R. Eleazar, "The matter may be compared to the case of a householder who had two cows, one strong, the other weak.
> B.   "On which one does he place the burden? Is it not on the strong one?
> C.   "Thus the Holy One, blessed be He, does not impose trials upon the wicked. Why not? Because they cannot endure: 'But the wicked are like the troubled sea' (Isa. 57:20).
> D.   "Upon whom does he impose trials? Upon the righteous: 'The Lord tries the righteous' (Ps. 11:5); 'And it came to pass after these things that god tried Abraham' (Gen. 22:1); 'And it came to pass after these things that his master's wife cast her eyes on Joseph' (Gen. 39:7)."

The exegetical parable serves a narrative, which is not a commonplace phenomenon in our document. But second look shows that what is at stake is the exegesis of Ps. 11:5, and the parable exactly matches the requirement of that base verse, that is, an illustration of why the burden of a trial is placed on the strong, not the weak cow/person. The formal construction then is a bit complex but not deceiving. The contrast between Hanina's healing of Yohanan, B-F, and Hanina's unwillingness to heal himself, G-L, yields the exegesis, M-N, a word of praise of Hanina by Yohanan, so it seems to me, who does not want to impose his suffering on others. That then yields the exegetical parable, which services Ps. 11:5. So the exegetical focus of the parable is autonomous of the narrative, No. 1, which is well served nonetheless.

CHAPTER THREE

SONG OF SONGS RABBAH
PARASHAH THREE

XXXVIII:ii.1-43 forms a vast Scripture-story amplifying Song 3:4.
At XL.i.23-29, in connection with "What is that coming up from
the wilderness, like a column of smoke, perfumed with myrrh and
frankincense, with all the fragrant powders of the merchant?" (Song
3:6), we find Tosefta Kippurim's narrative complement to Mishnah-
tractate Yoma 3:11, reproduced verbatim. That passage is discussed
ad loc. in Volume I. It is primary to Tosefta's complement to the
Mishnah and is parachuted down here for thematic reasons.

XL:i

12. A. In what form did he make his appearance to him?

B. R. Hama b. R. Hanina said, "He appeared to him in the form
of the angel that served the wicked Esau: 'For since I have seen
your face as one sees the face of a god' (Gen. 33:10).

C. "He said to him, 'Your face is like the face of your guardian
angel.'"

D. "The matter may be compared to a king who had a savage dog
and a tame lion. What did the king do?

E. "The king would take his lion and sick him against the son,
saying, 'If the dog comes to have a fight with the son, he will
say to the dog, "The lion cannot have a fight with me, [how]
are you going to make out in a fight with me?"'

F. "So if the nations come to have a fight with Israel, the Holy
One, blessed be He, says to them, 'Your angelic prince could
not stand up to Israel, and as to you, how much the more so!'"

The angel that wrestled with Jacob is at issue. The exegetical parable, XL:i.12D-F, tracks the verse subject to exegesis. All that is generic is the king/prince.

XLIII:ii

1. A. [Supply: "King Solomon made himself a palanquin, from the
wood of Lebanon. He made its posts of silver, its back of gold,
its seat of purple; it was lovingly wrought within by the daughters of Jerusalem:"]

    B.   R. Yudan b. R. Ilai interpreted the verses to speak of the ark:

    C.   "'... a palanquin': this is the ark."

    2.   A.   [Supply: "a palanquin:"]

            B.   What is a palanquin?

            C.   A litter.

    3.   A.   The matter may be compared to the case of a king who had an only daughter, who was beautiful, pious, and gracious.

            B.   Said the king to his staff, "my daughter is beautiful, pious, and gracious, and yet you do not make her a litter? Make her a litter, for it is better that the beauty of my daughter should appear from within a litter."

            C.   So said the Holy One, blessed be He, "My Torah is beautiful, pious, and gracious, and yet you do not make an ark for it?

            D.   "It is better that the beauty of my Torah should appear from within the ark."

The exegetical parable leaves no doubt that the simile begins in the cited verse, inviting the explanation of why a litter is required for the Torah, 3.C-D, and that question is answered by A-B.

XLIV:ii

    1.   A.   "... with the crown with which his mother crowned him:"

            B.   Said R. Yohanan, "R. Simeon b. Yohai asked R. Eleazar b. R. Yosé, saying to him, 'Is it possible that you have heard from your father [Yosé b. R. Halafta] the meaning of the phrase, "with the crown with which his mother crowned him"?'

            C.   "He said to him, 'Yes.'

            D.   "He said to him, 'And what was it?'

    E.   "He said to him, 'The matter may be compared to the case of a king who had an only daughter, whom he loved exceedingly, calling her "My daughter."

    F.   "'But he loved her so much that he called her, "My sister," and he loved her so much that he called her, "My mother."

    G.   "'So did the Holy One, blessed be He, exceedingly love Israel, calling them, "My daughter." That is shown in this verse: "Listen, O daughter, and consider" (Ps. 45:11).

    H.   "'Then he loved them so much that he called them, "My sister," as in this verse, "Open to me, my sister, my love" (Song 5:2).

    I.   "'Then he loved them so much that he called them, "My mother," as in this verse, "Listen to me, my people, and give ear to me, my nation" (Isa. 51:4), and the word for "my nation" is written "my mother."'"

J.   R. Simeon b. Yohai stood up and kissed him on his head and said, "If I had come only to hear from your mouth this explanation, it would have sufficed."

The exegetical parable is explicitly generated by the task of explaining the cited verse and makes sense only in that context. Then the progression from daughter to sister to mother makes sense, and every detail responds to the base-verse and its requirement.

XLIV:II

2.   A.   [Supply: "with the crown with which his mother crowned him":]
B.   Said R. Hanina b. R. Isaac, "We have made the rounds of the entire Scripture and have not found evidence that Bath-Sheba made Solomon her son a crown, and yet you say, 'with the crown with which his mother crowned him'!
C.   "But just as a crown is studded with precious stones and pearls, so the tent of meeting was marked off with blue and purple, crimson and linen."
3.   A.   R. Joshua of Sikhnin taught in the name of R. Levi: "When the Holy One, blessed be He, said to Moses, 'Make me a tabernacle,' Moses might have brought four poles and spread over them [skins to make] the tabernacle.
B.   "But this is not how the Holy One, blessed be He, did it. Rather, he took him above and showed him on high red fire, green fire, black fire, and white fire. He then said to him, 'Make me a tabernacle like this.'
C.   "Moses said to the Holy One, blessed be He, 'Lord of the ages, where am I going to get red fire, green fire, black fire, or white fire?'
D.   "He said to him, 'After the pattern which is shown to you on the mountain' (Ex. 25:40)."
4.   A.   Said R. Abun [Pesiqta deRab Kahana I:III.10: R. Berekhiah in the name of R. Levi], "[The matter may be compared to the case of] a king who had a beautiful icon.
B.   "He said to the manager of his household, 'Make me one like this.'
C.   "He said to him, 'My lord, O king, how can I make one like this ?'
D.   "He said to him, 'You in accord with your raw materials and I in accord with my glory.'
E.   "So said the Holy One, blessed be He, to Moses, 'See and make.'

F.   "He said to him, 'Lord of the world, am I god that I can make something like this?'

G.   "He said to him, 'After the pattern which is shown to you on the mountain' (Ex. 25:40)."

5.   A.   R. Berekhiah in the name of R. Bezalel: "The matter may be compared to the case of a king who appeared to his household manager clothed in a garment covered entirely with precious stones.

B.   "He said to him, 'Make me one like this.'

C.   "He said to him, 'My lord, O king, how can I make one like this [Pesiqta: where am I going to get myself a garment made entirely of precious stones]?'

D.   "So said the Holy One, blessed be He, to Moses, 'Make me a tabernacle.'

E.   "He said to him, 'Lord of the world, can I make something like this?'

F.   "He said to him, 'See and make.'

G.   "He said to him, 'Lord of the world, am I god that I can make something like this?'

H.   "He said to him, 'After the pattern which is shown to you on the mountain' (Ex. 25:40)."

The exegetical parables, No. 4, 5, are primary at Pesiqta deRab Kahana I:III.10, where they form part of the exposition of Num. 7:1, "On the day that Moses completed the setting up of the Tabernacle, he anointed and consecrated it." They respond to Ex. 25:40, "After the pattern shown you on the mountain." Then, at No. 4, we have a king who has is manager make an icon like the one he shows him, and at No. 5, it is a garment. In both cases the parable is particular to its exegetical task and makes sense only in that connection.

CHAPTER FOUR

SONG OF SONGS RABBAH
PARASHAH FOUR

XLVIII:v

1. A.   Another interpretation of the verse, "... behind your veil. Your hair is like a flock of goats moving down the slopes of Gilead (Song 4:3):"

16. A.   [In the version of Genesis Rabbah XXXII:X.1:] [Supply: "And the waters prevailed so mightily upon the earth that all the high mountains under the whole heaven were covered, the waters prevailed above the mountains, covering them fifteen cubits deep" (Gen. 7:19):]

B.   R. Jonathan went up to pray in Jerusalem. When he went by the Palatinus, a Samaritan saw him and asked him, "Where are you going?"

C.   He said to him, "To pray in Jerusalem."

D.   He said to him, "Wouldn't it be better for you to pray on this holy mountain and not on that dunghill?"

E.   He said to him, "Why is it regarded as blessed?"

F.   He said to him, "Because it was not submerged by the water of the Flood."

G.   For a moment R. Jonathan lost his learning in the law. His ass driver said to him, "Sir, give me permission and I shall answer him."

H.   He said to him, "Go ahead."

I.   He said to him, "If this place falls into the category of mountains, then it is written, 'And it covered all the high mountains' (Gen. 7:19). And if it does not fall into the category of mountains, then Scripture had no need to make special reference to it [since obviously it was submerged]."

J.   At that moment R. Jonathan got off the ass and mounted the ass-driver on it for a span of three *mils*, and he recited in his regard the following verses of Scripture:

K.   "'There shall not be barren among you, male or female, or among your cattle' (Deut. 7:14), even among your cattle drivers.

L.   "'No weapon that is formed against you shall prosper, and every tongue that shall rise against you in judgment you shall condemn' (Isa. 54:17).

M.   "'Your empty heads are like pomegranates split open'
(Song 4:3), meaning that even the emptiest head among
you is as full of good replies as a pomegranate is full of
seeds.

N.   "'behind your veil:' needless to say, the modest and
self-controlled among you."

1.   *On what basis does the narrative attain coherence, e.g., what is the action
or event that precipitates the telling of the tale?* So far as we have a narrative, it concerns the sage who lost his learning and the unlettered
Israelite who successfully intervened. That is the impact of the climactic passage, J-M. In that context, the debate on the status of the
Samaritan's mountain is secondary and without the tension and
resolution imparted by the action of forgetting the learning, all we
have is a dramatized exchange of ideas.

2.   *What point of conflict or intersection of wills accounts for the telling of the
tale and how is the point of tension resolved?* As noted, the sage loses his
learning in a moment of conflict, and the humble man takes over
and wins the argument for the Torah.

3.   *How, in light of other, comparable, pieces of writing and the data that
they yield, is the narrative classified, and what are its indicative formal qualities, e.g., long or short, complex or simple?* The complexity emerges in the
mixture of the substantive dispute and the formal setting thereof.

XLIX:i

1.   A.   "Your two breasts are like two fawns (Song 4:5):"

B.   This refers to Moses and Aaron.

J.   Just as one breast is not larger than the other, so Moses and
Aaron were the same: "These are Moses and Aaron" (Ex. 6:27),
"These are Aaron and Moses" (Ex. 6:26), so that in knowledge
of the Torah Moses was not greater than Aaron, and Aaron
was not greater than Moses.

2.   A.   R. Abba said, "The matter may be compared to the
case of a king who had two first-rate pearls, which he put
in the balance.

B.   "This one was not greater than that, and that was
not greater than this.

C.   "So Moses and Aaron were equal."

3.   A.   Said R. Hanina b. R. Pappa, "Blessed is the
Omnipresent, who has chosen these two brothers.

B.   "For they were created only for the Torah and
the glory of Israel."

4.   A.   R. Joshua of Sikhnin in the name of R. Levi:

"There were two species of snakes in Alexandria, one of which induced cold, the other heat.

B.   "There was a case in which physicians sent for some of them and made a compound out of them with which they healed [snake bites]."

The exegetical parable illustrates the equality of Moses and Aaron as two pearls; it has no embedded, implicit action but is just a simile. The Ma'aseh, XLIX:i.4, serves to instantiate the basic proposition.

LVI:i

1.   A.   "A garden locked is my sister, my bride, [a garden locked, a fountain sealed] (Song 4:12):"

B.   R. Judah b. R. Simon in the name of R. Joshua b. Levi: "[The matter may be compared to the case of] a king who had two daughters, an older and a younger, and who did not take time out to marry them off but left them for many years and went overseas.

C.   "The daughters went and took the law into their own hands, and married themselves off to husbands. And each one of them took her husband's signature and his seal.

D.   "After a long time the king came back from overseas and heard people maligning his daughters, saying, 'The king's daughters have already played the whore.'

E.   "What did he do? He issued a proclamation and said, 'Everybody come out to the piazza,' and he came and went into session in the antechamber [holding court there].

F.   "He said to them, 'My daughters, is this what you have done and have ruined yourselves?'

G.   "Each one of them immediately produced her husband's signature and his seal.

H.   "He called his son-in-law and asked, 'To which of them are you the husband?'

I.   "He said to him, 'I am the first of your sons-in-law, married to your elder daughter.'

J.   "He said to him, 'And what is this?'

K.   "He said to him, 'This is my signature and my seal.'

L.   "And so with the second.

M.   "Then the king said, 'My daughters have been guarded from fornication, and you malign and shame them! By your lives, I shall carry out judgment against you.'

N.   "So too with the nations of the world: since they taunt Israel and say, '"And the Egyptians made the people of Israel work with rigor" (Ex. 1:13), if that is what they could make them do in labor, how much the more so with their bodies and with their wives'!'

> O.   "Then said the Holy One, blessed be He, 'A garden locked is
> my sister, my bride.'"

The protracted account of matters does not transform the exegetical parable into a free-standing narrative adapted for illustrative purposes. For the details of the staged exchange responding to the malign talk, E-M, respond to the requirements of N-O. Yet what is lacking at N is the counterpart to the attestation of the valid marriages, G-L. In other words, what is lacking in the exegetical parable is the detailed application of the simile to the case, and the "so too…," clause hardly suffices.

LVI:1

8.   A.   [Supply from Leviticus Rabbah XXXII:V.2: Another interpretation of "A garden locked" (Song 4:12):] R. Phineas in the name of R. Hiyya bar Abba, "Because the Israelites locked themselves up and avoided licentious sexual behavior with the Egyptians, they were redeemed from Egypt. On that account was 'your being sent forth' [that is, 'your shoots'] 'are an orchard of pomegranates with all choicest fruits.' That interpretation is in line with the following: 'And it came to pass, when Pharaoh sent forth… ' (Ex. 13:17). [The shoots of Song 4:13) calls to mind the "sending forth' of Pharaoh, and the Israelites were sent forth by virtue of the fact that they had protected the integrity of their 'shoots,' that is, their offspring.]

> B.   R. Simeon b. Yohai taught on Tannaite authority, "[The Egyptians were] in the position of someone who inherited a piece of ground that was a dumping ground. The heir was lazy, so he went and sold it for some trifling sum. The buyer went and worked hard and dug up in the dump heap and found a treasure, and with it he built himself a big palace. The buyer would walk about the marketplace, with servants following in a retinue, all on the strength of that treasure that he had bought with the dump heap.
>
> C.   "The seller, when he saw this, he began to choke, saying, 'Woe, what I have lost!'
>
> D.   "So too, when the Israelites were in Egypt, they were enslaved in mortar and bricks, and they were held in contempt by the Egyptians. But when they saw them with their standards, encamped at the sea, in royal array, the Egyptians began to choke, saying, 'Woe, what have we sent forth from our land!'
>
> E.   "That is in line with this verse, 'And it came to pass [a word that contains consonants that can be read, 'woe,'] when Pharaoh had let the people go' (Ex. 13:17)."

9.   A.   Said R. Jonathan, "They were in the position of someone who had a field the size of a kor who went and sold it for a piddling sum.

B.   "The buyer went and dug wells in it and made in it gardens and orchards.

C.   "When the seller saw this, he began to choke, saying, 'Woe, what I have lost!'

D.   "So too, when the Israelites were in Egypt, they were enslaved in mortar and bricks, and they were held in contempt by the Egyptians. But when they saw them with their standards, encamped at the sea, in royal array, the Egyptians began to choke, saying, 'Woe, what have we sent forth from our land!'

E.   "That is in line with this verse, 'And it came to pass [a word that contains consonants that can be read, 'woe,'] when Pharaoh had let the people go' (Ex. 13:17)."

10.   A.   R. Yosé says, "They were in the position of someone who had a grove of cedars, who went and sold it for a piddling sum.

B.   "The buyer went and made of the wood boxes, chests, towers and carriages.

C.   "When the seller saw this, he began to choke, saying, 'Woe, what I have lost!'

D.   "So too, when the Israelites were in Egypt, they were enslaved in mortar and bricks, and they were held in contempt by the Egyptians. But when they saw them with their standards, encamped at the sea, in royal array, the Egyptians began to choke, saying, 'Woe, what have we sent forth from our land!'

E.   "That is in line with this verse, 'And it came to pass [a word that contains consonants that can be read, 'woe,'] when Pharaoh had let the people go' (Ex. 13:17)."

The task of the several exegetical parables is to capture the loss inflicted upon themselves by the Egyptians when they sent forth the Israelites, and the Egyptians' recognition of that loss. The first, 8.B-C+D, tracks the exegetical assignment, D-E being realized at B-C; the second, No. 9, matching the first; and the third, No. 10, following suit.

CHAPTER FIVE

SONG OF SONGS RABBAH
PARASHAH FIVE

LXI:I

6. A. [I come to my garden, my sister, my bride, I gather my myrrh with my spice, I eat my honeycomb with my honey, I drink my wine with my milk. Eat, O friends, and drink; drink deeply, O lovers! (Song 5:1):] "Eat, O friends:" this refers to the princes.

   B. "drink deeply, O lovers:" this refers to the nobles.

   C. Why does [the Song] refer to the princes as friends?

   D. Said R. Simeon b. Yosina, "[The reason is that the princes and nobles are given special standing in the conditions of their dedicatory-offerings, which no other individuals are ever accorded, as I shall now explain:] In every other circumstance an individual does not present as an offering a sin-offering made as a free-will-offering [but only as an obligatory one], while here a sin-offering is brought voluntarily.

   E. "In every other circumstance the offering brought by an individual does not override the restrictions involving uncleanness and the Sabbath, while here the offering brought by an individual does override the restrictions involving uncleanness and the Sabbath.

   F. "In all other circumstances, an individual does not present a sin-offering except in the case of a[n unwitting] sin, while here an individual does present a sin-offering not in the case of a[n unwitting] sin."

7. A. [In connection with the anomalous rules governing the offering of the princes,] another explanation of the phrase, "Eat, O friends:"

   B. Said R. Berekhiah, "The matter may be compared to the case of a king who made a banquet and invited guests, and a dead creeping thing fell into the soup. If the king had declined to eat it, all of them would have declined to eat it. The king put out his hand [to serve himself] so everybody else did too. [That accounts for the acceptance of the offerings under the special rules, setting aside restrictions ordinarily in force.]"

8. A. [In connection with the anomalous rules governing the offering of the princes,] said R. Yannai, "The matter may be com-

     pared to the case of a king who made a banquet and invited
     guests to come to him, and he went around among them, say-
     ing to them, 'I hope you like it, I hope you enjoy it.'"

9. A. [In connection with the anomalous rules governing the offer-
     ing of the princes,] said R. Abbahu, "The matter may be com-
     pared to the case of a king who made a banquet and invited
     guests to come, and when they had eaten and drunk, he said,
     'Take this good helping and give it to the host.'

  B. "Thus here: 'I come to my garden, my sister, my bride, I gather
     my myrrh with my spice, I eat my honeycomb with my honey,'
     so you eat too.

  C. "'I drink my wine with my milk.' You too: 'Eat, O friends, and
     drink; drink deeply, O lovers.'"

The three Halakhic parables explain why the offering of the princes is subjected to rules different from the offering of private persons.
No. 7 has the king affirm special rules, No. 8 is not fully realized,
and No. 9 recasts the entire transaction.

LXXIV:I

9. A. ["His arms are rounded gold, set with jewels. His body is ivory
     work, encrusted with sapphires" (Song 5:14):] "encrusted with
     sapphires:"

  B. [Study of the Torah] drains the strength of people, for it is as
     hard as sapphire. [The words for encrusted and drain the strength
     use the same consonants.]

    11. A. R. Eliezer b. R. Simeon:

      B. Ass-drivers came to his father to buy grain from the
      town.

      C. They saw him sitting at the oven. His mother would
      take [a hot roll from the oven] and he would eat it, his
      mother would take [a hot roll from the oven] and he would
      eat it—until he ate up all the rolls.

      D. They said, "Woe! there is an evil snake in that man's
      belly. It appears that this one is going to bring a famine
      to the world."

      E. He heard what they were saying.

      F. When they went out to buy their burden of grain,
      he took their asses and brought them up to the roof.

      G. They came looking for their asses and did not find
      them.

      H. They raised their eyes and saw them situated on the
      roof.

      I. They went to his father and repeated the story to him.

      J. He said to them, "Is it possible that you made him
      hear some offensive statement?"

K.   They said to him, "No, my lord, but this is what happened."

L.   He said to them, "Then why did you call the evil eye down upon him [by grudging him his meal]? Was he eating something that belonged to you? Or is it your job to provide him with his meals? Is not the One who created him the one who also created his food? Still, go speak to him in my name, and he will bring them down for you."

M.   The latter miracle was more difficult than the former.

N.   When he brought them up, he brought them up one by one, but when he brought them down, he brought them down two by two.

O.   But when he was engaged in the study of the Torah, even his cloak he was unable to bear.

P.   That is in line with this verse: "encrusted with sapphires." [For study of the Torah drains the strength of people].

12.   A.   A member of the household in the establishment of Rabban Gamaliel had the habit of taking a basket carrying forty *seahs* of grain and bringing it to the baker.

B.   He said to him, "All this wonderful strength is in you, and you are not engaged in the Torah?"

C.   When he got involved in the Torah, he would begin to take thirty, then twenty, then twelve, then eight *seahs*, and when he had completed a book, even a basket of only a single *seah* he could not carry.

D.   And some say that he could not even carry his own hat, but others had to take it off him, for he could not do it.

E.   That is in line with this verse: "encrusted with sapphires." [For study of the Torah drains the strength of people].

1.   *On what basis does the narrative attain coherence, e.g., what is the action or event that precipitates the telling of the tale?* The first story, No. 11, finds its point in the contrast between the remarkable appetite and strength of the principal prior to taking up Torah-study, and the weakness that came over him afterward. Then the point of the whole is supplied by O. Without O-P, the narrative in two parts, taking the asses up to the roof, carrying them down, lacks all focus and point. The second story, No. 12, goes over the same ground but is not realized so dynamically.

2.   *What point of conflict or intersection of wills accounts for the telling of the*

tale and how is the point of tension resolved? The contrast between strength outside of Torah-study and weakness within resolves the intersection.

3.   *How, in light of other, comparable, pieces of writing and the data that they yield, is the narrative classified, and what are its indicative formal qualities, e.g., long or short, complex or simple?* No. 11 is a nicely articulated anecdote, with its setting of the stage, B-E, then the response, F-H, and the complaint, I-N. Had the story ended at that point, the issue would have been the father's response to the complaint, L, and the conclusion, M-N, the whole cohering as a standard miracle story. The imposition of the Torah-study exegesis changes the face altogether.

LXXVI:i

1.   A.   "His speech is most sweet (Song 5:16):"

3.   A.   [Leviticus Rabbah XXVII:VI.2ff.:] Said R. Samuel b. R. Nahman, "On three occasions the Holy One, blessed be He, came to engage in argument with Israel, and the nations of the world rejoiced, saying, 'Can these ever [dare] engage in an argument with their creator? Now he will wipe them out of the world.'

B.   "One was when he said to them, 'Come, and let us reason together, says the Lord' [Isa. 1:18]. When the Holy One, blessed be He, saw that the nations of the world were rejoicing, he turned the matter to [Israel's] advantage: 'If your sins are as scarlet, they shall be white as snow' [Isa. 1:18].

C.   "Then the nations of the world were astonished, and said, 'This is repentance, and this is rebuke? He has planned only to amuse himself with his children.'

D.   "[A second time was] when he said to them, 'Hear, you mountains, the controversy of the Lord' [Mic. 6:2], the nations of the world rejoiced, saying, 'How can these ever [dare] engage in an argument with their creator? Now he will wipe them out of the world.'

E.   "When the Holy One, blessed be He, saw that the nations of the world were rejoicing, he turned the matter to [Israel's] advantage: 'O my people, what have I done to you? In what have I wearied you? Testify against me' [Mic. 6:3]. 'Remember what Balak king of Moab devised' [Mic. 6:5].

F. "Then the nations of the world were astonished, saying, 'This is repentance, and this is rebuke, one following the other? He has planned only to amuse himself with his children.'

G. "[A third time was] when he said to them, 'The Lord has an indictment against Judah, and will punish Jacob according to his ways' [Hos. 12:2], the nations of the world rejoiced, saying, 'How can these ever [dare] engage in an argument with their creator? Now he will wipe them out of the world.'

H. "When the Holy One, blessed be He, saw that the nations of the world were rejoicing, he turned the matter to [Israel's] advantage. That is in line with the following verse of Scripture: 'In the womb he [Jacob = Israel] took his brother [Esau = other nations] by the heel [and in his manhood he strove with God. He strove with the angel and prevailed, he wept and sought his favor]'" (Hos. 12:3-4).

4. A. Said R. Yudan [b. R. Simeon], "The matter may be compared to a widow who was complaining to a judge about her son. When she saw that the judge was in session and handing out sentences of punishment by fire, pitch, and lashes, she said, 'If I report the bad conduct of my son to that judge, he will kill him now.' She waited until he was finished. When he had finished, he said to her, 'Madam, this son of yours, how has he behaved badly toward you?'

B. "She said to him, 'My lord, when he was in my womb, he kicked me.'

C. "He said to her, 'Now has he done anything wrong to you?'

D. "She said to him, 'No.'

E. "He said to her, 'Go your way, there is nothing wrong in the matter [that you report].'

F. "[Lev. R. adds:] "So, when the Holy One, blessed be He, saw that the nations of the world were rejoicing, he turned the matter to [Israel's] advantage:

G. "'In the womb he took his brother by

> the heel' (Mic. 12:3). [Then the nations of the world were astonished, saying, 'This is repentance and this is rebuke, one following the other? He has planned only to amuse himself with his children.']"
>
> H. R. Eleazar b. R. Simon said, "The God of Jacob, our father, has paid honor to him."

The exegetical parable, A-E, does not actually match the situation that it is meant to clarify. The widowed mother does not match God, and the matter is not turned to the son's advantage, so the son also does not match Israel of the parable. Here the parable at best is adapted to its context but does not meet its requirements in any striking fashion.

LXXVI:1

8.   A.   Another interpretation of the verse, "His speech is most sweet:"

      B.   The matter may be compared to the case of a king who scolded his son, and the son was afraid and lost heart.

      C.   When the king saw that his son had lost heart, he began to hug and kiss him and appease him, saying to him, "What's with you? Are you not my only son? Am I not your father?"

      D.   So when the Holy One, blessed be He, spoke: "I am the Lord your God," their spirit forthwith departed.

      E.   Since they had died, the angels began to hug and kiss them, saying to them, "What's with you? Don't be afraid! 'You are children of the Lord your God' (Dt. 14:1)."

      F.   And the Holy One, blessed be He, sweetened the word in their mouths and said to them, "Are you not my children? 'I am the Lord your God.' You are my people, you are precious to me."

      G.   So he began to appease them until their souls were restored, and they began to entreat him.

      H.   Thus: "His speech is most sweet."

Israel is the prince, God the king, and the exegetical parable works well. Just as the king encourages the prince, so God encourages Israel. Only E is somewhat awry. Otherwise the parable closely serves the case it is meant to clarify.

CHAPTER SIX

SONG OF SONGS RABBAH
PARASHAH SIX

LXXVIII:ı

1.   A.   "My beloved has gone down to his garden, to the beds of spices, [to pasture his flock in the gardens, and to gather lilies]:"

      B.   Said R. Yosé b. R. Hanina, "As to this verse, the beginning of it is not the same as the end, and the end not the same as the beginning.

      C.   "The verse had only to say, 'My beloved has gone down to pasture in his garden,' but you say, 'in the gardens'!

      D.   But 'my beloved' is the Holy One, blessed be He;

      E.   "'to his garden' refers to the world.

      F.   "'to the beds of spices' refers to Israel.

      G.   "'to pasture his flock in the gardens' refers to synagogues and schoolhouses.

    H.   "'and to gather lilies' speaks of picking [taking away in death] the righteous that are in Israel."

2.   A.   What is the difference between when old folks die and when young people die?

      B.   R. Judah and R. Abbahu:

      C.   R. Judah says, "When a candle goes out on its own, it is good for it and good for the wick, but when the candle does not go out on its own, it is bad for it and bad for the wick."

      D.   R. Abbahu said, "When a fig is picked in its season, it is good for it and good for the fig tree. When it is not picked in its season, it is bad for it and bad for the fig tree."

3.   A.   There was the case involving R. Hiyya b. R. Abba and his disciples, and some say, R. Aqiba and his disciples, and some say, R. Joshua and his disciples.

      B.   They had the custom of going into session and studying under a fig tree. Every day the owner of the fig tree would get up in the morning and pick his fig.

      C.   They said, "We should change our place, perhaps he suspects us [of stealing his fruit]."

      D.   What did they do? They went and held their sessions in another location.

E.   The owner of the fig tree got up but did not find them. He went and looked for them until he found them, He said to them, "My lords, there was a single religious duty that you were carrying out for me, and you want to hold it back from me!"

F.   They said to him, "God forbid!"

G.   "Then why did you leave your place and go into session in another location?"

H.   They said, "We were concerned that you might suspect us."

I.   He said to them, "God forbid. But I shall tell you on what account I get up early to pick my fig. It is because once the sun shines on the figs, they get rotten."

J.   They immediately returned to their place.

K.   One day they found that he had not gathered. They took some of them and opened them up and found them wormy.

L.   They said, "Well did the master of the fig tree speak. And if he knows the season of his fig and picks it, so does the Holy One, blessed be He, know when it is the season of the righteous to remove them, so he takes them up."

1.   *On what basis does the narrative attain coherence, e.g., what is the action or event that precipitates the telling of the tale?* The story functions as a parable, with A-K illustrating L. But it is not a parable, it is specific, one-time, concrete. The story is in these parts: A-D, E-J, K, L— a somewhat odd composition. But if we take out the component required by the context—"the master of the fig tree…"—we have A-D vs. E-J, a balanced transaction, in which the merit accruing to the master of the fig tree is the focus, and his affirmation of the sages and the importance of their Torah-study form the center of the matter.

2.   *What point of conflict or intersection of wills accounts for the telling of the tale and how is the point of tension resolved?* The tension is between the perception of the disciples and that of the owner of the fig tree, the former being scrupulous about the property of others, the latter generous in his appreciation of the sages' work.

3.   *How, in light of other, comparable, pieces of writing and the data that they yield, is the narrative classified, and what are its indicative formal qualities, e.g., long or short, complex or simple?* If we ignore the redactional components, it is a simple set of matched transactions.

LXXVIII:ı

> 4. A. ["My beloved has gone down to his garden, to the beds of spices, to pasture his flock in the gardens, and to gather lilies" (Song 6:2):] Said R. Samuel b. R. Nahman, "[The matter may be compared] to the case of a king who had an orchard and planted in it rows of nut trees, apple trees, and pomegranates, and handed them over to his son.
>
> B. "When the son did the father's will, the king would go and make the rounds all over the world and see which planting was particularly attractive and would uproot it and bring it and plant it in that orchard. But when his son did not carry out his will, the king would see which planting in the orchard was particularly fine, and he would uproot that one.
>
> C. "So is the case with Israel: when they carry out the will of the Omnipresent, he picks out a righteous person among the nations of the world, for instance, Jethro or Rahab, and brings him and cleaves him to Israel. But when Israel does not do the will of the Holy One, blessed be He, he identifies a righteous, upright, virtuous, and God-fearing person among them and takes him up from their midst."

The lily-gathering is now amplified in an exegetical parable. When Israel does God's will, God gathers the righteous of the nations and brings them to Israel. But when Israel does not do God's will, then God takes a righteous Israelite away from Israel and gathers him in. The Mashal, B, of the king and the prince goes over the same ground with precision.

LXXVIII:ı

> 7. A. When R. Bun b. R. Hiyya died, R. Zira went up to take leave of him: "'Sweet is the sleep of a working man' (Qoh. 5:11):
>
> B. "Let me tell you what R. Bun resembles:
>
> C. "A king who had a vineyard, which he hired workers to keep. Now there was one worker there, who was paid for his work more than all the others.
>
> D. "When the king saw how remarkably zealous he was at his work, he took him

by the hand and began walking with him up and down.

E. "At evening the workers came to collect their wages, and that worker came to collect his wage along with them. And the king gave him his wage the same as theirs.

F. "They workers began to complain and said to him, 'Our Lord, King, we worked hard all day long, and this one worked only two or three hours for the day, but he takes the same wage that we do!'

G. "The king said to them, 'Why are you complaining? This one accomplished in two or three hours what you people did not accomplish in the entire day of work!'

H. "So R. Bun b. R. Hiyya accomplished in the twenty-eight years in which he studied the Torah what an accomplished disciple did not accomplish in a hundred years."

I. Said R. Yohanan, "Whoever is engaged in Torah study in this world, even in the world to come will not be accorded the right to sleep,

J. "but they will bring him to the house of study of Shem and Aber, Abraham, Isaac, Jacob, Moses and Aaron.

K. "And how long? Until: 'I will make you a great name, like the name of the great ones that are in the earth' (2 Sam. 7:9)."

The parable cannot be called exegetical, since the governing verse, A, emerges only implicitly at I-J. The parable concerns Bun alone, and makes its point at H/G.

LXXXI:1

1. A. ["Turn away your eyes from me, for they disturb me—Your hair is like a flock of goats, moving down the slopes of Gilead (Song. 6:5):] "Turn away your eyes from me:"

B. R. Azariah in the name of R. Judah b. R. Simon: "[The matter may be compared] to the case of a king who was enraged against the queen and pushed her out and drove her away from the palace.

C.   "What did she do? She went and pressed her face against a pillar outside the palace.

D.   "When the king went by, the king said, 'Take her away from before me, for I can't bear it.'

E.   "Thus when the court is in session and decrees fasts and individuals afflict themselves, the Holy One, blessed be He, says, 'I can't bear it.'"

The base-verse has to illustrate a case in which God is disturbed to look upon Israel, and for that purpose the exegetical parable invokes the king and the queen, now inventing a case in which the king is disturbed by the sight of the queen, thus an exact match for the program of the base-verse. But the application, E, is then predetermined: we require a case in which what the King is disturbed to see is evidence that his rejection of the Queen, Israel, contradicts the facts of the case. Israel repents, and God cannot bear to see the signs of repentance, during the spell of separation—a very subtle realization indeed. So the parable is exact for what is to be realized.

LXXXVII:I

1.   A.   ["I went down to the nut orchard to look at the blossoms of the valley, to see whether the vines had budded, whether the pomegranates were in bloom" (Song 6:11):] Another explanation of the phrase, "I went down to the nut orchard:"

B.   Said R. Joshua b. Levi, "The Israelites are compared to a nut tree:

C.   "just as a nut tree is pruned and improved thereby, for, like hair that is trimmed and grows more abundantly, and like nails that are trimmed and grow more abundantly,

D.   "so is the case with Israel, for they are pruned of the return on their work, which they gave to those who labor in the Torah in this world, and it is for their good that they are so pruned, for that increases their wealth in this world and the reward that is coming to them in the world to come."

Now the exegetical parable abandons the narrative voice of a story-teller altogether and suffices with the static simile. The comparison is not to what a king does with a queen or prince, but to the character of the nut tree and what is done with it. Then the point of comparison is how Israel is "pruned" of part of its wealth in favor of support of Torah-study, which produces a more abundant crop in the end.

LXXXVII:i

9.   A.   ["I went down to the nut orchard to look at the blossoms of
          the valley, to see whether the vines had budded, whether the
          pomegranates were in bloom" (Song 6:11):] Another explana-
          tion of the phrase, "I went down to the nut orchard:"
     B.   just as in the case of a nut, a stone breaks it,
     C.   so the Torah is called a stone, [and] the impulse to do evil is
          called a stone.
     D.   The Torah is called a stone: "And I will give you the tablets of
          stone" (Ex. 24:12).
     E.   The impulse to do evil is called a stone: "And I will take away
          the stony heart out of your flesh" (Ezek. 36:26).
          F.   Said R. Levi, "[The matter may be compared to the
               case of] a lonely spot, which is infested with terror-
               ists. What does the king do? He assigns there brigades
               to guard the place so that the terrorists will not at-
               tack travelers on the way.
          G.   "So said the Holy One, blessed be He, 'The Torah
               is called a stone, and the impulse to do evil is called
               a stone.
          H.   "'Let stone guard stone.'"

The desired proposition is, the Torah overcomes the impulse to do
evil, C. For that purpose the simile, B, is invoked. Then, F-H, an
exegetical parable serves to make the same point. Now there is the
king and the exemplary action. The Torah is like the royal brigade,
the impulse to do evil like the terrorists. Then the parable is invented for its exegetical task.

LXXXVIII:i

1.   A.   "Before I was aware, my fancy set me in a chariot beside my
          prince (Song 6:12):"
     B.   It was taught on Tannaite authority by R. Hiyya, "The matter
          may be compared to the case of a princess who went out gath-
          ering stray sheaves.
     C.   "The king turned out to be passing and recognized that she
          was his daughter.
     D.   He sent out his friend to take her and seat her with him in the
          carriage.
     E.   "Now her girlfriends were surprised at her and said, 'Yester-
          day you were gathering stray sheaves, and today you are seated
          in a carriage with the king.'
     F.   "She said to them, 'Just as you are surprised at me, so I am
          surprised at myself, and I recited in my own regard the follow-
          ing verse of Scripture, 'Before I was aware, my fancy set me in
          a chariot beside my prince.'
     G.   "Thus too when the Israelites were enslaved in Egypt in mor-

tar and bricks, they were rejected and despised in the view of
the Egyptians.

H.   "But when they were freed and redeemed and made prefects
        over everyone in the world, the nations of the world expressed
        surprise, saying, 'Yesterday you were working in mortar and
        bricks, and today you have been freed and redeemed and made
        prefects over everyone in the world!'

I.   "And the Israelites replied to them, 'Just as you are surprised
        at us, so we are surprised at ourselves,' and they recited in their
        own regard, 'Before I was aware, my fancy set me in a chariot
        beside my prince.'"

The exegetical parable is articulated in correspondence to the exegetical task. The king/princess motif serves, with God the king, Israel the princess. Then Israel has been enslaved but is now redeemed
and made prefect over the nations, and Israel is surprised at the shift
in its situation. The parable then replicates that transaction at D-F.
The only odd moment is at B-C, why the princess was gathering
sheaves and estranged from the king is not explained and has no
corresponding moment in the application of the parable.

LXXXVIII:i

5.   A.   Another explanation of the verse, "'Before I was aware, my fancy
             set me in a chariot beside my prince:'"

     B.   Scripture speaks of the Community of Israel.

     C.   The Community of Israel says to the nations of the world, "'Do
             not rejoice against me, O my enemy; though I have fallen, I
             shall arise' (Mic. 7:8).

     D.   "When I dwelled in darkness, the Holy One, blessed be He,
             brought me forth to light: 'Though I sit in darkness, the Lord
             is a light to me' (Mic. 7:8)."

     E.   So in her own regard she recited the verse, "Before I was aware,
             my fancy set me in a chariot beside my prince."

         6.   A.   Justus, a tailor in Sepphoris, went up to the govern-
                      ment and was received by the king.

              B.   The king said to him, "Ask me for something, and I
                      shall give it to you."

              C.   He said to him, "Make me the duke of our locale."

              D.   The king gave it to him.

              E.   After he had assumed the position, he left it.

              F.   And those who knew him said, "It's the same man,"
                      but others who knew him said, "It's not the same."

              G.   One of them said to them, "When he goes through
                      the market, if he glances at that tailor's seat on which
                      he used to sit and stitch, it is the same man, but if
                      not, it is not the same man."

> H. He passed through the market and began to look at the stool on which he had sat and stitched, so they knew that he was the same man.
>
> I. He said to them, "You are surprised at me, but I am more surprised at myself than you are."
>
> J. And they recited in his regard the verse, "Before I was aware, my fancy set me in a chariot beside my prince,"
>
> K. meaning, with me the Prince, the Eternal, walked.

Here is a narrative that veers very close to the exegetical parable. All that is lacking is the explicit language of comparison: "a parable: to what is the matter comparable?" Otherwise we have the governing exegesis, E, realized at I-J+K, and the story that is spun out of the components of the planned exegesis. Since we have the king as well, all that violates the ordinary program of the parable is the limiting detail: the named figure, Justus, and the specific place. The stick-figures that populate exegetical parables are standard: no motivation, no explanation for attitude or action, and little activity. What we have, then, is a concretization of the exegetical parable of the king and the princess, LXXXVIII:i.1.

CHAPTER SEVEN

SONG OF SONGS RABBAH
PARASHAH SEVEN

XCVI:i.5-6-6 form a vast scriptural story amplifying the narrative of Nebuchadnezzar and Israelite idol worship in his time. XCVII:i.18 sets forth a scriptural story on Nebuchadnezzar and Daniel and idolatry. I have not reproduced those important extensions of the corresponding Scripture-narratives, which do not figure in this study.

XC:I

3.   A. [How graceful are your feet in sandals, O queenly maiden! Your rounded thighs are like jewels, the work of a master hand (Song 7:1):] Said R. Berekhiah, "This is how the two pinnacles of the age, R. Eliezer and R. Joshua, have interpreted the verse, 'How graceful are your feet in sandals, O queenly maiden:'

B. "'How beautiful were your festival pilgrims, who locked the door against all suffering [for the words for sandals and lock the door share the same consonants].'"

XC:I

4.   A. There was the case of someone who forgot to lock the doors of his house when he went up for the pilgrim festival.

B. And when he came home, he found a snake wound around the rings of his door.

XC:I

5.   A. There was another case of someone who forgot and did not bring his chickens into his house when he went up for the pilgrim festival.

B. When he came home, he found cats torn to pieces before them.

XC:I

6.   A. There was another case of someone who forgot and did not bring his pile of grain into the house when he went up for the pilgrim festival.

XC:I

    B.   When he came home, he found lions surrounding the wheat.

7.   A.   Said R. Phineas, "There was the case of two rich brothers who were in Ashkelon, who had wicked gentile neighbors, who said, 'When these Jews go up to pray in Jerusalem, we shall go into their houses and clean them out.'

    B.   "The time came and they went up.

    C.   "The Holy One, blessed be He, set up for them angels in their likeness, and they would go in and come out of their houses.

    D.   "When they came home from Jerusalem, they divided up what they had brought with them among all their neighbors.

    E.   "They said to them, 'Where were you?'

    F.   "They said to them, 'In Jerusalem.'

    G.   "'When did you go up?'

    H.   "'On such-and-such a day.'

    I.   "They said, 'Blessed is the God of the Jews, whom you have not abandoned, and who has not abandoned you! We thought, "When these Jews go up to pray in Jerusalem, we shall go into their houses and clean them out." But your God has sent angels in your likeness, who came out and went into your houses because you had faith in him.'

    J.   "This fulfills the verse, 'How graceful are your feet in sandals, O queenly maiden.'"

The first three Ma'asim, Nos. 3-6, all register the same point, which is that God protects the property of those who absent themselves at home to make a pilgrimage on a festival. No. 7 is a more elaborate version of the same motif. The reason the stories are inserted here is articulated at 7.J. These Ma'asim have nothing in common with Halakhic ones.

XC:II

1.   A.   Another explanation of the verse, "How graceful are your feet in sandals, O queenly maiden:"

    B.   [The word for sandals is so written that it can be read,] in two closings [or: completions, with reference to the concluding days of the festivals of Tabernacles and Passover, as will be spelled out presently].

2.   A.   Said R. Hama b. R. Hanina, "The matter may be compared to two peddlers who came to a town. One of them took up the matter with the other, saying to his fellow, 'If we both open our shops together in this town, we shall bring down the price. You open your stall in your week, and I shall do so in my week.'"

The concluding days of Passover are separate from those of the Festival by a long span of time, so that each will be observed not in competition with the other. The exegetical parable is meant to explain that fact, but it lacks an explicit statement of how the matter is clarified by the simile.

XC:ii

4.   A.   Said R. Joshua b. Levi, "The Concluding Day of the Festival [the Eighth Day of Solemn Assembly] was suitable to be distanced fifty days from the Festival, corresponding to the Conclusion of Passover [which is Pentecost, fifty days after Passover].

B.   "But as to the Concluding Day of the Festival, since it marks the passage from summer to winter, it is not a time for going and coming.

C.   "The matter may be compared to the case of a king who had many daughters, some of them married and living near by, some of them married and living far off.

D.   "One day all of them came to greet the king, their father.

E.   "Said the king, 'Those who are married and living nearby can go and come as they like, but those who are married and living at a distance cannot come and go anytime they like.

F.   "'So while they are all with me, come, let us celebrate a single banquet for them all and rejoice with them all.'

G.   "So as to the Concluding Day of Passover [Pentecost], since the season is passing from winter to summer, said the Holy One, blessed be He, 'These are days for going and coming.'

H.   "But as to the Concluding day of the Festival, since the days are passing from summer to winter, with the roads dusty and hard for walking, therefore the [Eighth Day of Solemn Assembly] is not distanced by fifty days [from the opening days of Tabernacles, in the way in which Pentecost is separated from the opening days of Passover by fifty days] [for,] said the Holy One, blessed be He, 'These are not days for going and coming. But while they are here, let us celebrate a single banquet for them all and rejoice with them all.'

I.   "Therefore Moses admonishes the Israelites, saying to them, 'On the eighth day you shall have a solemn assembly' (Num. 29:35).

J.   "Thus: 'How graceful are your feet in sandals, O queenly maiden.'"

The exegetical parable, C-F, closely matches the problem that occupies the expositor, G-H, since what requires explanation, why one festival is separated from another by fifty days, while that is not the case for the other festival, treating Pentecost and Passover as a comparable construction to Tabernacles and The Eighth Day of Solemn Assembly. The case of the king and the princesses accommodates the difference that is explained.

XC:III

4.   A.   "Your rounded thighs are like jewels [the work of a master hand (Song 7:1)]:"

    B.   [Since the word for jewels and for illnesses share the same consonants, the sense is this:] how many illnesses are on its account,

    C.   how many circumcised babies die on its account!

        5.   A.   Said R. Nathan, "There was this case. I came to the town of Cappadocia, and there was a woman who produced male children. When they were circumcised, they died. The first was circumcised and died, so too the second, so too the third. The fourth she brought before me, and I examined its flesh and found it pale. I looked at it and I did not find in it blood of the circumcision. They asked me, 'Should we circumcise him?'

            B.   "I said to them, 'Wait and let him be, until the blood of circumcision is produced. For we have learned there: "As to the infant and the sick person, they are not to be circumcised until they get well."

            C.   "They let him be, then circumcised him and he turned out to live, and they produced as his name, 'Nathan,' after me.'

            D.   "That is in line with this verse: 'like jewels.'"

The *Ma'aseh* is self-contained and involves an autobiographical tale.

XC:III

7.   A.   ["How graceful are your feet in sandals, O queenly maiden! Your rounded thighs are like jewels, the work of a master hand"

(Song 7:1):]. And who made it ["like jewels"]?

B.   R. Menahema said, "'the work of a master hand:'

C.   "the work of the master hand of the Holy One, blessed be He, in this world."

8.   A.   Said R. Samuel, "The matter may be compared to the case of a king who had an orchard, planted row by row of nuts, apples, pomegranates, and he handed them over to his son, saying to him, 'My son, I ask of you only that when these plantings bring their first fruit, you present it to me and let me taste it, so that I may see the work of my hands and take pleasure in you.'

B.   "So said the Holy One, blessed be He, to the Israelites, 'My children, I ask of you only that when a first son is born to any of you, he be sanctified to my name: "Sanctify to me all the firstborn" (Ex. 13:2).

C.   "'And when you go up for the pilgrim festivals, you bring him up and all your males to appear before me.'

D.   "Therefore Moses admonishes Israel: 'Three times... in the year' (Ex. 23:14)."

The exegetical parable derives its task from B-C, which require a case in which the prince show the king the produce of the king's orchards. The reason for the inclusion of the whole is the base verse's reference to the pilgrim festivals, but the parable and its reference-point are complete in A-B.

XCI:I

13.   A.   [Your navel is a rounded bowl, that never lacks mixed wine. Your belly is a heap of wheat, encircled with lilies (Song 7:2):] R. Nehemiah in the name of R. Abun says, "The nations of the world have no planting, nor sowing, nor root.

B.   "The three matters derive from a single verse of Scripture: 'They are scarcely planted, scarcely sown, scarcely has their stock taken root in the earth' (Is. 40:24).

C.   "But the Israelites have a planting: 'And I will plant them in this land' (Jer. 32:41); they have a sowing: 'And I will sow her to me in the land' (Hos. 2:25); they have a root: 'In days to come Jacob shall take root' (Isa. 27:6)."

14.   A.   To what may the matter be compared?

> B.   The straw, chaff, and stubble argued with one another.
> C.   This one says, "On my account the field is sown," and that one says, "On my account the field is sown."
> D.   The wheat said to them, "Wait for me until the threshing floor arrives, and we shall see for whom the field is sown."
> E.   The threshing floor arrived, and when they were brought into the threshing floor, the household came out to winnow it.
> F.   The chaff was gone with the wind.
> G.   He took the straw and tossed it on the ground.
> H.   He took the stubble and burned it up.
> I.   He took the wheat and made it into a pile.
> J.   Those who passed by, whoever saw it, kissed it: "Kiss the wheat" (Ps. 2:12).
> K.   So it is with the nations of the world:
> L.   These say, "We are Israel, and on our account the world has been made," and those say, "We are Israel, and on our account the world has been made,"
> M.   so Israel says to them, "Wait until the day of the Holy One, blessed be He, comes, and we shall then know on whose account the world has been made: 'For behold the day comes, it burns as a furnace' (Mal. 4:1); 'You shall fan them and the wind shall carry them away' (Isa. 41:16).
> N.   "But of Israel Scripture says, 'And you shall rejoice in the Lord, you shall glory in the Holy One of Israel' (Isa. 41:16)."

The exegetical parable works its way through the issue of Israel and the nations, K-M, though the parable enters into details not required by L, that is, there is no counterpart in "the nations of the world" to chaff, straw, and stubble, only wheat vs. everything else. But that close exposition of the parable does not signal the adaptation of a ready-made simile. Nonetheless, the argument among the straw, chaff, and stubble, is not the point of K-M, but rather, the argument between Israel/wheat and everything else, and B omits all reference to the wheat, so there are some disjunctures not to be ignored.

CII:1

6. A. [The mandrakes give forth fragrance, and over our doors are all choice fruits, new as well as old, which I have laid up for you, O my beloved (Song 7:13):] "and over our doors are all choice fruits:"

    B. Members of the household of R. Shila and rabbis:

    C. Members of the household of R. Shila said, "The matter [of 'choice fruits, new as well as old'] may be compared to the case of a virtuous woman, to whom her husband left sparse possessions and little money for expenses [when he went overseas]. When her husband came back, she said to him, 'Remember what you left me, and see what I have collected for you and what I have also added for you beyond that!'"

    D. And rabbis say, "The matter [of 'choice fruits, new as well as old'] may be compared to a king who had an orchard, which he gave to a tenant-farmer. What did the tenant-farmer do? He filled baskets of figs from the produce of the orchard and put them at the gate of the orchard. Now when the king passed by and saw all this increase, he said, 'All this increase is at the doorway of the orchard—then in the orchard how much the more so!'

    E. "So take the case of the earlier generations, the men of the great assembly, Hillel and Shammai, and Rabban Gamaliel the Elder. Then the latter generations, R. Yohanan b. Zakkai, R. Eliezer and R. Joshua, R. Meir and R. Aqiba and their disciples—how much the more so!

    F. "And in their regard Scripture says, 'new as well as old, which I have laid up for you, O my beloved.'"

The exegetical task is defined at E, God has laid up new as well as old, not only Hillel and Shammai and Gamaliel but also the newer generations, Yohanan b. Zakkai, Eliezer and Joshua, Aqiba, and Meir. That is captured in neither of the two exegetical Meshalim. C has a virtuous woman who increases the husband's capital, and D has a tenant farmer impress the landholder ("king") with a small part of the crop. In neither case do I see how the earlier/later motif figures in the parable itself, dictating its articulation.

CHAPTER EIGHT

SONG OF SONGS RABBAH
PARASHAH EIGHT

CVII:ɪ

6.   A. ["Who is that coming up from the wilderness, leaning upon her beloved? Under the apple tree I awakened you. There your mother was in travail with you, there she who bore you was in travail" (Song 8:5)] "There your mother was in travail with you:"

    B. Did she really go into labor there?

    C. Said R. Berekhiah, "The matter may be compared to the case of someone who went into a dangerous place and was saved from the danger.

    D. "His friend met him and said to him, 'Did you go through that perilous passage? What perils you have escaped! Your mother really bore you there! How much anguish you have survived! It's as though you were reborn today!'"

The assignment undertaken by the parable is to respond to B's question of the base-verse, and the parable is spelled out a C-D: "Your mother really bore you there" means, it is as if you were reborn today. The simile is to Israel in the wilderness. The exposition then shows how the parable has responded to its exegetical task and leaves no doubt that we have an exegetical parable, pure and simple.

CIX:ɪ

4.   A. ["Many waters cannot quench love, neither can floods drown it. If a man offered for love all the wealth of his house, it would be utterly scorned" (Song 8:7): "it would be utterly scorned:"

        B. R. Yohanan was going up on foot from Tiberias to Sepphoris, and R. Hiyya b. R. Abba was attending to him. They came by a field. Said R. Yohanan, "That field belonged to me, but I sold it to pay the expenses of laboring in the Torah."

        C. They came by a vineyard. Said R. Yohanan, "That vineyard belonged to me, but I sold it to pay the expenses of laboring in the Torah."

        D. They came by an olive grove. Said R. Yohanan the same thing, ["That olive grove belonged to me, but I sold it to pay the expenses of laboring in the Torah."]

E. Then R. Hiyya b. R. Abba began crying.

F. He said to him, "How come you're crying?"

G. He said to him, "I am crying because you have left nothing for your old age."

H. He said to him, "Hiyya, my son, is what I have done such a light thing in your eyes? For I have sold something which is given for six days [of God's labor], for it is said, 'For in six days did the Lord make' (Ex. 20:11), while the Torah took forty days to be given: 'And he was there with the Lord for forty days' (Ex. 34:28); 'Then I abode in the mount forty days' (Dt. 9:9)."

I. When R. Yohanan died, his generation recited in his regard this verse: "'If a man offered for love all the wealth of his house,' – that is, for the love with which R. Yohanan loved the Torah,

J. "'it would be utterly scorned,' – [Simon, p. 310, n. 4: such love could not be assessed in money]."

1. *On what basis does the narrative attain coherence, e.g., what is the action or event that precipitates the telling of the tale?* The story is in three units, the first two of them continuous. B-D, E-H, I-J. The point of the details of B-D emerges at the end, H. B-D is explained by E-H. I-J is tacked on for redactional reasons, explaining how the anecdote belongs to its context.

2. *What point of conflict or intersection of wills accounts for the telling of the tale and how is the point of tension resolved?* The conflict is between the value of real estate and the value of Torah-study; the point then is, Torah-study serves as well as real estate serves and is more valuable.

3. *How, in light of other, comparable, pieces of writing and the data that they yield, is the narrative classified, and what are its indicative formal qualities, e.g., long or short, complex or simple?* The anecdote is simple and works itself out in the contrast between the two obvious units.

CXI:III

3.   C. ["We have a little sister, and she has no breasts. What shall we do for our sister, on the day when she is spoken for?] 8:9 If she is a wall, we will build upon her a battlement of silver; but if she is a door, we will enclose her with boards of cedar. 8:10 I was a wall, and my breasts were like towers; then I was in his eyes as one who brings peace (Song 8:9-10):] "I was a wall:"

D. Said R. Aibu, "Said the Holy One, blessed be He, 'I am going to make an advocate for Israel among the nations of the world.'

E. "And what is it? It is the echo: 'Except the Lord of hosts had left to us a very small remnant' (Isa. 1:9)."

4.   A.   It has been taught on Tannaite authority:
      B.   Once the final prophets, Haggai, Zechariah, and
Malachi had died, the Holy Spirit ceased from Israel.
      C.   Even so, they would make use of the echo.

CXI:iii

5.   A.   There was the case of sages voting in the up-
           per room of the house of Gedia in Jericho. An echo
           came forth and said to them, "There is among you
           one man who is worthy of receiving the Holy Spirit,
           but his generation is not suitable for such to hap-
           pen.
           B.   They set their eyes upon Hillel the Elder.
           C.   When he died, they said in his regard, "Woe
           for the modest one, woe for the pious one, the dis-
           ciple of Ezra."

CXI:iii

6.   A.   There was another case, in which the Israel-
           ite sages took a vote, in the vineyard in Yavneh.
           B.   Now were they really *in* a vineyard! Rather,
           [they were like a vineyard, for] this was the
           Sanhedrin, that sat in rows and rows, lines and lines,
           like a well-ordered vineyard.
           C.   An echo came forth and said to them, "There
           is among you one man who is worthy of receiving
           the Holy Spirit, but his generation is not suitable
           for such to happen.
           D.   They set their eyes upon Samuel the Younger.
           E.   When he died, they said in his regard, "Woe
           for the modest one, woe for the pious one, the dis-
           ciple of Hillel the Elder.

CXI:iii

9.   A.   There was the case in which Yohanan, the
           high priest, heard an echo come forth from the
           Most Holy Place, saying, "The young men who
           went out to war have won at Antioch."
           B.   They wrote down that day and that hour, and
           that is how matters were: on that very day they
           had won their victory.

CXI:iii

10.   A.   There was the case in which Simeon the Righ-
           teous heard an echo come forth from the Most Holy
           Place, saying, "The action has been annulled that
           the enemy has planned to destroy the Temple, and
           Caius Caligula has been killed and his decrees an-
           nulled.
           B.   This he heard in Aramaic.

The cases set forth anecdotes of a biographical character. CXI:iii.4 explains the insertion of the composite, which has no place in this context.

CXII:III

10.   A. [Supply: "O Lord, our Lord, how glorious is your name in all the earth! whose majesty is rehearsed in the heavens" (Ps. 8:2):]

B. R. Joshua of Sikhnin in the name of R. Levi: "What is written here is not 'your majesty' but 'whose majesty is rehearsed,'

C. "your majesty is therein, your happiness is therein, it makes you happy that your Torah should be in heaven."

D. "He said to them, 'No, the desire does not come from you [and it is none of your business].'"

11.   A. Said R. Yudan, "The matter may be compared to the case of a man who had a son with stumped fingers. What did he do? He took him to a silk worker to teach him the craft. He began to look at his fingers. He said, 'The very essence of this craft is acquired only with the fingers. How is this one going to learn?'

B. "Thus: 'No, the desire does not come from you [and it is none of your business].'

C. "So when the Holy One, blessed be He, wanted to give the Torah to Israel, the ministering angels tried to intervene against Israel and to intervene before the Holy One, blessed be He, saying, 'Lord of the world, your majesty is therein, your happiness is therein, it makes you happy that your Torah should be in heaven.'

D. "He said to them, 'No, the desire does not come from you [and it is none of your business].

E. "'It is written therein, "And if a woman has an issue of her blood for many days" (Lev. 15:25). Now is there a woman in your midst? Thus: No, the desire does not come from you [and it is none of your business].

F. "Further it is written therein, "When a man dies in a tent" (Num. 19:14). Now is there death among you? Thus: No, the desire does not come from you [and it is none of your business].'

G. "That is why Scripture praises [Moses]: 'You have ascended on high, you have taken away your captive' (Ps. 68:19)."

The parable is formed in line with its exegetical task, which is to explain why the ministering angels could not intervene and keep the Torah in heaven. The simile is precise: the angels have no need for the Torah, which does not pertain to them any more than silk-weaving does to the son with stumped fingers. The same matter now continues.

CXII:III

12. A. [Supply: "You have ascended on high, you have taken away your captive" (Ps. 68:19):]

B. Said R. Aha, "This refers to the laws that apply to mortals,

C. "for instance, the laws governing men and women who have suffered a flux, women in their menstrual period and after child birth.

D. "Thus: 'No, the desire does not come from you [and it is none of your business].'"

13. A. And rabbis say, "The matter may be compared to the case of a king who was marrying off his daughter outside of town.

B. "The townsfolk said to him, 'Our lord, our king, it is praiseworthy and right that your daughter should be with you in town.'

C. "He said to them, 'What difference does it make to you?'

D. "They said to him, 'Perhaps tomorrow you may go to her and live with her and stay with her because of your love for her.'

E. "He said to them, 'My daughter I shall marry off out of town, but I shall stay with you in town.'

F. "Thus when the Holy One, blessed be He, was planning to give the Torah to the Israelites, the ministering angels said to the Holy One, blessed be He, 'Lord of the world, 'you are the one whose majesty is over heaven,' your happiness is therein, your glory and your praise is that your Torah should be in heaven.'

G. "He said to them, 'What difference does it make to you?'

H. "They said to him, "Perhaps tomorrow you will bring your Presence to rest among the creatures below.'

I. "Said to them the Holy One, blessed be He, 'My Torah is what I am sending to the creatures below, but I shall continue to dwell among the creatures of the upper world.

> J. "'I shall give my daughter with her marriage settle-
> ment in another town, so she may be honored with
> her husband for her beauty and charm, for she is
> a princess, and they will honor her. But I shall dwell
> with you among the creatures of the upper world.'
>> K. "And who made this matter explicit?
>> It was Habakkuk: 'His glory covers the
>> heavens and the earth is full of his praise'
>> (Hab. 3:3)."

The second exegetical parable for Ps. 68:19 deals with a different
matter, namely, the angels' fear that God would take up residence
on earth, rather than remaining with them I heaven. He assures them
that the Torah goes to mankind, but he remains in Heaven. Then
the Torah is represented by the daughter, God by the king, and the
exegetical parable hews closely to its task of realizing in ordinary
terms the relationship that Scripture as read by the exegete means
to set forth.

CXIII:ɪ

1.   A.   ["My vineyard, my very own, is for myself; you, O Solomon, may
     have the thousand, and the keepers of the fruit two hundred" (Song
     8:12):] "My vineyard, my very own, is for myself:"
     B.   R. Hiyya taught on Tannaite authority, "The matter may be com-
     pared to the case of a king who was angry with his son and handed
     him over to his servant. What did he do? He began to beat him with
     a club. He said to him, 'Don't obey your father.'
     C.   "The son said to the servant, 'You big fool! The very reason that
     father handed me over to you was only because I was not listening
     to him, and you say, "Don't listen to father"!'
     D.   "So too, when sin had brought it about that the house of the sanc-
     tuary should be destroyed and Israel sent into exile to Babylonia,
     Nebuchadnezzar said to them, 'Do not listen to the Torah of your
     father in heaven, but rather, "fall down and worship the image that
     I have made" (Dan. 3:15).'
     E.   "The Israelites said to him, 'You big fool! The very reason that
     the Holy One, blessed be He, has handed us over to you is because
     we were bowing down to an idol: "She saw... the images of the
     Chaldeans portrayed with vermilion" (Ezek. 23:14), and yet you say
     to us, "fall down and worship the image that I have made" (Dan.
     3:15). Woe to you!'
     F.   "It is at that moment that the Holy One, blessed be He, said,
     'My vineyard, my very own, is for myself.'"

The exegetical parable closely follows the exposition, D-F, drawing
from and adapting only the king/prince relationship, but otherwise

simply translating the transaction of D-E into the terms of the narrative.

CXIV:i

1.   A.   "O you who dwell in the gardens, my companions are listen-
            ing for your voice; let me hear it" (Song 8:13:
      B.   R. Nathan in the name of R. Aha said, "The matter may be
            compared to the case of a king who got mad at his staff and
            imprisoned them. What did the king do? He took all his offic-
            ers and staff and went to listen to what they were saying [in
            prison to one another].
      C.   "He heard that they were saying, 'Our lord, the king, is our
            praise, he is our life. May we never fail our lord, the king, forever.'
      D.   "He said to them, 'My children, raise your voices so that the
            my companions who are near by you may hear.'
      E.   "Thus even though the Israelites are occupied with their daily
            work all six days of creation, on the Sabbath day they get up
            carly and come to the synagogue and recite the *Shema* and pass
            before the ark and proclaim the Torah and conclude with the
            words of the prophet.
      F.   "And the Holy One, blessed be He, says to them, 'My chil-
            dren, raise your voices so that the my companions may hear.'

The key to the exegetical parable lies at E-F, translated into the case
of the king and his staff, B-C+D. Then Israel forms the imprisoned
staff, whose continuing loyalty, even in the prison of workdays, is
exemplary and is meant to win over the favor of the angels, the other
component of the divine retinue.

CXV:ii.3

      A.   "Make haste, my beloved, and be like a gazelle or a young stag
            upon the mountains of spices" (Song 8:14):
      B.   Said R. Levi, "The matter may be compared to the case of a
            king who made a banquet and invited guests. Some of them
            ate and drank and said a blessing to the king, but some of them
            ate and drank and cursed the king.
      C.   "The king realized it and considered making a public display
            at his banquet and disrupting it. But the matron [queen] came
            and defended them, saying to him, 'My lord, O king, instead
            of paying attention to those who ate and drank and cursed you,
            take note of those who ate and drank and blessed you and praised
            your name.'
      D.   "So is the case with Israel: when they eat and drink and say a
            blessing and praise and adore the Holy One, blessed be He, he
            listens to their voice and is pleased. But when the nations of
            the world eat and drink and blaspheme and curse the Holy One,
            blessed be He, with their fornication of which they make men-

> tion, at that moment the Holy One, blessed be He, gives thought
> even to destroy his world.
>
> E. "But the Torah comes along and defends them, saying, 'Lord
>   of the world, instead of taking note of these, who blaspheme
>   and spite you, take note of Israel, your people, who bless and
>   praise and adore your great name through the Torah and
>   through song and praise.'
>
> F. "And the Holy Spirit cries out, '"Make haste, my beloved:" flee
>   from the nations of the world and cleave to the Israelites.'"

The base-verse speaks of God's making haste and fleeing: from what?
The answer lies at D-E: God tarries to hear the praise and adora-
tion of Israel, but hastens to abandon the blasphemy of the nations.
But God does not destroy the nations, E, by reason of Israel's pro-
pitiation, and the Torah/the queen, C/E calls attention to Israel's
redemptive power to save the nations of the world. This daring
message dictates the narrative of the exegetical parable and imparts
a subtlety to the matter, such as we have seen only at a few passages.

CHAPTER NINE

NARRATIVES IN
SONG OF SONGS RABBAH

The Song of Songs finds a place in the Torah because for Rabbinic Judaism the collection of love-songs in fact speaks about the relationship between God and Israel. So the entire compilation of systematic exegesis of the Song of Songs, Song of Songs Rabbah, rests on parabolic thinking and explores a coherent generative metaphor. The intent of the compilers is to turn everyday experience—the love of husband and wife—into a metaphor of God's love for Israel and Israel's love for God. Then, when Solomon's song says, "O that you would kiss me with the kisses of your mouth! For your love is better than wine," (Song 1:2), the Rabbinic exegetes think of how God kissed Israel, e.g., at Sinai. So Song of Songs Rabbah thus joins metaphor to theology, symbol to structure, in setting forth the entire Rabbinic system. It is hardly surprising that the preferred narrative type for this document is the exegetical parable. No other classification of narrative writing competes.

I. *The Authentic Narrative*

The items set forth here capture the attention of the documentary hypothesis. That is because we are able to compare and contrast the authentic narratives of the present document with those of another of the same classification, that is, another of the Rabbah-Midrash-compilations, specifically, Lamentations Rabbah, companion for the present probe.

What we shall now see is that the narratives of Song of Songs Rabbah bear in common three traits that set them apart from those of Lamentations Rabbah. First, all are brief, anecdotal, and biographical, involving stories focused upon individual, named authorities. Those of Lamentations Rabbah will present a striking contrast, for they tend to be protracted, and, more important, their issues vastly transcend the individual and are defined by the condition of corporate Israel. Second, the topic of the narratives of Song of Songs Rabbah throughout is clearly defined: the rules of the Torah and its study. The issue of the narratives of Lamentations Rabbah is not Torah and its study but (predictably) the fate of Israel and the explanation of its sorry condition. Third, the authentic narratives surveyed in this chapter barely qualify as authentic, since the indicative trait, the realization of the teleological logic that imposes sense upon the whole only at the end, may be discerned only with great difficulty. The counterpart narratives of Lamentations Rabbah fit well into that definition.

The upshot is, the insistence of the documentary hypothesis that each Rabbinic compilation be read, to begin with, as an autonomous statement of its own, produces consequential results and explains the data that we have in hand. We now turn to the selected items, reviewing them briefly and classifying them one by one.

1.   I:i.7. Another interpretation of the verse, "Do you see a man who is diligent in his business" (Prov. 22:29): this refers to this is R. Hanina. They say: One time he saw people of his village bringing whole-offerings and peace-offerings up [on a pilgrimage to the Temple]. He said, "All of them are bringing peace-offerings to Jerusalem, but I am not bringing up a thing! What shall I do?" Forthwith he went out to the open fields of his town, the unoccupied area of his town, and there he found a stone. He went and plastered it and polished it and painted it and said, "Lo, I accept upon myself the vow to bring it up to Jerusalem."

   This anecdote barely qualifies as an authentic narrative. The diligence of Hanina lies in his exemplary devotion to the task, and heaven's response thereto.

2.   XIX:I,7. R. Eleazar Hisma went to a certain place. The people said to him, "Does my lord know how to recite the Shema's blessings?" He said to them, "No." They said to him, "Is this R. Eleazar, the man for whom people make such a fuss? It is for nothing that people call you 'my lord!'" His face turned white. He went to R. Aqiba, and he looked sick. He said to him, "What's with you? You look sick." He told the story to him. He said to him, "Does my lord wish to learn?" He said to him, "Yes." After he had learned, he went to the same place. They said to him, "Does my lord know how to recite the Shema's blessings? He said to them, "Yes." They said to him, "Lo, Eleazar has regained the power of speech," and they called him R. Eleazar Hisma [= who can speak].

   The anecdote explains how the sage mastered the el-

  ementary liturgical rites, explaining the meaning of his
  nickname, Hisma.

3. XXXIII:ii.1 R. Yohanan was punished with suffering from gallstones
  for three years and a half. R. Hanina came up to visit him. He said
  to him, "How're you doing?" He said to him, "I have more than I
  can bear." He said to him, "Don't say that. But say, 'The faithful
  God.'" When the pain got severe, he would say, "Faithful God,"
  and when the pain became greater than he could bear, R. Hanina
  would come in to him and say something over him, and he restored
  his soul. After some time R. Hanina became ill, and R. Yohanan
  came up to visit him. He said to him, "How're you doing? He said
  to him, "How hard is suffering. He said to him, "Yes, but the reward is still greater." He said to him, "I don't want either them or
  their reward." He said to him, "Why don't you say that word that
  you said over me and restored my soul?" He said to him, "When I
  was up and about, I served as a pledge for others, but now that I
  am within, I don't need anybody else to serve as a pledge for me.
  He said to him, "It is written, 'he pastures his flock among the lilies': the rod of the Holy One, blessed be He, draws near only to
  people whose hearts are as soft as lilies."

> Hanina healed Yohanan, but he found it difficult to
> bear up under the same torment and could not heal
> himself. Virtue requires soft-heartedness, to which God
> responds. The story does cohere through its climactic
> conclusion.

4. XLVIII:v.16. ["And the waters prevailed so mightily upon the earth
  that all the high mountains under the whole heaven were covered,
  the waters prevailed above the mountains, covering them fifteen cubits deep" (Gen. 7:19):] R. Jonathan went up to pray in Jerusalem.
  When he went by the Palatinus, a Samaritan saw him and asked
  him, "Where are you going?" He said to him, "To pray in Jerusalem." He said to him, "Wouldn't it be better for you to pray on
  this holy mountain and not on that dunghill, because it was not
  submerged by the water of the Flood. For a moment R. Jonathan
  lost his learning in the law. His ass driver said to him, "Sir, give
  me permission and I shall answer him."

> The simple ass-driver kept his wits about him, while
> the learned master could not cope with the challenge
> of disputation with the Samaritan. The climax comes
> at the end: the humblest of Israelites, the ass-driver,
> are full of Torah-learning.

5. LXXIV:i.11 ["His arms are rounded gold, set with jewels. His body
  is ivory work, encrusted with sapphires" (Song 5:14):] "encrusted

with sapphires:" [Study of the Torah] drains the strength of people, for it is as hard as sapphire. [The words for encrusted and drain the strength use the same consonants.] R. Eliezer b. R. Simeon: Ass-drivers came to his father to buy grain from the town. They saw him sitting at the oven. His mother would take [a hot roll from the oven] and he would eat it, his mother would take [a hot roll from the oven] and he would eat it—until he ate up all the rolls. They said, "Woe! there is an evil snake in that man's belly. It appears that this one is going to bring a famine to the world. He heard what they were saying. When they went out to buy their burden of grain, he took their asses and brought them up to the roof They came looking for their asses and did not find them. They raised their eyes and saw them situated on the roof. When he brought them up, he brought them up one by one, but when he brought them down, he brought them down two by two. But when he was engaged in the study of the Torah, even his cloak he was unable to bear. That is in line with this verse: "encrusted with sapphires." [For study of the Torah drains the strength of people].

6.   LXXIV:i.12. A member of the household in the establishment of Rabban Gamaliel had the habit of taking a basket carrying forty *seahs* of grain and bringing it to the baker. He said to him, "All this wonderful strength is in you, and you are not engaged in the To-rah?" When he got involved in the Torah, he would begin to take thirty, then twenty, then twelve, then eight *seahs,* and when he had completed a book, even a basket of only a single *seah* he could not carry. That is in line with this verse: "encrusted with sapphires." [For study of the Torah drains the strength of people].

> The two narratives contain the same lesson, which is that Torah-study involves diminishing one's physical strength. How that moral shapes the entire antecedent complex is not obvious to me. But it is situated as the climactic statement and the compositions loosely qualify as narratives.

7.   CIX:I.4 ["Many waters cannot quench love, neither can floods drown it. If a man offered for love all the wealth of his house, it would be utterly scorned" (Song 8:7): "it would be utterly scorned:" R. Yohanan was going up on foot from Tiberias to Sepphoris, and R. Hiyya b. R. Abba was attending to him. They came by a field. Said R. Yohanan, "That field belonged to me, but I sold it to pay the expenses of laboring in the Torah." They came by a vineyard. Said R. Yohanan, "That vineyard belonged to me, but I sold it to pay the expenses of laboring in the Torah." Then R. Hiyya b. R. Abba began crying. He said to him, "I am crying because you have left nothing for your old age." He said to him, "Hiyya, my son, is

what I have done such a light thing in your eyes? For I have sold
something which is given for six days [of God's labor], for it is said,
'For in six days did the Lord make' (Ex. 20:11), while the Torah
took forty days to be given: 'And he was there with the Lord for
forty days' (Ex. 34:28); 'Then I abode in the mount forty days' (Dt.
9:9)."

> The contrast between investing in real estate and in-
> vesting in Torah-study is the point of this narrative,
> making the whole cohere. Torah-study is far more
> valuable and reliable as an investment. Here at any
> rate we have an authentic narrative, since the point
> of the prior details registers at the end and imparts co-
> gency to what has gone before.

The authentic narratives of Song of Songs Rabbah turn out to limit
themselves to a single theme, and that is not the same one as defines the paramount program of Lamentations Rabbah theme (as
we shall see in chapter sixteen). Of the narratives of Song of Songs
Rabbah, numbers 2 through 7 involve the theme of Torah-study and
its priority. Only No. 1 completely omits the theme of Torah-learning. No. 3 specifies the virtue that Torah-study is meant to incul-
cate, which is soft-heartedness, corresponding to physical weakness.
So we may say that, when the compilers of the document resorted
to writing that can claim the status of narrative (excluding narratives signified as *Mashal* or *Ma'aseh*, the former distinguished in substance, the latter mostly in formal marker), the narrative concerns
itself with the virtues of Torah-study and its outcome. These facts
take on meaning in the comparison with the counterpart writing of
Lamentations Rabbah, with its quite different and distinctive focus
and theme.

But the evidence of a handful of narratives of a common character in a vast compilation such as is constituted by Song of Songs
Rabbah is hardly proportionate: we cannot claim to have discov-
ered a rule of narrative writing for Song of Songs Rabbah and only
for that compilation. What we do know is that this theme, no other
theme, is expressed in the exemplary anecdote set forth in the foregoing catalogue. That represents an accurate description of what we
have found, no more than that. But the contrast to Lamentations
Rabbah and its thematic definition of narratives takes on consequence
by reason of the fact now in hand. It represents a documentary
choice, not a random phenomenon.

II. *The Mashal*

The whole of Song of Songs serves as a *Mashal* for the Rabbinic sages. We therefore cannot find surprising the compilers' resort to the exegetical parable as a principal medium of their exposition.

What defines the parable is the announcement that a case or proposition may be approached through a simile, an account of a transaction the components of which are comparable in character or relationship to the case or proposition at hand. That account, like the *Ma'aseh*, then may, but need not, report an anecdote, involving a transaction comparable to the one at hand but more readily accessible in its simplicity of detail than the one at hand.

The question that engages us in the present context is, does the *Mashal* stand on its own, or does it require the exegetical context to bear specific meaning? At stake is the autonomy of the parable: does it represent writing distinct from documentary tasks but then adapted to the realization of those tasks? Or is the parable integral to the documentary writing of Song of Songs Rabbah in particular? That is the question that guided analysis in chapters one through eight, the results of which are recapitulated here. The answer, as readers may already have intuited, is that the parable in Song of Songs Rabbah is more often an invention of the exegete of a particular passage than an adaptation by him of a ready-made narrative of exemplary quality. In three-fourths of the exegetical parables, the relationships and transactions and even static similes that comprise the parables of our compilation respond to the exegetical tasks of a highly particular sort and are explicitly linked to the accomplishment of those tasks. Those items were written in the context of compiling this particular document. In one fourth, the matter is ambiguous, for reasons to be specified. I can identify no parabolic narrative that stands autonomous of an exegetical context. These entries may or may not have responded to the tasks of compiling an exegetical exposition of Song of Songs Rabbah in particular.

To set off the parable from its context, I underline the parabolic component of the composition.

a. The Halakhic Mashal

1.   LXI:i.7. [In connection with the anomalous rules governing the offering of the princes,] another explanation of the phrase, "Eat, O friends:" Said R. Berekhiah, "The matter may be compared

to the case of a king who made a banquet and invited guests, and a dead creeping thing fell into the soup. If the king had declined to eat it, all of them would have declined to eat it. The king put out his hand [to serve himself] so everybody else did too.

2.   LXI:i.8. [In connection with the anomalous rules governing the offering of the princes,] said R. Yannai, "The matter may be compared to the case of a king who made a banquet and invited guests to come to him, and he went around among them, saying to them, 'I hope you like it, I hope you enjoy it.'"

3.   LXI:i. 9. [In connection with the anomalous rules governing the offering of the princes,] said R. Abbahu, "The matter may be compared to the case of a king who made a banquet and invited guests to come, and when they had eaten and drunk, he said, 'Take this good helping and give it to the host.' Thus here: 'I come to my garden, my sister, my bride, I gather my myrrh with my spice, I eat my honeycomb with my honey,' so you eat too. "'I drink my wine with my milk.' You too: 'Eat, O friends, and drink; drink deeply, O lovers.'"

> The task of the triplet of Halakhic parables is to explain the indicated matter, why God accepts the offerings under special rules, setting aside normal restrictions. The parables are particular to their Halakhic case.

The Halakhic *Mashal* cannot be characterized as an important narrative option in this document. That is hardly surprising, since Song of Songs Rabbah has no Halakhic burden of any weight. But it is of interest that the tiny corpus of Halakhic parables is wholly documentary in origin.

b. The Exegetical Mashal

By contrast, the compilation undertakes a systematic reading of the Song of Songs, and it is hardly surprising that the principal narrative form is the exegetical parable. We shall now see that most, though not all, parables take shape in response to the particular exegetical task at hand and do not derive from a generic corpus available for adaptation to a local task.

1.-6.   [I.iv.1-2. Another interpretation of "The Song of Songs" This is in line with the following verse of Scripture: "And more so because Qohelet was wise; [he also taught the people knowledge, yes, he pondered and sought out and set in order many proverbs]" (Qoh. 12:9): "And more so because Qohelet was wise;

he also taught the people knowledge, yes, he pondered and sought out and set in order many proverbs" (Qoh. 12:9): He pondered" words of the Torah, and "he sought out" words of the Torah. He made "handles" for the Torah. For you find that before Solomon came along, there was no parable [Hebrew: *dugma*, e.g., paradigm].

The foregoing sets the stage for the elaborate set of parabolic similes that follows. All six go over the ground of I.iv.6, each in its own way.

I:iv.3-7. 3A. R. Nahman said, "[The matter may be compared] to the case of a huge palace that had many doors, so whoever came in would wander from the path to the entry. A smart fellow came along and took a skein of string and hung the string on the way to the entry, so everybody came and went following the path laid out by the skein. 3B. R. Nahman said the matter in yet another way: "[The matter may be compared] to the case of a reed marsh that no one could enter. A smart fellow came along and took a scythe and cut the reeds, so everybody began to go in and come out by chopping down the reeds. 4. Said R. Yosé, "[The matter may be compared] to the case of a basket full of produce but lacking a handle so no one could lift it up. A smart fellow came along and made handles for it, so people began to carry it about holding on to the handles. 5. Said R. Shila, "[The matter may be compared] to the case of a big jug full of boiling water but lacking a handle so no one could lift it up. A smart fellow came along and made handles for it, so people began to carry it about holding on to the handles. 6. Said R. Hanina, "[The matter may be compared] to the case of a deep well full of water, and the water was cold, sweet, and good, but no one could drink from it. A smart fellow came along and provided a rope joined with another rope, a cord joined with another cord, sufficiently long so people could draw water from the well and drink it, and then everybody began to draw and drink. So from one thing to the next, from one proverb to the next, Solomon penetrated into the secret of the Torah.

7. And rabbis say, "Let a parable not be despised in your view, for it is through the parable that a person can master the words of the Torah. The matter may be compared to the case of a king who lost gold in his house or pearls. Is it not through a wick that is worth a penny that he finds it again?

All six exegetical parables (3A, 3B, 4-7) illustrate the "handles" that Solomon made for the Torah, and none contains a detail that is extraneous to that task. Since there are no marks of adaptation of available, formed similes, all must be classified as not autonomous but exegetically-subordinate to the task at hand. Some contain no more than a simile, others resort to (pseudo-) narrative.

7.   I:v.1.   "If you seek words of the Torah like hidden treasures, the Holy One, blessed be He, will not withhold your reward; <u>The matter may be compared to the case of a person, who, if he should lose a penny or a pin in his house, will light any number of candles, any number of wicks, until he finds them.</u> Now the matter yields an argument *a fortiori*...

The exegetical parable portrays not a story but a case, what one would do, not what someone paradigmatically has done.

8.   II.ii.9.   R. Yohanan interpreted the verse ["O that you would kiss me with the kisses of your mouth"] to speak of the Israelites when they went up to Mount Sinai: The matter may be compared to the case <u>of a king who wanted to marry a woman, daughter of good parents and noble family. He sent to her a messenger to speak with her. She said, 'I am not worthy to be his serving girl. But I want to hear it from his own mouth.' When that messenger got back to the king, his face was full of smiles, but what he said was not grasped by the king. The king, who was astute, said, 'This one is full of smiles. It would appear that she has agreed. But what he says is not to be understood by me. It appears that she has said, 'I want to hear it from his own mouth.'</u> So the Israelites are the daughter of good parents. The messenger is Moses. The king is the Holy One, blessed be He.

Why does Israel want God to kiss her personally, meaning, what was at stake at Sinai? The parable answers that question and more: Israel wanted God's personal presence at its betrothal at Sinai, and God understood that fact from the elliptical way in which Moses conveyed the message, a very subtle reading of the transaction. The exegetical parable is generated by the task at hand, the point the exegete wishes to register, and is not adapted out of a ready-made simile, awaiting definition for an occasion.

9-12. II.ii.14. R. Azariah, and some say R. Eliezer and R. Yosé b. R. Hanina and rabbis: R. Eliezer says, "The matter may be compared

to the case of <u>a king who had a wine cellar. The first guest
came to him first, and he mixed a cup for him and gave it to
him. A second came and he mixed a cup for him and gave it
to him When the son of the king came, he gave him the whole
cellar.</u> So the First Man was commanded in respect to seven
commandments. As to Noah, a further commandment was assigned to him. The Israelites, by contrast, made their own all
of the religious duties, positive and negative alike."

II.ii.17. R. Yosé b. R. Hanina and rabbis say, "<u>The matter may be
compared to the case of a king who was divvying up rations
to his legions through his generals, officers, and commanders. But when the turn of his son came, he gave him his rations with his own hand.</u>"

II.ii.18. R. Isaac says, "<u>The matter may be compared to a king who
was eating sweetmeats, And when the turn of his son came,
he gave him his rations with his own hand.</u>"

II.ii.19. Rabbis say, "<u>The matter may be compared to the case of a
king who was eating meat. And when the turn of his son came,
he gave him his rations with his own hand.</u>"

> The four exegetical parables cover the same ground:
> how and why the king varied his practice to show fa-
> vor to the prince. While they prove diverse, all of them
> respond to the same exegetical challenge: why does
> God deal personally with Israel, not through interme-
> diaries, and not in such a way as to treat Israel as
> equivalent to the nations.

13.   II.ii.20. R. Abbahu, and some say the following in the name of R.
Judah, and R. Nehemiah: R. Nehemiah said, "[The matter of 'O that
you would kiss me with the kisses of your mouth!' may be compared
to] <u>two colleagues who were occupied with teachings of the law. This
one states a general principle of law, and that one states a general
principle of law.</u>

> This is hardly a parable, in the sense in which a par-
> able asks for some sort of action or movement. It is,
> rather, a simile, pure and simple. How the simile
> matches the case it is meant to clarify is not obvious
> to me.

14.   IV:i.1 "Draw me after you, let us make haste. The king has brought
me into his chambers. We will exult and rejoice in you; we will extol
your love more than wine; rightly do they love you" (Song 1:4): Said
R. Meir, "When the Israelites stood before Mount Sinai to receive
the Torah, said to them the Holy One, blessed be He, 'Shall I really
give you the Torah? Bring me good sureties that you will keep it, and
then I shall give it to you. They said to him, 'Lord of the ages, our

fathers are our sureties for us. He said to them, 'Your fathers themselves require sureties.' To what is the matter comparable? To someone who went to borrow money from the king. He said to him, 'Bring me a surety, and I shall lend to you. He went and brought him a surety. He said to him, 'Your surety has to have a surety. He went and brought him another surety. He said to him, 'Your surety has to have a surety. When he had brought him yet a third surety, he said to him, 'You should know that it is on this one's account that I am lending to you. So when the Israelites stood to receive the Torah, he said to them, 'Shall I really give you my Torah? Bring me good sureties that you will keep it, and then I shall give it to you.'"

> I see no detail of the parable that does not realize the exegetical program: borrow money, surety, surety for a surety, surety for the surety's surety—why so many, if not for the exegetical transaction, "your fathers themselves require…." So the parable strikes me as utterly dependent upon the case it is meant to generalize and render accessible.

15. IV:iii. 10. R. Berekhiah in the name of R. Judah b. R. Ilai: "It is written, 'And Moses led Israel onward from the Red Sea' (Ex. 15:22): He led them on from the sin committed at the sea. They said to him, 'Moses, our lord, where are you leading us?' They said to him, 'Indeed, wherever you go and lead us, we are with you.' "The matter is comparable to the case of one who went and married a woman from a village. He said to her, 'Arise and come with me. She said to him, 'From here to where? She said to him, 'Wherever you go and take me, I shall go with you.' So said the Israelites, 'My soul cleaves to you' (Ps. 63:9)."

> The prevailing metaphor, Israel is God's bride, generates the simile, and the implicit narrative of the parable, "Wherever you go and take me, I shall go," flows from the exegetical context.

16. IV.v.3 [Supply: Another interpretation of the verse, "We will exult and rejoice in you:"] The matter [of the situation of the Israelites] may be compared to the case of a noble lady, whose husband, the king, and whose sons and sons-in-law went overseas. They came and told her, "Your sons are coming home." She said, "What difference does it make to me? Let my daughters-in-law rejoice." When her sons-in-law came home, they said to her, "Your sons-in-law are coming." So she said, "What difference does it make to me? Let my daughters rejoice." When they told her, "The king, your husband, is coming," she said, "This is the occasion for whole-hearted rejoicing, waves upon waves of joy!" So in the age to come the prophets will come and say to Jerusalem, "Your sons come from afar" (Isa. 60:4), and she will say, "What difference does that make to me?" But when they said to

her, "Lo, your king comes to you, he is triumphant and victorious" (Zech. 9:9), she will say, "This is the occasion for whole-hearted rejoicing!"

> The exegetical problem does not require more than the "sons," but once we have the queen with sons and daughters, the rest follows. Still, it is not so obvious that the parabolic narrative follows the exegetical challenge, for, in the bulk of the cases, the details of the parable match those of the case that is metaphorized, and here that is not precisely the case.

17. IX:ii.1. "I compare you, my love, [to a mare of Pharaoh's chariots]:" Said R. Eliezer, "The matter may be compared to the case of <u>a princess who was kidnapped, and her father was ready to redeem her. But she gave indications to the kidnappers, saying to them, 'I am yours, I belong to you, and I am going after you.' Said her father to her, 'What are you thinking? Is it that I do not have the power to redeem you? I would have you hold your peace [using the same word as 'compare you'], yes, be silent.'</u> So when the Israelites were encamped at the sea, and the Egyptians pursued after them and overtook them in camp by the sea' the Israelites, fearful, gave indicates to the Egyptians, saying to them, 'We are yours, we belong to you, and we are going after you.' Said to them the Holy One, blessed be He, 'What are you thinking? Is it that I do not have the power to redeem you?'" (Ex. 14:9)

> The key to the case is "fearful." That explains why the Israelites/princess identified with Egyptians/kidnappers, and accounts for God's/the King's assurance that he has the power to rescue her. Then the parable in each detail matches the exegetical case.

18. X:iii.3. [Supply: "Command the children of Israel and say to them" (Num. 28:2):] The matter provokes a parable: to what may it be compared? To the case of <u>a queen who was departing from this life. She said to him, "By the life of my lord, the king, I command you concerning my children!" He said to her, "Instead of giving me orders concerning my children, give my children orders concerning me!"</u> So when Moses said before the Holy One, blessed be He, "Lord of the world, since you remove me from the world, at least let me know what sort of leaders you are going to provide for the Israelites." ..."Instead of giving me instructions concerning my children, give instructions to my children concerning me!" That is in line with this verse: "Command the children of Israel and say to them" (Num. 28:2).

> The departing Moses is told to provide for God's requirements, as the departing Queen instructs the chil-

dren about taking care of the children and is told to watch out for the King. Here is an instance of modeling the parable after the case.

19.   XII:ii.1. [Taking up Song 1:12,] R. Phineas in the name of R. Hoshaia said, "'While the king,' the King of kings of kings, the Holy One, blessed be He, 'was on his couch,' in the firmament, ['my nard gave forth its fragrance'], he had already anticipated [his descent on Mount Sinai] [Simon, p. 79, n. 4: by enveloping the mountain in flames and smoke], thus: 'And it came to pass on the third day, while it was yet morning, that there were thunders... upon the mount' (Ex. 19:16)." It may be compared to the case of <u>a king who decreed, "On such and such a day, I shall enter town. The townsfolk slept all night, so when the king came and found them sleeping, he had the trumpets and horns sounded. The prince of that town woke the people up and brought them forth to receive the king. The king walked before them until he reached his palace.</u> Thus the Holy One, blessed be He, anticipated [his descent on Mount Sinai]: "And it came to pass on the third day, while it was yet morning, that there were thunders... upon the mount" (Ex. 19:16). The Israelites had been sleeping all that night, for the sleep of Pentecost is very pleasant, and the night is brief Came the Holy One, blessed be He, and found them sleeping. So he had the trumpets and horns sounded That is in line with this verse: "And it came to pass on the third day, while it was yet morning, that there were thunders... upon the mount" (Ex. 19:16).

> God forewarns Israel of his imminent arrival as the king tells the town he is en route, and the medium—thunder/trumpets—is comparable. So the parable tracks the case.

20.   XIX:i.5 ["a lily of the valleys." (Song 2:1):] R. Azariah in the name of R. Judah in the name of R. Simon [interpreted the cited verse to speak of Israel before Mount Sinai]. The matter may be compared to <u>a king who had an orchard. He planted in it rows upon rows of figs, grapevines, and pomegranates. After a while the king went down to his vineyard and found it filled with thorns and brambles. He brought woodcutters and cut it down. But he found in the orchard a single red rose. He took it and smelled it and regained his serenity and said, 'This rose is worthy that the entire orchard be saved on its account.'</u> So too the entire world was created only on account of the Torah. For twenty-six generations the Holy One, blessed be He, looked down upon his world and saw it full of thorns and brambles. But he found in the world a single red rose, Israel, that was destined to stand before Mount Sinai and to say before the Holy One, blessed be He, 'Whatever the Lord has said we shall do and we shall obey' (Ex. 24:7).

> The exact match between the parable and the theo-

logical myth—"Israel the single red rose"—is self-evident.

21. XIX:I,6 R. Hanan of Sepphoris interpreted the verse to speak of acts of loving kindness [that one may do by helping others carry out their liturgical obligations]: <u>Ten men entered a synagogue to say their prayers, but they did not know how to say the Shema and go before the ark to recite the Prayer. But there was among them one who did know how to say the Shema and to go before the ark. Among them, he was 'like a lily among brambles.'</u>

> Here we have not a narrative parable but a mere simile, a case meant to realize a situation, not a narrative meant to compare with a vivid transaction.

22. XX:I.6. ["As an apple tree among the trees of the wood so is my beloved among young men. With great delight I sat in his shadow, and his fruit was sweet to my taste" (Song 2:3):] R. Judah b. R. Simon made two statements: Just as an apple costs only a penny, but you can smell its fragrance any number of times, So said Moses to the Israelites, 'If you wish to be redeemed, you may be redeemed for a simple matter.' They may be compared to <u>someone who had sore feet and he went to all the physicians for healing and was not healed. Then he came to one, who said to him, 'If you want to be healed, you can be healed in a simple way. Plaster your feet with bullshit.'</u> So said Moses to the Israelites, 'If you wish to be redeemed, you may be redeemed for a simple matter.'

> The exegetical task is to find a simile to a redemption through a simple matter, and the exegetical parable supplies a simile, which is made into a narrative simply by the "he went to all the physicians... until he came to one...." That is not a very dramatic narrative.

23. XX:i.7. ["As an apple tree among the trees of the wood so is my beloved among young men. With great delight I sat in his shadow, and his fruit was sweet to my taste" (Song 2:3):] R. Judah b. R. Simon made another statement: The matter may be compared to the case of <u>a king who had a precious stone and a pearl. His son came along and said to him, 'Give it to me.' He said to him, 'It is yours, it belongs to you, and I give it over to you.'</u> So said the Israelites before the Holy One, blessed be He, "'The Lord is my strength and my song'" (Ex. 15:2) Said to them the Holy One, blessed be He, 'It is yours, it belongs to you, and I give it over to you.'

> The foregoing judgment pertains here as well. What is needed is a simile for a donation, and the king/prince supply the players in a static transaction.

24. XXII:i.2. ["Sustain me with raisins refresh me with apples; for I am sick with love" (Song 2:3]): R. Simeon b. Yohai taught on Tannaite authority, "When the Israelites came forth from Egypt, what were they like? They were comparable to <u>a prince who recovered from an illness. Said his tutor [to the king], 'Let your son go to school.' Said the king to him, 'My son has not yet recovered his full color. For he has become pale because of his illness. Let my son take it easy and enjoy himself for three months with food and drink, and then he can go back to school.'</u> So when the Israelites went forth from Egypt, there were among them those who had been deformed through the slave labor of mortar and bricks. The ministering angels said to him, 'Lo, the time has come. Give them the Torah.' Said to them the Holy One, blessed be He, 'My children have not yet recovered their full color on account of the slave labor of mortar and bricks.

    Here we have an active transaction, not just a simile for a situation, in an exegetical parable that hews to the situation of Israel after leaving Egypt.

25. XXXI:i.6. "O my dove, in the clefts of the rock" (Song 2:14):] It was taught on Tannaite authority by the house of R. Ishmael, "When the Israelites went forth from Egypt, to what were they to be compared? To <u>a dove that fled from a hawk and flew into the cleft of a rock and found a serpent hidden there. It went in but could not, because the snake was hidden there, and it tried to go backward but could not, because the hawk was standing outside. What did the dove do? It began to cry out and beat its wings, so that the owner of the dove-cote should hear and come and save it.</u> That is what the Israelites were like at the sea.

    The simile describes a situation, not an event, and the situation of the parable exactly matches that of Israel at the sea.

26. XXXI:I.7."O my dove, in the clefts of the rock" (Song 2:14)] R. Judah in the name of R. Hama of Kefar Tehumin: "The matter may be compared to <u>the king who had an only daughter and wanted to listen to her converse. What did he do? He circulated an announcement and said, 'Let everybody assemble in the piazza.' When they had come forth, what did he do? He made a gesture to his servants, and they suddenly fell on her like thugs. She began to cry out, 'Father, father, save me.' He said, 'Had I not treated you in this way, you would not have cried out and said, "Father, save me."</u> So when the Israelites were in Egypt, the Egyptians enslaved them, and they begin to cry out and look upward to the Holy One, blessed be He: 'And it came to pass in the course of those many days that the king of Egypt died, and the children of Israel signed by reason of the bondage, and they cried' (Ex. 2:23).

The parabolic narrative responds to the exegetical challenge, point by point. No detail of the parable is extraneous or out of phase.

27. XXXIII:II.2: "The matter may be compared to the case of <u>a householder who had two cows, one strong, the other weak. On which one does he place the burden? Is it not on the strong one?</u> "Thus the Holy One, blessed be He, does not impose trials upon the wicked. Why not? Because they cannot endure: 'But the wicked are like the troubled sea' (Isa. 57:20) Upon whom does he impose trials? Upon the righteous: 'The Lord tries the righteous' (Ps. 11:5),

> The simile of the two cows contains no story or action, only an observation, quickly translated into its exegetical elements.

28. XL:i.12: "The matter may be compared <u>to a king who had a savage dog and a tame lion. What did the king do?</u> "The king would take his lion and sick him against the son, saying, 'If the dog comes to have a fight with the son, he will say to the dog, "The lion cannot have a fight with me, [how] are you going to make out in a fight with me?"'" So if the nations come to have a fight with Israel, the Holy One, blessed be He, says to them, 'Your angelic prince could not stand up to Israel, and as to you, how much the more so!'

> Here is another situation constructed as a simile. The lion cannot fight with the prince, how can the dog do it? This too is a simile lacking narrative movement. The dependence of the simile upon the exegetical situation is self-evident.

29. XLIII:ii.3 ["King Solomon made himself a palanquin, from the wood of Lebanon. He made its posts of silver, its back of gold, its seat of purple; it was lovingly wrought within by the daughters of Jerusalem "'... a palanquin': this is the ark." The matter may be compared to the case of <u>a king who had an only daughter, who was beautiful, pious, and gracious. Said the king to his staff, "my daughter is beautiful, pious, and gracious, and yet you do not make her a litter? Make her a litter, for it is better that the beauty of my daughter should appear from within a litter."</u> So said the Holy One, blessed be He, "My Torah is beautiful, pious, and gracious, and yet you do not make an ark for it? It is better that the beauty of my Torah should appear from within the ark."

> The princess and the Torah are what is compared, and the message of the king about the princess replicates the message of God about the Torah, an exact simile.

30. XLIV:ii. 1. "... with the crown with which his mother crowned him:"

The matter may be compared to the case <u>of a king who had an only</u> <u>daughter, whom he loved exceedingly, calling her "My daughter."</u> <u>But he loved her so much that he called her, "My sister," and he</u> <u>loved her so much that he called her, "My mother."</u> So did the Holy One, blessed be He, exceedingly love Israel, calling them, "My daughter." Then he loved them so much that he called them, "My sister," Then he loved them so much that he called them, "My mother."

> The three stages, daughter/sister/mother, are matched for Israel, in an exegetical parable built on the foundations of Scripture's requirement.

31. XLIV:ii.3, 4. R. Joshua of Sikhnin taught in the name of R. Levi: "When the Holy One, blessed be He, said to Moses, 'Make me a tabernacle,' Moses might have brought four poles and spread over them [skins to make] the tabernacle. But this is not how the Holy One, blessed be He, did it. Rather, he took him above and showed him on high red fire, green fire, black fire, and white fire. He then said to him, 'Make me a tabernacle like this.' Moses said to the Holy One, blessed be He, 'Lord of the ages, where am I going to get red fire, green fire, black fire, or white fire?' He said to him, 'After the pattern which is shown to you on the mountain' (Ex. 25:40)." Said R. Abun [Pesiqta deRab Kahana I:III.10: R. Berekhiah in the name of R. Levi], "[The matter may be compared to the case of] <u>a king who</u> <u>had a beautiful icon He said to the manager of his household, 'Make</u> <u>me one like this.' He said to him, 'My lord, O king, how can I make</u> <u>one like this ?' He said to him, 'You in accord with your raw mate-</u> <u>rials and I in accord with my glory.'</u> So said the Holy One, blessed be He, to Moses, 'See and make.' He said to him, 'Lord of the world, am I god that I can make something like this?' He said to him, 'After the pattern which is shown to you on the mountain' (Ex. 25:40)."

32. XLIV:ii.5 R. Berekhiah in the name of R. Bezalel: "The matter may be compared to the case of <u>a king who appeared to his household</u> <u>manager clothed in a garment covered entirely with precious stones</u> <u>He said to him, 'Make me one like this.' He said to him, 'My lord,</u> <u>O king, how can I make one like this [Pesiqta: where am I going to</u> <u>get myself a garment made entirely of precious stones]?</u> "So said the Holy One, blessed be He, to Moses, 'Make me a tabernacle.' He said to him, 'Lord of the world, can I make something like this?' He said to him, 'See and make.' He said to him, 'Lord of the world, am I god that I can make something like this?' He said to him, 'After the pattern which is shown to you on the mountain' (Ex. 25:40)."

> In the case of both parables, the exchange between the king and the major domo is hardly so elaborate as the exegetical precipitant expects. The main point in both cases is simply that the king supplies a model to be followed by the major domo, a simple enough point,

which yields no dynamic narrative but only a simile: it is like the case of a king who said....

33. XLIX:i.1. "Your two breasts are like two fawns (Song 4:5):" This refers to Moses and Aaron. Just as one breast is not larger than the other, so Moses and Aaron were the same: "These are Moses and Aaron" R. Abba said, "The matter may be compared to the case of <u>a king who had two first-rate pearls, which he put in the balance. This one was not greater than that, and that was not greater than this.</u> So Moses and Aaron were equal."

Once more the simile suffices to clarify the scriptural situation. It matches that situation and involves no activity.

34. LVI:I1 "A garden locked is my sister, my bride, [a garden locked, a fountain sealed] (Song 4:12):" R. Judah b. R. Simon in the name of R. Joshua b. Levi: "[The matter may be compared to the case of] <u>a king who had two daughters, an older and a younger, and who did not take time out to marry them off but left them for many years and went overseas. The daughters went and took the law into their own hands, and married themselves off to husbands. And each one of them took her husband's signature and his seal. After a long time the king came back from overseas and heard people maligning his daughters, saying, 'The king's daughters have already played the whore.' What did he do? He issued a proclamation and said, 'Everybody come out to the piazza,' and he came and went into session in the antechamber [holding court there]. He said to them, 'My daughters, is this what you have done and have ruined yourselves?' Each one of them immediately produced her husband's signature and his seal. Then the king said, 'My daughters have been guarded from fornication, and you malign and shame them! By your lives, I shall carry out judgment against you.</u> So too with the nations of the world: since they taunt Israel and say, '"And the Egyptians made the people of Israel work with rigor" (Ex. 1:13), if that is what they could make them do in labor, how much the more so with their bodies and with their wives'!'

The parable is elaborate and the details vastly exceed what is required for the exegetical point to come to clarification. Indeed, the relationship is disproportionate, and the stages in the parabolic narrative serve no exegetical purpose.

35. LVI:i.8. [Another interpretation of "A garden locked" (Song 4:12): R. Phineas in the name of R. Hiyya bar Abba, "Because the Israelites locked themselves up and avoided licentious sexual behavior with the Egyptians, they were redeemed from Egypt. On that account was 'your being sent forth' that is, 'your shoots' 'are an orchard of pome-

granates with all choicest fruits.' That interpretation is in line with the following: 'And it came to pass, when Pharaoh sent forth... ' (Ex. 13:17).] R. Simeon b. Yohai taught on Tannaite authority, "[The Egyptians were] in the position of <u>someone who inherited a piece of ground that was a dumping ground. The heir was lazy, so he went and sold it for some trifling sum. The buyer went and worked hard and dug up in the dump heap and found a treasure, and with it he built himself a big palace. The buyer would walk about the market-place, with servants following in a retinue, all on the strength of that treasure that he had bought with the dump heap. The seller, when he saw this, he began to choke, saying, 'Woe, what I have lost!'</u> So too, when the Israelites were in Egypt, they were enslaved in mortar and bricks, and they were held in contempt by the Egyptians. But when they saw them with their standards, encamped at the sea, in royal array, the Egyptians began to choke, saying, 'Woe, what have we sent forth from our land!'

36. LVI:i.9 Said R. Jonathan, "They were in the position of <u>someone who had a field the size of a kor who went and sold it for a piddling sum. The buyer went and dug wells in it and made in it gardens and or-chards. When the seller saw this, he began to choke, saying, 'Woe, what I have lost!'</u> So too, when the Israelites were in Egypt, they were enslaved in mortar and bricks, and they were held in contempt by the Egyptians. But when they saw them with their standards, encamped at the sea, in royal array, the Egyptians began to choke, saying, 'Woe, what have we sent forth from our land!'

37. LVI:i.10 R. Yosé says, "They were in the position <u>of someone who had a grove of cedars, who went and sold it for a piddling sum. The buyer went and made of the wood boxes, chests, towers and carriages. When the seller saw this, he began to choke, saying, 'Woe, what I have lost!'</u> So too, when the Israelites were in Egypt, they were en-slaved in mortar and bricks, and they were held in contempt by the Egyptians. But when they saw them with their standards, encamped at the sea, in royal array, the Egyptians began to choke, saying, 'Woe, what have we sent forth from our land!'"

> The task of the exegetical parable is to explain how the Israelites were held in contempt by the Egyptians because they were slaves, but when they saw them with their standards in array, they realized the dignity and value of Israel. That yields three parables, the improve-ment of the land that was inherited and neglected but then sold to someone who (1) built a palace, or who (2) dug wells and created a garden, or (3) cut down trees and made boxes, chests, and the like. The parables go over common ground, in all three instances carrying out the same assignment in the same way.

38. "His speech is most sweet (Song 5:16): Said R. Yudan [b. R. Simeon], "The matter may be compared to <u>a widow who was complaining to a judge about her son. When she saw that the judge was in session and handing out sentences of punishment by fire, pitch, and lashes, she said, 'If I report the bad conduct of my son to that judge, he will kill him now.' She waited until he was finished. When he had finished, he said to her, 'Madam, this son of yours, how has he behaved badly toward you?' She said to him, 'My lord, when he was in my womb, he kicked me.' He said to her, 'Now has he done anything wrong to you?' She said to him, 'No.' He said to her, 'Go your way, there is nothing wrong in the matter [that you report].'</u> So, when the Holy One, blessed be He, saw that the nations of the world were rejoicing, he turned the matter to [Israel's] advantage.

> Here the parable vastly outweighs in detail and in scope the exegetical assignment and scarcely matches that assignment. The parable of the mother who suppresses her complaint strikes me as out of phase with its exegetical context.

39. LXXVI:i.8 Another interpretation of the verse, "His speech is most sweet:" The matter may be compared to the case of <u>a king who scolded his son, and the son was afraid and lost heart. When the king saw that his son had lost heart, he began to hug and kiss him and appease him, saying to him, "What's with you? Are you not my only son? Am I not your father?"</u> So when the Holy One, blessed be He, spoke: "I am the Lord your God," their spirit forthwith departed. And the Holy One, blessed be He, sweetened the word in their mouths and said to them, "Are you not my children? 'I am the Lord your God.' You are my people, you are precious to me. So he began to appease them until their souls were restored, and they began to entreat him. Thus: "His speech is most sweet."

> God scolded Israel, which lost heart, and God responded by showing Israel his love, just like the king and the prince of the parable, another exegetical parable that translates the message into an engaging narrative.

40. LXXVIII:i.4. ["My beloved has gone down to his garden, to the beds of spices, to pasture his flock in the gardens, and to gather lilies" (Song 6:2):] Said R. Samuel b. R. Nahman, "[The matter may be compared] to the case <u>of a king who had an orchard and planted in it rows of nut trees, apple trees, and pomegranates, and handed them over to his son. When the son did the father's will, the king would go and make the rounds all over the world and see which planting was particularly attractive and would uproot it and bring it and plant it in that orchard. But when his son did not carry out his will, the king</u>

would see which planting in the orchard was particularly fine, and he would uproot that one. So is the case with Israel: when they carry out the will of the Omnipresent, he picks out a righteous person among the nations of the world, for instance, Jethro or Rahab, and brings him and cleaves him to Israel. But when Israel does not do the will of the Holy One, blessed be He, he identifies a righteous, upright, virtuous, and God-fearing person among them and takes him up from their midst."

> The parable once more precisely replicates the transaction of the verse of Scripture as interpreted by the sages, Jethro and Rahab corresponding to the attractive plantings God found abroad and brought back to Israel. But Israel loses its virtuous personalities when it does not do God's will.

41. LXXXI:il. "Turn away your eyes from me:" The matter may be compared] to the case of a king who was enraged against the queen and pushed her out and drove her away from the palace. What did she do? She went and pressed her face against a pillar outside the palace. When the king went by, the king said, 'Take her away from before me, for I can't bear it.' Thus when the court is in session and decrees fasts and individuals afflict themselves, the Holy One, blessed be He, says, 'I can't bear it.'"

> The queen shows her remorse by pressing her face against the pillar, and the king is moved and avoids the spectacle, as God avoids the spectacle of Israel's remorseful fasting and affliction. No detail of the exegetical parable parts company from the verse as read by the Rabbinic interpreter.

42. LXXXVII:I.1. "I went down to the nut orchard:" The Israelites are compared to a nut tree: "just as a nut tree is pruned and improved thereby, for, like hair that is trimmed and grows more abundantly, and like nails that are trimmed and grow more abundantly, so is the case with Israel, for they are pruned of the return on their work, which they gave to those who labor in the Torah in this world, and it is for their good that they are so pruned, for that increases their wealth in this world and the reward that is coming to them in the world to come."

> The simile is precisely matched to the case it is meant to illuminate, but there is no effort to tell a story either through the parable or through its generative application.

43. LXXXVII:i.9. ["I went down to the nut orchard to look at the blossoms of the valley, to see whether the vines had budded, whether the

pomegranates were in bloom" (Song 6:11):] Another explanation of
the phrase, "I went down to the nut orchard:" just as in the case of
a nut, a stone breaks it, so the Torah is called a stone, [and] the impulse
to do evil is called a stone. The Torah is called a stone. The impulse
to do evil is called a stone: "And I will take away the stony heart out
of your flesh" (Ezek. 36:26). Said R. Levi, "[The matter may be compared to the case of] a lonely spot, which is infested with terrorists.
What does the king do? He assigns there brigades to guard the place
so that the terrorists will not attack travelers on the way. So said the
Holy One, blessed be He, 'The Torah is called a stone, and the impulse to do evil is called a stone. 'Let stone guard stone.'"

> The exegetical parable compares the Torah to the
> brigades. But this does not exactly replicate the thought
> of the exegete, since he calls the Torah, a stone, which
> guards the impulse to do evil, a stone. So we should
> expect the simile to match both elements, and it does
> not do so. For the match to work precisely, the ter-
> rorists would have to match the royal troops.

44. LXXXVIII:i.1. "Before I was aware, my fancy set me in a chariot
beside my prince (Song 6:12):" "The matter may be compared to the
case of a princess who went out gathering stray sheaves. The king
turned out to be passing and recognized that she was his daughter.
He sent out his friend to take her and seat her with him in the carriage. Now her girlfriends were surprised at her and said, 'Yesterday
you were gathering stray sheaves, and today you are seated in a carriage
with the king.' She said to them, 'Just as you are surprised at me, so
I am surprised at myself, and I recited in my own regard the following verse of Scripture, 'Before I was aware, my fancy set me in a chariot
beside my prince.' Thus too when the Israelites were enslaved in Egypt
in mortar and bricks, they were rejected and despised in the view of
the Egyptians. But when they were freed and redeemed and made
prefects over everyone in the world, the nations of the world expressed
surprise, saying, 'Yesterday you were working in mortar and bricks,
and today you have been freed and redeemed and made prefects over
everyone in the world! "And the Israelites replied to them, 'Just as
you are surprised at us, so we are surprised at ourselves,' and they
recited in their own regard, 'Before I was aware, my fancy set me in
a chariot beside my prince.'"

> The exegetical parable works precisely to replicate in
> its terms the details of the reading of the cited verse,
> the whole being a verbatim match. Why the princess
> was out gathering stray sheaves is unexplained, and the
> disjuncture only highlights the correspondence of the
> parable and the transaction it embodies.

45. XC:ii.1. Another explanation of the verse, "How graceful are your feet in sandals, O queenly maiden:" [The word for sandals is so written that it can be read,] in two closings [or: completions, with reference to the concluding days of the festivals of Tabernacles and Passover, as will be spelled out presently]. 2. Said R. Hama b. R. Hanina, "The matter may be compared to <u>two peddlers who came to a town. One of them took up the matter with the other, saying to his fellow, 'If we both open our shops together in this town, we shall bring down the price. You open your stall in your week, and I shall do so in my week.'"</u>

> We have no guidance here on how the parable realizes the transaction that is at issue.

46. XC:ii.4. Said R. Joshua b. Levi, "The Concluding Day of the Festival [the Eighth Day of Solemn Assembly] was suitable to be distanced fifty days from the Festival, corresponding to the Conclusion of Passover [which is Pentecost, fifty days after Passover]. But as to the Concluding Day of the Festival, since it marks the passage from summer to winter, it is not a time for going and coming. The matter may be compared to the case <u>of a king who had many daughters, some of them married and living near by, some of them married and living far off. One day all of them came to greet the king, their father. Said the king, 'Those who are married and living nearby can go and come as they like, but those who are married and living at a distance cannot come and go anytime they like. So while they are all with me, come, let us celebrate a single banquet for them all and rejoice with them all.'</u> So as to the Concluding Day of Passover [Pentecost], since the season is passing from winter to summer, said the Holy One, blessed be He, 'These are days for going and coming.' But as to the Concluding day of the Festival, since the days are passing from summer to winter, with the roads dusty and hard for walking, therefore the [Eighth Day of Solemn Assembly] is not distanced by fifty days [from the opening days of Tabernacles, in the way in which Pentecost is separated from the opening days of Passover by fifty days] [for,] said the Holy One, blessed be He, 'These are not days for going and coming. But while they are here, let us celebrate a single banquet for them all and rejoice with them all.'"

> The rather complex case captured in the parable shows the same precision of match as do the exegetical parables. We see that the parable transcends its exegetical task and serves as a medium of clarification and illumination, now explaining the details of the sacred calendar. The "So as to the…" component leaves no doubt that the parable is constructed to clarify the case, tracking as it does the elements that require explanation.

47.   XC:iii.8 Said R. Samuel, "The matter may be compared to the case
of <u>a king who had an orchard, planted row by row of nuts, apples,</u>
<u>pomegranates, and he handed them over to his son, saying to him,</u>
<u>'My son, I ask of you only that when these plantings bring their first</u>
<u>fruit, you present it to me and let me taste it, so that I may see the</u>
<u>work of my hands and take pleasure in you.'</u> So said the Holy One,
blessed be He, to the Israelites, 'My children, I ask of you only that
when a first son is born to any of you, he be sanctified to my name:
"Sanctify to me all the firstborn" (Ex. 13:2).

> The "I ask of you only…," transaction with the first-
> born produces the "I ask of you only the first fruit of
> the plantings." The parable's prolix details, nuts,
> apples, pomegranates, contribute nothing, but affect
> nothing.

48.   XCI:i.13. "The nations of the world have no planting, nor sowing,
nor root. But the Israelites have a planting: 'And I will plant them in
this land' (Jer. 32:41); they have a sowing: 'And I will sow her to me
in the land' (Hos. 2:25); they have a root: 'In days to come Jacob
shall take root' (Isa. 27:6). To what may the matter be compared?
<u>The straw, chaff, and stubble argued with one another. This one says,</u>
<u>"On my account the field is sown," and that one says, "On my ac-</u>
<u>count the field is sown." The wheat said to them, "Wait for me until</u>
<u>the threshing floor arrives, and we shall see for whom the field is sown."</u>
<u>The threshing floor arrived, and when they were brought into the</u>
<u>threshing floor, the household came out to winnow it. He took the</u>
<u>wheat and made it into a pile</u>. So it is with the nations of the world:
These say, "We are Israel, and on our account the world has been
made," and those say, "We are Israel, and on our account the world
has been made," so Israel says to them, "Wait until the day of the
Holy One, blessed be He, comes, and we shall then know on whose
account the world has been made: 'For behold the day comes, it burns
as a furnace' (Mal. 4:1); 'You shall fan them and the wind shall carry
them away' (Isa. 41:16).

> The eschatological resolution of conflict for the status
> of Israel generates the parabolic counterpart: the con-
> flict of straw, chaff, and stubble. What is left out of the
> conflict portrayed by the parable is the wheat, which
> of course stands for Israel. But that is necessary to the
> transaction: "Wait until the day of the Holy One
> comes…." Israel has to be above the fray—that is the
> point of the exegesis—and so has to be omitted from
> the nations' competition.

49.   CII:i.6 A. [The mandrakes give forth fragrance, and over our doors

are all choice fruits, new as well as old, which I have laid up for you, O my beloved (Song 7:13):] "and over our doors are all choice fruits:" Members of the household of R. Shila said, "The matter [of 'choice fruits, new as well as old'] may be compared to the case of a virtuous woman, to whom her husband left sparse possessions and little money for expenses [when he went overseas]. When her husband came back, she said to him, 'Remember what you left me, and see what I have collected for you and what I have also added for you beyond that!'"

50.   CII:i.6 B And rabbis say, "The matter [of 'choice fruits, new as well as old'] may be compared to a king who had an orchard, which he gave to a tenant-farmer. What did the tenant-farmer do? He filled baskets of figs from the produce of the orchard and put them at the gate of the orchard. Now when the king passed by and saw all this increase, he said, 'All this increase is at the doorway of the orchard— then in the orchard how much the more so!' So take the case of the earlier generations, the men of the great assembly, Hillel and Shammai, and Rabban Gamaliel the Elder. Then the latter generations, R. Yohanan b. Zakkai, R. Eliezer and R. Joshua, R. Meir and R. Aqiba and their disciples—how much the more so!

> As I said in chapter seven, I do not see how the exegetical parable intersects with the transaction, either at No. 49 or at No. 50. No. 49 is left without an explicit application. No. 50 is supposed to show how if the early generations attained Torah-learning, the later ones achieved still more. None of this bears any close correspondence to the parabolic materials. The problem lies in the "so take the case..." component.

51.   CVII:i.6. ["Who is that coming up from the wilderness, leaning upon her beloved? Under the apple tree I awakened you. There your mother was in travail with you, there she who bore you was in travail" (Song 8:5)] "There your mother was in travail with you: Did she really go into labor there? Said R. Berekhiah, "The matter may be compared to the case of someone who went into a dangerous place and was saved from the danger. His friend met him and said to him, 'Did you go through that perilous passage? What perils you have escaped! Your mother really bore you there! How much anguish you have survived! It's as though you were reborn today!'"

> Berekhiah explicitly links the parable to the transaction that is captured by the parable: "It's as though you were reborn today" is the key language: having escaped death in the dangerous place and having been saved. The parable then captures the situation of Israel in the wilderness.

52. CXII:iii.10-11. [Supply: "O Lord, our Lord, how glorious is your name in all the earth! whose majesty is rehearsed in the heavens" (Ps. 8:2):] R. Joshua of Sikhnin in the name of R. Levi: "What is written here is not 'your majesty' but 'whose majesty is rehearsed,' your majesty is therein, your happiness is therein, it makes you happy that your Torah should be in heaven." He said to them, 'No, the desire does not come from you [and it is none of your business].'" 11. Said R. Yudan, "The matter may be compared to the case of <u>a man who had a son with stumped fingers. What did he do? He took him to a silk worker to teach him the craft. He began to look at his fingers. He said, 'The very essence of this craft is acquired only with the fingers. How is this one going to learn?</u> Thus: 'No, the desire does not come from you [and it is none of your business].' So when the Holy One, blessed be He, wanted to give the Torah to Israel, the ministering angels tried to intervene against Israel and to intervene before the Holy One, blessed be He, saying, 'Lord of the world, your majesty is therein, your happiness is therein, it makes you happy that your Torah should be in heaven.' He said to them, 'No, the desire does not come from you [and it is none of your business].

> The point of the transaction is God's rebuke to the angels in giving the Torah to men: the angels simply cannot use it, any more than the apprentice with stumps for fingers can use the knowledge of silk-weaving: he just doesn't have the capacity. The exegetical parable then hews closely to the line of the transaction that is portrayed, the key language being "No, the desire does not come from you [and it is none of your business]."

53. CXII:iii.13. And rabbis say, "The matter may be compared to the case <u>of a king who was marrying off his daughter outside of town. The townsfolk said to him, 'Our lord, our king, it is praiseworthy and right that your daughter should be with you in town. Perhaps tomorrow you may go to her and live with her and stay with her because of your love for her.' He said to them, 'My daughter I shall marry off out of town, but I shall stay with you in town.'</u> Thus when the Holy One, blessed be He, was planning to give the Torah to the Israelites, the ministering angels said to the Holy One, blessed be He, 'Lord of the world, 'you are the one whose majesty is over heaven,' your happiness is therein, your glory and your praise is that your Torah should be in heaven. Perhaps tomorrow you will bring your Presence to rest among the creatures below.' Said to them the Holy One, blessed be He, 'My Torah is what I am sending to the creatures below, but I shall continue to dwell among the creatures of the upper world. I shall give my daughter with her marriage settlement in another town, so she may be honored with her husband for her beauty and charm, for

she is a princess, and they will honor her. But I shall dwell with you among the creatures of the upper world.'

>The issue is congruent with the preceding: the angels' concern that God not abandon Heaven runs parallel to their concern to keep the Torah in Heaven But now the issue is God, not the Torah. The shift in the parabolic narrative once more attests to the origin of the parable in the transaction that is portrayed by it.

54. CXIII:i.1. ["My vineyard, my very own, is for myself; you, O Solomon, may have the thousand, and the keepers of the fruit two hundred" (Song 8:12):] "My vineyard, my very own, is for myself:" R. Hiyya taught on Tannaite authority, "The matter may be compared to the case of <u>a king who was angry with his son and handed him over to his servant. What did he do? He began to beat him with a club. He said to him, 'Don't obey your father. The son said to the servant, 'You big fool! The very reason that father handed me over to you was only because I was not listening to him, and you say, "Don't listen to father"!'</u> So too, when sin had brought it about that the house of the sanctuary should be destroyed and Israel sent into exile to Babylonia, Nebuchadnezzar said to them, 'Do not listen to the Torah of your father in heaven, but rather, "fall down and worship the image that I have made" (Dan. 3:15). The Israelites said to him, 'You big fool! The very reason that the Holy One, blessed be He, has handed us over to you is because we were bowing down to an idol: "She saw... the images of the Chaldeans portrayed with vermilion" (Ezek. 23:14), and yet you say to us, "fall down and worship the image that I have made" (Dan. 3:15). Woe to you!'

>The exegetical parable exactly replicates the case it is meant to realize, as the repetition of the operative language shows clearly.

55. CXIV:i.1. "O you who dwell in the gardens, my companions are listening for your voice; let me hear it" (Song 8:13): R. Nathan in the name of R. Aha said, "The matter may be compared to the case of <u>a king who got mad at his staff and imprisoned them. What did the king do? He took all his officers and staff and went to listen to what they were saying [in prison to one another]. He heard that they were saying, 'Our lord, the king, is our praise, he is our life. May we never fail our lord, the king, forever. He said to them, 'My children, raise your voices so that the my companions who are near by you may hear.'</u> Thus even though the Israelites are occupied with their daily work all six days of creation, on the Sabbath day they get up early and come to the synagogue and recite the *Shema* and pass before the ark and proclaim the Torah and conclude with the words of the prophet. And the Holy One, blessed be He, says to them, 'My children, raise

> your voices so that the my companions may hear.'
>
> The world finds its simile in a prison, to which Israel is sentenced for daily work; on the Sabbath Israel expresses its true convictions, for God's angelic retinue to hear too. The correspondences require that the weekdays be compared to a prison, which does not really work well here.

56. CXV:ii.3 "Make haste, my beloved, and be like a gazelle or a young stag upon the mountains of spices" (Song 8:14): Said R. Levi, "The matter may be compared to the case of <u>a king who made a banquet and invited guests. Some of them ate and drank and said a blessing to the king, but some of them ate and drank and cursed the king. The king realized it and considered making a public display at his banquet and disrupting it. But the matron [queen] came and defended them, saying to him, 'My lord, O king, instead of paying attention to those who ate and drank and cursed you, take note of those who ate and drank and blessed you and praised your name.'</u> So is the case with Israel: when they eat and drink and say a blessing and praise and adore the Holy One, blessed be He, he listens to their voice and is pleased. But when the nations of the world eat and drink and blaspheme and curse the Holy One, blessed be He, with their fornication of which they make mention, at that moment the Holy One, blessed be He, gives thought even to destroy his world. But the Torah comes along and defends them, saying, 'Lord of the world, instead of taking note of these, who blaspheme and spite you, take note of Israel, your people, who bless and praise and adore your great name through the Torah and through song and praise.' And the Holy Spirit cries out, '"Make haste, my beloved:" flee from the nations of the world and cleave to the Israelites.'"

> The queen is counterpart to the Torah, Israel to those that bless god for his beneficence, the nations to those that do not. The components of the exegetical parable respond to the transaction that is portrayed, and at issue is preserving the world despite the sinfulness of the nations. The Torah contains the record of Israel's salvation of the world.

The exegetical parables ordinarily, but not invariably, are constructed to restate in general terms a transaction portrayed by Scripture as interpreted by the exegetes of Song of Songs Rabbah. These parables are particular to the case and explicitly interpreted in exactly that way: 1-6, 7, 8, 9-12, 14, 15, 17, 18, 19, 20, 21, 22, 23, 24, 25, 26, 27, 28, 29, 30, 33, 35, 36, 37, 39, 40, 41, 42, 44, 46, 47, 48, 51,

52, 53, 54, 56—45 in all. The three Halakhic parables likewise respond to the exegetical challenge.

These parables do not precisely match the case they are meant to realize: 13, 16, 31-32, 34, 38, 43, 45, 49-50, 55—11 in all. Those that on the surface can serve for some purpose other than the specific one at hand in general involve a more elaborate transaction than those particular to the terms of the verse that is amplified.

The upshot is, 48 out of 59 parables, or 80%, assuredly originate within the framework of the documentary writing, and the other 20% may or may not undertake a comparable documentary task. Parabolic writing, like narrative writing, defined one of the media for the accomplishment of the tasks facing compilers of documents. If they drew upon a corpus of extra-documentary writing, e.g., broadly circulating parables, fully formed and available through a labor of adaptation, there is slight evidence in Song of Songs Rabbah to suggest so.

C. The Biographical Mashal

The advent of the biographical Mashal shows us how the genre served purposes not contemplated in the materials compiled for the earlier documents, from the Mishnah through the Tannaite Midrash-compilations.

1. LXXVIII:i.7 When R. Bun b. R. Hiyya died, R. Zira went up to take leave of him: "'Sweet is the sleep of a working man' (Qoh. 5:11): Let me tell you what R. Bun resembles: <u>A king who had a vineyard, which he hired workers to keep. Now there was one worker there, who was paid for his work more than all the others. When the king saw how remarkably zealous he was at his work, he took him by the hand and began walking with him up and down. At evening the workers came to collect their wages, and that worker came to collect his wage along with them. And the king gave him his wage the same as theirs. They workers began to complain and said to him, 'Our Lord, King, we worked hard all day long, and this one worked only two or three hours for the day, but he takes the same wage that we do!' The king said to them, 'Why are you complaining? This one accomplished in two or three hours what you people did not accomplish in the entire day of work!'</u> So R. Bun b. R. Hiyya accomplished in the twenty-eight years in which he studied the Torah what an accomplished disciple did not accomplish in a hundred years."

    The parabolic narrative of the king and the accomplished worker is elaborate but well-focused on its problem.

The biographical parable does not pretend to respond to the exegetical challenge of Qohelet 5:11. It takes as its problem the case of Bun b. R. Hiyya's remarkable achievement in learning. Clearly, the parable is concerned with Bun's early death: does he attain the reward for Torah-learning that would have corresponded to the achievements of a long life. Yes, he does, because in his short life he did what others take a whole lifetime to accomplish. If that is the point, then there can be no doubt that the parable responds to the case, and so far as the case contributes to the accomplishment of the documentary task, the parable likewise is documentary.

HALAKHIC PARABLES OF SONG RABBAH
PARABLE PARTICULAR TO ITS HALAKHIC SETTING: ALL
PARABLE NOT PARTICULAR TO ITS HALAKHIC SETTING:—

EXEGETICAL PARABLES OF SONG RABBAH
PARABLE PARTICULAR TO ITS EXEGETICAL SETTING: 45
PARABLE NOT PARTICULAR TO ITS EXEGETICAL SETTING: 11

That carries us back to the question already introduced, Do the parables circulate independent of their documentary context? In approximately four-fifths of the instances, the parable is constructed in response to the case it is meant to clarify through a process of imaginative generalization. It is comprised therefore by the counterpart-players or counterpart-transactions set forth by the components of the verse subject to clarification and application. The parable then is integral to the exegetical process, applying the principle of the verse under discussion to exemplary cases. That is made explicit in the vast majority of instances.

So we ask: has the exegetical task provoked the parable, or did the parable take shape independent of the exegetical circumstance? The governing criterion is the question: is the parable in every last detail particular to the exegetical context, or is it necessary to adjust the parable to that context? We know that such a necessity comes into play when a detail of a parable proves superfluous, playing no role in the exposition of the base-verse or context. Overall, then, the answer to the question is, in Song of Songs Rabbah, in constructing parables the exegetical task is primary, the construction of a pertinent, illuminating simile only secondary and derivative.

What, then, can have circulated beyond the limits of the document in its exegetical framework? Very little. I see no evidence of a free-floating, vast corpus of similes and exemplary narratives, snatched from on high and adapted to local purposes. Rather, I see the evidence of a mode of thought, involving similes and metaphors of transactions. In the formation of most, though not all, exegetical parables in our document, the generative force derives not from the fixed conventions of the abstract players, the king, the prince but from the transactions they embody, and these transactions are particular to the verse under study as set forth by the Rabbinic exegetes. Like chess pieces, the nameless kings and princes and queens are moved hither and yon, to reconstitute a relationship or a transaction in terms analogous to mathematical symbols: purely abstract, very precise.

III. *The Maʿaseh*

In Song of Songs Rabbah, the marker, Maʿaseh, gives diverse signals, and loses all specificity. To understand what that means, we must recall that the *Maʿaseh* in the Mishnah and the Tosefta signifies a very particular function and form: a function in law as precedent or exemplary case, and a form of severely limited and austere narrative description: such happened and sages ruled in so-and-so a manner. Then other documents took over and used the received form in their own ways. For example, in Sifré to Deuteronomy it takes on traits unfamiliar in its counterparts in the Mishnah, Tosefta, and Sifra (not to mention Sifré to Numbers!).

To spell this out: In the Mishnah and the Tosefta, the marker, *Maʿaseh*, signals a Halakhic precedent or case. In the Halakhic compilations, that is the principal use to which the *Maʿaseh* is put. Of the narratives and pseudo-narratives of the Mishnah, 80% are *Maʿasim,* and of these, most are Halakhic *Maʿasim:* cases or precedents. Given the character of the Mishnah that is a predictable outcome. The Tosefta follows suit, with *Maʿasim* forming just under 80% of its narrative or pseudo-narrative corpus. The majority of Sifra's counterparts follow suit, but the tiny corpus of *Maʿasim* encompasses incidents or situations bearing no particular, Halakhic charge, e.g., Eliezer's prediction of the student's imminent demise, and the crops in the time of Simeon b. Shatah. In Sifré to Numbers I found not a single Halakhic *Maʿaseh,* and the matched triplet of *Maʿasim* that I did find produced a pattern—one comprised by the situation/transaction/outcome—that I could not link to any exegetical problem or plan, other than that defined by the narrative context. Here again, the marker, *Ma'aseh*, bears no fixed signals as to the task or plan of the narrative that follows.

In Sifré to Deuteronomy we witnessed the emergence of a type of *Ma'aseh* we did not find in a prior document, the exegetical *Ma'aseh*, comparable to the exegetical *Mashal*. By that characterization I mean, the focus of the *Ma'aseh* is on the interpretation of a verse of Scripture, not on the realization of a Halakhic norm, or on the provision of a case for analysis. Most of the *Ma'asim* of Sifré to Deuteronomy are exegetical in the simple sense that they illustrate or clarify the meaning of a verse of Scripture; they bear no autonomous standing outside of that exegetical task. That is what I mean in comparing the exegetical *Ma'aseh* to the exegetical parable: the function is the same.

With these facts in mind, we now address those compositions of Song of Songs Rabbah that bear the marker, *Ma'aseh*, translated "case" or counterparts. What we see is chaos.

1. IV:v. 2. Another interpretation of the verse, "We will exult and rejoice in you:" Said R. Idi, "There was the case of a woman in Sidon, who lived with her husband for ten years and did not produce offspring. They came before R. Simeon b. Yohai and wanted to be parted from one another. He said to them, "By your lives! Just as you were joined to one another with eating and drinking, so you will separate from one another only with eating and drinking." They followed his counsel and made themselves a festival and made a great banquet and drank too much. When his mind was at ease, he said to her, "My daughter, see anything good that I have in the house! Take it and go to your father's house!" What did she do? After he fell asleep, she made gestures to her servants and serving women and said to them, "Take him in the bed and pick him up and bring him to my father's house."

    Without the indicated marker, this composition would fall into the classification of authentic narratives, since the whole holds together only at the climax and conclusion.

2. VI:ii.5. [Do not gaze at me because I am swarthy, because the sun has scorched me" (Song 1:6):] And said R. Isaac, "There was the case [*Ma'aseh*] of a local noblewoman who had an Ethiopian slave-girl, who went down to draw water from the well with her friend. She said to her friend, 'My friend, tomorrow my master is going to divorce his wife and take me as his wife.' The other said to her, 'Why?' It is because he saw her hands dirty.' She said to her, 'You big fool! Let your

ears hear what your mouth is saying. Now if concerning his wife, who
is most precious to him, you say that because he saw her hands dirty
one time, he wants to divorce her, you, who are entirely dirty, scorched
from the day of your birth, how much the more so!' So too, since the
nations of the world taunt the Israelites, saying, 'This nation has exchanged its glory [for naught],' as in the verse, 'They exchanged their
glory for an ox that eats grass' (Ps. 106:20), the Israelites reply to them,
'Now if we who are in that condition for an hour and have incurred
liability on that account, as for you, how much the more so!'

> This is labeled *Ma'aseh* but in fact conforms to the stan-
> dard pattern of the *Mashal*. I underline the parabolic-
> like component of the composition, with the exegeti-
> cal application closely followed by the requirements of
> the case.

3. XLIX:i.1 "Your two breasts are like two fawns (Song 4:5):" This refers to Moses and Aaron. R. Joshua of Sikhnin in the name of R.
Levi: "There were two species of snakes in Alexandria, one of which
induced cold, the other heat. There was a case in which physicians
sent for some of them and made a compound out of them with which
they healed [snake bites]."

> Here is a more conventional *Ma'aseh*, though lacking
> any Halakhic or exegetical task to perform. The per-
> tinence is clear, the point is not.

4   LXXVIII:i.1 "My beloved has gone down to his garden, to the beds
of spices, [to pasture his flock in the gardens, and to gather lilies]:"
"'and to gather lilies' speaks of picking [taking away in death] the
righteous that are in Israel." What is the difference between when
old folks die and when young people die? R. Abbahu said, "When a
fig is picked in its season, it is good for it and good for the fig tree.
When it is not picked in its season, it is bad for it and bad for the fig
tree." 3. There was the case involving R. Hiyya b. R. Abba and his
disciples, and some say, R. Aqiba and his disciples, and some say, R.
Joshua and his disciples. They had the custom of going into session
and studying under a fig tree. Every day the owner of the fig tree
would get up in the morning and pick his fig. They said, "We should
change our place, perhaps he suspects us [of stealing his fruit]." What
did they do? They went and held their sessions in another location.
The owner of the fig tree got up but did not find them. He went and
looked for them until he found them, He said to them, "My lords,
there was a single religious duty that you were carrying out for me,
and you want to hold it back from me!" They said to him, "God forbid!" Then why did you leave your place and go into session in another
location?" They said, "We were concerned that you might suspect
us." He said to them, "God forbid. But I shall tell you on what ac-

count I get up early to pick my fig. It is because once the sun shines on the figs, they get rotten."

> The *Ma'aseh* illustrates the exegesis of the base verse, "to gather lilies," in line with Abbahu's reading of the matter. The rather extended story, showing the virtue of the disciples of sages, leads to the climactic point: the householder gathers the figs in its proper time ("in its season").

5.   XC:I 3. ["How graceful are your feet in sandals, O queenly maiden! Your rounded thighs are like jewels, the work of a master hand" (Song 7:1):] Said R. Berekhiah, "This is how the two pinnacles of the age, R. Eliezer and R. Joshua, have interpreted the verse, 'How graceful are your feet in sandals, O queenly maiden:' How beautiful were your festival pilgrims, who locked the door against all suffering [for the words for sandals and lock the door share the same consonants].'"
XC:I.4. There was the case of someone who forgot to lock the doors of his house when he went up for the pilgrim festival. And when he came home, he found a snake wound around the rings of his door.

6.   XC:I 5. There was another case of someone who forgot and did not bring his chickens into his house when he went up for the pilgrim festival. When he came home, he found cats torn to pieces before them.

7   XC:I 6. There was another case of someone who forgot and did not bring his pile of grain into the house when he went up for the pilgrim festival. When he came home, he found lions surrounding the wheat.

8.   XC:I 7. Said R. Phineas, "There was the case of two rich brothers who were in Ashkelon, who had wicked gentile neighbors, who said, 'When these Jews go up to pray in Jerusalem, we shall go into their houses and clean them out.' The Holy One, blessed be He, set up for them angels in their likeness, and they would go in and come out of their houses. When they came home from Jerusalem, they divided up what they had brought with them among all their neighbors. They said to them, 'Where were you?' They said to them, 'In Jerusalem.' When did you go up?' 'On such-and-such a day.' They said, 'Blessed is the God of the Jews, whom you have not abandoned, and who has not abandoned you! We thought, "When these Jews go up to pray in Jerusalem, we shall go into their houses and clean them out." But your God has sent angels in your likeness, who came out and went into your houses because you had faith in him.' This fulfills the verse, 'How graceful are your feet in sandals, O queenly maiden.'"

> The four cases, Nos. 5-8, all illustrate the same proposition, which is the exegetical one: the door is locked against suffering, so pilgrims do not pay a price for making the holy trip.

9. XC:iii.5. Said R. Nathan, "There was this case. I came to the town of Cappadocia, and there was a woman who produced male children. When they were circumcised, they died. The first was circumcised and died, so too the second, so too the third. The fourth she brought before me, and I examined its flesh and found it pale. I looked at it and I did not find in it blood of the circumcision. They asked me, 'Should we circumcise him?' I said to them, 'Wait and let him be, until the blood of circumcision is produced. For we have learned there: "As to the infant and the sick person, they are not to be circumcised until they get well." They let him be, then circumcised him and he turned out to live, and they produced as his name, 'Nathan,' after me.'"

> Without the marker, *Ma'aseh*, what we have is a sage-story, such as we meet in The Fathers According to R. Nathan text A, below, chapter seventeen: the climax is that the ruling saved the life of the child, who also could be circumcised without ill-effect.

10. CXI:iii.5. There was the case of sages voting in the upper room of the house of Gedia in Jericho. An echo came forth and said to them, "There is among you one man who is worthy of receiving the Holy Spirit, but his generation is not suitable for such to happen.
11. CXI:iii.6. There was another case, in which the Israelite sages took a vote, in the vineyard in Yavneh. An echo came forth and said to them, "There is among you one man who is worthy of receiving the Holy Spirit, but his generation is not suitable for such to happen. They set their eyes upon Samuel the Younger.
12. CXI:iii.9 There was the case in which Yohanan, the high priest, heard an echo come forth from the Most Holy Place, saying, "The young men who went out to war have won at Antioch." They wrote down that day and that hour, and that is how matters were: on that very day they had won their victory.
13. CXI:iii.10 There was the case in which Simeon the Righteous heard an echo come forth from the Most Holy Place, saying, "The action has been annulled that the enemy has planned to destroy the Temple, and Caius Caligula has been killed and his decrees annulled.

> These four *Ma'asim* illustrate the working of the echo. It is a thematic composite.

None of the *Ma'asim* of Song of Songs Rabbah replicates the indicative traits—whether formal or functional—of the *Ma'aseh* in Mishnah-Tosefta. No. 1 is a standard narrative, bearing no Halakhic datum. Nos. 2, 4 present nothing other than exegetical parables. No. 2 serves an exegetical purpose. No. 3 presents a case that preserves an illustrative fact. Nos. 5-8, 10-13 set forth *Ma'asim* that illustrate propositions and preserve exemplary facts, none of which bears either an exegetical or a Halakhic burden. No. 9 is marked *Ma'aseh* but sets forth a standard narrative. In all, *Ma'aseh* has lost all specific meaning or signification.

IV. Not Classified

I do not know what to make of this item:

1.   LXXXVIII:i.5 Another explanation of the verse, "'Before I was aware, my fancy set me in a chariot beside my prince:" Scripture speaks of the Community of Israel. The Community of Israel says to the nations of the world, "'Do not rejoice against me, O my enemy; though I have fallen, I shall arise' (Mic. 7:8). When I dwelled in darkness, the Holy One, blessed be He, brought me forth to light: 'Though I sit in darkness, the Lord is a light to me' (Mic. 7:8) So in her own regard she recited the verse, "Before I was aware, my fancy set me in a chariot beside my prince." Justus, a tailor in Sepphoris, went up to the government and was received by the king. The king said to him, "Ask me for something, and I shall give it to you." He said to him, "Make me the duke of our locale." The king gave it to him. After he had assumed the position, he left it. And those who knew him said, "It's the same man," but others who knew him said, "It's not the same." One of them said to them, "When he goes through the market, if he glances at that tailor's seat on which he used to sit and stitch, it is the same man, but if not, it is not the same man." He passed through the market and began to look at the stool on which he had sat and stitched, so they knew that he was the same man. He said to them, "You are surprised at me, but I am more surprised at myself than you are." And they recited in his regard the verse, "Before I was aware, my fancy set me in a chariot beside my prince."

     The item qualifies as an exegetical narrative. It could be adapted as an exegetical parable, but in its present form is too elaborate to qualify. The climactic moment is lost, at least as I see it, in the ex-tailor's "I am more surprised than you are...."

I see no marker, Ma'aseh, nor are the indicators of the parable present. "And they recited in his regard the verse...," does not serve as the counterpart to the parable's "so is Israel...," and equivalents. The story's climax, "You are surprised at me but I am more surprised...," hardly links in an obvious way to the exegetical context. So I am lost to classify the narrative or to make sense of it.

V. *Song of Song Rabbah's Narratives in Canonical Context*

We have now prepared the way to address the issue that this probe raises in reference to the several documents subject to examination: do narratives of various types participate in the thought of the document or embody extra-documentary reflection, beyond the limits of their context in Song of Songs Rabbah? These questions produce the answers that settle the issue.

1. *Do anomalous or asymmetric compositions or composites attest to thought that takes place beyond the limits of the documents subject to the rules and symmetry of the canon?* The narratives and pseudo-narratives realize the documentary program and are tightly linked to the exegetical or expository task, as seen in the details that follow:

A. The Authentic Narrative: No. 1 illustrates how Heaven collaborates with the pilgrim; Nos. 2-6 all endorse Torah-study.

B. The *Mashal:*

The Halakhic *Mashal:*.the three Halakhic parables all answer a question particular to the Halakhic context that they address.

The Exegetical *Mashal:* Only the parables not generated by the exegetical task come under consideration. The forty-five classified as exegetical in origin obviously belong within the framework of the document. That leaves these: No. 13, a Torah-parable; No. 16, a parable that overspreads the limits of the case but remains well within the doctrinal limits of the composition; No. 31-2, as with No. 16; No. 34: the exegetical proposition of the asymmetrical parable is documentary; No. 38 is doctrinally coherent with the document; No. 43: a Torah-tale; No. 45: the parable is supposed to explain a detail of the Halakhah, how it does so is unclear; Nos. 49=50 are Torah-statements; No. 55 concerns how Israel remains loyal to God, even under difficult circumstances.

The Biographical *Mashal:* this is a Torah-story, pure and simple.

C. The *Ma'aseh* : No. 1 attests to enduring love; No. 2 is a parable that affirms Israel's enduring loyalty to God; No. 3 is null; No. 4 is a Torah-narrative; Nos. 5-8 affirm the pilgrimage and God's protection of pilgrims; No. 9 shows the wisdom of the sage; Nos. 10-13 affirm heavenly echoes as media of communication between God and certain Israelites, including priests and sages.

D. Not Classified: I do not know the point of the item, so I cannot assess its position on the classical issues of the Rabbinic canon.

To answer the question: No, the narrative and pseudo-narrative writings find a place entirely within the frame of reference of the documentary compositions and composites of Song of Songs Rabbah. They do not provide access to some other viewpoint or system than the Rabbinic one that defines the documentary program. Not only so, but Song of Song Rabbah's compilers have adapted the narrative and pseudo-narrative writing to their larger purpose and task, which is that of exegesis of the Song of Songs within the hermeneutics of the fully-realized Rabbinic Judaism.

2. *Does non-documentary, narrative writing exhibit readily-discernible patterns of form and meaning as does documentary writing? If so, what are these patterns and how are we to classify and to interpret them?* For the exegetical parables, which define the principal narrative form of the document, the pattern is clear: a parable is formed to state in generic terms ("king/prince/queen") the proposition that exegesis of the verse under consideration yields. For the authentic narratives, the paramount theme concerns Torah-study, its requirements and rewards. There is a non-documentary corpus of motifs on which documentary writers draw, images that embody fixed relationships such as king/prince, king/queen, and the like. That corpus is generic, and its items make no impact upon the documentary adaptation thereof for particular purposes and occasions. As to patterns of form and meaning accessible in the narrative writing, our probe produces no more than the stick-figures of king/prince and the like, and these do not adumbrate a system beyond or different from the Rabbinic one that predominates in this compilation.

3. *At what point in the process that yielded the canonical writings as we know them did documentary considerations intervene, and what is the meaning of that intervention? When and under what circumstances did documentary considerations give way to writing utterly indifferent to its documentary venue?* Song of Songs Rabbah begins with the generative exegetical principle that the scriptural book portrays the love of God and Israel. That paramount principle animates the narratives and pseudo-narratives of the Midrash-compilation. So, as I see it, documentary considerations intervened from the very outset of all writing for this compilation and shaped, also, the narrative component as well. Those considerations account for the paramount status accorded to the exegetical parable among the narrative or pseudo-narrative compositions of the

compilation. Stated simply: documentary considerations everywhere govern, and non-documentary writing forms a negligible component of the document, which, start to finish, knows precisely what it wishes to say and says it.

PART TWO

NARRATIVES IN LAMENTATIONS RABBAH
FORMS, TYPES AND DISTRIBUTION

CHAPTER TEN

LAMENTATIONS RABBAH
THE PETIHTAOT

I have omitted two sizable composites that resemble, but, within the
definition of narrative that governs in this study, do not qualify as,
narratives: Scripture-stories, dealt with briefly in the introduction and
further in chapter seventeen.

XXIII.i.19-43 form a huge Scripture-story, that is, an amplification of verses of Scripture in such a way as to weave fresh narratives into Scripture's own narratives. The systematic exposition of
the intersecting verse follows a fixed form: citation of a phrase or a
clause, with a brief exposition of the pertinent application to the
destruction of the temple. What is impressive is the reading of the
aged king's reflections upon old age as a metaphor for the events of
the destruction of the first temple. The insertions of secondary amplifications, interpolations of various sorts, and the like, scarcely
confuses the matter, since the basic form is so well established and
consistent throughout. The important interpolations are Nos. 20-23,
34-40, all of which is to compare the individual's with the nation's
old age, is fully achieved.

Along these same lines XXXIV.i.1-15 form a large Scripture-story,
amplifying Jer. 9:10-12 and other passages. This is certainly the least
successful *petihta*, since there is no pretense at discovering an intersecting verse or appealing to a base verse. What we have at 1.A is
simply a verse that, later on, is meant to serve as a prooftext, nothing more. The real point of interest begins at No. 2, the disposition
of Jeremiah after the destruction. Nos. 3, 4, 5, 6 work on that same
theme. No. 6 then invokes the verse cited at No. 1. No. 7 addresses
a further clause in that same verse, and No. 8 does the same, drawing in its wake the remainder of the materials. So the whole is meant
to amplify the theme of Jeremiah, the land, and the fate of God,
after the destruction, and the verse that is subjected to some sustained interest forms part of that larger thematic essay. The passage

does not constitute a coherent narrative, though it contains narrative-elements.

II:1.

3.   A.   Rabbi [Judah the Patriarch] would dispatch R. Assi and R. Ammi to go out and inspect the condition of the towns of the land of Israel.

   B.   They would go into a town and say to the people, "Bring us the guardians of the town."

   C.   So the people would produce the captain of the guard and the senator and say to them, "Here are the guardians of the town."

   D.   They said to them, "These are the guardians of the town? These are those who ravage the town."

   E.   They said to them, "Then who are the guardians of the town?"

   F.   They said to them, "They are the scribes and teachers, who dwell upon, repeat, and keep the Torah day and night."

   G.   That is in line with that which is said: "And you will dwell upon it day and night" (Josh. 1:8).

   H.   And so too: "Except the Lord build the house, they labor in vain who build it" (Ps. 127:1).

1.   *On what basis does the narrative attain coherence, e.g., what is the action or event that precipitates the telling of the tale?* The contrast between the this-worldly guardians and the scribes and teachers imparts coherence to all details and focuses the story on its main point.

2.   *What point of conflict or intersection of wills accounts for the telling of the tale and how is the point of tension resolved?* As indicated, the contrast between the intuitive answer to the question and the Torah's answer is what precipitates and resolves the tension of the story.

3.   *How, in light of other, comparable, pieces of writing and the data that they yield, is the narrative classified, and what are its indicative formal qualities, e.g., long or short, complex or simple?* The story works as an exchange of opinions, there is not much action, only dialogue given a dramatic setting.

II.11.

   1.   A.   ["Alas! Lonely sits the city once great with people!" (Lamentations 1:1):] "Thus says the Lord of hosts: 'Summon the dirge-singers, let them come; send for the skilled women, let them come.' [Let them quickly start a wailing for us, that our eyes may run with tears, our pupils flow with water. For the sound of wailing is heard from Zion, How are we despoiled! How greatly are we shamed!]" (Jer. 9:16-18).

   B.   R. Yohanan and R. Simeon b. Laqish and rabbis [comment on the cited verse in different ways].

2. A. R. Yohanan said, "The matter [of the exile of Israel, then Judah] may be compared to the case of a king who had two sons. He lost his temper with the first, took a stick and beat him and threw him out of the house.

B. "He said, 'Woe for this one! From what luxury he has been thrown out!'

C. "He lost his temper with the second, took a stick and beat him and threw him out of the house.

D. "He said, 'I am the one [who is at fault], for my way of bringing them up is no good.'

E. "So when the Ten Tribes went into exile, the Holy One, blessed be He, began to recite for them the following verse: 'Woe is they, for they have strayed from me' (Hos. 7:13).

F. "But when Judah and Benjamin went into exile, it is as though the Holy One, blessed be He, said, 'Woe is me for my hurt' (Jer. 10:19)."

3. A. R. Simeon b. Laqish said, "The matter may be compared to the case of a king who had two sons. He lost his temper with the first, took a stick and beat him and the son writhed and perished.

B. "He then lamented for him.

C. "He lost his temper with the second, took a stick and beat him and the son writhed and perished.

D. "He said, 'Now I don't have the strength to lament for them, but summon the dirge-singers, let them come; send for the skilled women, let them come.'

E. "So when the Ten Tribes went into exile, the Holy One, blessed be He, began to lament for them: 'Hear you this word that I take up in lamentation over you, O house of Israel' (Amos 5:1).

F. "But when Judah and Benjamin went into exile, it is as though the Holy One, blessed be He, said, 'now I do not have the strength to lament for them, but "Summon the dirge-singers, let them come; send for the skilled women, let them come." Let them quickly start a wailing for us, [that our eyes may run with tears, our pupils flow with water].'

G. "What is written is not 'for them' but 'for us,'

H. "'it is for me and for them.'

I. "'that our eyes may run with tears, our pupils flow with water:'

J. "What is written is not, 'their eyes,' but 'our eyes,'

K. "'mine and theirs.'"

4. A. Rabbis say, "The matter may be compared to the case of a king who had twelve sons, and two of them died. He began to take comfort in the ten.

B. "Then another two died, and he began to take comfort from the eight.

C. "Then another two died, and he began to take comfort from the six.

> D. "Then another two died, and he began to take comfort from the four.
>
> E. "Then another two died, and he began to take comfort from the two.
>
> F. "Then when all of them had died, he began to mourn for them [all]: 'Alas! Lonely sits the city once great with people!'"

The three exegetical parables, Nos. 2, 3, and 4, work their way from Scripture to the illustrative case constructed by the narrative. But the basis is the contrast between God's disposition of the ten northern tribes and of those of Judea. In the former case, God threw the sons out, in the latter, he blames himself and takes the burden on himself, 2.E-F then contrasting with 2.A-D, which tracks the matter. No. 3 goes over the same ground, contrasting the Ten tribes with Judah and Benjamin, now as to God's response to the exile of each, once more a product of Scripture's facts. No. 4 shifts the ground entirely, and I do not see how the parable has been generated by Scripture's case. The point is now that God speaks at Lamentations 1:1, and the elaborate exposition, two by two, is hardly necessary.

XXIV.ii.

> 1. A. ["The Valley of Vision Pronouncement. What can have happened to you that you have gone, all of you, up on the roofs, O you who were full of tumult, you clamorous town, you city so gay? Your slain are not the slain of the sword, nor the dead of battle. Your officers have all departed; they fled far away; your survivors were all taken captive, taken captive without their bows. That is why I say, 'Let me be, I will weep bitterly. Press not to comfort me for the ruin of my poor people.' For my Lord God of Hosts had a day of tumult and din and confusion—Kir raged in the Valley of Vision, and Shoa on the hill; while Elam bore the quiver in troops of mounted men, and Kir bared the shield—and your choicest lowlands were filled with chariots and horsemen; they stormed at Judah's gateway and pressed beyond its screen. You gave thought on that day to the arms in the Forest House, and you took note of the many breaches in the city of David. And you collected the water of the Lower Pool; and you counted the houses of Jerusalem and pulled houses down to fortify the wall; and you constructed a basin between the two walls for the water of the old pool. But you gave no thought to him who planned it, you took no note of him who designed it long before. My Lord God of Hosts summoned on that day weeping and lamenting, to tonsuring and girding with sackcloth' (Isaiah 22:1-14)":]Another interpretation of the passage, "My Lord God of Hosts summoned on that day to weeping and lamenting, to tonsuring and girding with sackcloth:"

B.   When the Holy One, blessed be He, considered destroying the house of the sanctuary, he said, "So long as I am within it, the nations of the world cannot lay a hand on it.

C.   "I shall close my eyes to it and take an oath that I shall not become engaged with it until the time of the end."

D.   Then the enemies came and destroyed it.

E.   Forthwith the Holy One, blessed be He, took an oath by his right hand and put it behind him: "He has drawn back his right hand from before the enemy" (Lam. 2:3).

F.   At that moment the enemies entered the sanctuary and burned it up.

G.   When it had burned, the Holy One, blessed be He, said, "I do not have any dwelling on earth any more. I shall take up my presence from there and go up to my earlier dwelling."

H.   That is in line with this verse: "I will go and return to my place, until they acknowledge their guilt and seek my face" (Hos. 5:15).

I.   At that moment the Holy One, blessed be He, wept, saying, "Woe is me! What have I done! I have brought my Presence to dwell below on account of the Israelites, and now that they have sinned, I have gone back to my earlier dwelling. Heaven forfend that I now become a joke to the nations and a source of ridicule among people."

J.   At that moment Metatron came, prostrated himself, and said before him, "Lord of the world, let me weep, but don't you weep!"

K.   He said to him, "If you do not let me weep now, I shall retreat to a place in which you have no right to enter, and there I shall weep."

L.   That is in line with this verse: "But if you will not hear it, my soul shall weep in secret for pride" (Jer. 13:17).

2.   A.   Said the Holy One, blessed be He, to the ministering angels, "Let's go and see what the enemies have done to my house."

B.   Forthwith the Holy One, blessed be He, and the ministering angels went forth, with Jeremiah before them.

C.   When the Holy One, blessed be He, saw the house of the sanctuary, he said, "This is certainly my house, and this is my resting place, and the enemies have come and done whatever they pleased with it!"

D.   At that moment the Holy One, blessed be He, wept, saying "Woe is me for my house! O children of mine—where are you? O priests of mine—where are you? O you who love me—where are you? What shall I do for you? I warned you, but you did not repent."

E.   Said the Holy One, blessed be He, to Jeremiah, "Today I am like a man who had an only son, who made a marriage canopy for him, and the son died under his marriage canopy. Should you not feel pain for me and for my son?

F.   "Go and call Abraham, Isaac, Jacob, and Moses from their graves, for they know how to weep."

G.   He said before him, "Lord of the world, I don't know where Moses is buried."

H.   The Holy One, blessed be He, said to him, "Go and stand at the bank of the Jordan and raise your voice and call him, 'Son of Amram, son of Amram, rise up and see your flock, which the enemy has swallowed up!'"

I.   Jeremiah immediately went to the cave of Machpelah and said to the founders of the world, "Arise, for the time has come for you to be called before the Holy One, blessed be He."

J.   They said to him, "Why?"

K.   He said to them, "I don't know," because he was afraid that they would say to him, "In your time this has come upon our children!"

L.   Jeremiah left them and went to the bank of the Jordan and cried out, "Son of Amram, son of Amram, rise up, for the time has come for you to be called before the Holy One, blessed be He."

M.   He said to him, "What makes this day so special, that I am called before the Holy One, blessed be He?"

N.   He said to them, "I don't know."

O.   Moses left him and went to the ministering angels, for he had known them from the time of the giving of the Torah. He said to them, "You who serve on high! Do you know on what account I am summoned before the Holy One, blessed be He?"

P.   They said to him, "Son of Amram! Don't you know that the house of the sanctuary has been destroyed, and the Israelites taken away into exile?"

Q.   So he cried and wept until he came to the fathers of the world. They too forthwith tore their garments and put their hands on their heads, crying and weeping, up to the gates of the house of the sanctuary.

R.   When the Holy One, blessed be He, saw them, forthwith: "My Lord God of Hosts summoned on that day to weeping and lamenting, to tonsuring and girding with sackcloth."

S.   Were it not stated explicitly in a verse of Scripture, it would not be possible to make this statement.

T.   And they went weeping from this gate to that, like a man whose deceased lies before him,

U.   and the Holy One, blessed be He, wept, lamenting, "Woe for a king who prospers in his youth and not in his old age."

1.   *On what basis does the narrative attain coherence, e.g., what is the action or event that precipitates the telling of the tale?* Here we have a massive composite of a coherent, narrative character, a narrative not interwoven with verses of Scripture or dependent on a scriptural pas-

sage for structure and order. No. 1.B-I form a complete narrative, how God behaved when the Temple fell. At issue here is how God allowed the destruction to take place and then how he responded to the destruction, leading up to J-K, God has to weep, lest he retreat to weep outside of the world altogether. No. 2 carries the matter forward, now with a colloquy with Jeremiah, then Moses, who mourn for the destruction along with God.

2.   *What point of conflict or intersection of wills accounts for the telling of the tale and how is the point of tension resolved?* The unfolding narrative leads to the point that God shared in the rites of mourning for the Temple along with the prophets and the patriarchs. God calls on the saints to mourn along with him, and they do.

3. *How, in light of other, comparable, pieces of writing and the data that they yield, is the narrative classified, and what are its indicative formal qualities, e.g., long or short, complex or simple?* I cannot point in the documents examined to this point to comparable constructions of such extensive and intensive qualities. And the unitary narrative continues at XXIV:ii.3, following.

XXIV:ii.

3. A. Said R. Samuel bar Nahman, "When the Temple was destroyed, Abraham came before the Holy One, blessed be He, weeping, pulling at his beard and tearing his hair, striking his face, tearing his clothes, with ashes on his head, walking about the temple, weeping and crying, saying before the Holy One, blessed be He,

 B. "'How come I am treated differently from every other nation and language, that I should be brought to such humiliation and shame!'

 C. "When the ministering angels saw him, they too [Cohen, *Lamentations Rabbah* (London, 1948: Soncino), p. 43:] composed lamentations, arranging themselves in rows, saying,

 D. "'the highways lie waste, the wayfaring man ceases' (Isa. 33:8)."

 E. "What is the meaning of the statement, 'the highways lie waste'?

 F. "Said the ministering angels before the Holy One, blessed be He, 'The highways that you paved to Jerusalem, so that the wayfarers would not cease, how have they become a desolation?'

 G. "'the wayfaring man ceases:'

 H. "Said the ministering angels before the Holy One, blessed be He, 'How have the ways become deserted, on which the Israelites would come and go for the pilgrim festivals?'

 I. "'You have broken the covenant:'

 J. "Said the ministering angels before the Holy One, blessed be

He, 'Lord of the world, the covenant that was made with their father, Abraham, has been broken, the one through which the world was settled and through which you were made known in the world, that you are the most high God, the one who possesses heaven and earth.'

K.   "'He has despised the cities:'

L.   "Said the ministering angels before the Holy One, blessed be He, 'You have despised Jerusalem and Zion after you have chosen them!'

M.   "Thus Scripture says, 'Have you utterly rejected Judah? Has your soul loathed Zion?' (Jer. 14:19).

N.   "'He regards not Enosh:'

O.   "Said the ministering angels before the Holy One, blessed be He, 'Even as much as the generation of Enosh, chief of all idol worshippers, you have not valued Israel!'

P.   "At that moment the Holy One, blessed be He, responded to the ministering angels, saying to them, 'How come you composing lamentations, arranging themselves in rows, on this account?'

Q.   "They said to him, 'Lord of the world! It is on account of Abraham, who loved you, who came to your house and lamented and wept. How come you didn't pay any attention to him?'

R.   "He said to them, 'From the day on which my beloved died, going off to his eternal house, he has not come to my house, and now "what is my beloved doing in my house" (Jer. 11:15)?'

S.   "Said Abraham before the Holy One, blessed be He, 'Lord of the world! How come you have sent my children into exile and handed them over to the nations? And they have killed them with all manner of disgusting forms of death! And you have destroyed the house of the sanctuary, the place on which I offered up my son Isaac as a burnt-offering before you!?'

T.   "Said to Abraham the Holy One, blessed be He, 'Your children sinned and violated the whole Torah, transgressing the twenty-two letters that are used to write it: "Yes, all Israel have transgressed your Torah" (Dan. 9:11).'

U.   "Said Abraham before the Holy One, blessed be He, 'Lord of the world, who will give testimony against the Israelites, that they have violated your Torah?'

V.   "He said to him, 'Let the Torah come and give testimony against the Israelites.'

W.   "Forthwith the Torah came to give testimony against them.

X.   "Said Abraham to her, 'My daughter, have you come to give testimony against the Israelites that they have violated your religious duties? and are you not ashamed on my account? Remember the day on which the Holy One, blessed be He, peddled you to all the nations and languages of the world, and no one wanted to accept you, until my children came to Mount

Sinai and they accepted you and honored you! And now are you coming to give testimony against them on their day of disaster?'

Y. "When the Torah heard this, she went off to one side and did not testify against them.

Z. "Said the Holy One, blessed be He, to Abraham, 'Then let the twenty-two letters of the alphabet come and give testimony against the Israelites.'

AA. "Forthwith the twenty-two letters of the alphabet came to give testimony against them.

BB. "The aleph came to give testimony against the Israelites, that they had violated the Torah.

CC. "Said Abraham to her, 'Aleph, you are the head of all of the letters of the alphabet, and have you now come to give testimony against the Israelites on the day of their disaster?'

DD. "'Remember the day on which the Holy One, blessed be He, revealed himself on Mount Sinai and began his discourse with you: "I [*anokhi*, beginning with aleph] am the Lord your God who brought you out of the Land of Egypt, out of the house of bondage" (Ex. 20:2).

EE. "'But not a single nation or language was willing to take you on, except for my children! And are you now going to give testimony against my children?'

FF. "Forthwith the aleph went off to one side and did not testify against them.

GG. "The bet came to give testimony against the Israelites.

HH. "Said Abraham to her, 'My daughter, have you come to give testimony against my children, who are meticulous about the Five Books of the Torah, at the head of which you stand, as it is said, "In the beginning [*bereshit*] God created…" (Gen. 1:1)?'

II. "Forthwith the bet went off to one side and did not testify against them.

JJ. "The gimel came to give testimony against the Israelites.

KK. "Said Abraham to her, 'Gimel, have you come to give testimony against my children, that they have violated the Torah? Is there any nation, besides my children, that carries out the religious duty of wearing show-fringes, at the head of which you stand, as it is said, "Twisted cords [*gedelim*] you shall make for yourself" (Dt. 22:12).'

LL. "Forthwith the gimel went off to one said and did not testify against them.

MM. "Now when all of the letters of the alphabet realized that Abraham had silenced them, they were ashamed and stood off and would not testify against Israel.

NN. "Abraham forthwith commenced speaking before the Holy One, blessed be He, saying to him, 'Lord of the world, when I was a hundred years old, you gave me a son. And when he had already reached the age of volition, a boy thirty-seven years of age, you told me, "offer him up as a burnt-offering before me"!

OO. "'And I turned mean to him and had no mercy for him, but I myself tied him up. Are you not going to remember this and have mercy on my children?'

PP. "Isaac forthwith commenced speaking before the Holy One, blessed be He, saying to him, 'Lord of the world, when father said to me, "God will see to the lamb for the offering for himself, my son" (Gen. 22:8), I did not object to what you had said, but I was bound willingly, with all my heart, on the altar, and spread forth my neck under the knife. Are you not going to remember this and have mercy on my children!'

QQ. "Jacob forthwith commenced speaking before the Holy One, blessed be He, saying to him, 'Lord of the world, did I not remain in the house of Laban for twenty years? And when I went forth from his house, the wicked Essau met me and wanted to kill my children, and I gave myself over to death in their behalf. Now my children are handed over to their enemies like sheep for slaughter, after I raised them like fledglings of chickens. I bore on their account the anguish of raising children, for through most of my life I was pained greatly on their account. And now are you not going to remember this and have mercy on my children?'

RR. "Moses forthwith commenced speaking before the Holy One, blessed be He, saying to him, 'Lord of the world, was I not a faithful shepherd for the Israelites for forty years? I ran before them in the desert like a horse. And when the time came for them to enter the land, you issued a decree against me in the wilderness that there my bones would fall. And now that they have gone into exile, you have sent to me to mourn and weep for them.'

SS. "This is in line with the proverb people say: 'When it's good for my master, it's not good for me, but when its bad for him, it's bad for me!'

TT. "Then Moses said to Jeremiah, 'Go before me, so I may go and bring them in and see who will lay a hand on them.'

UU. "Said to him Jeremiah, 'It isn't even possible to go along the road, because of the corpses.'

VV. "He said to him, 'Nonetheless.'

WW. "Forthwith Moses went along, with Jeremiah leading the way, until they came to the waters of Babylon.

XX. "They saw Moses and said to one another, 'Here comes the son of Amram from his grave to redeem us from the hand of our oppressors.'

YY. "An echo went forth and said, 'It is a decree from before me.'

ZZ. "Then said Moses to them, 'My children, to bring you back is not possible, for the decree has already been issued. But the

Omnipresent will bring you back quickly.' Then he left them.

AAA. "Then they raised up their voices in weeping until the sound rose on high: 'By the rivers of Babylon there we sat down, yes, we wept' (Ps. 137:1).

BBB. "When Moses got back to the fathers of the world, they said to him, 'What have the enemies done to our children?'

CCC. "He said to them, 'Some of them he killed, the hands of some of them he bound behind their back, some of them he put in iron chains, some of them he stripped naked, some of them died on the way, and their corpses were left for the vultures of heaven and the hyenas of the earth, some of them were left for the sun, starving and thirsting.'

DDD. "Then they began to weep and sing dirges: 'Woe for what has happened to our children! How have you become orphans without a father! How have you had to sleep in the hot sun during the summer without clothes and covers! How have you had to walk over rocks and stones without shoes and sandals! How were you burdened with heavy bundle of sand! How were your hands bound behind your backs! How were you left unable even to swallow the spit in your mouths!'

EEE. "Moses then said, 'Cursed are you, O sun! Why did you not grow dark when the enemy went into the house of the sanctuary?'

FFF. "The sun answered him, 'By your life, Moses, faithful shepherd! They would not let me nor did they leave me alone, but beat me with sixty whips of fire, saying, "Go, pour out your light."'

GGG. "Moses then said, 'Woe for your brilliance, O temple, how has it become darkened? Woe that its time has come to be destroyed, for the building to be reduced to ruins, for the school children to be killed, for their parents to go into captivity and exile and the sword!'

HHH. "Moses then said, 'O you who have taken the captives! I impose an oath on you by your lives! If you kill, do not kill with a cruel form of death, do not exterminate them utterly, do not kill a son before his father, a daughter before her mother, for the time will come for the Lord of heaven to exact a full reckoning from you!'

III. "The wicked Chaldeans did not do things this way, but they brought a son before his mother and said to the father, 'Go, kill him!' The mother wept, her tears flowing over him, and the father hung his head.

JJJ. "And further Moses said before him, 'Lord of the world! You have written in your Torah, "Whether it is a cow or a ewe, you shall not kill it and its young both in one day" (Lev. 22:28).

KKK. "But have they not killed any number of children along with their mothers, and yet you remain silent!'

LLL. "Then Rachel, our mother, leapt to the fray and said to the

Holy One, blessed be He, 'Lord of the world! It is perfectly self-evident to you that your servant, Jacob, loved me with a mighty love, and worked for me for father for seven years, but when those seven years were fulfilled, and the time came for my wedding to my husband, father planned to substitute my sister for me in the marriage to my husband. Now that matter was very hard for me, for I knew the deceit, and I told my husband and gave him a sign by which he would know the difference between me and my sister, so that my father would not be able to trade me off. But then I regretted it and I bore my passion, and I had mercy for my sister, that she should not be shamed. So in the evening for my husband they substituted my sister for me, and I gave my sister all the signs that I had given to my husband, so that he would think that she was Rachel.

MMM. "'And not only so, but I crawled under the bed on which he was lying with my sister, while she remained silent, and I made all the replies so that he would not discern the voice of my sister.

NNN. "'I paid my sister only kindness, and I was not jealous of her, and I did not allow her to be shamed, and I am a mere mortal, dust and ashes. Now I had no envy of my rival, and I did not place her at risk for shame and humiliation. But you are the King, living and enduring and merciful. How come then you are jealous of idolatry, which is nothing, and so have sent my children into exile, allowed them to be killed by the sword, permitted the enemy to do whatever they wanted to them?!'

OOO. "Forthwith the mercy of the Holy One, blessed be He, welled up, and he said, 'For Rachel I am going to bring the Israelites back to their land.'

PPP. "That is in line with this verse of Scripture: 'Thus said the Lord: A cry is heard in Ramah, wailing, bitter weeping, Rachel weeping for her children. She refuses to be comforted for her children, who are gone. Thus said the Lord, Restrain your voice from weeping, your eyes from shedding tears; for there is a reward for your labor, declares the Lord; they shall return from the enemy's land, and there is hope for your future, declares the Lord: your children shall return to their country'" (Jer. 31:15-17)."

1. *On what basis does the narrative attain coherence, e.g., what is the action or event that precipitates the telling of the tale?* The whole of XXIV.ii.3 forms a unitary and well-crafted composition, with no important interpolations or imperfections of any kind. I see these sub-units of the exposition: C-O, the systematic exposition of Is. 33:8, which forms the prologue to P, God's response to the accusation of the angels. Then we come to the unit of the encounter with Abraham, Q-NN.

Abraham rebukes God for sending his children into exile, which opens the way to the testimony of the Torah, then of the twenty-two letters of the alphabet of which the Torah is comprised. Abraham ultimately defends Israel through the *zekhut* he attained at the binding of Isaac. Isaac follows, PP, then Jacob, QQ, and Moses, RR. That completes that unit. What follows is the progress of Moses and Jeremiah to Babylon, TT-AAA. Moses returns and reports to the patriarchs, a new sub-unit, BBB-DDD. Moses then rebukes the sun, the Temple, and imposes an oath on the captors, EEE-III; the sub-unit continues with Moses' address to God and concludes there. Then comes Rachel, LLL-OOO+PPP, at which the exposition comes to its climax and conclusion. The entire story holds together through the figure of Rachel, who accomplishes what none of the prior saints is able to do: move God to forgive and grant Israel a hope in its future. This strikes me as a key passage on the power of women to accomplish the systemic reversals at crucial points. This is a unitary story, with Rachel the critical figure. What Abraham/Isaac/Jacob/Moses/Jeremiah cannot do, Rachel does. The story without her fails, falling apart into free-standing paragraphs, but with her registers its point on the divine pathos.

2.   *What point of conflict or intersection of wills accounts for the telling of the tale and how is the point of tension resolved?* The conflict is between God's indictment of Israel and the plea for grace and forgiveness by Abraham, Isaac, Jacob, Moses, and Jeremiah, and it is resolved with the plea of Rachel.

3. *How, in light of other, comparable, pieces of writing and the data that they yield, is the narrative classified, and what are its indicative formal qualities, e.g., long or short, complex or simple?* This vast, complex narrative is utterly different from any authentic narrative we have encountered in the documents probed in the present study. It is not only protracted but exquisitely balanced, with details matched throughout, and patterns repeated for effect.

CHAPTER ELEVEN

LAMENTATIONS RABBAH
PARASHAH ONE

XXXV:v.

1. A. ["How lonely sits] the city that was full of people" (Lamentations 1:1):

B. R. Samuel taught on Tannaite authority, "There were twenty-four main streets in Jerusalem. Each thoroughfare had twenty-four side-turnings; each side-turning twenty-four roads; each road twenty-four streets; each street twenty-four courts; each court twenty-four houses; and each court residents double the number of those who came out of Egypt.

C. "This illustrates the statement: 'Judah and Israel are as numerous as the sand on the sea shore' (1 Kgs. 4:20).

D. "That is the sense of the verse, 'the city that was full of people.'"

    2. A. Said R. Eleazar, "There was a case involving a caravan in which there was a merchant who was leading three hundred camels bearing pepper.

    B. "He came by Tyre and found a certain tailor, sitting at the gate. He said to him, 'What are you selling?'

    C. "He said to him, 'Pepper.'

    D. "He said to him, 'Sell me a little.'

    E. "He said to him, 'No, for all of it is for one [purchaser].'

    F. "He said to him, 'You are going to sell it only to the Jewish town.'

    G. "He came to the Jewish town and found another tailor sitting at the gate. He said to him, 'What are your camels carrying?'

    H. "He said to him, 'Keep cutting.'

    I. "He said to him again, 'What are you selling?'

    J. "He said to him, 'Keep sewing.'

    K. "He said to him, 'Tell me what you are carrying, and if I can, I shall buy it, and if not, I shall bring you to someone who will buy it all.'

    L. "He said to him, 'Pepper.'

    M. "He took him to a house, and showed him a pile of coins, saying to them, 'Look at this money. Does it circulate in your land?' [The other was satisfied and made the

sale,] and he took his leave and went off in peace.
N.   "After he had left, he went out to walk in the market place. He met one of his friends, who said to him, 'What are you bringing here?'
O.   "He said to him, 'Pepper.'
P.   "He said to him, 'If you have a little, sell it to me for a hundred denars, for I have a party to give.'
Q.   "He said to him, 'I have already sold it to a certain tailor, but I'll tell him to give you a little of it.'
R.   [Following Cohen, p. 70:] "He went and found the house full of buyers, so that those who were in the first room secured an ounce each, and those in the second room half an ounce each, while those in the third received no attention at all."
S.   "That is the sense of the verse, 'the city that was full of people.'"

The *Ma'aseh*, illustrating the populous character of Israel, is in these parts: B-F, Tyre; G-M, N-R. R states the goal of the construction, to illustrate how numerous was the Jewish population. Here the marker does not signify a Halakhic or an exegetical program at all. The purpose of the story is realized, finally, at R, but it is difficult to argue that the whole takes on cogency only at that point.

XXXV:v.

3.   A.   ["How lonely sits] the city that was full of people:"] [Cohen, p. 70:] If you wish to know how many multitudes there were in Jerusalem, you can ascertain it from the priests.
B.   R. Joshua of Sikhnin in the name of R. Levi said, "To what may the matter be compared?
C.   "To a large heap that stood in the market-place, and no one could estimate its volume. There was a smart man there, who said to them, 'If you want to come to an estimate of its volume, you may come to an estimate based on the amount of priestly ration that is separated from it.'
D.   "So if you want to estimate the population of the Israelites you make an estimate based on the priesthood.
E.   "That is in line with this verse: 'And Solomon offered for the sacrifice of peace-offerings, which he offered to the Lord, twenty-two thousand oxen and a hundred and twenty-thousand sheep' (I Kgs. 8:63)."

The exegetical parable, C, closely follows D+E, and I detect no free-

standing parabolic materials that are adapted for the present purpose. Rather, the parable responds to its task, translating the components into its simile.

XXXV:vii.

1. A. "she that was great among the nations:"

    B. Has not "[How lonely sits the city that was] full of people" been
    said? Then why now say, "among the nations"?

    C. It means, great in learning.

2. A. "She that was a princess among the cities [has become a vas-
    sal]:"

    B. R. Huna in the name of R. Yosé said, "Wherever a Jerusalemite
    would go, they would set a place of honor for him and seat
    him there, so as to hear his wisdom."

    3. A. There is the following case [*ma'aseh*].

        B. There was a Jerusalemite who went to a town,
        where he was received by a friend. He spent some
        time there. The time came for him [to die], and he
        entrusted his property into the hands of his friend
        by whom he had been received.

        C. He said to him, "If my son comes to you and
        wants this property, if he does not carry out three
        acts of wisdom, do not give him this property."

        D. The people had agreed that none of them would
        show the house of his father's friend to a stranger
        [who might ask for it].

        E. The son heard and went to that place, and he
        knew the name of the man. He came and sat at the
        gate of the town. He saw someone carrying a load
        of twigs. He said to him, "Will you sell those twigs?"

        F. He said to him, "Yes."

        G. He said to him, "Take the price and go, carry
        the wood to So-and-so."

        H. He followed him until he came to the house of
        that man.

        I. He called to them, "Take away this load."

        J. He said, "Who ordered it?"

        K. He said to him, "You did not tell me, but they
        belong to the man who is following me." [This is
        the first clever act of the son, in finding the house.]

        L. He came down and greeted him, saying to him,
        "Who are you?"

        M. He said to him, "I am the son of that
        Jerusalemite, who died here with you."

        N. He took him in and made a meal for him.

        O. Now that man had a wife and two sons and
        two daughters. They sat down to eat, and he set

before them five chickens."

P.   He said to him, "Take and divide it up [among us]."

Q.   He said to him "That is not mine to do, for I am a guest."

R.   He said to him, "Please me."

S.   He took one bird and gave it to the master of the house and his wife, the next and set it for his two sons, and the third and set it before the two daughters, and took the remaining two for himself."

[This is the second clever act of the son.]

T.   He said to him, "How is that for a division?"

U.   He said to him, "But did I not say to you that I am a guest, and the honor is not mine? Nonetheless, I divided matters up quite properly. You and your wife and one chicken are three; your two sons and a chicken are three; and your two daughters and a chicken are three; and I and the two chickens are three."

V.   The next day he made a meal for him and brought before them one chicken. He said to the guest, "Take and divide it up."

W.   He said to him "That is not mine to do, for I am a guest."

X.   He said to him, "Please me."

Y.   He took the head and set it before the master of the house, the entrails and set them before the wife, the thighs for the sons, the wings for the daughters, and the body for himself.

Z.   He said to him, "How is that for a division?"

AA. He said to him, "But did I not say to you that I am a guest, and the honor is not mine? Nonetheless, I divided matters up quite properly.

BB. "I gave you the head, because you are the head of the house, the entrails to your wife, because children issue from the womb, the thighs to your sons, the pillar of the house, the wings for your two daughters, because they are going to fly away from your house and go to their husbands.

CC. "And I took for myself the [body which is shaped like a] boat [so Cohen, p. 74], because in a boat I came.

DD. "So now give me the inheritance left by my father, so that I may go along."

EE. "So he went and give him his inheritance and he went along."

1.   *On what basis does the narrative attain coherence, e.g., what is the action or event that precipitates the telling of the tale?* The narrative, meant to illustrate the honor paid to Jerusalemites by reason of their wisdom, bears the marker, *Ma'aseh*, but must be classified as an authentic narrative. A-C+D set the stage. Then there are these chapters of problem-solving through wisdom: D-K, L-U, V-CC, with the denouement, DD-EE. The unfolding in three parts, plus the prologue and the epilogue, is smooth and uninterrupted. The parts cohere as they unfold, a single pattern governing their articulation. I cannot claim that DD-EE impose cogency upon the whole, which, rather, derives from the recurrent patterning of the action.

2.   *What point of conflict or intersection of wills accounts for the telling of the tale and how is the point of tension resolved?* The tension derives from the assignment: can the son solve the problems and so display requisite wisdom, and it is resolved in the unfolding of the three actions.

3.   *How, in light of other, comparable, pieces of writing and the data that they yield, is the narrative classified, and what are its indicative formal qualities, e.g., long or short, complex or simple?* The wisdom-story requires a prologue and an epilogue and tripartite action.

XXXV·vii

4.   A.   Four Jerusalemites went to Athens and were received by someone there. In the evening he made a meal for them. After they had eaten and drunk, he set four beds for them, one of them damaged [and supported by the next].

B.   After they had eaten and drunk, he said, "I'm going to listen, for the Jerusalemites are very smart. I'll go and lie down near them to know what they are saying."

C.   One of them woke up, the one sleeping in the damaged bed, and said, "Do you think that I am sleeping on a bed? I am sleeping only on the ground."

D.   The second woke up and said, "Are you surprised at that? The meat that we were eating tasted of dog."

E.   The third woke up and said, "Are you surprised at that? The wine that we drank tasted like the grave."

F.   The fourth awoke and said, "Are you surprised at that? The householder here is not the father of his son."

G.   At that moment the man said, "One of them spoke the truth, and three told lies."

H. He got up in the morning and went to the butcher, saying to him, "Here is some money, and give me the same meat that you gave me yesterday."

I. He said to him, "I don't have any left."

J. He said, "What was there special about it?"

K. He said to him, "I had one lamb which was sucking, but its dam died, and I had a bitch, so the lamb sucked from her. When you came in the evening, I was out of meat when you came to buy some, and I had nothing else so I gave you some of this."

L. He said to himself "Two of them told the truth and two lied."

M. He went to the wine-dealer and said to him, "Give me some of the wine that you sold me last night."

N. He said to him, "I don't have any left."

O. He said to him, "What was there special about it?"

P. He said to him, "I had one vine, planted over my father's grave. I pressed the grapes and poured the wine into casks. I was running out of wine when you came to buy some, and I had no choice but to give you some of that."

Q. He said to himself "Three of them told the truth and one lied."

R. He said, "I'm going to go and ask mother."

S. He went to his mother and said to her, "Whose son am I?"

T. She said to him, "Your father's son."

U. He said to her, "Tell me the truth, whose son am I? And if you don't tell me the truth, I'll cut off your head."

V. She said to him, "Your father was infertile. Did I do wrong by going and playing the whore so as to bring you all this property [that you have inherited from your putative father], so that it would not go to a third party?"

W. Then he said, "And are the Jerusalemites going to come to us and declare us all to be illegitimate?"

X. They made an agreement among themselves not to receive Jerusalemites [as guests].

5. A. A Jerusalemite came to Athens, but no one wanted to extend him hospitality, so he went to a stall.

B. After they had eaten and drink, he wanted to sleep there.

C. The owner of the stall said to him, "We have made an agreement among us that no one from Jerusalem will sleep among us until he has jumped three jumps."

D. He said to him, "I don't know how you people jump. You jump first, and I'll follow you."

E. He took one jump, then another, and a third, and ended up outside the stall. The Jerusalemite went and locked the door after him.

F. He said to him, "What's this?"

G. He said to him, "What you wanted to do to me, I have done to you."

6. A. An Athenian came to Jerusalem and went to the school house and found youngsters there, but their master was not present.

B. He asked them questions, and they answered him.

C. They said to him, "Let us make a deal that whoever is asked a question and cannot answer it will lose a piece of clothing."

D. They agreed.

E. They said to him, "You go first, for you are a sage."

F. He said to them, "You ask first, because you are locals."

G. They said to him, "Explain the following: Nine go out but eight come in, two pour out but one drinks, and twenty-four serve."

H. He could not explain these things to them. They took away his clothes.

I. He went to R. Yohanan, saying to him, "Is this how you act in your place? They strip guests naked."

J. He said to him, "Who stripped you?"

K. He said to him, "School children!"

L. He said to them, "Did they ask you something that you did not answer?"

M. He repeated the story to him.

N. He said to him, "Go and tell them: [Cohen, p. 78:] the nine which go in are the nine months of gestation, and the eight that come out are the eight days of circumcision,

O. "the two that pour are the two breasts that give milk, and the one that drinks is the baby,

P.   "and the twenty-four that serve are the twenty-four months of nursing."

Q.   He went and told them all this and they returned his clothing, and they recited in his regard, "If you had not plowed with my heifer, you would not have solved my riddle" (Judges 14:18).

7.   A.   An Athenian came to Jerusalem and came upon a child and gave him some money, saying to him, "Go, buy me cheese and eggs.

B.   When he came back, he said to him, "Tell me, as to these eggs, whence do they come, from a white chicken or a black one?"

C.   The child said to him, "You tell me, as to this cheese, where does it come from, white goats or black?

8.   A.   An Athenian came to Jerusalem and came upon a child and gave him some money, saying to him, "Go, buy me figs."

B.   He said to him, "Many thanks."

C.   He said to him, "Was it for nothing?"

D.   He said to him, "What do you want?"

E.   He said to him, "You with your mouth and I with my legs."

F.   He said to him, "Go and divide."

G.   There was an inferior portion, which the boy set before himself, and a better portion, before the visitor.

H.   He said to him, "Many thanks, well do people say that the Jerusalemites are very clever. Since the child knew that the money was mine, he chose the better portion and set it before me."

I.   When he was going, he said to him, "By your life! Let's cast lots. If yours comes up, you will take what's mine and if mine comes up, I'll take yours."

J.   They agreed, so the child got the man's portion.

9.   A.   An Athenian came to Jerusalem and came upon a child and gave him some money, saying to him, "Take this money and bring me something to eat now, with something left over for the way."

B.   He went and brought him salt.

C.   He said to him, "Did I tell you to bring me salt?"

D.   He said to him, "Something to eat and be satisfied, with something left over.

E.   "By your life, in this you will find something of which you can eat and be satisfied and leave something over for your trip."

10. A.   An Athenian came to Jerusalem and came upon a broken mortar. He took it and went to a tailor, saying to him, "Sew this broken mortar for me."

B.   He took out a handful of sand, saying to him, "Twist this into thread for me, and I'll sew the mortar."

11. A.   An Athenian came to Jerusalem and came upon a priest, saying to him, "How much of that load of wood will turn into smoke?"

B.   He said to him, "When it is damp, all of it, when it is dry, a third is smoke, a third ash, and a third fire."

C.   Where had the priest learned this?

D.   From the wood on the temple altar.

12. A.   An Athenian came to Jerusalem and wanted to learn wisdom.

B.   He worked for three and a half years and had learned nothing.

C.   When he came to leave, he bought a slave, blind in one eye. The one who had sold the slave said to him, "By your life, he is very clever and can see at a distance."

D.   When they had come out of the gate, the slave said to him, "Make haste, so we may overtake the caravan."

E.   He said to him, "Is there a caravan before us?"

F.   He said to him, "Yes, and there is a she-camel in front of us, blind in one eye; it has twins in its womb; it is carrying two skin bottles, one with wine, the other, vinegar; it is four miles away, and the camel driver is a gentile."

G.   He said to him, "How do you know that it is blind in one eye?"

H.   "Because one side of the path has been grazed by the camel, but not the other."

I.   "How do you know that it has twins in the womb?"

J.   "It lay down, and I saw the traces of two."

K.   "How do you know that it is carrying two skin bottles, one with wine, the other, vinegar:"

L.   "From the drippings. The ones of wine are absorbed in the ground, those of vinegar ferment."

M.   "How do you know that the camel driver is a gentile?"

N.   "He pissed in the middle of the road. A Jew

would go off to one side."

O.   "And how do you know that it is four miles away?"

P.   "Up to four miles you can make out the mark of the camel's hoof, but not beyond."

13.   A.   Someone from Athens was making fun of the locals of Jerusalem. They said, "Who will go and bring him to us?"

B.   One of them said, "I'll bring him to you, with his head shaved."

C.   He went to Athens and stayed with him.

D.   He was walking in the market place, and one of his sandals broke. He gave it to a workman, saying, "Take this *tremis* [a sizable sum of money] and fix this sandal."

E.   He said to him, "Are sandals so costly where you live?"

F.   He said to him, "When they are expensive, they cost ten *denars,* and when cheap, eight."

G.   He said to him, "If I come with you there bringing a stock of sandals, could you sell them?"

H.   He said to him, "Yes, but do not enter the place without me."

I.   He did so. When he got outside the gates, he sent word and called the other, who came out to him, receiving him and greeting him.

J.   He said to him, "What can we do for you, for we have agreed among ourselves not to let a stranger come in here to sell anything unless his head is shaven [and his face blackened]."

K.   He said to him, "What difference does shaving my head make to me if I sell my goods."

L.   He went and shaved his head, entered and took his seat in the middle of the market place, spreading out his sandals before him.

M.   Someone came by and said, "How much is this sandal?"

N.   He said to him, "They cost ten *denars.*"

O.   He said to him, "Show me a sandal for ten *denars!*" He hit him on the head with it and went away.

P.   Whoever came by did the same to him, until his head   was broken.

Q.   Afterward he came to him and said to him, "Did I pay you off so badly?"

R.   He said, "Don't ridicule the locals of Jerusalem any more."

14. A. A Samaritan set himself up as a dream-interpreter, ridiculing people.

B. Said R. Ishmael b. R. Yosé, "I shall go and see how this Samaritan is ridiculing people."

C. He went.

D. Someone came to him and said, "I saw in my dream an olive tree feeding oil."

E. He said to him, "The olive means light and oil means light; you will see a lot of light."

F. Said R. Ishmael b. R. Yosé, "May your spirit explode! That man has known [has committed incest with] his mother."

G. Someone else came to him, saying to him, "I saw in my dream one eye swallowing the other."

H. He said to him, "Your one eye is light and so the other, you will see much light."

I. Said R. Ishmael b. R. Yosé, "May your spirit explode! That man has two children, and one of them has committed incest with the other."

J. Someone else came to him, saying to him, "I saw in my dream that I swallowed a star."

K. He said to him, "You are light and a star is light, so light is added to light."

L. Said R. Ishmael b. R. Yosé, "May your spirit explode! That man has killed a Jew."

M. How did he know it? From the following: "Look now toward heaven and count the stars" (Gen. 15:5).

N. Another came to him and said, "I saw in my dream [Cohen, p. 81:] that I had three eyes."

O. He said to him, "You will see much light."

P. Said R. Ishmael b. R. Yosé, "May your spirit explode! That man is a baker; two eyes are his own, the third, the oven's."

Q. Another came to him and said, "I saw in my dream that I had four ears, and everybody was listening to me."

R. He said to him, "You will be very famous."

S. Said R. Ishmael b. R. Yosé, "May your spirit explode! That man is a thorn-gatherer, and when he carries them everybody runs away from him."

T. Another came to him and said, "I saw in my dream that I was carrying a notebook with twenty-four pages, written on one side and erased on the other."

U. He said to him, "You are rising to greatness, and your business affairs will be so many that you will have to write and erase."

V.   Said R. Ishmael b. R. Yosé, "May your spirit explode! That man has a garment of twenty-four patches, and he sews in one place and the garment is torn in another."

W.   Another came to him and said, "I saw in my dream that I was carrying a pole, with a bundle of lettuce tied to it."

X.   He said to him, "You are rising to greatness."

Y.   Said R. Ishmael b. R. Yosé, "May your spirit explode! That man has a store of wine that is going to sour, and everybody will come and take some of it in bottles and use it for pickling lettuce."

Z.   Another came to him and said, "I saw in my dream that everybody was pointing at me.

AA. He said to him, "You are rising to greatness and everybody is going to point at you as a gesture of praise."

BB. Said R. Ishmael b. R. Yosé, "Pay me the fee, and I'll interpret the dream for you."

CC. He said to him, "It has already been interpreted."

DD. The same man came back and said, "I saw in my dream that everybody was puffing at me with their cheeks and praising me with gestures of their fingers."

EE. He said to him, "You will become great, and everybody will praise you with his cheeks."

FF. Said R. Ishmael b. R. Yosé, "May your spirit explode! That man has a store of wheat, and when he dreamed people were pointing at him in praise, what it meant was that rain had dripped on it, and when he dreamed that people were puffing at him with their cheeks, it meant that the wheat had swelled up, and when he dreamed that people praised him with their fingers, it meant that the wheat had already sprouted, so he would get no profit from it."

15.   A.   A Samaritan said, "I want to go to see a certain sage of the Jews who makes fun of everybody [following Cohen, p. 82]."

B.   He said to him, "I saw in my dream four cedars, four sycamores, a hide stuffed with straw, and an ox riding on them."

C.   Said to him R. Ishmael b. R. Yosé, "The four cedars stand for four bedposts, the four sycamores stand for four legs of the bed, the hide stuffed with straw, the cords, the ox riding on them, the leather mattress on which you sleep. You are going to climb up into bed but not get out of it."

D.   And so it happened.

16.   A.   Another came and said to him, "In planting season I dreamed of an olive tree."

B.   He said to him, "You will see a lot of light."

C.   Another came and said to him, "In beating season I dreamed of olives."

D.   He said to him, "Prepare your loins for blows."

E.   He said to him, "My lord, the other got a good interpretation and I got a bad one!?

F.   He said to him, "May your spirit explode! He saw it at planting time, you at beating time."

17.   A.   There was the case of a disciple who was in session before R. Yohanan, who explained matters to no avail.

B.   He said to him, "What's wrong that you don't understand?"

C.   He said to him, "I saw in my dream three bad things, and I don't know what they mean."

D.   He said to him, "What are they?"

E.   He said to him, "In my dream I was told I would die in the month of Adar, would not see the month of Nisan, and would sow but not reap."

F.   He said to him, "These are good omens. 'Dying in Adar' means you will die in the glory of the Torah. 'Not seeing Nisan' means you will not experience trials [the words for Nisan and trials use the same consonants].' 'Sowing but not reaping' means you will not bury children who are born to you."

18.   A.   Another one said to him, "I dreamed that I did not have pants on."

B.   He said to him, "That is not a bad sign but a good one. When the Festival [of Tabernacles] comes, you will have nothing."

C.   How did he know? Because the word for leg and the word for festival are the same.

19.   A.   Someone came to R. Yosé b. Halafta and said, "I was shown in my dream, 'Go to Cappadocia and find your father's property.'"

B.   He said to him, "Did your father ever go to Cappadocia?"

C.   He said to him, "No."

D.   He said to him, "Go, count the twentieth beam in your house."

E.   He said to him, "There aren't twenty in all."

F.   He said to him, "Go, count from top to bottom and from bottom to top, and at the twentieth you will find your father's treasure."

G.   He did so and found the money and got rich.

H.   How did R. Yosé know? Because in Greek *kappa* means twenty and *dokoi* means beams.

20.   A.   There was the case of a woman who came to R. Eleazar and said, "I saw in my dream that the beam of the house was split."

B.   He said to her, "You will have a son."

C.   And that's what happened.

21.   A.   Another time she came and did not find him there, but did find his disciples. She said to them, "Where is your master?"

B.   They said to her, "What do you want of him?"

C.   She said to them, "Maybe you are as smart as your teacher about interpreting a dream I saw."

D.   They said to her, "Tell us what you want and we'll make sense of it for you."

E.   She said to them, "I saw in my dream that the beam of the house was split."

F.   They said to her, "You will bury your husband."

G.   She left, weeping.

H.   R. Eleazar heard and asked, "Why is she crying?"

I.   They said to him, "She came to bring you a question but did not find you."

J.   He said to them, "What did she want?"

K.   "The interpretation of a dream."

L.   "And what did you tell her?"

M.   They told him, and he said to them, "You have killed him, for is it not written, 'And it came to pass, as he interpreted it to us, so it was' (Gen. 41:13)?

N.   "And has not R. Yohanan said, 'A dream follows its interpretation, except in the case of wine. Some dream of drinking wine and it is a good sign, others dream of it and it is a bad sign.'"

O.   R. Abbahu said, "Dreams mean nothing for either good or ill."

22.   A.   There is the case of R. Joshua, who was walking on the way, and someone walking on the way saw him.

B.   He said to him, "What are you doing?"

C.   He said to him, "I am walking on the way."

D.   He said to him, "Well said, for [Cohen, p. 84:] robbers like you have trodden it [stealing private property and making it public property through usu-fruct].”

E.   He was walking along and found a child at a crossroad.

F.   He said to him, “What is the nearest way to town?”

G.   He said to him, “This way is near and far, and that is far and near.”

H.   R. Joshua went on the one that was near and far. But as he got near the wall, there were gardens and orchards surrounding it, so he could not get into town.

I.   He went back to the child and said to him, “My child, did you not say to me that this way is near and far?”

J.   He said to him, “My lord, you are a great sage in Israel. Did I not say to you that this is far and near, and that is near and far?”

K.   At that moment said R. Joshua, “Happy are you O Israel, that all of you are sages, from your youngest to your oldest!”

L.   He went further and came upon another child, who was holding a covered dish.

M   He said to him, “What is in that dish?”

N.   He said to him, “If my mother wanted you to know what is in it, she would not have told me to cover it.”

O.   He went further and came upon another child, to whom he set the question, “What is the water of the city like?”

P.   He said to him, “Don’t worry, the garlic and onions are plentiful.”

Q.   He went into the town and found a little girl standing and filling a pitcher of water from a cistern. He said to her, “Give me some water.”

R.   She said to him, “For you and for your ass.”

S.   After he had drunk and was turning away, he said to her, “My daughter, you have acted like Rebecca.”

T.   She said to him, “I acted like Rebecca, but you have not behaved like Eliezer [by giving me a gift, in line with Gen. 24].”

23.   A.   [Following Cohen, p. 85:] It has been taught on Tannaite authority: They leave over peah of a dish prepared in a boiling pot and it goes without saying, of one prepared in a tightly covered stew

pot.
B.   There is the following precedent:
C.   R. Joshua b. Hananiah lodged with a widow, and she brought him a dish on the first day, and he ate it and did not leave peah; the second day and he did not leave peah; and as to the third day, what did she do? She oversalted a dish of pounded grain, and when he tasted it, he did not touch it.
D.   She said to him, "Why did you leave aside the dish of pounded grain?"
E.   He said to her, "I had already eaten during the day."
F.   She said to him, "If you had already eaten during the day, why didn't you decline the bread in the way in which you declined the grain? Maybe you left it over as peah? And why did you not leave peah from the two dishes you ate as you left it from this pounded grain?"
G.   Said R. Joshua, "No one ever got the better of me in an argument than those children and this widow and the little girl:
H.   "so exemplifying the verse, 'she that was great among the nations.'"

1.   *On what basis does the narrative attain coherence, e.g., what is the action or event that precipitates the telling of the tale?* The complex of wisdom-stories follows transparent patterns. XXXV:vii.4 is in these parts: 4.A-G, H-L, M-Q, R-V, W-X, that is, a prologue, a tripartite construction of matched parts, and an epilogue. No. 5 is in these parts: 5.A-C, D-E, F-G, that is, a problem, a solution, and an explanation. No. 6 begins with a prologue, A-F, which sets the stage; then come G-H, I-M, N-Q, a different pattern from the foregoing, but highly patterned nonetheless. No. 7 is unitary, so too No. 8, 9, following the same pattern. Nos. 10-11 conform to the same rules of presentation. No. 12 is in these parts: A-C, the prologue, DF, with F systematically expounded at G-H, I-J, K-L, M-N, and O-P, five components in all. No. 13 sets up its problem at A-B, then solves it at C-H, which is expounded at I-J, L-P, and an epilogue at Q-R. Nos. 14-21 break away from the complex of Athenian/Jerusalem-wisdom stories; they are joined by their common topic, dream-interpretation. No. 22 reverts to the wisdom-pattern, now in these units: 22.A-D, E-G, H-J+K, L-N, O-P, Q-R, S-T. The *Maʿaseh*, No. 23, is in these parts: C-E, F, G-H, now connecting the entire pertinent complex. The composite holds together in the indicated ways, and

the individual entries form anecdotes with the stated purpose imposing coherence on each one respectively.

2.   *What point of conflict or intersection of wills accounts for the telling of the tale and how is the point of tension resolved?* The tension is between the wisdom of the one party and the obtuseness of the other.

3.   *How, in light of other, comparable, pieces of writing and the data that they yield, is the narrative classified, and what are its indicative formal qualities, e.g., long or short, complex or simple?* The construction of a sustained composite out of narratives has no counterpart in the documents we have examined in this exercise, and the specific narratives also find no match in the documents already treated.

XXXVIII.ɪ.

1.   A.   "The roads to Zion mourn, for none come to the appointed feasts (Lamentations 1:4):"

B.   Said R. Huna, "Everyone seeks its proper mate.

C.   "There was a case in which a wild bitch who climbed up a rock to mate with a male."

This is an odd Ma'aseh indeed.

XXXIX:ɪɪ.

1.   A.   "Her foes have become the head, her enemies prosper" (Lamentations 1:5) "because the Lord has made her suffer for the multitude of her transgressions; her children have gone away, captives before the foe" (Lamentations 1:6): For three and a half years Vespasian surrounded Jerusalem, with four generals with him: the general of Arabia, Africa, Alexandria, and [Cohen:] Palestine.

2.   A.   In Jerusalem were three rich men, any one of whom had the resources to feed the city for five years: Ben Sisit, Ben Kalba-Shabua, and Naqdimon Ben Gurion.

B.   And there also was Ben Battiah, son of Rabban Yohanan b. Zakkai's daughter, who was in charge of the stores.

C.   He went and burned all the stores.

D.   Rabban Yohanan ben Zakkai heard and cried, "Woe!"

E.   People went and said, "Lo, your friend said, 'woe.'"

F.   He sent and summoned him, saying to him, "Why did you cry, 'woe'?"

G.   He said to him, "I did not say 'woe' but 'wow.'"

H.   He said to him, "Why did you say 'wow'?"

I.   He said to him, "I was thinking that so long as the stores were available, the people of the city would not give themselves up to make sorties and do battle and engage the enemy."

J.   Through the difference between "woe" and "wow," Rabban Yohanan ben Zakkai was saved.

K.   This verse of Scripture applies to him: "The excellency of knowledge is that wisdom preserves the life of the one who has it" (Qoh. 7:12).

3.   A.   Three days later Rabban Yohanan ben Zakkai went out to stroll in the market, and he saw people boiling straw and drinking the water.

B.   He said, "Can people who boil straw and drink the water stand before the armies of Vespasian? The simple fact is that I have to get myself out of here."

C.   Rabban Yohanan sent to Ben Battiah, "Get me out of here."

D.   He said to him, "We have agreed that no one is going to get out except for a corpse."

E.   He said to him, "Get me out as a corpse."

F.   R. Eliezer carried him at the head, R. Joshua at the feet, and Ben Battiah walked in front. When they got to the gates, the guards wanted to stab the corpse. Ben Battiah said to them, "Do you want people to say that when our teacher died, they stabbed his body?" They let them pass.

G.   When they had passed the gates, they carried him to the cemetery and left him there and went back to the city.

4.   A.   Rabban Yohanan b. Zakkai emerged and went among Vespasian's troops, saying to them, "Where is the king?"

B.   They went and told Vespasian, "A Jew wants you."

C.   He said to them, "Bring him along."

D.   When he came in, he said, *"Vive domine Imperator!"*

E.   Vespasian said to him, "You greet me as a king but I am not, and if the king hears, he will assassinate me."

F.   He said to him, "If you are not a king, you will be, because the temple will be destroyed only by the power of a king: 'And Lebanon shall fall by a mighty one' (Isa. 10:34)."

5.   A.   They took [Rabban Yohanan ben Zakkai] and put him inside the innermost of seven rooms and asked him what time of night it was.

B. He told them.

C. They asked him, "What time of the day is it?"

D. He told them.

E. How did he know it?

F. From his study [he kept repeating traditions, and these told him the passage of time].

6. A. They took [Rabban Yohanan ben Zakkai] and put him inside the innermost of seven rooms and asked him what time of night it was.

B. He told them.

C. They asked him, "What time of the day is it?"

D. He told them.

E. How did he know it?

F. From his study [he kept repeating traditions, and these told him the passage of time].

7. A. Three days later Vespasian went to wash at Gophna. After he had bathed, he came out and put on his shoes. But when he had put on one of his shoes, they brought him a writing from Rome that the king had died and the citizens of Rome had crowned him king.

B. He wanted to put on the other shoe and he could not put it on his foot.

C. He sent for Rabban Yohanan ben Zakkai and asked, "Can you tell me why all these years I have been able to put on these shoes, but when I put on one of them and wanted to put on the other, it would not go on my foot?"

D. He said to him, "You have heard good news: 'A good report makes the bones fat' (Prov. 15:30)."

E. "And what shall I do to get it on?"

F. He said to him, "If you have an enemy, or some one you owe, let him walk in front of you, and your flesh will shrink: 'A broken spirit dries bones' (Prov. 17:22)."

8. A. The generals began to speak in parables before him: "As to a cask in which a snake has nested, what is to be done with it?"

B. He said to him, "Bring a charmer and charm the snake."

C. Said Amgar [Cohen: Pangar], "Kill the snake and break the cask."

D. "If a snake nested in a tower, what is to be done with it?"

E. "Bring a charmer and charm the snake, and leave the tower be."

F. Said Amgar, "Kill the snake and burn the tower."

G. Said Rabban Yohanan ben Zakkai, "All neighbors who do injury do it to their neighbors: Instead of defending us, you argue for the prosecution against us."

H. He said to him, "By your life! It is for your benefit that I have said what I said. So long as the temple is standing, the nations will envy you. But if it is destroyed, they will not envy you."

I. Said to him Rabban Yohanan ben Zakkai, "The heart truly knows whether it is woven or crooked [that is, what your intention really is]."

9. A. Vespasian said to Rabban Yohanan ben Zakkai, "Ask for something, and I shall give it to you."

B. He said to him, "I ask you to leave the city and go away."

C. He said to him, "The citizens of Rome did not make me king except to carry out public policy, and you tell me to leave the city and go away?! Ask something else, and I will do it."

D. He said to him, "I ask you to leave the western gate, which leads to Lydda, and spare everyone who leaves up to the fourth hour."

10. A. After he had come and conquered the city, he said to him, "If you have a relative there, send and bring him out."

B. He sent R. Eliezer and R. Joshua to bring out R. Saddoq, whom they found at the city gate.

C. When he came, Rabban Yohanan stood up before him.

D. Vespasian asked, "Are you honoring this emaciated old man?"

E. He said to him, "By your life, if in Jerusalem there had been one more like him, even though your army were twice as big, you would not have been able to take the city."

F. He said to him, "What is his power?"

G. He said to him, "He eats a single fig, and on the strength it gives him, he teaches a hundred sessions at the academy."

H. "Why is he so thin?"

I. "Because of his many abstinences and fasts."

J. Vespasian called physicians, who fed him little by little with food and drink until he recovered his strength.

K. [Saddoq's] son, Eleazar, said to him, "Father,

give them their reward in this world, lest they have merit on your account in the world to come."

L.   He gave them [Cohen:] calculation by fingers and scales for weighing.

11.   A.   When they had conquered the city, he divided the destruction of the four ramparts to the four generals, with the western one to Pangar.

B.   Heaven had decreed that the western wall should never be destroyed.

C.   The three other generals destroyed their parts, but he did not destroy his.

D.   He sent and summoned him and said, "Why did you not destroy your part?"

E.   He said to him, "If I had destroyed my part as the others destroyed theirs, the kingdoms that will arise after you would never know about the great glory of what you have destroyed. But when people look [at the western wall], they will say, 'See the power of Vespasian from what he destroyed!'"

F.   He said to him, "By your life, you have spoken well. But because you have disobeyed my orders, I decree for you that you go up and throw yourself off the top of the gate. If you live, you live, if you die, you die."

G.   He went up, threw himself off, and died.

H.   So did the curse of Rabban Yohanan ben Zakkai stick to him.

1.   *On what basis does the narrative attain coherence, e.g., what is the action or event that precipitates the telling of the tale?* I have tried to divide the whole into what seem to me its obviously distinct units, but the narrative in general flows from unit to unit. Let us consider the cogency of the individual units, then how the whole holds together. No. 2 shows how Yohanan b. Zakkai saved himself from the zealot by dissimulation. It certainly is a coherent narrative. No. 3 carries forward that story of Jerusalem under siege and Yohanan's decision to escape. Here the pattern is the same as before: Yohanan saves himself through his wisdom. No. 4 carries the narrative forward, and once more Torah saves the sage. Nos. 5, 6 do not greatly enrich the narrative but do repeat its main point. No. 7 follows suit. No. 8 has the general engage in a debate with the sage, and No. 9-10 complete the story of Yohanan. From that perspective No. 11 is tacked on. But each unit has its climactic moment, and most of them cohere around the proposition that, in this way, in that way, the sage's mastery of Torah saved the situation.

2. *What point of conflict or intersection of wills accounts for the telling of the tale and how is the point of tension resolved?* The tension derives from the situation of siege and the issue of how the sage saves himself and the Torah, repeatedly resolved by appeal to the Torah.

3. *How, in light of other, comparable, pieces of writing and the data that they yield, is the narrative classified, and what are its indicative formal qualities, e.g., long or short, complex or simple?* This protracted, complex, continuous narrative sets forth the stages in the destruction of the Temple as these pertain to the Torah-sage, from the siege to the escape to the denouement.

XLIII.i.

3.   A.   Another interpretation of the clause, "Her uncleanness was in her skirts" (Lamentations 1:9):

    B.   There was a place located lower than Jerusalem, called Tophet.

      4.   A.   R. Yosé said, "[The Targum translates it] the valley of Bar Hinnon."

          B.   "There was a hollow idol set up there, inside seven rooms, holding a copper plate in its hand, on which a fire pan was placed. When someone brought an offering of flour, one chamber was opened for him; when he brought one of doves and pigeons, two, of a lamb, three, of a ram, four, of a calf, five, of an ox, six. But when someone brought an offering of his child, seven were opened for him. They put the child on the copper plate, lit the fire pan beneath, and sang before the idol, 'May the sacrifice be pleasant and sweet to you.'

          C.   "Why do they do this? So the parents should not hear the groans of their children and retract."

      5.   A.   There was a priest who went to someone who had many children and said to him, "Such and such a statue has told me to come to you, for I have heard that you have many children, so you should offer up one of them."

          B.   He said to him, "They are not subject to my domination. One works in gold, one in silver, one with sheep, one with herds. I have one young son, who is in the house of his master. Wait until he comes from the house of his master, and I shall give him to you, and you may go and offer him up."

          C.   Said to him the Holy One, blessed be He, "Of all the sons that you had, you could offer to an idol only this one, who is consecrated to Heaven!"

      6.   A.   R. Judah b. R. Simon in the name of R. Levi b. Parta: "The matter may be compared to the case of a noble woman to whom her lover said, 'Warm some food up for me.'

B.   "She took the portrait of the king and burned it up to heat the food.

C.   "Said the king to her, 'Of all the things you had in the palace, you could heat up food for your lover only with my portrait!'

D.   "So said the Holy One, blessed be He, to that wicked man, 'Of all the sons that you had, you could offer to an idol only this one, who is consecrated to my name!'

E.   "That is in line with the following verse: 'Moreover you have taken your sons and your daughters, whom you bore to me, and these you have sacrificed to them to be devoured' (Ezek. 16:20).

F.   "Therefore: 'therefore her fall is terrible,' she has come under terrible trials."

The parable, 6.A-C, realizes the message of D, which in turn recapitulates the *Ma'aseh*, 5.C. It is a complex construction, but the place and shaping of the parable seem clear.

XLIV.i.

1.   A.   "The enemy has stretched out his hands over all her precious things" (Lamentations 1:10):

B.   You find that when the gentiles entered the sanctuary, with them came the Ammonites and Moabites.

C.   Everyone was running to plunder the silver and gold, but the Ammonites and Moabites went running to plunder the scroll of the Torah,

D.   so as to remove from there the statement, "An Ammonite and a Moabite shall not enter the assembly of the Lord" (Dt. 23:4).

2.   A.   R. Judah b. R. Simon in the name of R. Levi bar Parta: "To what may they be compared?

B.   "To a fire that happened in the palace of the king, and everybody ran to plunder the silver and gold, but the slave ran to plunder [Cohen, p. 114] his title deed.

C.   "So when the gentiles entered the sanctuary, with them came the Ammonites and Moabites.

D.   "Everyone was running to plunder the silver and gold, but the Ammonites and Moabites went running to plunder the scroll of the Torah, so as to remove from there the statement, 'An Ammonite and a Moabite shall not enter the assembly of the Lord' (Dt. 23:4)."

As in the foregoing, we first have a pseudo-narrative, XLIV:i.1, and then a parable that recapitulates the pseudo-narrative, 2.C-D, now comparing the Ammonites and Moabites to slaves out to plunder the title that binds them to the master.

"... for these things I weep" invites a long sequence of martyrologies. Most of these are authentic narratives, as I shall show. While our problem is not the character of the document's composites, perspective on the whole does illuminate the character of the parts. I begin, then, with a brief account of the construction that follows, L.i.1-15. Nos. 1, 2, 3 (which serves Ezek. 5:10), 4, 5; these are enriched with materials on how the spoiled suffered in particular, Nos. 6, 7, 8, + 10, and these items serve Dt. 28:56 and related verses; then another, and principal, martyrology, Hannah and her seven sons, parachuted down with no clear reason other than a general thematic affinity, No. 8. No. 11 reverts back to the base verse, as though we had been given anything remotely suggesting an amplification of a disciplined character, and No. 12 moves us on to the next clause. Here we do find something enriching, which is the recurrent interest in showing how God suffers with Israel and for Israel. No. 13 then proceeds to the next theme – one can hardly call it a sustained amplification of anything to do with the cited verse. This yields a sizable interpolation of Messiah-materials, none of them pretending to have been framed for the purposes of our document. The sequence runs from No. 13 to the end.

L.i.

1. A. "For these things I weep; my eyes flow with tears; for a comforter is far from me, one to revive my courage; my children are desolate, for the enemy has prevailed" (Lamentations 1:16):

   B. Vespasian—may his bones be pulverized!—filled three ships with men and women of the nobility of Jerusalem, planning to place them in the brothels of Rome. When they had embarked on the sea, they said, "Is it not enough for us that we have angered our God in his holy house? Shall we now outrage him overseas as well?"

   C. They said to the women, "Do you want such a thing?"

   D. They said to them, "No."

   E. They said, "Now if these, who are built for sexual relations, do not want it, as to us, how much the more so!"

   F. They said to them, "Do you think that if we throw ourselves into the sea, we shall have a portion in the world to come?"

   G. The Holy One, blessed be He, enlightened them with

this verse: "The Lord said, I will bring them back from Bashan, I will bring them back from the depths of the sea" (Ps. 68:23).

H.   "I will bring them back from Bashan: ""I will bring them back from between the teeth of lions."

I.   "I will bring them back from the depths of the sea:" this is meant literally.

J.   The first company stood up and said, "Surely we had not forgotten the name of our God or spread forth our hands to a strange God" (Ps. 44:21), and threw themselves into the sea.

K.   The second company went and said, "No, but for your sake we are killed all day long" (Ps. 44:23), and they threw themselves into the sea.

L.   The third company went and said, "Would not God search this out? For he knows the secrets of the heart" (Ps. 44:22), and they threw themselves into the sea.

M.   And the Holy Spirit cried, "For these things I weep."

1.   *On what basis does the narrative attain coherence, e.g., what is the action or event that precipitates the telling of the tale?* The story is in these parts: B-E, F-G+H-I, then J-L+M. The story reaches its climax in the suicides of J-L, on which basis the antecedent units cohere. Without the climax of J-L, there is no narrative.

2.   *What point of conflict or intersection of wills accounts for the telling of the tale and how is the point of tension resolved?* The tension concerns whether God will retrieve the martyrs from the sea, and God's response to the suicides, J-L+M, resolves it.

3. *How, in light of other, comparable, pieces of writing and the data that they yield, is the narrative classified, and what are its indicative formal qualities, 'e.g., long or short, complex or simple?* The working out of the narrative in triplets is the obvious structural quality of the composition.

L.i.

2.   A.   "For these things I weep:"

B.   Hadrian—may his bones be pulverized—set up three guards, one in Emmaus, one in Kefar Leqatia, and the third in Bethel in Judah.

C.   He thought, "Whoever escapes the one will be caught by the other."

D.   He sent forth a proclamation, saying, "Wherever a Jew is located, let him come out, because the king wants to assure him."

E.   The heralds made this announcement and caught

Jews, in line with this verse: "And Ephraim is become like a silly dove, without understanding" (Hos. 7:11).

F. [The Jews who were caught were taunted:] "Instead of asking that the dead be resurrected, pray that those alive will not be caught."

G. Those who understood did not come out of hiding, but those who did not gathered in the valley of Bet Rimmon.

H. [Hadrian] said to his general, "Before I am done eating this piece of cake and chicken leg, I want to be able to look for a single one of these yet alive and not find him."

I. He surrounded them with the legions and slaughtered them, so the blood streams as far as Cyprus.

J. And the Holy Spirit cried, "For these things I weep."

1. *On what basis does the narrative attain coherence, e.g., what is the action or event that precipitates the telling of the tale?* The parts, B-D, Hadrian's plan, E-G, the realization of the plan, H-I, climax and conclude with I: one way or the other, the Romans under Hadrian captured the Jewish fighters and killed them. Until that point, the prior units do not cohere, there is no narrative.

2. *What point of conflict or intersection of wills accounts for the telling of the tale and how is the point of tension resolved?* The important point is to show how silly the Jews were, to believe the Romans' promises. But that fulfills the prophecy of Hosea. Nonetheless, God mourns.

3. *How, in light of other, comparable, pieces of writing and the data that they yield, is the narrative classified, and what are its indicative formal qualities, e.g., long or short, complex or simple?* The simple anecdote is in three units, and captures a variety of incidents in a single pattern.

L.i.

3. A. There was the case of one band that was hidden in a cave. They said to one of them, "Go out and bring us one of those who were killed," which they ate.

B. One day they said, "Let one of us go and if he finds something, let him bring it, and we shall have something to eat."

C. He went out and found his father killed, and he buried him and marked the spot.

D. He came back and said, "I found nothing."

E. Another one of them went out, in the direction of that deceased and found the body and brought it back to them and they ate it.

F. Afterward they said to him, "Where did you find this corpse?"

G.   He said to them, "In such and such a place."

H.   "And what was the mark?"

I.   He told them.

J.   The other said, "Woe is me, I have eaten the flesh of my father."

K.   This exemplifies the verse: "Therefore the fathers shall eat the sons in the midst of you, and the sons shall eat their fathers" (Ezek. 5:10).

1.   *On what basis does the narrative attain coherence, e.g., what is the action or event that precipitates the telling of the tale?* The climactic moment comes in the match between the incident and the verse of Scripture, and the story is told to show how Ezekiel's prophecy has been realized in fact. The parts, A, B-D, E-I+J-K, provide for three components of the unitary account, but without J-K, the whole lacks a point.

2.   *What point of conflict or intersection of wills accounts for the telling of the tale and how is the point of tension resolved?* The tension is between the incident and its interpretation, and it is resolved by J-K, as noted.

3.   *How, in light of other, comparable, pieces of writing and the data that they yield, is the narrative classified, and what are its indicative formal qualities, e.g., long or short, complex or simple?* The pattern of the stories to this point focuses on the fulfillment of the prophecies, showing that these things about which God mourns were foreordained in response to Israel's own conduct, all in accord with the prophets' visions.

L.i.4 = CXIX.i.2

4.   A.   The wife of Trajan—may his bones be pulverized—gave birth to a child on the ninth of Ab, while the Jews were observing rites of mourning, and the child died on Hanukkah.

B.   They said to one another, "What shall we do? Shall we kindle the Hanukkah lights or not?"

C.   They said, "Let us light them, and what will be will be."

D.   They went and slandered the Jews to him, saying to his wife, "When your son was born, these Jews went into mourning, and when he died, they lit their lamps."

E.   She sent and said to her husband, "Instead of conquering the barbarians, come and conquer these Jews, who have rebelled against you.

F.   He had made a calculation that the trip would take ten days but the winds carried him and brought him in five days.

G.   He came into the synagogue and found the Jews

occupied with this verse of Scripture: "The Lord will bring a nation against you from afar, from the end of the earth, as the vulture swoops down" (Dt. 28:49).

H.   He said to them, "I am he. I thought that I would come to you in ten days, but I came in five."

I.   He surrounded them with his legions and killed them.

J.   He said to the women, "Submit to my legions, and if not, I shall do to you what I did to your husbands."

K.   They said to him, "Then what you did to the men do to the women."

L.   He surrounded them with his legions and killed them.

M.   So their blood mingled with the blood of the others and streamed as far as Cyprus.

N.   And the Holy Spirit cried, "For these things I weep."

1.   *On what basis does the narrative attain coherence, e.g., what is the action or event that precipitates the telling of the tale?* The units are A-D. E-H, I-M, the whole reaching its purpose in the martyrdom accepted by the women, who are the true martyrs: they had a choice.

2.   *What point of conflict or intersection of wills accounts for the telling of the tale and how is the point of tension resolved?* The contrast between the slander of Trajan's wife and the heroic martyrdom of the Israelites' wives underscores the tension between the stoic conduct of the Israelites—"Let us light them, and what will be will be"—and their fate. Israel accepted its fate, men and women alike.

3.   *How, in light of other, comparable, pieces of writing and the data that they yield, is the narrative classified, and what are its indicative formal qualities, e.g., long or short, complex or simple?* The tripartite construction signals the plan of the convention that guides the author in expounding the anecdote.

L.i.

5.   A.   There was the case of the two children of R. Saddoq, high priest, who were taken captive, one a boy, the other a girl, each falling to a different officer.

B.   This one went to a whore and handed over the boy as her fee [for sex].

C.   That one went to a storekeeper and handed over the girl as his fee for wine.

D.   This exemplifies the verse of Scripture, "And they have given a boy for a harlot and sold a girl for wine" (Joel 4:3).

E.   After some days the whore went to the storekeeper and said to him, "I have a Jewish boy and he is ready for that girl you have. Let's match them up with one another,

and whatever they produce as a child we can divide among
us.

F.   They did so. They closed them up in a room, and
the girl started crying. The boy asked her, "Why are you
crying?"

G.   She said to him, "Woe for this daughter of the high
priest who has gone and wed a slave."

H.   He said to her, "Who is your father?"

I.   She said to him, "I am the daughter of Saddoq, the
high priest."

J.   He said to her, "Where did you used to live?"

K.   She said to him, "In Jerusalem, in the upper market
place."

L.   He said to her, "What was the mark of the house?"

M.   She told him, "Such and so."

N.   He said to her, "Did you have a brother or sister?"

O.   She said to him, "I had a brother, with a mole on
his shoulder. When he would come home from school, I
would uncover it and kiss it."

P.   He said to her, "If you were to see it, would you recognize it?"

Q.   She said to him, "Yes."

R.   He bared his shoulder, and they recognized one another, embraced, and kissed, until their souls expired.

S.   And the Holy Spirit cried, "For these things I weep."

1.   *On what basis does the narrative attain coherence, e.g., what is the action
or event that precipitates the telling of the tale?* The units, A-D, E-F, G-R,
leads to R: they recognized one another and died together. Omitted is a hint as to why they did not know one another to begin with.

2.   *What point of conflict or intersection of wills accounts for the telling of the
tale and how is the point of tension resolved?* The tension is established at
A-D, the separation of the children and what would be their fate,
and it is resolved at R, the whole heading toward that climactic
moment.

3.   *How, in light of other, comparable, pieces of writing and the data that
they yield, is the narrative classified, and what are its indicative formal qualities, e.g., long or short, complex or simple?* The simple conventional pattern governs the exposition of the anecdote.

L.ɪ.

6.   A.   There was the case of Miriam [Buber: Martha],
daughter of Boethus, that she was betrothed to Joshua b.
Gamla, and the king appointed him high priest.

B.   He married her.

C. One time she said, "I shall go and see how he reads in the Torah on the Day of Atonement."

D. What did they do for her? They brought out carpets from the door of her house to the door of the house of the sanctuary, so that her feet should not be exposed. Nonetheless, her feet were exposed.

E. When her husband died, sages decreed for her [a settlement of her marriage contract involving] two *seahs* of wine a day.

> F. But it has been taught, "They do not allot wine for a woman by the act of a court"? And why not? R. Hiyya b. Abba said, "It is a precaution against wantonness: 'Harlotry, wine, and new wine take away the heart' (Hos. 4:11)."
>
> G. And why then did they allot wine for her? R. Hezeqiah, R. Abbahu in the name of R. Yohanan: "It was for her cooking."
>
> H. And lo, we have learned: **But if she was nursing a child, they give her less work to do and give her higher alimony [M. Ket. 5:9F].**
>
> I. R. Joshua b. Levi commented [on this passage], "What do they add? Wine, because it makes the milk flow."

J. Said R. Eleazar bar Saddoq, "May I not see consolation, if I did not see that the troops tied her hair on the tails of horses and made her run from Jerusalem to Lud.

K. "In her regard I cited this verse: 'The tender and delicate woman among you, who would not set the sole of her foot on the ground because of delicateness and tenderness' (Dt. 28:56)."

L.ı.

7. A. There was the case of Miriam, daughter of Naqdimon, for whom sages allotted the sum of five hundred gold *denars* for the purchase of perfumes daily.

B. Nonetheless, she went and cursed them, saying to them, "May you have to make exactly the same allotment to your daughters!"

C. Said R. Aha, "So we replied after her, 'Amen.'"

D. Said R. Eleazar b. R. Saddoq, "May I not see consolation, if I did not see her gathering barley from beneath the hooves of the horses in Akko.

E. "In her regard I cited this verse: 'If you do not know, O you fairest among women, go forth by the footsteps of the flock and feed your kids' (Song 1:8).

F. "Read the consonants for the word 'your kids' as

> though they spelled 'your bodies' [Cohen, p. 129, n. 4:
> 'If you know not how to observe the Torah, then the time
> will come when you will have to go out among the foot-
> steps of the flocks to seek grain to feed your bodies']."

The two *Ma'asim*, L.i.6, 7, and 8, repeat the same two-part program:
the luxury enjoyed by the woman, contrasted with her fate in the
aftermath of the calamity. Thus L.i.6A-E register that Miriam's feet
did not even touch the bare ground, and she was accorded lavish
support from her husband's estate. Then, J-K, comes the contrast.
L.i.7 follows the same model, A-C, D-E+F.

L.i.

> **8.**   A.   There is the case of Miriam, daughter of Tanhum,
> who was taken captive and ransomed in Akko. They
> brought her a shift, and she went down to immerse in the
> sea, and the waves came and swept it off, so she got an-
> other and went down to immerse in the sea, and the waves
> came and swept it off.
> B.   When she saw this, she said, "Let the Collector [God]
> collect the debt. [The waves exact punishment for my
> sins.]"
> C.   Since she had accepted the divine decree upon her-
> self, the Holy One, blessed be He, gestured to the sea and
> it returned her garments.

Here is a *Ma'aseh* that records a miracle: Miriam was humiliated by
the sea. When she recognized that it was punishment for sin, God
indicated to the sea to cease tormenting her. We note that the traits
of the authentic narrative, a tripartite construction climaxing at the
third of the three components, are lacking.

L.i.

> **9.**   A.   There was the case of Miriam, daughter of Tanhum,
> who was taken captive with her seven sons with her.
> B.   The ruler took and imprisoned them within seven
> rooms.
> C.   Then he went and brought the eldest and said to him,
> "Bow down before the idol."
> D.   He said to him, "God forbid! I will not bow down
> before the idol."
> E.   "Why not?"
> F.   "Because it is written in the Torah, 'I am the Lord
> your God' (Ex. 20:2)."
> G.   He forthwith had him taken off and killed.
> H.   Then he went and brought the next and said to him,
> "Bow down before the idol."

I.   He said to him, "God forbid! I will not bow down before the idol."

J.   "Why not?"

K.   "Because it is written in the Torah, 'You shall have no other gods before me' (Ex. 20:3)."

L.   He forthwith had him taken off and killed.

M.   Then he went and brought the next and said to him, "Bow down before the idol."

N.   He said to him, "God forbid! I will not bow down before the idol."

O.   "Why not?"

P.   "Because it is written in the Torah, 'For you shall not bow down to any other god' (Ex. 34:14)."

Q.   He forthwith had him taken off and killed.

R.   Then he went and brought the next and said to him, "Bow down before the idol."

S.   He said to him, "God forbid! I will not bow down before the idol."

T.   "Why not?"

U.   "Because it is written in the Torah, 'He who sacrifices unto the gods, except for the Lord only, shall be utterly destroyed' (Ex. 22:19)."

V.   He forthwith had him taken off and killed.

W.   Then he went and brought the next and said to him, "Bow down before the idol."

X.   He said to him, "God forbid! I will not bow down before the idol."

Y.   "Why not?"

Z.   "Because it is written in the Torah, 'Hear O Israel, the Lord our God, the Lord is one' (Dt. 6:4)."

AA. He forthwith had him taken off and killed.

BB. Then he went and brought the next and said to him, "Bow down before the idol."

CC. He said to him, "God forbid! I will not bow down before the idol."

DD. "Why not?"

EE. "Because it is written in the Torah, 'For the Lord your God is in the midst of you, a God great and awful' (Dt. 7:21)."

FF. He forthwith had him taken off and killed.

GG. Then he went and brought the youngest and said to him, "My child, bow down before the idol."

HH. He said to him, "God forbid! I will not bow down before the idol."

II.   "Why not?"

JJ.   "Because it is written in the Torah, 'Know this day

and lay it to your heart that the Lord, he is God in heaven above and on earth beneath, there is none else' (Dt. 4:39).

KK. "Furthermore, we have taken an oath to our God that we will not exchange him for any other: 'You have sworn the Lord this day to be your God' (Dt. 26:17). And as we swore to him, so he swore to us not to exchange us for another people: 'And the Lord has sworn you this day to be his own treasure' (Dt. 26:18)."

LL. He said to him, "Your brothers have had their fill of years and life and have had happiness, but you are young and have not. Bow down before the idol, and I will show you favor."

MM.   He said to him, "It is written in our Torah, 'The Lord shall reign for ever and ever' (Ex. 15:128), 'The Lord is king for ever, the nations have perished out of his land' (Ps. 10:16).

NN. "You are nothing, and his enemies are nothing. A human being lives today and is gone tomorrow, rich today and poor tomorrow, but the Holy One, blessed be He, lives and endures for all eternity."

OO.He said to him, "I will toss my ring to the earth in front of the idol. You just pick it up. Then people will know that you have obeyed Caesar."

PP. He said to him, "Woe to you, Caesar, if you fear mortals, who are no different from you, shall I not fear the King of kings of kings, the Holy One, blessed be He, the God of the universe?"

QQ. He said to him, "And is there a divinity in the world?"

RR.   He said to him, "Woe to you, Caesar, and have you seen a world without rules?"

SS. He said to him, "And does your God have a mouth?"

TT.He said to him, "And concerning your idol it is written, 'They have a mouth but cannot speak' (Ps. 115:5). But in connection with our God: 'By the word of the Lord the heavens were made' (Ps. 33:6)."

UU. He said to him, "And does your God have eyes?"

VV.   He said to him, "In regard to your idol it is written, 'They have eyes but do not see' (Ps. 115:5) but in connection with our God it is written, 'The eyes of the Lord that run to and fro through the whole earth' (Zech. 4:10)."

WW. He said to him, "And does your God have ears?"

XX. He said to him, "In regard to your idol it is

written, 'They have ears but they do not hear' (Ps. 115:6), but in connection with our God it is written, 'And the Lord listened and heard' (Mal. 3:16)."

YY. He said to him, "And does your God have a nose?"

ZZ. He said to him, "In regard to your idol it is written, 'They have noses but do not smell' (Ps. 115:6), but in connection with our God it is written, 'And the Lord smelled the sweet odor' (Gen. 8:21)."

AAA.   He said to him, "And does your God have hands?"

BBB.   He said to him, "In regard to your idol it is written, 'They have handles but they do not handle' (Ps. 115:7), but in connection with our God it is written, 'Yes, my hand has laid the foundation of the earth' (Isa. 48:13)."

CCC.   He said to him, "And does your God have feet?"

DDD.   He said to him, "In regard to your idol it is written, 'They have feet but they do not walk' (Ps. 115:7), but in connection with our God it is written, 'And his feet shall stand in that day on the Mount of Olives' (Zech. 14:4)."

EEE.   He said to him, "And does your God have a throat?"

FFF.   He said to him, "In regard to your idol it is written, 'Neither do they speak with their throat' (Ps. 115:7), but in connection with our God it is written, 'And sound goes out of his mouth' (Job 37:2).

> GGG. He said to him, "If he has all of these traits, how come he does not save you from my power as he saved Hananiah, Mishael, and Azariah from the power of Nebuchadnezzar?"

> HHH. He said to him, "Hananiah, Mishael, and Azariah were meritorious, and they fell into the hands of a meritorious king, while we are guilty and have fallen into the hands of a guilt-ridden and cruel king.

> III.   [Following Cohen, p. 132,] "And as for ourselves, our lives are forfeit to heaven. If you do not kill us, the Holy One, blessed be He, has many bears, wolves, snakes, leopards, and scorpions to kill us.

> JJJ.   "But the Holy One, blessed be He, has given us over into your hand only so as to exact from you vengeance for our blood in the future."

KKK. He immediately gave the order to put him to death.

LLL. His mother said to him, "By your life, Caesar, give me my son, so I may hug and kiss him."

MMM. They gave her her son, and she took out her breasts and gave him milk.

NNN. She said to him, "By your life, Caesar, kill me first, then him."

OOO. He said to her, "I cannot do that, for it is written in your Torah, 'And whether it be cow or ewe, you shall not kill it and its young in one day' (Lev. 22:28)."

PPP. "You wicked man! Now have you kept all of the commandments of the Torah except for this one alone?"

QQQ. He immediately gave the order to put him to death.

RRR. His mother threw herself upon her child and hugged and kissed him, saying to him, "My son, go tell Abraham, our father, 'My mother says to you, "Do not take pride, claiming, I built an altar and offered up my son, Isaac."

SSS. "'Now see, my mother built seven altars and offered up seven sons in one day.

TTT. "'And yours was only a test, but I really had to do it.'"

UUU. While she was hugging him, the king gave the order, and they killed him in her arms.

VVV. When he was put to death, sages calculated the matter of the child's age and found that he was two years, six months, and six and a half hours old.

WWW. At that moment all the nations of the world cried out and said, "What kind of God do these people have, who does such things to them! 'No, but for your sake, we are killed all day long' (Ps. 44:23)."

XXX. They say that after some

> days the woman went mad and
> threw herself from the roof and died:
> "She who has borne seven lan-
> guished" (Jer. 15:9).
> YYY.   An echo came forth: "A joy-
> ful mother of children" (Ps. 113:9).
> ZZZ.And the Holy Spirit cried,
> "For these things I weep."

1.   *On what basis does the narrative attain coherence, e.g., what is the action or event that precipitates the telling of the tale?* The famous narrative of the mother and her seven sons in its present formulation is in these parts: prologue, A-B, the first six sons and their steadfastness to martyrdom, C-G, H-L, M-Q, R-V, WAA, BB-FF, in a uniform pattern, with the youngest breaking the pattern at GG-OO, then the theological disputation between the youngest and Caesar, PP-FFF, then the disputation on divine capacity to perform miracles, GGG-KKK, then the scene of the martyrdom of mother and son, LLL-QQQ, then the mother's complaint to Abraham, RRR-UUU, and the denouement, VVV-WWW. It is difficult to maintain that the whole coheres only in the light of the conclusion, at UUU. But if we treat the primary component of the story as the martyrdom of the six older brothers, setting off that of the seventh, then we should see A-FF as coherent by reason of GG-PP, and then the prior acts of martyrdom reach their climax and take on cogency with the declaration of the youngest of the brothers. Then the rest is a secondary addition, as indicated in my margins, with only one obvious gloss, VVV-WWW.

2.   *What point of conflict or intersection of wills accounts for the telling of the tale and how is the point of tension resolved?* The tension is between the Caesar and the Israelite sons and their mother, the sons dying for theological truth, embodied in the capacity of the youngest to participate in the two-part disputation, then the mother serving a different function altogether in the narrative. According to my division of the composite, the narrative tension concerns the conduct of the youngest, who resists the easy temptation and insists on theological purity to the very end; and who is given a two-part disputation.

3. *How, in light of other, comparable, pieces of writing and the data that they yield, is the narrative classified, and what are its indicative formal qualities, e.g., long or short, complex or simple?* The complexity and development

of the composite-narrative distinguish the whole from the other narratives in our document.

L.ɪ.

      10. A. They said concerning Doeg, son of Joseph, that he died and left a young son to his mother, who would measure him by handbreadths and give his weight in gold to Heaven year by year.

            B. When the earthworks besieged Jerusalem, she slaughtered him by her own hand and ate him.

                  C. And in her regard Jeremiah laments, saying, "See, Lord, and consider to whom you have done this? Shall women eat their fruit, the children that are dandled in the hands" (Lam. 2:20)?

                  D. And the Holy Spirit answered, "Shall the priest and prophet be slain in the sanctuary of the Lord" (Zech. 2:20),

                  E. with reference to Zechariah son of Jehoiada.

"They said concerning…," functions like *Ma'aseh*, which marks not a fully articulated story but a case. The version at LXXVI:i.1 explicitly marks the anecdote with the marker, *Ma'aseh*.

L.ɪ.

13. A.   "for a comforter is far from me, one to revive my courage:"

     B.   What is the name of the royal messiah?

     C.   R. Abba bar Kahana said, "The Lord is his name: 'And this is the name with which he shall be called: "The Lord is our righteousness"' (Jer. 23:66)."

            G. R. Joshua said, "His name is 'shoot:' 'Behold, a man whose name is Shoot, and who shall shoot up out of his place and build the temple of the Lord' (Zech. 6:12)."

            H. R. Yudan in the name of R. Aibu: "His name is Comforter: 'for a comforter is far from me, one to revive my courage.'"

           14. A. The following case sustains the position of R. Yudan in the name of R. Aibu:

                B. There was a man who was ploughing, and one of his oxen lowed.

                C. An Arab came by and said to him, "What are you?"

                D. He said to him, "I am a Jew."

                E. He said to him, "Untie your ox and your plough."

                F. He said to him, "Why?"

                G. He said to him, "Because the house of the sanctuary of the Jews has been destroyed."

                H. He said to him, "How do you know?"

I.   He said to him, "I know from the lowing of your ox."

J.   While he was engaged with him, the ox lowed again.

K.   He said to him, "Harness your ox and tie on your plough, for the redeemer of the Jews has been born."

L.   He said to him, "What is his name?"

M.   He said to him, "His name is Menahem [Redeemer]."

N.   "And as to his father, what is his name?"

O.   He said to him, "Hezekiah."

P.   He said to him, "And where do they live?

Q.   He said to him, "In Birat Arba in Bethlehem in Judah."

R.   That man went and sold his oxen and sold his plough and bought felt clothing for children. He went into one city and left another, went into one country and left another, until he got there. All the villagers came to buy from him. But the woman who was the mother of that infant did not buy from him. He said to her, "Why didn't you buy children's felt clothing from me?"

S.   She said to him, "Because [Cohen, p. 137:] a hard fate is in store for my child."

T.   He said to her, "Why?"

U.   She said to him, "Because at his coming the house of the sanctuary was destroyed."

V.   He said to her, "We trust in the Master of the world that just as at his coming it was destroyed, so at his coming it will be rebuilt."

W.   He said to her, "Now you take for yourself some of these children's felt garments."

X.   She said to him, "I haven't got any money."

Y.   He said to her, "What difference does it make to you! Take them now, and after a few days I'll come and collect."

Z.   She took the clothes and went away. After a few days that man said, "I'm going to go and see how that infant is doing."

AA.   He came to her and said to her, "As to that child, how is he doing?"

BB.   She said to him, "Didn't I tell you that [Cohen, p. 137] a hard fate is in store for him? Misfortune has dogged him.

CC.   "From the moment [you left], strong

winds have come and a whirlwind and swept him off and have gone on."

DD. He said to her, "Did I not say to you that just as at his coming it was destroyed, so at his coming it will be rebuilt?"

15. A. Said R. Abun, "Why should I have to derive from an Arab [support for the position of R. Aibu, "His name is Comforter: 'for a comforter is far from me, one to revive my courage'"],

B. "for is there not an explicit verse of Scripture that says, 'And Lebanon shall fall by a mighty one' (Isa. 10:34), followed by 'And there shall come forth a shoot out of the stock of Jesse and a twig shall grow forth out of his roots' (Isa. 11:1) [and that shows that the day on which the temple is destroyed, the Messiah will be born (Cohen, p. 137, n. 5)]."

1. *On what basis does the narrative attain coherence, e.g., what is the action or event that precipitates the telling of the tale?* The introduction of the marker, Ma'aseh, does not change the fact that we have a fully-realized narrative. It is in these parts: B-J matched by K-Q, then R-V, concluded by W-DD, the destruction of the Temple matched by the advent of the Messiah, then the recapitulation of that pattern, marked by the climax: the disappearance of the baby-Messiah for the moment: "Just as at his coming it was destroyed, so at his coming it will be rebuilt." The coherence of the counterpart narratives, then, B-Q, R-V, is complemented by the outcome, W-DD, a tripartite composition. Either of the two statements of the match of the advent of the Messiah and the rebuilding of the Temple without the concluding unit will leave a false impression; only the climactic unit, the disappearance, states the entire message.

2. *What point of conflict or intersection of wills accounts for the telling of the tale and how is the point of tension resolved?* The tension is between the destruction of the Temple and Israel's condition, resolved by the advent of the Messianic infant, twice-over, then resolved by the statement that for the moment, he has disappeared.

3. *How, in light of other, comparable, pieces of writing and the data that they yield, is the narrative classified, and what are its indicative formal qualities, e.g., long or short, complex or simple?* The tripartite construction is familiar.

L.ɪɪ.

1. A. ["Zion stretches out her hands" (Lam. 1:17). Better: "For these things I weep" (Lam. 1:16):]

B. "Oh that my head were waters, and my eyes a fountain of tears that I may weep day and night for the slain of the daughter of my people" (Jer. 8:23).

C. Who said this verse?

D. If you wish to suggest that Jeremiah said it, it is not possible for someone not to eat, drink, or sleep [and only to mourn and weep all day long].

E. But it is only the Holy One, blessed be He, who said it, for he never sleeps: "Behold, he who keeps Israel neither slumbers nor sleeps" (Ps. 121:4).

2. A. Said R. Abba b. Kahana in the name of R. Levi, "It is written, 'And God said, 'Let the waters under the heavens be gathered together into one place' (Gen. 1:9).

B. "The Holy One, blessed be He, said, 'Let the waters gather themselves to me for the purpose that I will achieve through them.'"

C. Said R. Haggai in the name of R. Isaac, "The matter may be compared to the case of a king who built a palace and gave residences in it to people who lacked the power of speech. They would get up in the morning and greet the king by making appropriate gestures with their fingers and with flag-signals. The king thought to himself, 'Now if these, who lack the power of speech, get up in the morning and greet me by means of gestures, using their fingers and flag-signals, if they had full powers of speech, how much the more so!'

D. "So the king gave residences in the palace to people possessed of full powers of speech. They got up and took possession of the palace [and seized it]. They said, 'This palace no longer belongs to the king. The palace now belongs to us!'

E. "Said the king, 'Let the palace revert to its original condition.'

F. "So too, from the very beginning of the creation of the world, praise for the Holy One, blessed be He, went upward only from water. That is in line with the verse of Scripture which states, 'From the roar of many waters' (Ps. 93:4). And what praise did they proclaim? 'The Lord on high is mighty' (Ps. 93:4).

G. "Said the Holy One, blessed be He, 'Now if these [waters], which have neither mouth nor power of speech, so praise me, when mortals are created, how much the more so!'

H.   "The generation of Enosh went and rebelled against him, the generation of the flood went and rebelled against him, the generation of the dispersion went and rebelled against him.

I.   "The Holy One, blessed be He, said, 'Let these be taken away and let those [that were here before, that is, the primeval waters] come back.'

J.   "That is in line with the following verse of Scripture: 'And the rain was upon the earth forty days and forty nights' (Gen. 7:12)."

The exegetical parable, C-E, tracks the sense of the verse subject to clarification, F, G-I+J. G is realized by the people in the palatial residence who lacked the power of speech, F-G, then H by D, I by E. The parable has no autonomous existence and is not adapted from some independent corpus of stories.

No. 3 continues L.ii.1.E, cited above.

L.ii.

1.   A.   ["Zion stretches out her hands" (Lam. 1:17). Better: "For these things I weep" (Lam. 1:16):]

B   "Oh that my head were waters, and my eyes a fountain of tears that I may weep day and night for the slain of the daughter of my people" (Jer. 8:23).

C.   Who said this verse?

D.   If you wish to suggest that Jeremiah said it, it is not possible for someone not to eat, drink, or sleep [and only to mourn and weep all day long].

E.   But it is only the Holy One, blessed be He, who said it, for he never sleeps: "Behold, he who keeps Israel neither slumbers nor sleeps" (Ps. 121:4).

    3.   A.   R. Judah b. R. Simon said, "The matter may be compared to a shepherd who had only a staff and basket. He went and gathered a flock for himself. On one occasion wolves came and tore the flock to pieces.

        B.   "He said, 'I shall go back to my staff and basket.'

        C.   "So the shepherd is the Holy One, blessed be He: 'Give ear, O Shepherd of Israel, you who lead Israel like a flock, you who are enthroned on the cherubim, shine forth' (Ps. 80:2).

        D.   "The sheep are Israel: 'And you are my sheep, the sheep of my pasture' (Ezek. 34:31).

> E.   "'Wolves came and tore the flock into pieces'
> refers to the enemies who entered the temple.
> F.   "At that moment, the Holy One, blessed be He,
> said, 'Oh that my head were waters, and my eyes
> a fountain of tears that I may weep day and night
> for the slain of the daughter of my people' (Jer. 8:23)."

The exegetical parable, 3.A-B, spelled out at C-F, sticks closely to
the task, spelling out in an elaborate way the union of the parable
and the case. God is the shepherd, and "go back to my staff and
my basket" means, God reverts to his initial condition of having
nothing but what he started out with, having lost Israel and the
Temple.

LV.i.

2.   A.   "Hear how I groan; there is none to comfort me. All my enemies have heard of my trouble; they are glad that you have
done it. Bring the day you have announced and let them be as
I am" (Lamentations 1:21): "they are glad that you have done
it:"

 B.   [Buber: Said R. Levi,"] This may be compared to the case of
a noble lady to whom the king said, "Do not lend anything to
your neighbors. Do not borrow from them anything either."

 C.   One time the king lost his temper with her and drove her out
of the palace. She made the rounds of all her neighbors but
they would not accept her. She went back to the palace. Said
the king to her, "You have nerve to come back!"

 D.   She said to him, "You are the one who did it. For you said,
'Do not lend anything to your neighbors. Do not borrow from
them anything either.' Had I been lending to them or borrowing from them, and something of mine was in their domain or
theirs in mine, wouldn't they have received me?"

 E.   So too when the Temple was destroyed, [the nations of the world
sent word everywhere to which the Israelites fled and shut them
out, so they appealed to God,] said Holy One, blessed be He,
to Israel, "You have nerve to come back to me!"

 F.   They said to him, "Lord of the world, did you not write in your
Torah, 'Neither shall you make marriage with them, your daughter you shall not give to his son, nor his daughter shall you take
for your son' (Dt. 7:3).

 G.   "If we had intermarried with them, would they not have accepted us?

 H.   "you have done it."

Why are the nations glad that God has done to Israel what he has
done? The exegetical parable answers that question. But the story

that it tells is a bit elaborate for the case it has chosen to illustrate. The case, E-G, suffices with the prohibition of dealing with the neighbors, without sending Israel around to them, C, D. So the parable does not exactly match its assigned case.

CHAPTER TWELVE

LAMENTATIONS RABBAH
PARASHAH TWO

LVII:III.
2. A.   ["How the Lord in his anger has set the daughter of Zion under a cloud! He has cast down from heaven to earth the splendor of Israel; he has not remembered his footstool in the day
of his anger" (Lamentations 2:1):] "He has cast down from
heaven to earth the splendor of Israel:"

   B.   R. Huna bar Aha in the name of R. Hanina b. R. Abbahu:
"The matter may be compared to the case of a king who had
a son.

   C.   "The son cried, so he put him on his knees. He cried some more,
so he held him in his arms. He cried some more, so he put him
up on his shoulders. The boy dirtied the father, so he threw
him to the ground, and he was not thrown down in the way
that he was lifted up. The lifting up was step by step, but the
throwing down was in a single angry gesture.

   D.   "So it is said, 'And I, I taught Ephraim to walk, taking them by
their arms' (Hos. 11:3). Then: 'I will make Ephraim ride, Judah
shall plow, Jacob shall break his clods' (Hos. 10:11). And finally: 'He has cast down from heaven to earth the splendor of
Israel.'"

LVII:III.
3. A.   Another comment on the verse, "He has cast down from heaven
to earth the splendor of Israel:"

   B.   R. Joshua b. R. Nahman said, "The matter may be compared
to the case of townsfolk who made a crown for the king. They
angered him, but he took it, and they angered him again, but
he took it.

   C.   "[Finally] he said, 'Are the town-folk not irritating me only
because of the crown that is set on my head? Here, take it, it's
thrown in your face!'

   D.   "So said the Holy One, blessed be He, 'Isn't it the fact that the
Israelites are angering me only because of the icon of Jacob
that is engraved on my throne? Here, take it, it's thrown in your
face!'

   E.   "Thus: 'He has cast down from heaven to earth the splendor
of Israel.'"

The base-verse has two elements, "cast down" and "splendor of Israel," and the two parables address the two components. Both exegetical parables address the same verse of Scripture, taking as their task the concretization of the metaphor that God has (1) cast down from heaven to earth (2) the splendor of Israel. LVII:iii.2 has the king and prince, and C tracks the steps of D; there is no unclarity in the match, no missing detail or extraneous detail. LVII:iii.3 takes a different problem, namely, the reference in the base-verse to "splendor of Israel," namely, Jacob. Jacob's icon is engraved on God's throne, D. The parable, B-C, then has God remove the crown/icon in anger by reason of the provocations he has endured. The match between 3.D-E and 3.B-C is not so exact as the other.

LVII:iv.

1.   A.   ["How the Lord in his anger has set the daughter of Zion under a cloud! He has cast down from heaven to earth the splendor of Israel; he has not remembered his footstool in the day of his anger" (Lamentations 2:1):] "he has not remembered his footstool in the day of his anger:"

      B.   Said R. Hanina b. Isaac, "The Holy One, blessed be He, does not call to mind the blood of the circumcision that is between the feet of the aged patriarch [an observation made possible by the fact that the words for footstool and blood use the same consonants].

      C.   "Thus: 'And Abraham was ninety-nine years old when he was circumcised in the flesh of his foreskin' (Gen. 17:24)."

2.   A.   Said R. Yudan, "The matter may be compared to the case of a king who captured his enemies, killed them, and whose subjects wallowed in the blood of his enemies.

      B.   "One time they angered the king and he drove them out of the palace. They said, 'Does not the king remember how we wallowed in the blood of his enemies?'

      C.   "So the Israelites said, 'Does he not remember the blood in Egypt: 'And they shall take of the blood and put it on the two sideposts and on the lintel' (Ex. 12:7)."

Yudan provides an exegetical parable to concretize Hanina's exegesis, 1.B-C. What he adds is the motivation for reminding the king of the loyalty of the subjects, which is supplied at B, "One day they angered the king and he drove them...." The exegetical task, to link the statement of Lamentations to the destruction of the Temple ("angered... and he drove them..."), is then accomplished in an obvious way.

The next composite is devoted to the Bar Kokhba war. Our interest is only in the narratives encompassed by this complex composite, which are Nos. 10 and 19, but let us consider the composite as a whole. Then in my discussion within the framework of the problem of this exercise I will take up only the items I classify as authentic narratives. The base verse refers to destroying without mercy all the habitations of Jacob, and that provokes an essay on the extent of the destruction—what was destroyed, the rich country and population—and the way in which it was destroyed—without mercy. The entire composition is parachuted down; there is scarcely pretense at exegesis. The complex of Bar Kokhba materials, Nos. 4ff., makes its appearance in other, more appropriate settings as well. An exegesis of Isa. 21:13 finds its place in No. 27, but this seems to me garbled and out of place; No. 27 should really end at F. Then from that point we have a distinct exercise, an exegesis of Isa. 21:13-15. But K draws us back to the earlier material. In all, the entire composite draws us far from the text that provides the structure for the whole. To save space, I present only Nos. 1-19.

LVIII:ıı.

1.   A.   ["The Lord has destroyed without mercy all the habitations of Jacob; in his wrath he has broken down the strongholds of the daughter of Judah; he has brought down to the ground in dishonor the kingdom and its rulers.(Lamentations 2:2):"

> **5.**   A.   When R. Aqiba saw Bar Koziba, he said, "This is the royal messiah."
>
> B.   R. Yohanan b. Torta said to him, "Aqiba, grass will grow from your cheeks and he will still not have come."
>
> **6.**   A.   R. Yohanan interpreted the verse, "The voice is the voice of Jacob" (Gen. 27:22) in this way: "The voice is the voice of Caesar Hadrian, who killed eighty thousand myriads of people at Betar."
>
> **7.**   A.   Eighty thousand trumpeters besieged Betar. There Bar Koziba was encamped, with two hundred thousand men with an amputated finger.
>
> B.   Sages sent word to him, saying, "How long are you going to produce blemished men in Israel?"
>
> C.   He said to them, "And what shall I do to examine them [to see whether or not they are brave]?"

> D.   They said to him, "Whoever cannot uproot a cedar of Lebanon do not enroll in your army."
>
> E.   He had two hundred thousand men of each sort [half with an amputated finger, half proved by uprooting a cedar].
>
> **8.**   A.   When they went out to battle, he would say, "Lord of all ages, don't help us and don't hinder us!"
>
> B.   That is in line with this verse: "Have you not, O God, cast us off? And do not go forth, O God, with our hosts" (Ps. 60:12).
>
> **9.**   A.   What did Bar Koziba do?
>
> B.   He could catch a missile from the enemy's catapult on one of his knees and throw it back, killing many of the enemy.
>
> C.   That is why R. Aqiba said what he said [about Bar Koziba's being the royal messiah].

No. 10 is the first authentic narrative in the composite.

LVIII:ii.

> 10.   A.   For three and a half years Hadrian besieged Betar.
>
> B.   R. Eleazar the Modiite was sitting in sack cloth and ashes, praying, and saying, "Lord of all the ages, do not sit in judgment today, do not sit in judgment today."
>
> C.   Since [Hadrian] could not conquer the place, he considered going home.
>
> D.   There was with him a Samaritan, who said to him, "My lord, as long as that old cock wallows in ashes, you will not conquer the city.
>
> E.   "But be patient, and I shall do something so you can conquer it today."
>
> F.   He went into the gate of the city and found R. Eleazar standing in prayer.
>
> G.   He pretended to whisper something into his ear, but the other paid no attention to him.
>
> H.   People went and told Bar Koziba, "Your friend wants to betray the city."
>
> I.   He sent and summoned the Samaritan and said to him, "What did you say to him?"
>
> J.   He said to him, "If I say, Caesar will kill me, and if not, you will kill me. Best that I kill myself and not betray state secrets."
>
> K.   Nonetheless, Bar Koziba reached the con-

clusion that he wanted to betray the city.

L.   When R. Eleazar had finished his prayer, he sent and summoned him, saying to him, "What did this one say to you?"

M.   He said to him, "I never saw that man."

N.   He kicked him and killed him.

O.   At that moment an echo proclaimed: "Woe to the worthless shepherd who leaves the flock, the sword shall be upon his arm and upon his right eye" (Zech. 11:17).

P.   Said the Holy One, blessed be He, "You have broken the right army of Israel and blinded their right eye. Therefore your arm will wither and your eye grow dark."

Q.   Forthwith Betar was conquered and Ben Koziba was killed.

R.   They went, carrying his head to Hadrian. He said, "Who killed this one?"

S.   They said, "One of the Goths killed him," but he did not believe them.

T.   He said to them, "Go and bring me his body."

U.   They went to bring his body and found a snake around the neck.

V.   He said, "If the God of this one had not killed him, who could have vanquished him?"

W.   That illustrates the following verse of Scripture: "If their Rock had not given them over...." (Dt. 32:30).

1.   *On what basis does the narrative attain coherence, e.g., what is the action or event that precipitates the telling of the tale?* The story is in these parts: 10.A-E, F-J, K-Q, R-W, thus: the setting, the action, the denouement. The setting is the power of the sage through his prayers to prevent the disaster, his humility. This is contrasted with the arrogance, expressed through physical action, of Bar Kokhba. 'forthwith....'' Then Hadrian acknowledges the supernatural power of the sage.

2.   *What point of conflict or intersection of wills accounts for the telling of the tale and how is the point of tension resolved?* The tension is between the purity and sanctity of the humble sage, dependant on God, and the arrogance and profanity of the Jewish general. That is resolved by the Roman emperor's concession that God, not the Roman army, has conquered Israel.

3. *How, in light of other, comparable, pieces of writing and the data that they yield, is the narrative classified, and what are its indicative formal qualities, e.g., long or short, complex or simple?* The complexity lies in the characterization of the players, each differentiated from the others, and the fully-realized program of the narrative.

11. A. They killed the inhabitants of Betar until their horses waded in blood up to their nostrils, and blood rolled along in stones the size of forty-*seah* and flowed into the sea for a distance of four miles.

  B. And should you suppose that Betar was near the sea, it was four miles away.

12. A. Hadrian owned a vineyard eighteen miles square, from Tiberias to Sepphoris.
  B. They surrounded it with a fence made of the bones of those killed at Betar.

13. A. Nor was it permitted that they might be buried until a certain king came and ordered it.
  B. R. Huna said, "On the day on which those killed at Betar were handed over for burial, they invoked the benediction, '... who are kind and deals kindly' [in the Grace after meals].
  C. "'... who are kind:' because the bodies had not putrefied.
  D. "'... and who deals kindly:' because they were handed over for burial."

14. A. For fifty-two years Betar held out after the destruction of the house of the sanctuary.
  B. And why was it destroyed?
  C. Because they lit lamps on the occasion of the destruction of the house of the sanctuary.

  15. A. [The following explains why the inhabitants of Betar hated Jerusalem.] They say that there was a place in which the councilors of Jerusalem would go into session, in the center of the city.
  B. Someone from Betar would go up for prayer, and they would say, "Do you want to become a councilor?"
  C. He said, "No."
  D. Someone would say to him, "Would you like to become a city magistrate?"
  E. He said, "No."
  F. Some would say to him, "I heard you

have an estate for sale. Will you sell it to me?"

G. He would say, "I never thought of it."

H. The Jerusalem would write out and send a deed of possession to the steward of the man from Betar, bearing the message, "If so-and-so [the owner] comes, do not let him enter the property, for he has sold it to me."

I. The man would exclaim, "Would that my leg had been broken, so that I could not have gone up to that corner."

J. That illustrates the verse of Scripture: "Our steps were checked, [we could not walk in our squares. Our doom is near, our days are done, alas, our doom has come]" (Lam. 4:18).

17. A. R. Yohanan said, "They found the brains of three hundred children dashed upon one rock,

B. "and three hundred baskets of Tefillin-boxes, each basket holding three *seahs,* so that there were nine hundred *seahs.*"

18. A. Rabban Simeon b. Gamaliel said, "There were five hundred schools in Betar, and in the smallest of them there were three hundred children.

B. "The children would say, 'When the enemy comes against us, with these styluses we shall go out to do battle with them and stab them.'

C. "But when sin brought it about that the enemy came against them, they wrapped up each child in his book and burned him, and I alone survived.

D. "In his own regard he recited this verse: 'My eye affected my soul, because of all the daughters of my city' (Lam. 3:51)."

LVIII:ii.

19. A. There were two brothers in Kefar Haruba, and no Roman could pass by there, for they killed him.

B. They decided, "The whole point of the thing is that we must take the crown and put it on our head and make ourselves kings."

C. They heard that the Romans were coming to fight them.

D. They went out to do battle, and an old man met them and said, "May the Creator be your help against them."

E. They said, "Let him not help us nor hinder us!"

F. Because of their sins, they went forth and were killed.

G. They went, carrying his head to Hadrian. He said, "Who killed this one?"

H. They said, "One of the Goths killed him," but he did not believe them.

I. He said to them, "Go and bring me his body."

J. They went to bring his body and found a snake around the neck.

K. He said, "If the God of this one had not killed him, who could have vanquished him?"

> L. That illustrates the following verse of Scripture: "If their Rock had not given them over...." (Dt. 32:30).

1. *On what basis does the narrative attain coherence, e.g., what is the action or event that precipitates the telling of the tale?* Like LVIII:ii.10, No. 19 underscores the arrogance of the Israelites and the power of God alone to overcome them. The point that imparts coherence to the whole is at K: "If the god of this one had not...." The components are A-B, C-F, G-K, and the rest follows.

2. *What point of conflict or intersection of wills accounts for the telling of the tale and how is the point of tension resolved?* The conflict contrasts arrogance on the part of the Israelite warriors with the humility of the Roman emperor, expressed at K.

3. *How, in light of other, comparable, pieces of writing and the data that they yield, is the narrative classified, and what are its indicative formal qualities, e.g., long or short, complex or simple?* The tripartite exposition is brief and anecdotal, unlike its counterpart, but the main points emerge with great clarity in both the Bar-Kokhba-version and the anonymous one.

LXIII.ı.

1. A. ["The Lord has scorned his altar, disowned his sanctuary; he has delivered into the hand of the enemy the walls of her palaces; a clamor was raised in the house of the Lord as on the day of an appointed feast" (Lamentations 2:7):] "The Lord has scorned his altar, disowned his sanctuary:"

      B. Said R. Haggai in the name of R. Isaac, "The matter may be compared to the case of townsfolk who set forth banquet-tables in honor of the king. They angered him, but he took it, and they angered him again, but he took it.

      C. "[Finally] he said, 'Are the town-folk not irritating me only because of the banquet-tables that they have set for me? Here, take it, it's thrown in your face!'

      D. "So said the Holy One, blessed be He, 'Isn't it the fact that the Israelites are angering me only because of the banquet-tables that they have set for me? Here, take it, it's thrown in your face!'

      E. "Thus: 'The Lord has scorned his altar, disowned his sanctuary.'"

See LVII:iii.3. Note: LXVI:i.1 is omitted because it is classified as a Scripture-story.

LXVII.ı.

1. A. "My eyes are spent with weeping, my soul is in tumult; my heart is poured out in grief because of the destruction of the daughter of my people, because infants and babes faint in the streets of the city" (Lamentations 2:11): "My eyes are spent with weeping:"

      B. Said R. Eleazar, "There is a limit that applies to the eye [so that if one cries too much, it damages the eye].

          C. "[C-G follow Cohen, p. 178:] There are three kinds of tears which are beneficial: tears caused by a drug, mustard, and collyrium.

          D. "But the tears caused by laughter are best of all.

          E. "There are three kinds of tears that are harmful: tears caused by smoke, weeping, and straining in a privy.

          F. "But the tears caused by the death of an adult child are worst of all."

             G. There was the case of a woman whose adult son died. She wept over him nightly, until her eyelashes fell out. She went to a physician, who said to her, "Paint your eyes with this eye-paint that I give you, and you will recover."

2. A. "My eyes are spent with weeping, my soul is in tumult; my heart is poured out in grief because of the destruction of the daughter of my people, because infants and babes faint in the streets

of the city" (Lamentations 2:11): "my soul is in tumult, my heart is poured out in grief because of the destruction of the daughter of my people:"

B. There was the case of a man whose adult son died, and he wept over him nightly, until his liver dropped.

C. He said, "My liver has dropped from weeping over him, but it has made no difference." [Cohen, p. 179, n. 1: In like manner Israel's weeping brought them no relief, because God had taken no notice of it.]

The two *Ma'asim*, LXVII:i.1.G and 2.B-C, illustrate the generalizations to which they are attached, 1.F and 2.A. Neither could serve as the basis for exegetical parables, but both function as do that category of parables.

LXVIII.i.

2. A. [They cry to their mothers, "Where is bread and wine?" as they faint like wounded men in the streets of the city, as their life is poured out on their mothers' bosom (Lamentations 2:12):" "as they faint like wounded men in the streets of the city, as their life is poured out on their mothers' bosom:"

B. There is the case of a woman who said to her husband, "Take a bracelet or earring, go to the market, and buy something so we shall eat and not die."

C. He did so, but found nothing to buy, writhed, and died.

D. She said to her son, "Go, see what your father is doing."

E. He went to the market and found him dead in the market place, began weeping for him, writhed and died by his side.

F. That is in line with this verse: "as they faint like wounded men in the streets of the city:" this refers to the husband and adult son.

G. "as their life is poured out on their mothers' bosom:" this refers to her infant son, who wanted to suck but found no milk, so he writhed and died.

Though marked with the signal, *Ma'aseh*, with a king and queen in place of the woman and her husband/son, we would have a familiar kind of exegetical parable.

LXXVI.i.

1. A. "Look, O Lord, and see! With whom have you dealt thus? Should women eat their offspring, the children of their tender care? Should priest and prophet be slain in the sanctuary of the Lord?" (Lamentations 2:20):

B. There is the case of Doeg, son of Joseph, who died and left a young son to his mother, who would measure him by handbreadths and give his weight in gold to Heaven year by year.

C. When the earthworks besieged Jerusalem, she slaughtered him by her own hand and ate him.

D. Jeremiah lamented him before the Omnipresent, "Look, O Lord, and see! With whom have you dealt thus? Should women eat their offspring, the children of their tender care?"

E. To this the Holy Spirit replied, "Should priest and prophet be slain in the sanctuary of the Lord," speaking of Zechariah, son of Jehoiada.

The *Ma'aseh*, LXXVI.i.1B-C = L.i.10, serves like an exegetical parable to illustrate the cited verse, with the difference that the details are particular to the case, rather than a king/queen/prince.

CHAPTER THIRTEEN

LAMENTATIONS RABBAH
PARASHAH THREE

LXXIX:ii.

1. A. "I am the man [who has seen affliction under the rod of his wrath; he has driven and brought me into darkness without any light; surely against me he turns his hand again and again the whole day long]" (Lamentations 3:1-3):"

   B. Said R. Joshua of Sikhnin in the name of R. Levi, "The community of Israel says before the Holy One, blessed be He, 'Lord of the ages, I am he, and I am experienced in whatever you bring upon me' [following Buber; Cohen: 'I am indeed experienced in sufferings; what pleaseth thee is beneficial to me.']

   C. "The matter may be compared to the case of a noble lady, against whom the king grew angry. He drove her out of the palace. What did she do? She went and pressed her face against the pillar.

   D. "The king passed by and saw her and said to her, 'You have gall [to cling to the palace after you were driven out]!'

   E. "She said to him, 'My lord, king, this is proper for me, this is good for me, this is right for me, for no other woman took you but for me.'

   F. "The king said to her, 'No, but I am the one who rejected all other women on account of you.'

   G. "She said to him, 'No, but they are the ones who did not accept you.'

   H. "So the Holy One, blessed be He, said to the community of Israel, 'You have gall [Cohen, p. 189, n. 2: by praying to me after being driven into exile].'

   I. "The community of Israel replied, 'Lord of the world, this is proper for me, this is good for me, this is right for me, for no other nation accepted the Torah except for us.'

   J. "He said to her, 'No, but I am the one who rejected all other nations on account of you.'

   K. "She said to him, 'How come you went with your Torah around to all the other nations for them to reject it?'

   L. "'And he said, The Lord came from Sinai and rose from Seir to them' (Dt. 33:2), but they rejected it.

M.   "Then he offered it to the sons of Ishmael: 'He shined forth from Mount Paran' (Dt. 33:2), but they rejected it.

N.   "Finally he offered it to Israel, who accepted it: 'And he came forth from the myriads holy, at his right hand was a fiery Torah for them' (Dt. 33:2), 'All that the Lord has spoken we will do and obey' (Ex. 24:7)."

The key to the priority of the exegetical task, H-N, in the formation of the exegetical parable, C-G, lies in the implausibility of E/ G, which can fit only in the well-established pattern that the nations rejected the Torah and Israel alone accepted it. In any event, the match, C-G/H-N, has no close connection to 1.A-B. I take it the tie lies in the base-verse, "surely against me he turns his hand again and again the whole day long," since B is hardly an obvious link to the parable.

LXXXI.i.

3.   A.   ["He has walled me about so that I cannot escape; he has put heavy chains on me; Although I call and cry for help, he shuts out my prayer; he has blocked my ways with hewn stones, he has made my paths crooked" (Lamentations 3:7-9)]: "though I call and cry for help, he shuts out my prayer:"

B.   R. Aha and Rabbis:

C.   R. Aha said, "Whoever says his prayers with the congregation finds that his prayer is heard.

D.   "To what may the matter be compared? To the case of ten men who made a crown for the king, and a poor man came along and helped out.

E.   "What did the king say? 'Shall I not put on this crown [merely] on account of that poor man?'

F.   "The king forthwith accepts the crown and puts it on his head.

G.   "So if there are ten righteous persons standing in the synagogue and saying their prayers, and a wicked man is standing with them, what does the Holy One, blessed be He, say?

H.   "'On account of that wicked man shall I not accept the prayer? I shall accept it as is.'"

I.   And rabbis say, "Whoever says his prayers after the congregation says theirs finds that his actions are spelled out [and scrutinized in detail].

J.   "To what may the matter be compared? To the case of a king, whose sharecroppers and staff came before his presence to honor him. One person came late. Said the king, 'Let the wine bottle be stopped up for him.'

K.   "What made this [insult] come about? That the man came late.

L.   "So too, whoever says his prayers after the congregation says theirs finds that his actions are spelled out [and scrutinized in detail].

> M.   "That is in line with this verse of Scripture: 'though
> I call and cry for help, he shuts out my prayer.'
> N.   "The word 'shuts out' is written as though it read 'for
> it has finished,' [meaning, because the congregation had
> finished their prayer]."

The exegetical parables, C-H, I-L+M-N, deal with cases of shut-
ting out prayer, either because someone does not pray with the congregation or who says his prayers after the congregation have said
theirs, the same thing twice. G-H dictate the program of C-F. The
important point, G-H, is that God hears the prayers of the congregation despite the presence of the wicked man, which is not precisely the point that C announces. The parable, I-K, is closer in its
articulation to the point of L. But we cannot find that exact match
between the parable and the proposition that has generated it that
we usually notice.

LXXXIV.i.

1.   A.   "He has made my teeth grind on gravel and made me cower
          in ashes" (Lamentations 3:16):
     B.   There is the case of the son of R. Hanina b. Teradion,
          who joined up with guerillas. He snitched on them, and
          they killed him.
     C.   His father went and found him in the wilderness, with his
          mouth full of dirt and gravel.
          D.   A few days later they put him in a coffin and
          out of respect for his father, they wanted to have a
          eulogy said for him. The father would not permit
          it. He said to them, "Let me speak concerning my
          son."
          E.   He commenced by citing this verse: "Neither
          have I hearkened to the voice of my teachers, nor
          inclined my ear to those who taught me. I was well
          nigh in all evil in the midst of the congregation and
          assembly" (Prov. 5:13-14).
          F.   His mother commenced by citing this verse over
          him: "A foolish son is a vexation to his father, and
          bitterness to her that bore him" (Prov. 17:25).
          G.   His sister cited this verse: "Bread of falsehood
          is sweet to a man, but afterwards his mouth will be
          filled with gravel" (Prov. 20:17).

The *Ma'aseh* is in two parts, B-C, D-G. The first component forms
an ordinary *Ma'aseh*, that is, a statement of something that has happened, B, and its consequence, C.

LXXXIV.i.

4. A. ["He has made my teeth grind on gravel and made me cower in ashes; my soul is bereft of peace, I have forgotten what happiness is; so I say, 'Gone is my glory, and my expectation from the Lord'" (Lamentations 3:16-18)] [A further illustration of the verse, "my soul is bereft of peace, I have forgotten what happiness is:"]

B. Said R. Eleazar b. R. Yosé, "There was the case of a woman who brought her son to a cook and said to him, 'Teach my son the trade.'

C. "He said to her, 'Leave him with me for five years, and I shall teach him how to make five hundred kinds of omelets.'"

D. Rabbi [Judah the Patriarch] heard and said, "That kind of luxury we have never seen" [after the destruction of the Temple, thus "my soul is bereft of peace, I have forgotten what happiness is"].

E. R. Simeon b. Halafta heard and said, "Of such luxury we have never even heard."

The *Ma'aseh*, B-C, is invoked for the reason specified at D. Standing on its own, it has no meaning and fits no context.

LXXXIV.i.

5. A. [A further illustration of the verse, "my soul is bereft of peace, I have forgotten what happiness is:"] R. Judah b. Betera came to Nisibis on the eve of the great fast [the Day of Atonement].

B. He ate and finished [eating prior to the fast].

C. The head of the community came to him to invite him. He said to him, "I have already eaten and completed eating [prior to the fast]."

D. He said to him, "Pay attention to me, [Cohen: 'Let my master favor me by coming to my house for the meal'], so that people should not say that the master paid no attention to me."

E. Since he insisted, the other went with him.

F. The head of the community [Cohen, p. 197:] thereupon instructed his young servant, saying, "Any course which you serve us once must not be repeated."

G. They brought before them eighty courses, and he took a small taste of each, and drink a cup of each jar of wine.

H. The host said to him, "My lord, Did you not say to me, 'I have already eaten and finished [the final meal prior to the Day of Atonement]'? Now you were served with eighty courses, and you took a small taste of each, and drank a cup of each jar of wine." [Cohen, p. 197, n. 3:

He made this remark to boast of his lavish hospitality and insinuate that his guest had previously had an insufficient meal.]

I.   He said to him, "Why is it that the appetite is called capacious [*nefesh*]? The more you give it, the more it expands [*nefishah*]."

1.   *On what basis does the narrative attain coherence, e.g., what is the action or event that precipitates the telling of the tale?* The parts of the story, A-E, F-I, cohere at the end, I, which explains how the master was able to eat so much as he did.

2.   *What point of conflict or intersection of wills accounts for the telling of the tale and how is the point of tension resolved?* The tension is between the insistent pretentiousness of the host and the patient endurance of the master, resolved at the simple explanation at the end.

3.   *How, in light of other, comparable, pieces of writing and the data that they yield, is the narrative classified, and what are its indicative formal qualities, e.g., long or short, complex or simple?* The anecdote is simple, brief, and trivial.

LXXXV.i.

2.   A.   "My soul continually thinks of it and is bowed down within me" (Lamentations 3:19):

B.   R. Hiyya taught, "The matter may be compared to the case of a king who went to battle and took his sons with him. One time they angered him, and he took an oath not to take them along again.

C.   "Then he remembered them and wept, saying, 'Would that my sons were with me, even though they anger me!'

D.   "[Cohen's text, not in Buber:] The king is the Holy One, blessed be He, and the sons are Israel. When the Israelites went forth to battle, the Holy One, blessed be He, would go with them. But when they angered him, he did not accompany them [Cohen, p. 199, n. 2: which caused their overthrow and exile]. When Israel was no longer in the land, he said, 'Would that Israel were with me, even though they anger me.'

E.   "That is in line with the following: 'Oh that I were in the wilderness, in a lodging place of wayfaring men' (Jer. 9:1): 'would that my people were with me as in the past when they were in the wilderness.'

F.   "'Son of man, when the house of Israel dwelled in their own land, they defiled it' (Ezek. 36:17). [Cohen, p. 199, n. 3: 'Would that Israel dwelt in their own land though they defiled it.']

G.   "And the present passage: 'My soul continually thinks of it and is bowed down within me.'"

The execution of the exegetical parable, D+E-G, leaves no doubt at the exact correspondence of the parable with the case at hand. The sole point of divergence is that at B, the king takes an oath not to take them along, while at D, God did not accompany Israel. I take it that the adjustment is required by the character of the parable. The king cannot leave himself behind, B, while the sons go out to battle. The important point comes at C, and there the match is exact and textual.

LXXXV.i.

4.   A.   "But this I call to mind and therefore I have hope" (Lamentations 3:21):

    B.   R. Abba bar Kahana said in the name of R. Yohanan, "The matter may be compared to the case of a king who took a wife and wrote out for her a document specifying a very large marriage-settlement: 'So many [Cohen:] state-apartments I am making ready for you, so many purple garments I am giving you.'

    C.   "Then he left her for many years and went overseas, and her neighbors aggravated her, saying, 'The king has abandoned you, gone overseas and will never return.'

    D.   "She wept and sighed, but she would go into her room and open and read her marriage-settlement. When she saw in the document, 'So many state-apartments I am making ready for you, so many purple garments I am giving you,' she took comfort.

    E.   "After days and years had gone by, the king came home. He said to her, 'My daughter, I am surprised that you were able to wait for me all these years.'

    F.   "She said to him, 'My lord, king, were it not for the marriage-settlement that you wrote out for me, with its generous settlement, my neighbors would have misled me.'

    G.   "So the nations of the world aggravate Israel, saying to them, 'Your God does not want you any more, he has hidden his face from you, he has removed his Presence from your midst and will return to you no more. [Buber's text: Come to us and we shall appoint you dukes, lords, and generals.]'

    H.   "And when the Israelites go into their synagogues and study houses and recite in the Torah: 'And I shall have respect for you and make you fruitful and multiply you... and I will set my tabernacle among you... and I will walk among you' (Lev. 26:9-11), they take comfort.

    I.   "Tomorrow, when the redemption comes, the Holy One, blessed be He, will say to the Israelites, 'My children, I am surprised that you were able to wait for me all these years.'

    J.   "And they will reply to him, 'Lord of all the ages, were it not for your Torah, which you have given to us, the nations of the

world would long ago have led us astray from you.'
K.   "That is in line with this verse: 'But this I call to mind
      and therefore I have hope.'
L.   "Now the word 'this' refers only to the Torah: 'And this
      is the Torah' (Dt. 4:44).
M.   "So David says, 'Unless your Torah had been my delight,
      I should then have perished in my affliction' (Ps. 119:92)."

The exegetical parable finds the hope in what Israel remembers, which is the promises in the torah of Israel's redemption; the Torah is the marriage-contract, and the correspondence of the parable to the exegetical task is exact.

LXXXVI.i.

5.   A.   "'The Lord is my portion,' says my soul, 'therefore I will hope
            in him'" (Lamentations 3:24):
      B.   R. Abbahu in the name of R. Yohanan said, "The matter may
            be compared to the case of a king who came into a town, and
            with him were his dukes, lords, and generals. The chief citi-
            zens of the town were sitting in the midst.
      C.   "This one said, 'I will take a duke to my house,' and another,
            'I will take a lord to my house,' and a third, 'I will take a gen-
            eral to my house.'
      D.   "Now there was one astute fellow there, who said, 'I shall take
            only the king alone, for all of the others pass on, but he never
            passes on.'
      E.   "So of the nations of the world, these serve the sun, those the
            moon, others wood, others stone.
      F.   "But the Israelites serve only the Holy One, blessed be He: 'The
            Lord is my portion,' says my soul, 'therefore I will hope in him,'"
      G.   "for I proclaim his unity twice a day: 'Hear O Israel, the
            Lord our God, the Lord is one.'"

The perfect correspondence between E-F and the exegetical parable leaves no anomalies in the parable, which originates in its assigned task.

XCVIII.i.

1.   A.   "You have taken up my cause, O Lord, you have redeemed
            my life. You have seen the wrong done to me, O Lord; judge
            you my cause" (lamentations 3:58-59):
      B.   Hadrian—may his bones rot!—proclaimed, "Whoever does not
            greet the king will be put to death."
      C.   A Jew passed by and greeted him.
      D.   He said, "Who are you?"
      E.   He said to him, "A Jew."
      F.   He said to him, "You, a Jew, pass the king and greet him! Take
            him out and kill him."

G.   Then another one passed by and did not greet him.

H.   The king asked, "Who are you?"

I.   "A Jew."

J.   He said to him, "You, a Jew, pass the king and do not greet him! Take him out and kill him."

K.   The senators said to him, "We don't really know what your policy is. This one who did not greet you, you kill, and that one who greeted you, you kill."

L.   He said to them, "Let me be! I know precisely how I am going to kill my enemies."

> M.   That is why the Community of Israel says, "You have taken up my cause, O Lord, you have redeemed my life. You have seen the wrong done to me, O Lord; judge you my cause."

> N.   And the Holy Spirit cries out, "You have seen all their vengeance, all their devices against me."

1. *On what basis does the narrative attain coherence, e.g., what is the action or event that precipitates the telling of the tale?* B-F, G-J, coalesce and reach their point at K-L. The exegetical after-word, M, N, then situate the narrative in context.

2. *What point of conflict or intersection of wills accounts for the telling of the tale and how is the point of tension resolved?* The conflict is between the two policies toward the passing Israelites, which apparently contradict. The resolution is at L.

3. *How, in light of other, comparable, pieces of writing and the data that they yield, is the narrative classified, and what are its indicative formal qualities, e.g., long or short, complex or simple?* The tripartite composition is unitary, simple, and brief; no detail is extraneous.

CHAPTER FOURTEEN

LAMENTATIONS RABBAH
PARASHAH FOUR

CII:i.

3.   A.   Another matter concerning "The precious sons of Zion, [worth their weight in fine gold, how they are reckoned as earthen pots, the work of a potter's hands!" (Lamentations 4:2):"

B.   What made them precious?

C.   When one of them was invited to a banquet, he would not go unless he was invited twice.

CII:ii.

1.   A.   There was the case of a man who was in Jerusalem and made a banquet. He said to his messenger, "Go and bring my friend, Qamsa."

B.   He went and brought to him his enemy, Bar Qamsa.

C.   The latter came in and sat himself among the invited guests.

D.   He said to him, "How is it that you are my enemy and you sit in my house? Get out of here."

E.   He said to him, "Since I have come, don't humiliate me. I'll pay you back for the cost of whatever I eat."

F.   He said to him, "You are not to recline at this banquet."

G.   He said to him, "Get out of here."

H.   R. Zechariah b. Eucolus, who was there, could have stopped it, but he did not intervene.

I.   Bar Qamsa then left. He said to himself, "Since these are feasting in luxury, I am going to go and inform against them at court."

J.   What did he do? He went to the ruler and said to him, "These sacrifices that you contribute [to the temple] they eat, and they offer others in their place [which are inferior]."

K.   He put him off [rejecting the charge].

L.   He went back to him again and said, "These sacrifices that you contribute [to the temple] they eat, and they offer others in their place [which are inferior]. If you don't believe me, send an hyparch and some animals for sacrifice back with me, and you will know that I am not a liar."

M. He sent with him a third-grown calf.

N. While they were on the way, the hyparch dozed off, and the other got up by night and secretly blemished the beasts [so that they could not be offered on the altar and had to be replaced].

O. When the priest saw it, he substituted others for them.

P. The king's agent said to him, "Why don't you offer the animals I brought?"

Q. He said to him, "I'll do it tomorrow."

R. He came on the third day, but the priest had not offered them up.

S. He sent word to the king, "That matter involving the Jews is true."

T. The king immediately came forth against the temple and destroyed it.

U. That is the source of the saying, "Because of the difference between Qamsa and Bar Qamsa, the temple was destroyed."

> V. R. Yosé said, "It was the self-effacing character of Zechariah b. Eucolus that burned the temple."

1. *On what basis does the narrative attain coherence, e.g., what is the action or event that precipitates the telling of the tale?* The opening unit, A-H, signals the continuity of an act of vengeance. That is set forth at I-M, and realized at N-R. Then comes the result, which imposes coherence on the antecedent parts and indicates their point. The purpose of the story is to account for the destruction of Jerusalem by invoking the poor conduct of the Jerusalemites.

2. *What point of conflict or intersection of wills accounts for the telling of the tale and how is the point of tension resolved?* The tension is between the triviality of the erroneously-delivered invitation and the formidable result of the error, underscored at U.

3. *How, in light of other, comparable, pieces of writing and the data that they yield, is the narrative classified, and what are its indicative formal qualities, e.g., long or short, complex or simple?* This simple, anecdotal narrative registers its point with great clarity.

CII:i.

2. A. Another matter concerning "The precious sons of Zion, [worth their weight in fine gold, how they are reckoned as earthen pots, the work of a potter's hands!]:"

B. What made them precious?

C. None of them produced a defective child in limb or a child blemished in body.

3. A. There was the case of Joshua b. Hananiah, who went to Rome.

B. He was told that there was a boy in prison, kept there for pederasty.

C. He went and saw there a youngster of beautiful eyes, a lovely face, curly locks, who was used for pederasty.

D. He stood by the door to find out his character, reciting to him this verse, "Who gave Jacob for a spoil, and Israel to the robbers" (Isa. 42:24).

E. The boy responded, "Did not the Lord? He against whom we have sinned, and in whose ways they would not walk, neither did they obey his Torah" (Isa. 42:24).

F. When he heard this, he wept and recited the verse, "The precious sons of Zion, [worth their weight in fine gold, how they are reckoned as earthen pots, the work of a potter's hands!]"

G. He said, "I call heaven and earth to witness against me, that I will not budge without ransoming him at any price they demand."

H. They say that he did not budge without ransoming him at any price they demanded.

I. And not much time went by before he became a teacher in Israel.

J. And what was his name? R. Ishmael b. Elisha.

1. *On what basis does the narrative attain coherence, e.g., what is the action or event that precipitates the telling of the tale?* The story reaches its climax at the conclusion: the boy became famous as a sage, but even in his youth, he saved his own life by his knowledge of the Torah. Thus A-E, F-H, set cohere only at I-J, which imparts meaning to each preceding detail.

2. *What point of conflict or intersection of wills accounts for the telling of the tale and how is the point of tension resolved?* The contrast between the boy's mastery of Torah and his fate is resolved by the sage's action, precipitated by the boy's own achievement.

3. *How, in light of other, comparable, pieces of writing and the data that they yield, is the narrative classified, and what are its indicative formal qualities, e.g., long or short, complex or simple?* It is a simple anecdote.

CVIII.i.

3. A. ["Now their visage is blacker than soot, they are not recognized in the streets; their skin has shriveled upon their bones, it has become as dry as wood" (Lamentations 4:8):] "they are not

recognized in the streets; their skin has shriveled upon their bones, it has become as dry as wood" (Lamentations 4:8):

B. Said R. Eliezer b. R. Sadoq, "There is the case of a poor man who came and stood at the door of father's house. Father said to me, 'My son, go and see whether or not he is a Jerusalemite.'

C. "I went and found a woman, whose hair had fallen out, so that you could not tell whether it was a man or a woman.

D. "She asked only for a preserved fig.

E. "That illustrates the verse: 'their skin has shriveled upon their bones, it has become as dry as wood.'"

The *Ma'aseh* illustrates the cited verse.

CXI.i.

2. A. "and he kindled a fire in Zion, which consumed its foundations" (Lamentations 4:11):

B. It is written, "A Psalm of Asaph. O God, the gentiles have come into your inheritance" (Ps. 79:1).

C. What is required is not "psalm" but "a weeping of Asaph" or "a lament of Asaph" or "a dirge of Asaph." So why say, "A psalm of Asaph"?

D. The matter may be compared to the case of a king who prepared a bridal canopy for his son. He fixed it up, plastered it, cemented and decorated it.

E. But the son angered the father, so he tore it down. He went into the room, tore the curtains, broke the rods.

F. The son's pedagogue began to sit and play [using a piece of rod as a flute].

G. They said to him, "The king has destroyed this chamber, and you are sitting and playing a song?"

H. He said to him, "I am playing a song because the king has poured out his anger on his son's bridal chamber, but not on his son."

I. So people said to Asaph, "The Holy One, blessed be He, has destroyed his sanctuary, and you are sitting and singing a psalm?"

J. He said to them, "That is precisely why I am singing a song, for the Holy One, blessed be He, has poured out his anger on wood and stones, but not on Israel."

K. That is in line with this verse: "and he kindled a fire in Zion, which consumed its foundations."

The exegetical parable tracks the assigned task, I-J, though the parable is considerably more elaborate than the situation it illustrates. Indeed, the details of the parable are disproportionate to their task. All that is generic, nonetheless, is the king/prince. The rest is particular to its case.

CXIX.i.2= L.i.4

>**4.** A. The wife of Trajan—may his bones be pulverized—gave birth to a child on the ninth of Ab, while the Jews were observing rites of mourning, and the child died on Hanukkah.
>
>B. They said to one another, "What shall we do? Shall we kindle the Hanukkah lights or not?"...

This item is dealt with above.

CHAPTER FIFTEEN

LAMENTATIONS RABBAH
PARASHAH FIVE

CXL:I = SIFRÉ DEUTERONOMY XLIII:III.7-8

1.   A.   "for Mount Zion which lies desolate; jackals prowl over it" (Lamentations 5:18):

B.   Rabban Gamaliel, R. Joshua, R. Eleazar b. Azariah, and R. Aqiba went to Rome. They heard the din of the city of Rome from a distance of a hundred and twenty miles.

C.   They all begin to cry, but R. Aqiba began to laugh.

D.   They said to him, "Aqiba, we are crying and you laugh?"

E.   He said to them, "Why are you crying?"

F.   They said to him, "Should we not cry, that idolators and those who sacrifice to idols and bow down to images live securely and prosperously, while the footstool of our God has been burned down by fire and become a dwelling place for the beasts of the field? So shouldn't we cry?"

G.   He said to them, "That is precisely the reason that I was laughing. For if those who outrage him he treats in such a way, those who do his will all the more so!"

2.   A.   There was the further case of when they were going up to Jerusalem. When they came to the Mount of Olives they tore their clothing. When they came to the Temple mount and a fox came out of the house of the Holy of Holies, they began to cry. But R. Aqiba began to laugh.

B.   "Aqiba, you are always surprising us. Now we are crying and you laugh?"

C.   He said to them, "Why are you crying?"

D.   They said to him, "Should we not cry, that from the place of which it is written, 'And the ordinary person that comes near shall be put to death' (Num. 1:51) a fox comes out? So the verse of Scripture is carried out: 'for Mount Zion which lies desolate; jackals prowl over it.'"

E.   He said to them, "That is precisely the reason that I was laughing. For Scripture says, 'And I will take for myself faithful witnesses to record, Uriah the priest and Zechariah the son of Jeberechiah' (Isa. 8:2).

> F.   "Now what is the relationship between Uriah and Zechariah? Uriah lived in the time of the first temple, Zechariah in the time of the second!
>
> G.   "But Uriah said, 'Thus says the Lord of hosts: Zion shall be plowed as a field, and Jerusalem shall become heaps' (Jer. 26:18).
>
> > H.   "And Zechariah said, 'There shall yet be old men and old women sitting in the piazzas of Jerusalem, every man with his staff in his hand for old age' (Zech. 8:4).
> >
> > I.   "And further: 'And the piazzas of the city shall be full of boys and girls playing in the piazzas thereof' (Zech. 8:5).
> >
> > J.   "Said the Holy One, blessed be He, 'Now lo, I have these two witnesses. So if the words of Uriah are carried out, the words of Zechariah will be carried out, while if the words of Uriah prove false, then the words of Zechariah will not be true either.'
> >
> > K.   "I was laughing with pleasure because the words of Uriah have been carried out, and that means that the words of Zechariah in the future will be carried out."
> >
> > L.   They said to him, "Aqiba, you have given us consolation. May you be comforted among those who are comforted."

1.   *On what basis does the narrative attain coherence, e.g., what is the action or event that precipitates the telling of the tale?* The matched stories, 1, 2A-G, extended at H-K, form a tight match and make sense only when joined. But each works on its own, since 1.E imparts coherence to No. 1, and the composite of 2.G-K does the same for No. 2. There, 2.E-F makes a more elaborate statement than 1.D. Remove 1.E and its counterpart and the two stories become gibberish, which shows how the whole aims at that climax and conclusion. The repetition of the program of No. 1 at No. 2 intensifies the effect of the whole but changes nothing. What we have are two authentic stories, coherent within the teleological logic that, in this study, signifies the authentic narrative.

2.   *What point of conflict or intersection of wills accounts for the telling of the tale and how is the point of tension resolved?* This question reinforces the foregoing. The contrast between expectation and reality, between Israel's standing and Israel's condition, creates a tension, precisely the tension that Aqiba resolves in his climactic statement.

3.   *How, in light of other, comparable, pieces of writing and the data that they yield, is the narrative classified, and what are its indicative formal qualities, e.g., long or short, complex or simple?* These exegetical narratives do more than form a dramatic setting for an exchange of set-piece speeches, since the setting and the interaction of the players and the setting form the basis for the story. Matching the two incidents is integral.

CHAPTER SIXTEEN

NARRATIVES IN
LAMENTATIONS RABBAH

The theme of Lamentations Rabbati, a systematic verse-by-verse commentary to the book of Lamentations with an elaborate prologue as well, is Israel's relationship with God. Its message concerning Israel and God is that, with special reference to the destruction of the Temple in 586 B.C.E and in 70 C.E., and to the catastrophe of Bar Kokhba's rebellion, the stipulative covenant set forth in the Torah governs that relationship. Therefore nothing is arbitrary, and everything that happens to Israel makes sense and bears meaning. With the covenant to explain events, Israel is not helpless before its fate but through its conduct controls its own destiny.

Accordingly, Lamentations Rabbah sets forth a covenantal theology, realized in history, in which Israel and God have mutually and reciprocally agreed to bind themselves to a common Torah. The rules of the relationship are such that an infraction triggers its penalty willy-nilly; but obedience to the Torah likewise brings the reward of redemption. The upshot is this: Israel suffers because of sin, God will respond to Israel's atonement, on the one side, and loyalty to the covenant in the Torah, on the other. And when Israel has attained the merit that accrues through the Torah, God will redeem Israel. In that theological framework the events of 586 and 70 and their counterparts make sense. But that theological proposition does not capture the way in which Lamentations Rabbah recasts and renews the book of Lamentations, only the way in which it imparts coherence to that work. What is genuinely fresh, yet completely authentic to the foundation-document, is the Rabbinic account of how God wept for, and with, Israel. And it is through authentic narrative, not through exegesis, parable, or precedent, that the Rabbinic sages say so.

I. *The Authentic Narrative*

While principally an exegetical composite, Lamentations Rabbah sets
forth a vast and highly articulated corpus of authentic narrative
writing. The main body of the authentic narratives of the document
focuses upon the theological challenge of the exile of ancient Israel
to Assyria and Babylonia, the destruction of the Second Temple,
and the loss of the war led by Bar Kokhba. A cognate theme addresses Israel's relationships with the nations, and both Israel's and
the nations' relationships with God, relationships defined by God's
loathing of idolatry. And within the framework of theodicy, the theme
of tragedy—the human suffering and sense of loss—is ever-present.
Since the book of Lamentations raises all these themes, we cannot
find puzzling their paramount position within its narrative component as well.

What is more striking is the selection of narrative as the medium
for exploring them. Exegesis did not fully realize the compilers' goals,
nor did parable or precedent—the other two forms of narrative
writing we have seen in the documents that earlier came to closure—
accomplish their purpose. Only telling the story in detail, in the model
of the resort to narrative by the Torah and the prophets of Scripture, served. Telling the story formed for the compilers a necessary
medium for setting forth the theological message, because, as we shall
see, the details of the story embody that message in exemplary, concrete terms, with a consequent power and effect that a mere statement of theological abstraction cannot attain.

That explains, also, why the kind of narrative—sustained, not brief
and anecdotal, realized in a fair amount of development and characterization and plot-development—devoted to the theological
themes of the biblical book of Lamentations differs from the kind
devoted to the theological themes of Torah-study and glorification
of the sage. These narratives, differentiated by subject-matter, are
brief, undeveloped, acted out by stick-men, with much dialogue and
little action, and without deep engagement with matters of emotion.
And, it goes without saying, while Torah- and sage-stories involve
only Israelites, the document's narratives of destruction and catastrophe that portray both the theodicy of Israel's responsibility and
the tragedy that has come upon Israel introduce important gentile
figures. Otherwise these classifications of players, e.g., kings and
queens, rarely occur outside the framework of parables, for exam-

ple. But even there it is ordinarily assumed that the king/prince/ queen all are Israelites, as are all actors.

The contrast between Lamentations Rabbah, with its high proportion of authentic narratives, and Song of Songs Rabbah, with its preference for exegetical parables over authentic narratives, thus is not to be missed. The difference is documentary: each compilation selects the kind of narrative that serves its larger mission, defined by its subject matter. Nonetheless, just as the Mishnah contains authentic narratives of considerable weight, so the later documents encompass a variety of narratives, not all of them matching the documentary preference. Thus, even in Lamentations Rabbah not all the narratives fall into a single pattern or theme and articulation. That fact explains why our task is now to classify all the narratives (authentic and otherwise) by gross indicative traits of topic, theme, or proposition. What we want to find out is whether the authentic narratives fall into a single topical classification. In each case, we shall therefore ask about topic and proposition, on the one side, and narrative character: short and simple or long and complex, only dialogue or action and dialogue. These taxonomic indicators, very cursorily defined item by item, bear slight weight for literary criticism, but for the religious analysis of the writing they serve quite well to differentiate types of authentic narratives.

1.   II:i.3. Rabbi [Judah the Patriarch] would dispatch R. Assi and R. Ammi to go out and inspect the condition of the towns of the land of Israel They would go into a town and say to the people, "Bring us the guardians of the town." So the people would produce the captain of the guard and the senator and say to them, "Here are the guardians of the town. They said to them, "These are the guardians of the town? These are those who ravage the town." They said to them, "Then who are the guardians of the town? They said to them, "They are the scribes and teachers, who dwell upon, repeat, and keep the Torah day and night."

>   TOPIC AND PROPOSITION: The topic is Torah-study, and the proposition is that Torah-study protects the city.

>   NARRATIVE CHARACTER: We have a brief, exemplary anecdote, executed through what is said rather than sequences of actions.

2.   XXIV.ii.1. When the Holy One, blessed be He, considered destroying the house of the sanctuary, he said, "So long as I am within it, the nations of the world cannot lay a hand on it, I shall close my

eyes to it and take an oath that I shall not become engaged with it until the time of the end." Then the enemies came and destroyed it. Forthwith the Holy One, blessed be He, took an oath by his right hand and put it behind him: "He has drawn back his right hand from before the enemy" (Lam. 2:3). At that moment the enemies entered the sanctuary and burned it up. When it had burned, the Holy One, blessed be He, said, "I do not have any dwelling on earth any more. I shall take up my presence from there and go up to my earlier dwelling." At that moment the Holy One, blessed be He, wept, saying, "Woe is me! What have I done! I have brought my Presence to dwell below on account of the Israelites, and now that they have sinned, I have gone back to my earlier dwelling. Heaven forfend that I now become a joke to the nations and a source of ridicule among people." At that moment Metatron came, prostrated himself, and said before him, "Lord of the world, let me weep, but don't you weep!" He said to him, "If you do not let me weep now, I shall retreat to a place in which you have no right to enter, and there I shall weep." Said the Holy One, blessed be He, to the ministering angels, "Let's go and see what the enemies have done to my house." Forthwith the Holy One, blessed be He, and the ministering angels went forth, with Jeremiah before them. When the Holy One, blessed be He, saw the house of the sanctuary, he said, "This is certainly my house, and this is my resting place, and the enemies have come and done whatever they pleased with it!" At that moment the Holy One, blessed be He, wept, saying "Woe is me for my house! O children of mine—where are you? O priests of mine—where are you? O you who love me—where are you? What shall I do for you? I warned you, but you did not repent." Said the Holy One, blessed be He, to Jeremiah, "Today I am like a man who had an only son, who made a marriage canopy for him, and the son died under his marriage canopy. Should you not feel pain for me and for my son? "Go and call Abraham, Isaac, Jacob, and Moses from their graves, for they know how to weep." He said to them, "I don't know." Moses left him and went to the ministering angels, for he had known them from the time of the giving of the Torah. He said to them, "You who serve on high! Do you know on what account I am summoned before the Holy One, blessed be He? They said to him, "Son of Amram! Don't you know that the house of the sanctuary has been destroyed, and the Israelites taken away into exile?" So he cried and wept until he came to the fathers of the world. They too forthwith tore their garments and put their hands on their heads, crying and weeping, up to the gates of the house of the sanctuary. When the Holy One, blessed be He, saw them, forthwith: "My Lord God of Hosts summoned on that day to weeping and lamenting, to tonsuring and girding with sackcloth."

TOPIC AND PROPOSITION: The destruction of the Temple

was mourned by God in heaven, who found himself engaged in debate by Jeremiah, Abraham, Isaac, Jacob, and Moses.

Narrative character: Attitudes and emotions figure, actions register, not only dialogue, and the players are treated as individuals, not merely as stick-figures. The narrative is autonomous of Scripture and its exegesis, and its principal point is that God wept at the destruction.

3.   XXIV:ii.3. Said R. Samuel bar Nahman, "When the Temple was destroyed, Abraham came before the Holy One, blessed be He, weeping, pulling at his beard and tearing his hair, striking his face, tearing his clothes, with ashes on his head, walking about the temple, weeping and crying, saying before the Holy One, blessed be He, How come I am treated differently from every other nation and language, that I should be brought to such humiliation and shame!' When the ministering angels saw him, they too composed lamentations, arranging themselves in rows, saying, 'the highways lie waste, the wayfaring man ceases' (Isa. 33:8)." Said the ministering angels before the Holy One, blessed be He, 'The highways that you paved to Jerusalem, so that the wayfarers would not cease, how have they become a desolation?' 'the wayfaring man ceases:' Said the ministering angels before the Holy One, blessed be He, 'How have the ways become deserted, on which the Israelites would come and go for the pilgrim festivals?' 'You have broken the covenant:' Said the ministering angels before the Holy One, blessed be He, 'Lord of the world, the covenant that was made with their father, Abraham, has been broken, the one through which the world was settled and through which you were made known in the world, that you are the most high God, the one who possesses heaven and earth.' 'He has despised the cities:' Said the ministering angels before the Holy One, blessed be He, 'You have despised Jerusalem and Zion after you have chosen them! Thus Scripture says, 'Have you utterly rejected Judah? Has your soul loathed Zion?' (Jer. 14:19). 'He regards not Enosh:' Said the ministering angels before the Holy One, blessed be He, 'Even as much as the generation of Enosh, chief of all idol worshippers, you have not valued Israel!' At that moment the Holy One, blessed be He, responded to the ministering angels, saying to them, 'How come you composing lamentations, arranging themselves in rows, on this account?' They said to him, 'Lord of the world! It is on account of Abraham, who loved you, who came to your house and lamented and wept. How come you didn't pay any attention to him?' He said to them, 'From the day on which my beloved died, going off to his eternal house, he has not come to my house, and

now "what is my beloved doing in my house" (Jer. 11:15)?' Said Abraham before the Holy One, blessed be He, 'Lord of the world! How come you have sent my children into exile and handed them over to the nations? And they have killed them with all manner of disgusting forms of death! And you have destroyed the house of the sanctuary, the place on which I offered up my son Isaac as a burnt-offering before you!?' Said to Abraham the Holy One, blessed be He, 'Your children sinned and violated the whole Torah, transgressing the twenty-two letters that are used to write it: "Yes, all Israel have transgressed your Torah" (Dan. 9:11).' Said Abraham before the Holy One, blessed be He, 'Lord of the world, who will give testimony against the Israelites, that they have violated your Torah?' He said to him, 'Let the Torah come and give testimony against the Israelites.' Forthwith the Torah came to give testimony against them. Said Abraham to her, 'My daughter, have you come to give testimony against the Israelites that they have violated your religious duties? and are you not ashamed on my account? Remember the day on which the Holy One, blessed be He, peddled you to all the nations and languages of the world, and no one wanted to accept you, until my children came to Mount Sinai and they accepted you and honored you! And now are you coming to give testimony against them on their day of disaster?' When the Torah heard this, she went off to one side and did not testify against them. Said the Holy One, blessed be He, to Abraham, 'Then let the twenty-two letters of the alphabet come and give testimony against the Israelites.' Forthwith the twenty-two letters of the alphabet came to give testimony against them. The aleph came to give testimony against the Israelites, that they had violated the Torah. Said Abraham to her, 'Aleph, you are the head of all of the letters of the alphabet, and have you now come to give testimony against the Israelites on the day of their disaster?' 'Remember the day on which the Holy One, blessed be He, revealed himself on Mount Sinai and began his discourse with you: "I [*anokhi*, beginning with aleph] am the Lord your God who brought you out of the Land of Egypt, out of the house of bondage" (Ex. 20:2). But not a single nation or language was willing to take you on, except for my children! And are you now going to give testimony against my children?' Forthwith the aleph went off to one side and did not testify against them

> TOPIC AND PROPOSITION: Continuous with the foregoing, this enormous narrative takes up the topic of God and the destruction, and repeats the proposition that God mourned, along with all of his hosts, on that occasion.
>
> NARRATIVE CHARACTER: The dialogue serves as the medium of the story: God and the angels, God and

> Abraham, Abraham and the letters of the alphabet, Isaac, Jacob, Moses, Jeremiah; there is ample described action; only when Rachel intervenes does God promise to restore Israel to the Land.

4.   XXXV:v.2. Said R. Eleazar, "There was a case involving a caravan in which there was a merchant who was leading three hundred camels bearing pepper. He came by Tyre and found a certain tailor, sitting at the gate. He said to him, 'What are you selling?' He said to him, 'Pepper.' He said to him, 'Sell me a little.' He said to him, 'No, for all of it is for one [purchaser].' He said to him, 'You are going to sell it only to the Jewish town.' He came to the Jewish town and found another tailor sitting at the gate. He said to him, 'What are your camels carrying?' He said to him, 'Pepper.' He took him to a house, and showed him a pile of coins, saying to them, 'Look at this money. Does it circulate in your land?' [The other was satisfied and made the sale,] and he took his leave and went off in peace. After he had left, he went out to walk in the market place. He met one of his friends, who said to him, 'What are you bringing here?' He said to him, 'Pepper.' He said to him, 'If you have a little, sell it to me for a hundred denars, for I have a party to give.' He said to him, 'I have already sold it to a certain tailor, but I'll tell him to give you a little of it.' He went and found the house full of buyers, so that those who were in the first room secured an ounce each, and those in the second room half an ounce each, while those in the third received no attention at all."

> Without the marker, *Ma'aseh*, we should have here nothing other than an authentic narrative, reaching its climax at the end-point, at which the point of the whole registers.

> TOPIC AND PROPOSITION: The story deals with the prosperity and populous character of the Jewish towns of the Land of Israel, and its proposition is that there were many people (Lam. 1:1), who lived well.

> NARRATIVE CHARACTER: He did this, he said that, with such-and-such a result—that simple pattern prevails.

5.   XXV:vii.3 There is the following case [*Ma'aseh*]. There was a Jerusalemite who went to a town, where he was received by a friend. He spent some time there. The time came for him [to die], and he entrusted his property into the hands of his friend by whom he had been received. He said to him, "If my son comes to you and wants this property, if he does not carry out three acts of wisdom, do not

give him this property. The people had agreed that none of them would show the house of his father's friend to a stranger [who might ask for it]. The son heard and went to that place, and he knew the name of the man. He came and sat at the gate of the town. He saw someone carrying a load of twigs. He said to him, "Will you sell those twigs?"

> TOPIC AND PROPOSITION: The wisdom of the Jerusalemite secures for the son the inheritance that the father has provided for him.

> NARRATIVE CHARACTER: Dialogue carries the story, with the clever son of the Jerusalemite systematically overcoming the obstacles by solving the riddles his father left for him. The parts cohere as they unfold, the repeated pattern imposing cogency on the parts.

6. XXXV:vii.4 Four Jerusalemites went to Athens and were received by someone there. In the evening he made a meal for them. After they had eaten and drunk, he set four beds for them, one of them damaged [and supported by the next]. After they had eaten and drunk, he said, "I'm going to listen, for the Jerusalemites are very smart. I'll go and lie down near them to know what they are saying." One of them woke up, the one sleeping in the damaged bed, and said, "Do you think that I am sleeping on a bed? I am sleeping only on the ground." The second woke up and said, "Are you surprised at that? The meat that we were eating tasted of dog." The third woke up and said, "Are you surprised at that? The wine that we drank tasted like the grave." The fourth awoke and said, "Are you surprised at that? The householder here is not the father of his son." At that moment the man said, "One of them spoke the truth, and three told lies."

7. XXXV:vii.5. A Jerusalemite came to Athens, but no one wanted to extend him hospitality, so he went to a stall. After they had eaten and drink, he wanted to sleep there. The owner of the stall said to him, "We have made an agreement among us that no one from Jerusalem will sleep among us until he has jumped three jumps." He said to him, "I don't know how you people jump. You jump first, and I'll follow you." He took one jump, then another, and a third, and ended up outside the stall. The Jerusalemite went and locked the door after him. He said to him, "What's this?" He said to him, "What you wanted to do to me, I have done to you."

8. XXXV:vii.6 An Athenian came to Jerusalem and went to the school house and found youngsters there, but their master was not present. They said to him, "Let us make a deal that whoever is asked a question and cannot answer it will lose a piece of clothing." They said to him, "Explain the following: Nine go out but eight come in, two

pour out but one drinks, and twenty-four serve." He could not explain these things to them. They took away his clothes. He went to R. Yohanan, saying to him, "Is this how you act in your place? They strip guests naked." He said to him, "Go and tell them: [Cohen, p. 78:] the nine which go in are the nine months of gestation, and the eight that come out are the eight days of circumcision,

9.   XXXV:vii.7. An Athenian came to Jerusalem and came upon a child and gave him some money, saying to him, "Go, buy me cheese and eggs. When he came back, he said to him, "Tell me, as to these eggs, whence do they come, from a white chicken or a black one?"

10.   XXXV:vii.8. An Athenian came to Jerusalem and came upon a child and gave him some money, saying to him, "Go, buy me figs." There was an inferior portion, which the boy set before himself, and a better portion, before the visitor. He said to him, "Many thanks, well do people say that the Jerusalemites are very clever. Since the child knew that the money was mine, he chose the better portion and set it before me."

11.   XXXV:vii.9. An Athenian came to Jerusalem and came upon a child and gave him some money, saying to him, "Take this money and bring me something to eat now, with something left over for the way." He went and brought him salt.

12.   XXXV:vii.10. An Athenian came to Jerusalem and came upon a broken mortar. He took it and went to a tailor, saying to him, "Sew this broken mortar for me." He took out a handful of sand, saying to him, "Twist this into thread for me, and I'll sew the mortar."

13.   XXXV:vii.11. An Athenian came to Jerusalem and came upon a priest, saying to him, "How much of that load of wood will turn into smoke?" He said to him, "When it is damp, all of it, when it is dry, a third is smoke, a third ash, and a third fire."

14.   XXXV:vii.12. An Athenian came to Jerusalem and wanted to learn wisdom. When he came to leave, he bought a slave, blind in one eye. The one who had sold the slave said to him, "By your life, he is very clever and can see at a distance." When they had come out of the gate, the slave said to him, "Make haste, so we may overtake the caravan. He said to him, "Is there a caravan before us?" He said to him, "Yes, and there is a she-camel in front of us, blind in one eye; it has twins in its womb; it is carrying two skin bottles, one with wine, the other, vinegar; it is four miles away, and the camel driver is a gentile."

15.   XXXV:vii.13. Someone from Athens was making fun of the locals of Jerusalem. They said, "Who will go and bring him to us?" One of them said, "I'll bring him to you, with his head shaved." He went to Athens and stayed with him. He was walking in the market place, and one of his sandals broke. He gave it to a workman, saying, "Take this *tremis* [a sizable sum of money] and fix this sandal." He said to him, "Are sandals so costly where you live?" He said to him, "When they are expensive, they cost ten *denars,* and when cheap, eight."

TOPIC AND PROPOSITION: The composite of ten patterned narratives goes over the topic of the competition of Jerusalem and Athens for wisdom in solving
riddles. The proposition is that the Israelites best the
Athenians at wisdom.

NARRATIVE CHARACTER: The narratives fully articulate
the wisdom through action that is explained, expressed
in exchanges of dialogue as well. Some are brief exchanges, others elaborate, but all adhere to the simple
pattern: challenge, response, deed, dialogue, throughout.

16.   XXXV:vii.14. A Samaritan set himself up as a dream-interpreter,
       ridiculing people. Said R. Ishmael b. R. Yosé, "I shall go and see
       how this Samaritan is ridiculing people." Someone came to him and
       said, "I saw in my dream an olive tree feeding oil." said to him,
       "The olive means light and oil means light; you will see a lot of light."
       R. Ishmael b. R. Yosé, "May your spirit explode! That man has
       known [has committed incest with] his mother."

17.   XXXV:vii.15. A Samaritan said, "I want to go to see a certain sage
       of the Jews who makes fun of everybody. He said to him, "I saw in
       my dream four cedars, four sycamores, a hide stuffed with straw,
       and an ox riding on them."

18.   XXXV:vii.16. Another came and said to him, "In planting season
       I dreamed of an olive tree." He said to him, "You will see a lot of
       light."

19.   XXXV:vii.17. There was the case of a disciple who was in session
       before R. Yohanan, who explained matters to no avail. He said to
       him, "What's wrong that you don't understand?" He said to him,
       "I saw in my dream three bad things, and I don't know what they
       mean."

20.   XXXV:vii.18.Another one said to him, "I dreamed that I did not
       have pants on." He said to him, "That is not a bad sign but a good
       one. When the Festival [of Tabernacles] comes, you will have noth-
       ing."

21.   XXXV:vii.19. Someone came to R. Yosé b. Halafta and said, "I
       was shown in my dream, 'Go to Cappadocia and find your father's
       property.'

22.   XXXV:vii.20. There was the case of a woman who came to R.
       Eleazar and said, "I saw in my dream that the beam of the house
       was split."

23.   XXXV:vii.21. Another time she came and did not find him there,
       but did find his disciples. She said to them, "Where is your mas-
       ter?" She said to them, "I saw in my dream that the beam of the
       house was split."

TOPIC AND PROPOSITION: The topic of the eight anecdotes is dream-interpretation, and the proposition is
that sages have the power to interpret dreams.

NARRATIVE CHARACTER: The encounter between the
dreamers and the interpreters is realized in exchanges
of dialogue; these scarcely qualify as authentic narratives at all.

24. XXXV:vii. 22. There is the case of R. Joshua, who was walking on
the way, and someone walking on the way saw him. He said to him,
"What are you doing?" He said to him, "I am walking on the way."
He said to him, "Well said, for robbers like you have trodden it [steal-
ing private property and making it public property through usu-
fruct]." He was walking along and found a child at a crossroad. He
said to him, "What is the nearest way to town?" He said to him,
"This way is near and far, and that is far and near."

25. XXXV.vii.23. It has been taught on Tannaite authority: They leave
over peah of a dish prepared in a boiling pot and it goes without
saying, of one prepared in a tightly covered stew pot. There is the
following precedent: R. Joshua b. Hananiah lodged with a widow,
and she brought him a dish on the first day, and he ate it and did
not leave peah; the second day and he did not leave peah; and as
to the third day, what did she do? She oversalted a dish of pounded
grain, and when he tasted it, he did not touch it. She said to him,
"Why did you leave aside the dish of pounded grain? He said to
her, "I had already eaten during the day." She said to him, "If you
had already eaten during the day, why didn't you decline the bread
in the way in which you declined the grain? Maybe you left it over
as peah? And why did you not leave peah from the two dishes you
ate as you left it from this pounded grain?" Said R. Joshua, "No
one ever got the better of me in an argument than those children
and this widow and the little girl "so exemplifying the verse, 'she
that was great among the nations.'"

      TOPIC AND PROPOSITION: The wisdom of the Israelite
      child even exceeds the cleverness of the sage, who
      acknowledges that fact.

      NARRATIVE CHARACTER: Action and comment, action
      and comment, set forth the riddle and then convey the
      resolution thereof.

26. XXXIX:ii.2. In Jerusalem were three rich men, any one of whom
had the resources to feed the city for five years: Ben Sisit, Ben Kalba-
Shabua, and Naqdimon Ben Gurion. And there also was Ben
Battiah, son of Rabban Yohanan b. Zakkai's daughter, who was in

charge of the stores. He went and burned all the stores. Rabban Yohanan ben Zakkai heard and cried, "Woe!" He sent and summoned him, saying to him, "Why did you cry, 'woe'?" He said to him, "I did not say 'woe' but 'wow.'" Through the difference between "woe" and "wow," Rabban Yohanan ben Zakkai was saved.

27. XXXIX:ii.3 Three days later Rabban Yohanan ben Zakkai went out to stroll in the market, and he saw people boiling straw and drinking the water. He said, "Can people who boil straw and drink the water stand before the armies of Vespasian? The simple fact is that I have to get myself out of here." Rabban Yohanan sent to Ben Battiah, "Get me out of here." He said to him, "We have agreed that no one is going to get out except for a corpse. He said to him, "Get me out as a corpse." R. Eliezer carried him at the head, R. Joshua at the feet, and Ben Battiah walked in front. When they got to the gates, the guards wanted to stab the corpse. Ben Battiah said to them, "Do you want people to say that when our teacher died, they stabbed his body?" They let them pass.

28. XXXIX:ii,4. Rabban Yohanan b. Zakkai emerged and went among Vespasian's troops, saying to them, "Where is the king?" They went and told Vespasian, "A Jew wants you." He said to them, "Bring him along." When he came in, he said, *"Vive domine Imperator!"* Vespasian said to him, "You greet me as a king but I am not, and if the king hears, he will assassinate me." He said to him, "If you are not a king, you will be, because the temple will be destroyed only by the power of a king: 'And Lebanon shall fall by a mighty one' (Isa. 10:34)."

29. XXXIX:ii,5. They took [Rabban Yohanan ben Zakkai] and put him inside the innermost of seven rooms and asked him what time of night it was. He told them. From his study [he kept repeating traditions, and these told him the passage of time].

30. XXXIX:ii,6. They took [Rabban Yohanan ben Zakkai] and put him inside the innermost of seven rooms and asked him what time of night it was. He told them. From his study [he kept repeating traditions, and these told him the passage of time].

31. XXXIX:ii,7. Three days later Vespasian went to wash at Gophna. After he had bathed, he came out and put on his shoes. But when he had put on one of his shoes, they brought him a writing from Rome that the king had died and the citizens of Rome had crowned him king. He wanted to put on the other shoe and he could not put it on his foot. He sent for Rabban Yohanan ben Zakkai and asked, "Can you tell me why all these years I have been able to put on these shoes, but when I put on one of them and wanted to put on the other, it would not go on my foot?" He said to him, "You have heard good news: 'A good report makes the bones fat' (Prov. 15:30)."

32. XXXIX:ii,8. The generals began to speak in parables before him: "As to a cask in which a snake has nested, what is to be done with

it?" He said to him, "Bring a charmer and charm the snake." Said Amgar [Cohen: Pangar], "Kill the snake and break the cask." If a snake nested in a tower, what is to be done with it?" Bring a charmer and charm the snake, and leave the tower be." Said Amgar, "Kill the snake and burn the tower."

33.   XXXIX:ii,9. Vespasian said to Rabban Yohanan ben Zakkai, "Ask for something, and I shall give it to you." He said to him, "I ask you to leave the city and go away." He said to him, "The citizens of Rome did not make me king except to carry out public policy, and you tell me to leave the city and go away?! Ask something else, and I will do it." He said to him, "I ask you to leave the western gate, which leads to Lydda, and spare everyone who leaves up to the fourth hour."

34.   XXXIX:ii,10. After he had come and conquered the city, he said to him, "If you have a relative there, send and bring him out." He sent R. Eliezer and R. Joshua to bring out R. Saddoq, whom they found at the city gate. When he came, Rabban Yohanan stood up before him. Vespasian asked, "Are you honoring this emaciated old man? He said to him, "By your life, if in Jerusalem there had been one more like him, even though your army were twice as big, you would not have been able to take the city."

35.   XXXIX:ii,11. When they had conquered the city, he divided the destruction of the four ramparts to the four generals, with the western one to Pangar. Heaven had decreed that the western wall should never be destroyed. The three other generals destroyed their parts, but he did not destroy his. He said to him, "If I had destroyed my part as the others destroyed theirs, the kingdoms that will arise after you would never know about the great glory of what you have destroyed. But when people look [at the western wall], they will say, 'See the power of Vespasian from what he destroyed!'"

> TOPIC AND PROPOSITION: The topic is the destruction of the Temple, and the proposition is that the sage had the wisdom to survive and secure the survival of the Torah.
>
> NARRATIVE CHARACTER: A series of ten connected anecdotes are strong together, all of them fairly brief and self-contained, and the connections between one and the next are formal, not substantive. The paramount medium is dialogue; there are very few sequences of described action.

36.   L.i.1. "For these things I weep; my eyes flow with tears; for a comforter is far from me, one to revive my courage; my children are desolate, for the enemy has prevailed" (Lamentations 1:16): Vespasian—may his bones be pulverized!—filled three ships with

men and women of the nobility of Jerusalem, planning to place them in the brothels of Rome. When they had embarked on the sea, they said, "Is it not enough for us that we have angered our God in his holy house? Shall we now outrage him overseas as well?" They said, "Now if these, who are built for sexual relations, do not want it, as to us, how much the more so!" They said to them, "Do you think that if we throw ourselves into the sea, we shall have a portion in the world to come?" The Holy One, blessed be He, enlightened them with this verse: "The Lord said, I will bring them back from Bashan, I will bring them back from the depths of the sea" (Ps. 68:23). "I will bring them back from the depths of the sea:" this is meant literally.

> TOPIC AND PROPOSITION: The topic is the aftermath of the destruction, the disposition of the captives, and the proposition is that the Israelites preferred death to profaning God's name, and they further attributed their fate to sin against God.

> NARRATIVE CHARACTER: Dialogue serves as the medium for the narrative.

37. L.i.2. "For these things I weep:" Hadrian—may his bones be pulverized—set up three guards, one in Emmaus, one in Kefar Leqatia, and the third in Bethel in Judah. He sent forth a proclamation, saying, "Wherever a Jew is located, let him come out, because the king wants to assure him." The heralds made this announcement and caught Jews, in line with this verse: "And Ephraim is become like a silly dove, without understanding" (Hos. 7:11). [The Jews who were caught were taunted:] "Instead of asking that the dead be resurrected, pray that those alive will not be caught." Those who understood did not come out of hiding, but those who did not gathered in the valley of Bet Rimmon. Hadrian] said to his general, "Before I am done eating this piece of cake and chicken leg, I want to be able to look for a single one of these yet alive and not find him." He surrounded them with the legions and slaughtered them, so the blood streams as far as Cyprus.

> TOPIC AND PROPOSITION: The topic is the aftermath of the defeat by Hadrian, and the proposition is that it was cruel and bloody.

> NARRATIVE CHARACTER: A combination of described action and dialogue sustains the narrative.

38. L.i.3. There was the case of one band that was hidden in a cave. They said to one of them, "Go out and bring us one of those who were killed," which they ate. One day they said, "Let one of us go

and if he finds something, let him bring it, and we shall have something to eat." He went out and found his father killed, and he buried him and marked the spot. He came back and said, "I found nothing." Another one of them went out, in the direction of that deceased and found the body and brought it back to them and they ate it. Afterward they said to him, "Where did you find this corpse? He said to them, "In such and such a place. "And what was the mark?" He told them. The other said, "Woe is me, I have eaten the flesh of my father."

> TOPIC AND PROPOSITION: The aftermath of the defeat by Hadrian produces a horror, and the proposition is that the prophecies of Scripture were realized in those days.

> NARRATIVE CHARACTER: They main action is carried by dialogue.

39.   L.i.4 = CXIX.i.2 The wife of Trajan—may his bones be pulverized—gave birth to a child on the ninth of Ab, while the Jews were observing rites of mourning, and the child died on Hanukkah. They said to one another, "What shall we do? Shall we kindle the Hanukkah lights or not?" They said, "Let us light them, and what will be will be." They went and slandered the Jews to him, saying to his wife, "When your son was born, these Jews went into mourning, and when he died, they lit their lamps." She sent and said to her husband, "Instead of conquering the barbarians, come and conquer these Jews, who have rebelled against you. He had made a calculation that the trip would take ten days but the winds carried him and brought him in five days. He came into the synagogue and found the Jews occupied with this verse of Scripture: "The Lord will bring a nation against you from afar, from the end of the earth, as the vulture swoops down" (Dt. 28:49). He said to them, "I am he. I thought that I would come to you in ten days, but I came in five." He surrounded them with his legions and killed them.

> TOPIC AND PROPOSITION: The defeat by Trajan is followed by blood suppression and martyrdom. The proposition is, Scripture has foretold these things.

> NARRATIVE CHARACTER: The dialogue is augmented by described action, and the whole is guided by Scripture, which reveals to Trajan what he is to do.

40.   L.i.5. There was the case of the two children of R. Saddoq, high priest, who were taken captive, one a boy, the other a girl, each falling to a different officer. This one went to a whore and handed over the boy as her fee [for sex]. That one went to a storekeeper

and handed over the girl as his fee for wine. This exemplifies the
verse of Scripture, "And they have given a boy for a harlot and sold
a girl for wine" (Joel 4:3). After some days the whore went to the
storekeeper and said to him, "I have a Jewish boy and he is ready
for that girl you have. Let's match them up with one another, and
whatever they produce as a child we can divide among us. They
did so. They closed them up in a room, and the girl started crying.
The boy asked her, "Why are you crying?" She said to him, "Woe
for this daughter of the high priest who has gone and wed a slave."
He said to her, "Who is your father?" She said to him, "I am the
daughter of Saddoq, the high priest." He said to her, "Did you have
a brother or sister?" She said to him, "I had a brother, with a mole
on his shoulder. When he would come home from school, I would
uncover it and kiss it." He said to her, "If you were to see it, would
you recognize it? She said to him, "Yes." He bared his shoulder,
and they recognized one another, embraced, and kissed, until their
souls expired.

> TOPIC AND PROPOSITION: The topic is the fate of the
> captives, and the proposition is that virtue of the Isra-
> elite captives persists even in captivity.

> NARRATIVE CHARACTER: Dialogue bears the narrative
> burden.

41.   L.i.9 There was the case of Miriam, daughter of Tanhum, who was
taken captive with her seven sons with her. The ruler took and imprisoned them within seven rooms. Then he went and brought the
eldest and said to him, "Bow down before the idol. He said to him,
"God forbid! I will not bow down before the idol." "Why not?" "Because it is written in the Torah, 'I am the Lord your God' (Ex. 20:2)."
He forthwith had him taken off and killed.... Then he went and
brought the youngest and said to him, "My child, bow down before the idol." He said to him, "God forbid! I will not bow down
before the idol. "Why not?" "Because it is written in the Torah,
'Know this day and lay it to your heart that the Lord, he is God in
heaven above and on earth beneath, there is none else' (Dt. 4:39).
"Furthermore, we have taken an oath to our God that we will not
exchange him for any other: 'You have sworn the Lord this day to
be your God' (Dt. 26:17). And as we swore to him, so he swore to
us not to exchange us for another people: 'And the Lord has sworn
you this day to be his own treasure' (Dt. 26:18)."

> TOPIC AND PROPOSITION: "The ruler" unnamed mar-
> tyrs the Israelites for declining to bow down to idols,
> engaging in a detailed disputation on matters of theo-
> logical truth in the process. The proposition is, the

pagan ruler is cruel and the Israelite sons and their mother valiant.

NARRATIVE CHARACTER: The mixture of dialogue and action is made up mostly of dialogue, which bears the main burden of the tale: the refutation of the views of paganism.

42. L.i.14. The following case sustains the position of R. Yudan in the name of R. Aibu: There was a man who was ploughing, and one of his oxen lowed An Arab came by and said to him, "What are you?" He said to him, "I am a Jew." He said to him, "Untie your ox and your plough because the house of the sanctuary of the Jews has been destroyed." He said to him, "How do you know?" He said to him, "I know from the lowing of your ox." While he was engaged with him, the ox lowed again. He said to him, "Harness your ox and tie on your plough, for the redeemer of the Jews has been born." He said to him, "What is his name?" He said to him, "His name is Menahem [Redeemer]." "And as to his father, what is his name?" He said to him, "Hezekiah." He said to him, "And where do they live? He said to him, "In Birat Arba in Bethlehem in Judah." That man went and sold his oxen and sold his plough and bought felt clothing for children. He went into one city and left another, went into one country and left another, until he got there. All the villag ers came to buy from him. But the woman who was the mother of that infant did not buy from him. He said to her, "Why didn't you buy children's felt clothing from me?" She said to him, "Because a hard fate is in store for my child, because at his coming the house of the sanctuary was destroyed."

TOPIC AND PROPOSITION: The topic is the destruction and restoration of the Temple, and the proposition is, just as at the Messiah's coming, the Temple was destroyed, so at his coming it will be rebuilt.

NARRATIVE CHARACTER: While dialogue predominates, there are important actions in the exposition, involving the sale of the ox and purchase of clothing as a way of finding the Messiah-child.

43. LVIII:ii.10. For three and a half years Hadrian besieged Betar. R. Eleazar the Modiite was sitting in sack cloth and ashes, praying, and saying, "Lord of all the ages, do not sit in judgment today, do not sit in judgment today." Since [Hadrian] could not conquer the place, he considered going home. There was with him a Samaritan, who said to him, "My lord, as long as that old cock wallows in ashes, you will not conquer the city. But be patient, and I shall do some-

thing so you can conquer it today." He went into the gate of the city and found R. Eleazar standing in prayer. He pretended to whisper something into his ear, but the other paid no attention to him. People went and told Bar Koziba, "Your friend wants to betray the city." He sent and summoned the Samaritan and said to him, "What did you say to him?" He said to him, "If I say, Caesar will kill me, and if not, you will kill me. Best that I kill myself and not betray state secrets." Nonetheless, Bar Koziba reached the conclusion that he wanted to betray the city. When R. Eleazar had finished his prayer, he sent and summoned him, saying to him, "What did this one say to you?" He said to him, "I never saw that man." He kicked him and killed him.

> TOPIC AND PROPOSITION: The arrogance of Bar Kokhba is the topic, and the proposition is that the humility of the sage could have saved Betar, but the arrogance of Bar Kokhba is the cause of its fall.

> NARRATIVE CHARACTER: Dialogue supplemented by described action as required carries the narrative.

44. LVIII:ii. 19. There were two brothers in Kefar Haruba, and no Roman could pass by there, for they killed him. They decided, "The whole point of the thing is that we must take the crown and put it on our head and make ourselves kings. They heard that the Romans were coming to fight them. They went out to do battle, and an old man met them and said, "May the Creator be your help against them." They said, "Let him not help us nor hinder us!" Because of their sins, they went forth and were killed. They went, carrying his head to Hadrian. He said, "Who killed this one?" They said, "One of the Goths killed him," but he did not believe them. He said to them, "Go and bring me his body." They went to bring his body and found a snake around the neck. He said, "If the God of this one had not killed him, who could have vanquished him?"

> TOPIC AND PROPOSITION: The arrogance of the Israelite warriors is the topic, and the proposition is the same as the foregoing.

> NARRATIVE CHARACTER: As above, action supplements the dialogue that conveys the narrative.

45. LXXXIV.i.5. R. Judah b. Betera came to Nisibis on the eve of the great fast [the Day of Atonement]. He ate and finished [eating prior to the fast]. The head of the community came to him to invite him. He said to him, "I have already eaten and completed eating [prior to the fast]." He said to him, "Pay attention to me so that people should not say that the master paid no attention to me." Since he insisted, the other went with him. The head of the community there-

upon instructed his young servant, saying, "Any course which you serve us once must not be repeated." They brought before them eighty courses, and he took a small taste of each, and drink a cup of each jar of wine.

> TOPIC AND PROPOSITION: The topic is hospitality, and the proposition is, the aggressive host is boastful.

> NARRATIVE CHARACTER: The narrative is carried out through the deeds of the host and his staff and the comments and dialogue thereon.

46. XCVIII.i.1 Hadrian—may his bones rot!—proclaimed, "Whoever does not greet the king will be put to death." A Jew passed by and greeted him. He said, "Who are you?" He said to him, "A Jew." He said to him, "You, a Jew, pass the king and greet him! Take him out and kill him." Then another one passed by and did not greet him. The king asked, "Who are you?" "A Jew." He said to him, "You, a Jew, pass the king and do not greet him! Take him out and kill him." The senators said to him, "We don't really know what your policy is. This one who did not greet you, you kill, and that one who greeted you, you kill." He said to them, "Let me be! I know precisely how I am going to kill my enemies."

> TOPIC AND PROPOSITION: The harsh repression of Hadrian is the topic, and the proposition is, God knows what is being done to Israel and will avenge their blood.

> NARRATIVE CHARACTER: The narrative depends entirely on dialogue for exposition.

47. CII:ii.1. There was the case of a man who was in Jerusalem and made a banquet. He said to his messenger, "Go and bring my friend, Qamsa." He went and brought to him his enemy, Bar Qamsa. He said to him, "How is it that you are my enemy and you sit in my house? Get out of here." He said to him, "Since I have come, don't humiliate me. I'll pay you back for the cost of whatever I eat." He said to him, "You are not to recline at this banquet." Bar Qamsa then left. He said to himself, "Since these are feasting in luxury, I am going to go and inform against them at court." What did he do? He went to the ruler and said to him, "These sacrifices that you contribute [to the temple] they eat, and they offer others in their place [which are inferior]."

> TOPIC AND PROPOSITION: The theme is the cause of the destruction of Jerusalem, and the proposition is that enmity within Israel and cruelty of one Israelite to another led to acts of sedition that culminated in the destruction of the Temple.

> NARRATIVE CHARACTER: Dialogue is the principal ve-
> hicle for telling the story.

48.   CII:i.2.Another matter concerning "The precious sons of Zion,
       [worth their weight in fine gold, how they are reckoned as earthen
       pots, the work of a potter's hands!]:" 3. There was the case of Joshua
       b. Hananiah, who went to Rome. He was told that there was a boy
       in prison, kept there for pederasty. He went and saw there a young-
       ster of beautiful eyes, a lovely face, curly locks, who was used for
       pederasty. He stood by the door to find out his character, reciting
       to him this verse, "Who gave Jacob for a spoil, and Israel to the
       robbers" (Isa. 42:24). The boy responded, "Did not the Lord? He
       against whom we have sinned, and in whose ways they would not
       walk, neither did they obey his Torah" (Isa. 42:24). When he heard
       this, he wept and recited the verse, "The precious sons of Zion,
       [worth their weight in fine gold, how they are reckoned as earthen
       pots, the work of a potter's hands!]"

> TOPIC AND PROPOSITION: The fate of the captives is the
> theme, and the proposition is, the knowledge of To-
> rah is what saved the captives from their fate.

> NARRATIVE CHARACTER: The exchanges of dialogue,
> including verses of Scripture, form the means for tell-
> ing the story.

49.   CXL:i.1 = Sifré Deuteronomy XLIII:iii.7-8 "for Mount Zion which
       lies desolate; jackals prowl over it" (Lamentations 5:18): Rabban
       Gamaliel, R. Joshua, R. Eleazar b. Azariah, and R. Aqiba went to
       Rome. They heard the din of the city of Rome from a distance of
       a hundred and twenty miles. They all begin to cry, but R. Aqiba
       began to laugh. They said to him, "Should we not cry, that idola-
       tors and those who sacrifice to idols and bow down to images live
       securely and prosperously, while the footstool of our God has been
       burned down by fire and become a dwelling place for the beasts of
       the field? So shouldn't we cry?" He said to them, "That is precisely
       the reason that I was laughing. For if those who outrage him he
       treats in such a way, those who do his will all the more so!" (2). There
       was the further case of when they were going up to Jerusalem. When
       they came to the Mount of Olives they tore their clothing. When
       they came to the Temple mount and a fox came out of the house
       of the Holy of Holies, they began to cry. But R. Aqiba began to
       laugh.

> TOPIC AND PROPOSITION: The topic is the destruction
> of the Temple, and the proposition is, just as proph-
> ecy of destruction is realized, so prophecy of restora-
> tion is sure to come true.

NARRATIVE CHARACTER: Dialogue the whole way.

Now to summarize the results within the framework of the documentary hypothesis, I ask, what are the traits of authentic narratives in Lamentations Rabbah, and do we find a correlation between the interests of the document and the narrative corpus contained therein? In other words, have the compilers responded to a documentary program in the selection or narration of narratives? To answer that question, let us review the rather unrefined results in hand. What we see is that the themes of the Midrash-compilation and of the biblical book to which it attends have defined the paramount themes of the narratives collected therein.

1. TORAH-STORY
No. 1 (anecdote)
2. PROSPERITY OF ISRAEL PRIOR TO THE DESTRUCTION
No. 4 (several sequences of action, realized in dialogue)
3. DESTRUCTION OF THE TEMPLE; ISRAEL'S SUFFERING AND MARTYRDOM IN CONSEQUENCE; THE MESSIAH & RESTORATION
No. 2 (protracted narrative); No. 3 (protracted narrative); Nos. 26-35 (sequence of connected anecdotes [chapters], action and dialogue combined; No. 36 (dialogue, interspersed with verses of Scripture); No. 37 (described action and dialogue); No. 38 (described action and dialogue); No. 39 (described action and dialogue); No. 40 (anecdote realized through described action and dialogue); No. 41 (protracted sequence of connected, patterned exchanges between principals); No. 42 (action and dialogue); No. 43 (action and dialogue); No. 44 (action and dialogue, anecdote); No. 44 (as before); No. 46 (anecdote, as before); No. 47 (protracted account, with motivation and characterization, to account for the war against Jerusalem); No. 48 (Torah-knowledge saves Israelites in captivity; anecdote); No. 49 (protracted, balanced accounts, realized in dialogue deriving from verses of Scripture)
4. THE WIT OF JERUSALEMITES OR ISRAELITE CHILDREN/THE OBTUSENESS OF ATHENIANS
No. 5-15, 24-25 (several sequences of action, realized in dialogue);

> 5. DREAM INTERPRETATION
> Nos. 16-23 (brief, anecdotal, effected entirely in *he said
> to him... he said to him...*)
> 6. HOSPITALITY
> No. 45 (anecdote: action and dialogue)

The two large blocks of narrative materials, Nos. 3 and 4, attend to the capacious, encompassing theme, Israel among the nations. They moreover directly respond to the theological issues of the book of Lamentations. No. 2 explicitly joins in that discussion, and No. 5 is tacked on for reasons that are clear in context. So a rule of composition governing Lamentations Rabbah is this: narrative materials will focus on the condition of Israel among the nations in general, and the specific historical events that make Israel's condition among the nations an acute crisis and frame the theological challenges implicit therein.

The criterion—thematic congruence—on its own presents no surprise: what else should we expect except that a document's compilers will choose what pertains to the document? Why find astonishing that the compilers of exegesis of a document will on the whole limit themselves to topically pertinent items? The answer to both questions is, because as to narrative, other documents' compilers accomplish their goals through other kinds of narrative writing than authentic narratives. These elsewhere moreover are few, hardly important in proportion to the whole of the other documents we have examined, e.g., Song of Songs Rabbah or the Mishnah or Sifra. Authentic narrative serves uniquely well for Lamentations Rabbah, because it was only by telling the story in an artful manner that the compilers of the document could say fully and completely and accurately what they wished to convey. Not only so, but when, in a moment we turn to the Fathers According to Rabbi Nathan Text A, we shall see that, for its part, that authorship chooses stories of a quite different character. These are topically specific, fixed chapters in lives of important sages, their origins, Torah-study, death-scenes for example. In other words, on its own, the program of Lamentations Rabbah cannot be fully understood as consequential, with its choices as to modes of narrative writing grasped as significant. But when compared and contrasted with other canonical compilations, the narrative repertoire of the document at hand is seen to effect choices and respond to a documentary assignment.

That raises the question: why this, not that? Why the enormous corpus of authentic narratives in a document, the companions of which contain, proportionately, only modest proportions of authentic narratives, or none at all? In other words, why has the authorship of Lamentations Rabbah chosen a medium for accomplishing its goals that other documents we have probed ignore or treat as only marginally useful? In the present context, the question may be framed simply: why does Song of Songs Rabbah opt for exegetical parables, while Lamentations Rabbah prefers protracted, complex, authentic narratives, many of them enormous and beautifully articulated? Asked in this way, the question answers itself. Song of Songs Rabbah comments on a parabolic text and chooses the pseudo-narrative medium of exegetical parables to respond thereto. So it reads the Song of Songs the way the Song of Songs reads Israel's relationship to God: through the medium of a simile, realized, then, as a parable. Lamentations Rabbah addresses the large theological questions raised in the book of Lamentations, which, in the manner of biblical prophecy from Joshua through Kings uses historical narrative to frame a theology of history. So it reads the book of Lamentations the way Lamentations reads Israel's history: as the tragic outcome of Israel's own conduct, but as a tragic moment in the biography of God.

So in formulating protracted, enormous, continuous stories, one after another, the framers of Lamentations Rabbah have matched the book on which they comment with the kind of writing—sustained, narrative history—that dominates in the passages of Scripture subject to amplification. Just as these represent theology in the medium of historical narrative, so authentic, historical narrative serves as the chosen medium for theology of history in Lamentations Rabbah. Scripture with its focus upon the theological meaning of concrete, specific historical events, forms the model. In both cases, the Midrash-compilers, those of Song of Songs Rabbah and of Lamentations Rabbah respond in their choices of narrative writing to the book of Scripture assigned to them by carrying forward the very modes of thought and expression of that book, selecting, respectively, the one, the exegetical parable, the other, the (historical) narrative.

I think the Rabbinic sages who compiled Lamentations Rabbah will claim to have found the ideal medium for their message, uniquely able to tell how on earth the Temple was lost, and how in heaven God wept. Only through narrative do such things gain plausibility; only that way do they become accessible to thought.

II. *The Mashal*

After reviewing the forty-nine authentic narratives of various kinds, some of them remarkable for their articulation, we find that by contrast and in proportion the corpus of exegetical parables is paltry. In Lamentations Rabbah the parable proves a subordinated medium of exegesis and exposition, eighteen in all against forty-nine authentic stories, many of them enormous. We find fourteen exegetical parables, a pair in the Halakhic realm occurs, and an—in this context—unfamiliar utilization of the parable makes its appearance as well. These findings suggest that the classification of types and uses of parables can sustain further refinement, as other documents are subjected to systematic taxonomy of narrative writing.

When we recall that Song of Songs Rabbah required no fewer than fifty-six exegetical parables, but yielded only seven authentic narratives, none of them comparable to the massive constructions we have just examined, the picture is clear. The compilers of each document knew precisely what types of narratives they required, and they accordingly subordinated the narrative to documentary purposes.

A. The Halakhic Mashal

These are the only items that carry forward the now-ancient resort to parables to clarify, by concretizing, the transactions implicit in Halakhic rulings.

1.   LXXXI.i.3 R. Aha and Rabbis. R. Aha said, "Whoever says his prayers with the congregation finds that his prayer is heard. To what may the matter be compared? To the case of <u>ten men who made a crown for the king, and a poor man came along and helped out. What did the king say? 'Shall I not put on this crown [merely] on account of that poor man?' The king forthwith accepts the crown and puts it on his head</u>. So if there are ten righteous persons standing in the synagogue and saying their prayers, and a wicked man is standing with them, what does the Holy One, blessed be He, say? On account of that wicked man shall I not accept the prayer? I shall accept it as is.'"

> How the Halakhic parable illustrates the primacy of praying in a quorum of ten is not fully clear. The point is ten righteous persons' prayers are not rejected because of the presence of one wicked person. The com-

parison is then drawn to the case of the ten men who made the crown and a poor man who helped out—not a close parallel to the case that is rendered. That the king does not reject the crown of the ten who made the crown because of the participation of the poor man who helped out hardly corresponds to the matter of the wicked eleventh man.

2.   LXXXI.i.3 And rabbis say, "Whoever says his prayers after the congregation says theirs finds that his actions are spelled out [and scrutinized in detail]. To what may the matter be compared? To the case of <u>a king, whose sharecroppers and staff came before his presence to honor him. One person came late. Said the king, 'Let the wine bottle be stopped up for him.' What made this [insult] come about? That the man came late.</u> So too, whoever says his prayers after the congregation says theirs finds that his actions are spelled out [and scrutinized in detail].

    Here is a much more exact parallel. Now the Halakhic parable has someone who comes late and who is punished on that account, having called attention to himself by his lateness. The application is then precise.

These two items deal with the Halakhic preference for prayer in a quorum over prayer individually recited. They do not deal with detail, only with the general principle, and one of them does not exactly match the transaction it is meant to realize. They represent a considerably less successful utilization of the parable for Halakhic discourse than the counterparts in the Halakhic Midrash-compilations, which is hardly surprising in the present context.

B. The Exegetical Mashal

At issue once more is whether the exegetical parable matches its setting and responds to its assignment or is free-standing and adapted for its present purpose. The criterion, as before, is whether the details track the exegetical task or correspond to them only approximately. We shall see that most, though not all, of the exegetical parables originate in the particular task at hand and concretize, in generic figures, the transaction portrayed by the verse subject to amplification. The recurrence of the king/God, the queen or the prince/Israel once more marks the parable as a convention of constructing similes, some static, some dynamic, rather than as a genre of narrative writing (if the distinction makes a difference).

3. II.ii.,2 ["Alas! Lonely sits the city once great with people!" (Lamentations 1:1):] "Thus says the Lord of hosts: 'Summon the dirge-singers, let them come; send for the skilled women, let them come.' [Let them quickly start a wailing for us, that our eyes may run with tears, our pupils flow with water. For the sound of wailing is heard from Zion, How are we despoiled! How greatly are we shamed!]" (Jer. 9:16-18). R. Yohanan said, "The matter [of the exile of Israel, then Judah] may be compared to the case of <u>a king who had two sons. He lost his temper with the first, took a stick and beat him and threw him out of the house. He said, 'Woe for this one! From what luxury he has been thrown out!' He lost his temper with the second, took a stick and beat him and threw him out of the house. He said, 'I am the one [who is at fault], for my way of bringing them up is no good.'</u> So when the Ten Tribes went into exile, the Holy One, blessed be He, began to recite for them the following verse: 'Woe is they, for they have strayed from me' (Hos. 7:13). But when Judah and Benjamin went into exile, it is as though the Holy One, blessed be He, said, 'Woe is me for my hurt' (Jer. 10:19)."

4. II.ii.3. R. Simeon b. Laqish said, "The matter may be compared to the case of <u>a king who had two sons. He lost his temper with the first, took a stick and beat him and the son writhed and perished. He then lamented for him. He lost his temper with the second, took a stick and beat him and the son writhed and perished. He said, 'Now I don't have the strength to lament for them, but summon the dirge-singers, let them come; send for the skilled women, let them come.'</u> So when the Ten Tribes went into exile, the Holy One, blessed be He, began to lament for them: 'Hear you this word that I take up in lamentation over you, O house of Israel' (Amos 5:1). But when Judah and Benjamin went into exile, it is as though the Holy One, blessed be He, said, 'now I do not have the strength to lament for them, but "Summon the dirge-singers, let them come; send for the skilled women, let them come." Let them quickly start a wailing for us, [that our eyes may run with tears, our pupils flow with water].'

5. II.ii.4. Rabbis say, "The matter may be compared to the case of <u>a king who had twelve sons, and two of them died. He began to take comfort in the ten. Then another two died, and he began to take comfort from the eight. Then when all of them had died, he began to mourn for them [all]:</u> 'Alas! Lonely sits the city once great with people!'"

> The exegetical parables, particular to the case, take up the amplification of Jer. 9:6-18. The key language is "how greatly we are shamed," and the point is, with the first exile, God blamed the Israelites, but with the

second, he blamed himself. The second parable picks
up on "send for the skilled women...," and the third
moves us back to our base-verse. This is a rather complex composite, dealing with a single theme in response
to two clauses of one verse and another verse altogether
as well. But there can be no doubt that the parables
respond to the challenge of exegesis.

6.   XXXV:v.3. ["How lonely sits]the city that was full of people:"] If
      you wish to know how many multitudes there were in Jerusalem,
      you can ascertain it from the priests. R. Joshua of Sikhnin in the
      name of R. Levi said, "To what may the matter be compared?
      To <u>a large heap that stood in the marketplace, and no one could
      estimate its volume. There was a smart man there, who said to
      them, 'If you want to come to an estimate of its volume, you may
      come to an estimate based on the amount of priestly ration that
      is separated from it.</u>' So if you want to estimate the population of
      the Israelites you make an estimate based on the priesthood.

      The point of the parable is explicitly stated and links
      the parable to its exegetical setting. There can be no
      doubt as to what provoked the composition of the
      parable.

7.   L.ii.2. Said R. Abba b. Kahana in the name of R. Levi, "It is written,
      'And God said, 'Let the waters under the heavens be gathered
      together into one place' (Gen. 1:9). The Holy One, blessed be He,
      said, 'Let the waters gather themselves to me for the purpose that
      I will achieve through them.' Said R. Haggai in the name of R.
      Isaac, "The matter may be compared to the case of <u>a king who
      built a palace and gave residences in it to people who lacked the
      power of speech. They would get up in the morning and greet the
      king by making appropriate gestures with their fingers and with
      flag-signals. The king thought to himself, 'Now if these, who lack
      the power of speech, get up in the morning and greet me by means
      of gestures, using their fingers and flag-signals, if they had full powers
      of speech, how much the more so!' So the king gave residences in
      the palace to people possessed of full powers of speech. They got
      up and took possession of the palace [and seized it]. They said,
      'This palace no longer belongs to the king. The palace now be-
      longs to us!' Said the king, 'Let the palace revert to its original
      condition.</u>' So too, from the very beginning of the creation of the
      world, praise for the Holy One, blessed be He, went upward only
      from water. That is in line with the verse of Scripture which states,
      'From the roar of many waters' (Ps. 93:4). And what praise did
      they proclaim? 'The Lord on high is mighty' (Ps. 93:4). Said the
      Holy One, blessed be He, 'Now if these [waters], which have neither

mouth nor power of speech, so praise me, when mortals are created, how much the more so!' The generation of Enosh went and
rebelled against him, the generation of the flood went and rebelled
against him, the generation of the dispersion went and rebelled
against him. The Holy One, blessed be He, said, 'Let these be
taken away and let those [that were here before, that is, the primeval waters] come back.' That is in line with the following verse
of Scripture: 'And the rain was upon the earth forty days and forty
nights' (Gen. 7:12)."

> Here is a more conventional exegetical parable, but a
> story is told through verses of Scripture, "So too... when
> mortals are created. how much the more so... Enosh...
> dispersion... flood..., then the flood..." In that context,
> the parable replicates the story, in abstract terms. Now
> we do not have specific figures, e.g., the generation of
> Enosh, but a comparable transaction. But the parable
> can lay claim to an autonomous standing and is not
> wholly dependent, detail by detail, on the exegetical
> setting.

8.   L.ii.3 But it is only the Holy One, blessed be He, who said it, for he
      never sleeps: "Behold, he who keeps Israel neither slumbers nor
      sleeps" (Ps. 121:4). R. Judah b. R. Simon said, "The matter may
      be compared to <u>a shepherd who had only a staff and basket. He
      went and gathered a flock for himself. On one occasion wolves
      came and tore the flock to pieces. He said, 'I shall go back to my
      staff and basket.'</u> So the shepherd is the Holy One, blessed be He.
      The sheep are Israel: 'And you are my sheep, the sheep of my
      pasture' (Ezek. 34:31. Wolves came and tore the flock into pieces'
      refers to the enemies who entered the temple. At that moment,
      the Holy One, blessed be He, said, 'Oh that my head were wa-
      ters, and my eyes a fountain of tears that I may weep day and
      night for the slain of the daughter of my people' (Jer. 8:23)."

      > The shepherd weeps for the loss of all his possessions
      > but the staff and basket, just as God, having lost Is-
      > rael to the wolves, weeps for the loss of whatever he
      > had. It is hard to see the parable as exegetical, since
      > the key action, "wolves came..." is left without a verse
      > to amplify or clarify. And "At that moment..." is left
      > hanging, since it is not part of the parable. Something
      > is awry in this exposition of the verses and the parable
      > of the bereft shepherd.

9.   LV.i.2. "Hear how I groan; there is none to comfort me. All my en-

emies have heard of my trouble; they are glad that you have done
it. Bring the day you have announced and let them be as I am"
(Lamentations 1:21): "they are glad that you have done it:" This
may be compared to the case of a noble lady to whom the king
said, "Do not lend anything to your neighbors. Do not borrow
from them anything either." One time the king lost his temper
with her and drove her out of the palace. She made the rounds
of all her neighbors but they would not accept her. She went back
to the palace. Said the king to her, "You have nerve to come back!"
She said to him, "You are the one who did it. For you said, 'Do
not lend anything to your neighbors. Do not borrow from them
anything either.' Had I been lending to them or borrowing from
them, and something of mine was in their domain or theirs in mine,
wouldn't they have received me?" So too when the Temple was
destroyed, [the nations of the world sent word everywhere to which
the Israelites fled and shut them out, so they appealed to God,]
said Holy One, blessed be He, to Israel, "You have nerve to come
back to me!" They said to him, "Lord of the world, did you not
write in your Torah, 'Neither shall you make marriage with them,
your daughter you shall not give to his son, nor his daughter shall
you take for your son' (Dt. 7:3). If we had intermarried with them,
would they not have accepted us? you have done it."

> The exegetical parable explains why "there is none to
> comfort me... they are glad you have done it..." Why
> Israel can blame God for her isolation is clear: by
> keeping his will, Israel isolated herself from the nations
> and when God turned against her, there was no where
> to turn. The parable tracks the exegesis; we should be
> hard put to understand the outcome were we to tell
> the parabolic story without the concrete application.

10. LVII:iii.2. ["How the Lord in his anger has set the daughter of Zion
     under a cloud! He has cast down from heaven to earth the splen-
     dor of Israel; he has not remembered his footstool in the day of
     his anger" (Lamentations 2:1): "He has cast down from heaven to
     earth the splendor of Israel:" R. Huna bar Aha in the name of R.
     Hanina b. R. Abbahu: "The matter may be compared to the case
     of a king who had a son. The son cried, so he put him on his knees.
     He cried some more, so he held him in his arms. He cried some
     more, so he put him up on his shoulders. The boy dirtied the fa-
     ther, so he threw him to the ground, and he was not thrown down
     in the way that he was lifted up. The lifting up was step by step,
     but the throwing down was in a single angry gesture. So it is said,
     'And I, I taught Ephraim to walk, taking them by their arms' (Hos.
     11:3). Then: 'I will make Ephraim ride, Judah shall plow, Jacob
     shall break his clods' (Hos. 10:11). And finally: 'He has cast down

from heaven to earth the splendor of Israel.'"

The relationship of God to Israel, conveyed in Lam. 2:1, is translated into the exegetical parable, sustained by further verses of Scripture. Here the verses mark the stages in the king's relationship to the child.

11. LVII:iii.3=LXIII.i.1. Another comment on the verse, "He has cast down from heaven to earth the splendor of Israel:" R. Joshua b. R. Nahman said, "The matter may be compared to the case of townsfolk who made a crown for the king. They angered him, but he took it, and they angered him again, but he took it. Finally] he said, 'Are the town-folk not irritating me only because of the crown that is set on my head? Here, take it, it's thrown in your face!' So said the Holy One, blessed be He, 'Isn't it the fact that the Israelites are angering me only because of the icon of Jacob that is engraved on my throne? Here, take it, it's thrown in your face!'

The exegetical parable takes up another component of the base-verse, "the splendor of Israel." Why the parable should yield Jacob as the crown/splendor of Israel is not clear; that is a given.

12. LXXIX:ii.1 "I am the man [who has seen affliction under the rod of his wrath; he has driven and brought me into darkness without any light; surely against me he turns his hand again and again the whole day long]" (Lamentations 3:1-3):" The matter may be compared to the case of a noble lady, against whom the king grew angry. He drove her out of the palace. What did she do? She went and pressed her face against the pillar. The king passed by and saw her and said to her, 'You have gall [to cling to the palace after you were driven out]!. She said to him, 'My lord, king, this is proper for me, this is good for me, this is right for me, for no other woman took you but for me.' The king said to her, 'No, but I am the one who rejected all other women on account of you.' She said to him, 'No, but they are the ones who did not accept you.' So the Holy One, blessed be He, said to the community of Israel, 'You have gall. The community of Israel replied, 'Lord of the world, this is proper for me, this is good for me, this is right for me, for no other nation accepted the Torah except for us.' He said to her, 'No, but I am the one who rejected all other nations on account of you.' She said to him, 'How come you went with your Torah around to all the other nations for them to reject it?'

At issue in the exegetical parable is God's insistence that he chose Israel, and Israel's insistence that the nations rejected God and that Israel was the only nation that accepted the Torah. Then the parable tracks the exegetical problem very closely, and captures Israel's merit in continuing to remain loyal to God even after the expulsion.

13. LXXXV.i.2. "My soul continually thinks of it and is bowed down within me" (Lamentations 3:19): Hiyya taught, "The matter may be compared to the case of a king who went to battle and took his sons with him. One time they angered him, and he took an oath not to take them along again. Then he remembered them and wept, saying, 'Would that my sons were with me, even though they anger me!' The king is the Holy One, blessed be He, and the sons are Israel. When the Israelites went forth to battle, the Holy One, blessed be He, would go with them. But when they angered him, he did not accompany them. When Israel was no longer in the land, he said, 'Would that Israel were with me, even though they anger me.'

Here is an exegetical parable that precisely matches the case it is meant to realize, with an explicit statement to that effect ("the king is... the sons are...").

14. LXXXV.i.4. "But this I call to mind and therefore I have hope:" (Lamentations 3:21): R. Abba bar Kahana said in the name of R. Yohanan, "The matter may be compared to the case of a king who took a wife and wrote out for her a document specifying a very large marriage-settlement: 'So many state-apartments I am making ready for you, so many purple garments I am giving you.' Then he left her for many years and went overseas, and her neighbors aggravated her, saying, 'The king has abandoned you, has gone overseas and will never return.' She wept and sighed, but she would go into her room and open and read her marriage-settlement. When she saw in the document, 'So many state-apartments I am making ready for you, so many purple garments I am giving you,' she took comfort. After days and years had gone by, the king came home. He said to her, 'My daughter, I am surprised that you were able to wait for me all these years.' She said to him, 'My lord, king, were it not for the marriage-settlement that you wrote out for me, with its generous settlement, my neighbors would have misled me.' So the nations of the world aggravate Israel, saying to them, 'Your God does not want you any more, he has hidden his face from you, he has removed his Presence from your midst and will return to you no more. Come to us and we shall appoint you dukes, lords, and generals. And when the Israelites go into their synagogues and study houses and recite in the Torah: 'And I shall have respect for you and make you fruitful and multiply you... and I will set my tabernacle among you... and I will walk among you' (Lev. 26:9-11), they take comfort. Tomorrow, when the redemption comes, the Holy One, blessed be He, will say to

the Israelites, 'My children, I am surprised that you were able to wait for me all these years.' And they will reply to him, 'Lord of all the ages, were it not for your Torah, which you have given to us, the nations of the world would long ago have led us astray from you.'

> The nations correspond to the neighbors, God to the king, Israel to the queen, and the transaction—Israel's hope despite it all—is exactly captured in this nearly perfect match. The one detail not followed in the parable is the "Come to us and we shall appoint you...." In that important detail, the parable adds up to less than the case it is supposed to replicate, and it is an important difference.

15. LXXXVI.i.5. "'The Lord is my portion,' says my soul, 'therefore I will hope in him'" (Lamentations 3:24): R. Abbahu in the name of R. Yohanan said, "The matter may be compared to the case of <u>a king who came into a town, and with him were his dukes, lords, and generals. The chief citizens of the town were sitting in the midst. This one said, 'I will take a duke to my house,' and another, 'I will take a lord to my house,' and a third, 'I will take a general to my house.' Now there was one astute fellow there, who said, 'I shall take only the king alone, for all of the others pass on, but he never passes on.'</u> So of the nations of the world, these serve the sun, those the moon, others wood, others stone. But the Israelites serve only the Holy One, blessed be He: 'The Lord is my portion,' says my soul, 'therefore I will hope in him,'"

> The exegetical parable captures Israel's insistence on God as her portion, while the nations accept lesser beings, because God is eternal.

16. CXI.i.2 "and he kindled a fire in Zion, which consumed its foundations" (Lamentations 4:11): It is written, "A Psalm of Asaph. O God, the gentiles have come into your inheritance" (Ps. 79:1). What is required is not "psalm" but "a weeping of Asaph" or "a lament of Asaph" or "a dirge of Asaph." So why say, "A psalm of Asaph"? The matter may be compared to the case of <u>a king who prepared a bridal canopy for his son. He fixed it up, plastered it, cemented and decorated it. But the son angered the father, so he tore it down. He went into the room, tore the curtains, broke the rods. The son's pedagogue began to sit and play [using a piece of rod as a flute]. They said to him, "The king has destroyed this chamber, and you are sitting and playing a song?" He said to him, "I am playing a song because the king has poured out his anger on his son's bridal chamber, but not on his son."</u> So people said to Asaph, "The Holy

One, blessed be He, has destroyed his sanctuary, and you are sitting and singing a psalm?" He said to them, "That is precisely why I am singing a song, for the Holy One, blessed be He, has poured out his anger on wood and stones, but not on Israel." That is in line with this verse: "and he kindled a fire in Zion, which consumed its foundations."

> There is no understanding the transaction of the parable without knowledge of the problem taken up by the exegete, Ps. 79:1's reference to a Psalm in response to the nations' having come into God's inheritance. Then the parable solves that problem, leaving no space between the problem and the solution, an exact transaction.

The distinction between the exegetical parable that responds to the problem defined by the verses and the sage's reading of them, and the exegetical parable that stands autonomous of its particular setting, registers with a minimum of subjective judgment.

C. The Parable Recapitulating a Narrative, Neither Halakhic Nor Exegetical

A hither-to-fore unfamiliar type of parable is one that, in a simile of a dynamic character, recapitulates a free-standing narrative, hence, "the narrative-recapitulative parable." It invokes no base-verse and does not realize the articulated result of the interpretation of Scripture at all. In this probe of ours, it first makes its appearance in Lamentations Rabbah. There are two blatant instances in which neither a Halakhic nor an exegetical task frames the assignment addressed by a parable. Rather, the narrative-recapitulative parable is comprised by a story responsive to a story, thus: the parable that renders abstract a concrete narrative.

17.   XLIII.i..5. There was a priest who went to someone who had many children and said to him, "Such and such a statue has told me to come to you, for I have heard that you have many children, so you should offer up one of them." He said to him, "They are not subject to my domination. One works in gold, one in silver, one with sheep, one with herds. I have one young son, who is in the house of his master. Wait until he comes from the house of his master, and I shall give him to you, and you may go and offer him up." Said to him the Holy One, blessed be He, "Of all the sons that you had, you could offer to an idol only this one, who is consecrated to Heaven!" R. Judah b. R. Simon in the name of

R. Levi b. Parta: "The matter may be compared to the case <u>of a noble woman to whom her lover said, 'Warm some food up for me.' She took the portrait of the king and burned it up to heat the food. Said the king to her, 'Of all the things you had in the palace, you could heat up food for your lover only with my portrait!'</u> So said the Holy One, blessed be He, to that wicked man, 'Of all the sons that you had, you could offer to an idol only this one, who is consecrated to my name!' ·

> It is difficult to imagine a more exact replication of the case than in the narrative-recapitulative parable, but it is not exegetical in a narrow sense, not being tied up to a particular verse of Scripture. Rather, we have a story that is perfectly clear in its own terms, followed by a metaphor built on the model of the transactions of the story—an odd construction indeed. Clearly, the study of the classification of parables here finds a classification distinct from the Halakhic and the exegetical types.

18.   XLIV.i.1. You find that when the gentiles entered the sanctuary, with them came the Ammonites and Moabites. Everyone was running to plunder the silver and gold, but the Ammonites and Moabites went running to plunder the scroll of the Torah, as to remove from there the statement, "An Ammonite and a Moabite shall not enter the assembly of the Lord" (Dt. 23:4). R. Judah b. R. Simon in the name of R. Levi bar Parta: "To what may they be compared? <u>a fire that happened in the palace of the king, and everybody ran to plunder the silver and gold, but the slave ran to plunder his title deed.</u> So when the gentiles entered the sanctuary, with them came the Ammonites and Moabites. Everyone was running to plunder the silver and gold, but the Ammonites and Moabites went running to plunder the scroll of the Torah, so as to remove from there the statement, 'An Ammonite and a Moabite shall not enter the assembly of the Lord' (Dt. 23:4)."

> The parable once more matches a narrative, "So when the gentiles...," with the transaction of the narrative repeated in the parable.

I do not know what to make of this imaginative extension of the possibilities of the parable beyond its Halakhic and exegetical frameworks. With a larger corpus of such parabolic exercises in hand, I should claim that the parable's development in Lamentations Rabbah responds to the impact of the authentic narrative. That is, with the authentic narrative dominant, the parable is asked to respond not only to Halakhic and exegetical problems but also to serve the extension and amplification of authentic narratives. But the corpus is slight and cannot bear so weighty a hypothesis.

D. The Parabolic Components of Lamentations Rabbah

Let me first summarize the classification of the parables that I have set forth:

> EXEGETICAL PARABLES: 3, 4, 5, 6, 7, 8, 9, 10, 11, 12, 13, 14, 15, 16
> HALAKHIC PARABLES: 1, 2
> NARRATIVE-RECAPITULATIVE PARABLES: 17, 18

Of the eighteen parables that I have identified, fourteen are particular to the exegetical setting. Those that on the surface can serve for some purpose other than the specific one at hand involve a more elaborate transaction than those particular to the terms of the verse that is amplified or the Halakhic ruling that is clarified.

> HALAKHIC PARABLES OF LAMENTATIONS RABBAH
> Parable particular to its Halakhic setting: 2
> Parable not particular to its Halakhic setting:—

> EXEGETICAL PARABLES LAMENTATIONS RABBAH
> Parable particular to its exegetical setting: 14
> Parable not particular to its exegetical setting:—[possibly
> 2, Nos. 8 and 14]

> NARRATIVE-RECAPITULATIVE PARABLES OF LAMENTATIONS RABBAH
> The issue of the exegetical setting does not pertain: 17, 18

Our sample is limited and sustains no global generalization. Not only so, but the proportion of the document as a whole that we have reviewed in this rubric is negligible. We do not deal with a principal part of the document. But it is equally clear that Lamentation Rabbah's framers have found uses for the *Mashal*, both Halakhic and exegetical, and now narrative-recapitulative, that escaped the attention of the compilers of the Mishnah and the Tosefta. Though the number of entries is modest, it is also well-delineated and each of the types bears uniform traits.

III. *The Ma'aseh*

Lamentations Rabbah contains a negligible number of *Ma'asim*. It is not a preferred narrative form. And most of the instances we do have serve a single documentary purpose. In this compilation of exegeses of a particular book of Scripture, the *Ma'aseh* signals a case that illustrates or realizes the point of a particular verse of Lamentations. The marker, *Ma'aseh,* signals a case, not a fully realized, authentic narrative, that is adapted to the documentary program. That is what we see in most of the following cases. Here, then, the *Ma'aseh* forms the counterpart to the exegetical parable, exhibiting this fixed difference: the parable introduces a nameless, generic stick-figure, while the *Ma'aseh* cites a particular person; both are exemplary. So both in the exegetical parable and in the exegetical *Ma'aseh* the documentary vocation governs.

[1.   XXXV:v.2. is marked as a *Ma'aseh*, but I have classified it as an authentic story.]

[2.   XXXV:vii.3 is marked as a *Ma'aseh*, but I have classified it as an authentic story.]

3.   XXXVIII.i.1. "The roads to Zion mourn, for none come to the appointed feasts (Lamentations 1:4):" Said R. Huna, "Everyone seeks its proper mate. There was a case in which a wild bitch who climbed up a rock to mate with a male."

> Here *Ma'aseh* signals not a Halakhic precedent or an example but a datum drawn from nature, illustrating the proposition of Huna.

4.   L.i. 6. There was the case of Miriam, daughter of Boethus, that she was betrothed to Joshua b. Gamla, and the king appointed him high priest. One time she said, "I shall go and see how he reads in the Torah on the Day of Atonement." What did they do for her? They brought out carpets from the door of her house to the door of the house of the sanctuary, so that her feet should not be exposed. Nonetheless, her feet were exposed. When her husband died, sages decreed for her [a settlement of her marriage contract involving] two *seahs* of wine a day. Said R. Eleazar bar Saddoq, "May I not see consolation, if I did not see that the troops tied her hair on the tails of horses and made her run from Jerusalem to Lud. "In her regard I cited this verse: 'The tender and delicate woman among you, who would not set the sole of her foot on the ground because of delicateness and tenderness' (Dt. 28:56)."

The *Ma'aseh* here realizes or embodies the cited verse

of Deuteronomy, thus serves as the equivalent to a parable.

5.   L.i.7. There was the case of Miriam, daughter of Naqdimon, for whom sages allotted the sum of five hundred gold *denars* for the purchase of perfumes daily. Said R. Eleazar b. R. Saddoq, "May I not see consolation, if I did not see her gathering barley from beneath the hooves of the horses in Akko. In her regard I cited this verse: 'If you do not know, O you fairest among women, go forth by the footsteps of the flock and feed your kids' (Song 1:8).

> Here again, the requirements of the exegesis are met by an example, not a generic embodiment such as a parable provides. But the cited verse has dictated the striking detail of the *Ma'aseh*.

6.   L.i.8. There is the case of Miriam, daughter of Tanhum, who was taken captive and ransomed in Akko. They brought her a shift, and she went down to immerse in the sea, and the waves came and swept it off, so she got another and went down to immerse in the sea, and the waves came and swept it off. When she saw this, she said, "Let the Collector [God] collect the debt. [The waves exact punishment for my sins.]" Since she had accepted the divine decree upon herself, the Holy One, blessed be He, gestured to the sea and it returned her garments.

> The point of the *Ma'aseh* is articulated, "Since she had accepted...." Here we have a specific incident that embodies the stated principle. Here what is realized is not the exegesis of a verse of Scripture but the theological outcome of the same matter.

7.   LXVII.i.1. "My eyes are spent with weeping" (Lam. 2:11): But the tears caused by the death of an adult child are worst of all." There was the case of a woman whose adult son died. She wept over him nightly, until her eyelashes fell out. She went to a physician, who said to her, "Paint your eyes with this eye-paint that I give you, and you will recover."

> The *Ma'aseh* illustrates the mourning for the death of an adult child by invoking a specific case, the whole serving an exegetical purpose, in connection with Lam. 2:11: why the tears caused by the death of an adult child are worst of all.

8.   LXVII.i.2. "my soul is in tumult, my heart is poured out in grief because of the destruction of the daughter of my people" (Lam. 2:11): There was the case of a man whose adult son died, and he wept

over him nightly, until his liver dropped. He said, "My liver has
dropped from weeping over him, but it has made no difference."
As above.

9.   LXVIII.i.2. [They cry to their mothers, "Where is bread and wine?"
      as they faint like wounded men in the streets of the city, as their
      life is poured out on their mothers' bosom (Lamentations 2:12):"
      "as they faint like wounded men in the streets of the city, as their
      life is poured out on their mothers' bosom:" There is the case of a
      woman who said to her husband, "Take a bracelet or earring, go
      to the market, and buy something so we shall eat and not die." He
      did so, but found nothing to buy, writhed, and died. She said to
      her son, "Go, see what your father is doing." He went to the mar-
      ket and found him dead in the market place, began weeping for him,
      writhed and died by his side.

      As above, an explicit exegesis through an exemplary
      case.

10.   LXXXIV.i.1 "He has made my teeth grind on gravel and made me
      cower in ashes" (Lamentations 3:16): There is the case of the son
      of R. Hanina b. Teradion, who joined up with guerillas. He snitched
      on them, and they killed him. His father went and found him in
      the wilderness, with his mouth full of dirt and gravel. A few days
      later they put him in a coffin and out of respect for his father, they
      wanted to have a eulogy said for him. The father would not permit
      it. He said to them, "Let me speak concerning my son." He com-
      menced by citing this verse: "Neither have I hearkened to the voice
      of my teachers, nor inclined my ear to those who taught me. I was
      well nigh in all evil in the midst of the congregation and assembly"
      (Prov. 5:13-14). His mother commenced by citing this verse over
      him: "A foolish son is a vexation to his father, and bitterness to her
      that bore him" (Prov. 17:25) His sister cited this verse: "Bread of
      falsehood is sweet to a man, but afterwards his mouth will be filled
      with gravel" (Prov. 20:17).

      The case illustrates the verse of Scripture, with spe-
      cial reference to Lam. 3:16/Prov. 20:17.

11.   LXXXIV.i.4 [He has made my teeth grind on gravel and made me
      cower in ashes; my soul is bereft of peace, I have forgotten what
      happiness is; so I say, "Gone is my glory, and my expectation from
      the Lord" (Lamentations 3:16-18)] [A further illustration of the verse,
      "my soul is bereft of peace, I have forgotten what happiness is:" Said
      R. Eleazar b. R. Yosé, "There was the case of a woman who brought
      her son to a cook and said to him, 'Teach my son the trade. He
      said to her, 'Leave him with me for five years, and I shall teach him
      how to make five hundred kinds of omelets.'" Rabbi [Judah the Pa-
      triarch] heard and said, "That kind of luxury we have never seen"

[after the destruction of the Temple, thus "my soul is bereft of peace, I have forgotten what happiness is"].

What is illustrated is how the luxurious life prior to the war gave way to extreme want.

12. CVIII.i.3. Said R. Eliezer b. R. Sadoq, "There is the case of a poor man who came and stood at the door of father's house. Father said to me, 'My son, go and see whether or not he is a Jerusalemite.' I went and found a woman, whose hair had fallen out, so that you could not tell whether it was a man or a woman. She asked only for a preserved fig. That illustrates the verse: 'their skin has shriveled upon their bones, it has become as dry as wood.'"

Once more, the *Ma'aseh* serves an exegetical purpose.

The purpose of the *Ma'aseh* in Lamentations Rabbah is primarily exegetical. The pseudo-narrative is asked to tell an illustrative story that closely responds to the attitude or doctrine of the cited verse of Scripture, or that tells a story showing its realization. The document decides what it wants out of a given narrative form, and since this is an exegetical document, the *Ma'aseh* serves to bear the burden of illustrating the meaning of a verse. That's what it does, and it is pretty much all that it does. The upshot is, the prior conventions associated with the marker, *Ma'aseh*, have completely vanished; there is no instance in Lamentations Rabbah in which the marker signals a case or a precedent of a Halakhic character.

IV. *Not Classified*

1. L.i.10 = LXXVI:i.1 They said concerning Doeg, son of Joseph, that he died and left a young son to his mother, who would measure him by handbreadths and give his weight in gold to Heaven year by year. When the earthworks besieged Jerusalem, she slaughtered him by her own hand and ate him.

What is awry is the marker, "they said concerning…."
With the substitution of *Ma'aseh*, we should have the sort of exemplary case of an exegetical character that the compilers of Lamentations Rabbah prefer and occasionally introduce.

V. *Lamentation Rabbah's Narratives in Canonical Context*

These results yield an economical response to the questions that
precipitate this study, as announced in the Preface and clarified in
the Introduction: does narrative writing open a door to a different
Judaic religious system from that otherwise dominant in the documentary writing of the canonical books of Rabbinic Judaism? Because the indicative traits of documents, as these govern rhetoric,
topic, and logic of coherent discourse, do not pertain to narrative
or pseudo-narrative writing, the question arises: does this other kind
of composition, anomalous in the context of the conventional documentary indicators, contain a corpus of ideas separate from those
embodied in the documentary compositions and composites? Or, on
the contrary, are we able to pick out traits of writing that are *just* as
particular to the document that contains said writing as the definitive qualities of rhetoric, topic, and logic of coherent discourse that
otherwise govern? For Lamentations Rabbah the answers are clear
and one sided. I have already signaled my judgment and the foundations for it: the authentic narratives signal their claim to a position integral to, characteristic of, the document at hand, as much
as do the exegetical corpus that forms the shank of the document.

*1.   Do anomalous or asymmetric compositions or composites attest to thought
that takes place beyond the limits of the documents subject to the rules and symmetry of the canon?* The narratives and pseudo-narratives realize the
documentary program and are tightly linked to the exegetical or
expository task, as seen in the details that follow:

> A. THE AUTHENTIC NARRATIVE
>
> DESTRUCTION, CAUSES AND CONSEQUENCES: The Torah-study
> narrative, No. 1, the prosperity of Israel before the destruc-
> tion, No. 4, and the entire group devoted to the destruction
> of the Temple, the theodicy and the tragedy, fall well within
> the Rabbinic system, narrowly defined.
>
> JERUSALEMITE/ATHENIAN CONTRASTS: I do not see what is
> distinctively Rabbinic in the stories about the cleverness of
> the Israelites and the obtuseness of the Athenians, and in
> most of these stories there is no appeal to Torah-learning,
> or, as with Joshua, where there is, Torah-learning is subor-
> dinated to the wit of the non-sage (thus: Israelite woman/
> child).
>
> DREAM-INTERPRETATION SEQUENCE: Nor, except for the con-
> text, is there anything particularly Rabbinic in the dream-
> interpretation-narratives (whether these be classified as au-

thentic or inauthentic narratives).

HOSPITALITY: The hospitality-story fits together with a variety of such expressions of high esteem for hospitality, which is deemed part of the imitation of God. That theme recurs in particularly-Rabbinic composites.

B. THE *MASHAL*

THE HALAKHIC *MASHAL*: Both of these items on the importance of a quorum fit well within the Rabbinic framework. THE EXEGETICAL *MASHAL*: Only the parables not generated by the exegetical task come under consideration. The forty-five classified as exegetical in origin obviously belong within the framework of the document. That leaves No. 8/L.ii.3, God's mourning for Israel; No. 14/LXXXV.i.4, Israel's hope despite its defeat.

THE PARABLE RECAPITULATING A NARRATIVE: No. 17/XLIII.i.5, the outrage committed by idolaters; No. 18/XLIV.i.1, the Moabites and Ammonites try to remove from the Torah the prohibition of their entering into Israel.

C. THE *MA'ASEH*

No. 3, There was a case in which a wild bitch who climbed up a rock to mate with a male; No. 4, Miriam, daughter of Boethus, 'The tender and delicate woman among you, who would not set the sole of her foot on the ground because of delicateness and tenderness' (Dt 28:56); No. 5 Miriam, daughter of Naqdimon, same outcome; No. 6 Since she had accepted the divine decree upon herself, the Holy One, blessed be He, gestured to the sea and it returned her garments; No. 7 There was the case of a woman whose adult son died. She wept over him nightly, until her eyelashes fell out; No. 8 There was the case of a man whose adult son died, and he wept over him nightly, until his liver dropped; No. 9 Woman whose husband and son died of starvation; No. 10 There is the case of the son of R. Hanina b. Teradion, who joined up with guerillas. He snitched on them, and they killed him; No. 11 How luxurious life before 70 was; No. 12 exegetical ma'aseh.

EXEGETICAL AND INTEGRAL: Of the *Ma'asim*, these realize an explicit, exegetical assignment: Nos. 4, 5, 7, 8, 9, 10, 11, 12. In addition, the following illustrates a theological principle: No. 6. No. 3 asks the case drawn from nature to realize Huna's saying.

NOT CLASSIFIED: No. 1 is exegetical.

To answer the question to which these data pertain: No, most of the narrative and pseudo-narrative writings find a place entirely within the frame of reference of the documentary compositions and composites of Lamentations Rabbah. The theme is particular to the document, the theological proposition characteristic of the Rabbinic system. They do not provide access to some other viewpoint or system than the Rabbinic-theological one that throughout defines the document's exegetical program.

But there is an exception, and it is not trivial. The one important corpus that exhibits no distinctively-Rabbinic theological traits concerns the Israelites/Jerusalemites and the Athenians. In form and in topic I see nothing that requires us to classify the narrative as Rabbinic. But if the Athenian/Jerusalemite, or Samaritan/Israelite (for dream-interpretation), narratives or anecdotes do not belong to the Rabbinic system in particular, they also do not point toward some other Judaic system, no other theological construction.

The set of stories is parachuted down into our document, which finds no objection to its point, but which also does not lay claim to provide a uniquely appropriate setting in which to register that point. So while most of the authentic narratives do belong to the document and do contribute to realizing its larger doctrinal and exegetical goals, some of the authentic narratives do not bear indicative markers of belonging here primarily, if not exclusively. Interrogating these other narratives on their systemic program yields nothing of special weight or interest.

2. *Does non-documentary, narrative writing exhibit readily-discernible patterns of form and meaning as does documentary writing? If so, what are these patterns and how are we to classify and to interpret them?* It suffices now to recapitulate the observation that the non-documentary authentic narratives of the destruction and its aftermath, on earth and in heaven, find story-telling the appropriate medium for their message. How else to portray God as mourning for the destruction, how else to engage the patriarchs, Moses, Jeremiah, and Rachel, in the confrontation with God on what God has brought about, I cannot begin to imagine. So the principal component of non-documentary writing in the form of authentic narrative presents itself as unique to the document, because it and it alone can say what the compilers wish to say in response to Lamentations and the events it portrays. Indeed, given the power of the narrative theme, the humanization of God in relationship to Israel in response to the calamities brought about within the very covenantal relationship of God and Israel, we may designate the authentic narratives of the destruction and its aftermath as essential and unique to the documentary task. Stated

simply: the non-documentary narrative writing to which we refer forms the sole possible medium for carrying to its climax the theological message of Lamentations Rabbah—but not of the book of Lamentations: God wept.

3. *At what point in the process that yielded the canonical writings as we know them did documentary considerations intervene, and what is the meaning of that intervention? When and under what circumstances did documentary considerations give way to writing utterly indifferent to its documentary venue?* Apart from the Jerusalemite/Athenian composite, which to be sure forms no small exception, documentary considerations of theology shape authentic narrative as normatively as they shape exegesis. Once work on the task of composing compositions and compiling composites to re-present the book of Lamentations the vastly augmented form of Lamentations Rabbah got under way, most, though not all of the documentary writing of narrative commenced as well. And that is assuredly the fact for the most important single corpus of authentic narratives, those devoted to the destruction and its consequences, and God's response thereto. As to when and under what circumstances writing indifferent to the documentary venue got under way, I do not perceive the data that would permit us to answer that question. But it is not a question that forms an impasse either, for those data, if not particular to the document, also do not corrupt its contents or contradict its paramount conceptions. They represent not a competing system, or even a coherent one, but bits and pieces of we know not what: the detritus of culture, not culture.

PART THREE

NARRATIVES IN THE FATHERS
ACCORDING TO RABBI NATHAN TEXT A:
FORMS AND TYPES IN COMPARISON
WITH THE FATHERS

CHAPTER SEVENTEEN

NARRATIVES IN THE FATHERS ACCORDING TO RABBI NATHAN TEXT A

I. From The Fathers, Lacking Narratives, to The Fathers According to Rabbi Nathan Text A, A Principal Medium for Narrative Writing in the Rabbinic Canon

In 250 C.E. tractate Abot, The Fathers, delivered its sagacious message through aphorisms assigned to named sages. A few centuries later—perhaps in 500 C.E.—Abot deR. Natan, The Fathers According to Rabbi Nathan, a vast secondary expansion of that same tractate, gave flesh and blood form to those sages, recasting the tractate by adding a sizable number of narratives about its named authorities. The authorship of The Fathers presented its teachings in the form of aphorisms, rarely finding it necessary to supply those aphorisms with a narrative setting and—as we saw in Volume One—never resorting to narrative of any kind for the presentation of its propositions. The testamentary authorship that compiled The Fathers According to Rabbi Nathan by contrast provided a vast amplification and supplement to The Fathers, introducing into its treatment of the received tractate a huge corpus of narratives of various sorts. In this way, the later authorship indicated that it found, in narrative in general, and stories about sages in particular, the preferred modes of discourse for presenting its message. Specifically, in The Fathers According to Rabbi Nathan, the story about the sage became the paramount and critical medium for the presentation of what was new in the message of its framers.

In The Fathers According to Rabbi Nathan Text A as analyzed in my *Judaism and Story*,[1] I find five species of the genus, narrative. I

---

[1] *Judaism and Story: The Evidence of The Fathers According to Rabbi Nathan.* Chi-

classify these as (1) *Mashal*/parable, (2) *Ma'aseh*/precedent, (3) pseudo-narrative, as already defined in volume one, meaning, a setting for a saying, (4) scriptural story, to be defined,[2] and (5) sage-story. The sage-story forms a largest proportion, by far, of the narratives in the document at hand.

I mean by "sage-story" a narrative with these distinctive and indicative traits:

(1)   a beginning, middle, and end;

(2)   tension and resolution;

(3)   characterization of the hero, accomplished through an account of motivation;

(4)   the story is told about a particular person and what that singular person said and did on a distinct and important occasion;

(5)   omission of close attention to citations of verses of Scripture as a main focus of discourse.

A Scripture-story not only focuses upon a scriptural theme or hero, it also encompasses vast explosions of allusions to or verbatim citations of verses of Scripture.

In part vi, below, I shall elaborate on these indicative traits and provide examples of the sage-story. What we shall see is that that type of narrative I call a sage-story is as distinctive to The Fathers According to Rabbi Nathan Text A as these three volumes have shown the *Ma'aseh* or case/precedent is to the Mishnah and the exegetical *Mashal* or parable is to the two Sifrés and the story of God's emotions in relationship to Israel is particular to Lamentations Rabbah.

II. *Comparing* The Fathers *to* The Fathers According to Rabbi Nathan

The Fathers According to Rabbi Nathan Text A presents two types of materials and sets them forth in a fixed order. The document contains (1) amplifications of sayings in The Fathers as well as (2) materials not related to anything in the original document. The order

---

cago, 1992: University of Chicago Press. Reprint: Binghamton, 2002: Global Publications, CLASSICS IN JUDAIC STUDIES series. This chapter goes over some of the main points of that monograph.

[2] Already alluded to in the introduction to this volume.

in which The Fathers According to Rabbi Nathan Text A arranges its types of material becomes immediately clear. First, our authorship presents amplifications of the prior document, and, only second, does it tack on its own message. The Fathers According to Rabbi Nathan Text A first of all presents itself as continuous with the prior document, and then shows itself to be connected to it. And, of course, where the authorship gives us compositions that are essentially new both in rhetoric and in logic and in topic, it is in that second set of materials that we shall find what is fresh. But at no point do I find in the relationships of the two writings a systematic effort on the part of the later authorship to show themselves autonomous of all that has gone before. We find no desire to give evidence of a relationship of total independence of prior tradition, whether we invoke rhetorical, logical, or topical criteria. But, as we shall see, that is deceiving. Our authorship does have a new message and does make use of a fresh medium, and, in the nature of things, the innovative topic and rhetoric draw in their wake a new logic of intelligible discourse as well.

Where the authorship of the later document has chosen to cite and amplify sayings in the earlier one,[3] that exercise comes first. There may be additional amplification, and what appears to augment often turns out to be quite new and to enter the second of our two categories, in the form of (i) proof texts drawn from Scripture, or (ii) parables, (iii) other sorts of stories, sometimes involving named sages, that illustrate the same point, and (iv) sequences of unadorned sayings, those not found also in The Fathers, that make the same point. These come later in a sequence of discourses in The Fathers According to Rabbi Nathan. Where an appendix of secondary materials on a theme introduced in the primary discourse occurs, it will

---

[3] On the movement of stories and sayings from earlier to later documents, see my *Extra- and Non-Documentary Writing in the Canon of Formative Judaism. III. Peripatetic Parallels*. Binghamton, 2001: Global Publications. ACADEMIC STUDIES IN THE HISTORY OF JUDAISM SERIES. Second edition, revised, of *The Peripatetic Saying: The Problem of the Thrice-Told Tale in Talmudic Literature*. Chico, 1985: Scholars Press for Brown Judaic Studies. I systematically pursued that problem in my earliest methodological exercises, *Development of a Legend. Studies on the Traditions Concerning Yohanan ben Zakkai*. Leiden, 1970: Brill. Reprinted: Binghamton, 2002: Global Publications. CLASSICS OF JUDAIC SERIES; *The Rabbinic Traditions about the Pharisees before 70*. Leiden, 1971: Brill. I-III. Second printing: Atlanta, 1999: Scholars Press for South Florida Studies in the History of Judaism, and *Eliezer ben Hyrcanus. The Tradition and the Man*. Leiden, 1973: Brill. Reprint: Binghamton, 2002: Global Publications, CLASSICS IN JUDAIC STUDIES SERIES.

be inserted directly after the point at which said theme is located in
the counterpart, in the later document, to that passage in the earlier one, and only afterward will the exposition of the saying in The
Fathers proceed to a further point. This general order predominates
throughout. It signifies a well-crafted document, not a haphazard
collection, arbitrarily arranged.

III. *The Forms of The Fathers According to Rabbi Nathan*

When we compare the basic structure of The Fathers and The Fathers According to Rabbi Nathan Text A we ask a simple question:
has the earlier document, The Fathers, dictated the traits of orga-
nization, proportion and balance characteristic of the later one? Or
does the new composition take an independent position of its own
on the choices made by the authorship of the earlier writing? If the
framers of The Fathers According to Rabbi Nathan Text A were to
adopt the policies of composition characteristic of The Fathers, then
we should anticipate further lists of wise sayings, arranged in the order
of names of The Fathers itself. If the authorship of The Fathers
According to Rabbi Nathan Text A should choose otherwise, then
anything is possible.

The answer is simply stated. The framework of The Fathers According to Rabbi Nathan Text A derives not from The Fathers but
from a plan conceived independent of the example of The Fathers.
It involves a number of components, some of them drawn from The
Fathers, some derived from the response to The Fathers, and some
altogether independent of The Fathers. The authorship of The Fathers has handed down to their successors of The Fathers According to Rabbi Nathan Text A the basic scheme of listing names and
assigning sayings to those names. But the framers of The Fathers
According to Rabbi Nathan Text A have followed the received lists
only in part—which is to say, they have exercised freedom of choice
even in dropping or ignoring what they wished. The authorship of
The Fathers has further provided sayings that demanded amplification, and also a model for how that secondary expansion is to be
worked out. Finally, on their own, the authorship of The Fathers
According to Rabbi Nathan Text A drew upon a variety of materials not included by that of The Fathers. In a purely formal framework, we may point to those fresh types of materials as a source for

what in The Fathers According to Rabbi Nathan Text A is new in not only a formal but also a programmatic and substantive sense.

IV. *The Topical Program of The Fathers and of The Fathers According to Rabbi Nathan: Points in Common, Points of Difference*

Recognizing the differences in the formal preferences of the authorship of The Fathers According to Rabbi Nathan Text A requires little exercise of taste and judgment. Matters are clear on the surface. When we turn to the more difficult but critical issue of changes in opinion and sensibility, we find that our own perspective intervenes. And yet, here too, if we survey the surface of matters and rely mainly on what is visible to the naked eye, we shall not err. What we now wish to know is precisely what views characterize the later, exegetical document but not the original, apothegmatic one.

The earlier document speaks only of the individual, who prepares in this world for the life of the world to come. The teleology of the system outlined by The Fathers, then, calls for the individual to prepare for judgment before God and promises eternal life. The Fathers According to Rabbi Nathan Text A is consistent and one-sided when it addresses not so much the individual as the nation, and promises not the life of the world to come (which, I take for granted, is assumed but systemically neutral in this context) but the age to come for corporate, holy Israel, as against this age, which belongs to the (undifferentiated) nations. In this shift of mythic categories the framers of The Fathers According to Rabbi Nathan Text A redefine the teleology at hand and focus it upon historical and social categories, rather than those that emerge from the life and death of the individual—a striking shift indeed.

Points of emphasis in The Fathers lacking all counterpart in restatement and development in The Fathers According to Rabbi Nathan Text A make three points. First, the study of the Torah alone does not suffice. One has also to make an honest living through work. In what is particular to The Fathers According to Rabbi Nathan Text A we find not that point but its opposite: one should study the Torah and other things will take care of themselves—a claim of a more supernatural character than the one in The Fathers. A second point of clear interest in the earlier document to which in the later one we find no response tells sages to accommodate their wishes to those of the community at large, to accept the importance of the government, to work in community, to practice self-abnegation and restraint in favor of the wishes of others. The sage here is less a supernatural figure than a political leader, eager to conciliate and reconcile the other.

The third and most important, indicative shift in the later document imparts to the teleological question an eschatological answer altogether lacking in the earlier one. If we were to ask the authorship of Abot to spell out their teleology, they would draw our attention to the numerous sayings about this life's being a time of preparation for the life of the world to come, on the one side, and to judgment and eternal life, on the other. The focus is on the individual and how he or she lives in this world and prepares for the next. The category is the individual, and, commonly in the two documents before us when we speak of the individual, we also find the language of this world and the world to come, *olam hazzeh, olam habbah.* The sequence of sayings about this world and the next form a stunning contrast to the ones about this age and the next age, *olam hazzeh, le'atid labo.* Here, moreover, the definitive category is social, therefore national, raising the issue not of the private person but of holy Israel. The concern then is what will happen to the nation in time to come, meaning the coming age, not solely the coming life of the individuals' resurrection. The systemic teleology shifts its focus to the holy people, and, alongside, to the national history of the holy people—now and in the age to come. So in the movement from this world and the world to come, to this age and the age to come, often expressed as the coming future, *le'atid labo,* we note an accompanying categorical shift in the definitive context: from individual and private life of home and family, to society and historical, public life. That shift then characterizes the teleological movement, as much as the categorical change. And, as we see, it is contained both in general and in detail in the differences we have noticed between The Fathers and The Fathers According to Rabbi Nathan.

In our sifting of details, we should not miss the main point. The Fathers According to Rabbi Nathan Text A differs from The Fathers in one aspect so fundamental as to change the face of the base-document completely. While the earlier authorship took slight interest in lives and deeds of sages, the later one contributed in a systematic and orderly manner the color and life of biography to the named but faceless sages of The Fathers. Let me state with emphasis:

The stories about sages make points that correspond to positions taken in statements of viewpoints particular to The Fathers According to Rabbi Nathan. The stories also contain those fresh points that differentiate the later from the earlier document.

That is to say, the national-eschatological interest of the later document, with its focus on living only in the Land of Israel, on the one side, and its contrast between this age, possessed by the gentiles, and the age to come, in which redeemed Israel will enjoy a paramount position, which has no counterpart in the earlier composition, emerges not only in sayings but also in stories about the critical issue, the destruction of Jerusalem and the loss of the Temple, along with the concomitant matter, associated with the former stories, about repentance and how it is achieved at this time. When we consider the contents of those stories, we see time and again that same national-salvific and eschatological teleology that eludes discovery in The Fathers.

Yet a further point of development lies in the notion that study of the Torah combined with various virtues, e.g., good deeds, fear of sin, suffices, with a concomitant assurance that making a living no longer matters. Here too the new medium of the later document—the stories about sages—bears the new message. For that conviction emerges not only explicitly, e.g., in the sayings of Hananiah about the power of Torah-study to take away many sources of suffering, Judah b. Ilai's that one should treat words of the Torah as the principal, earning a living as trivial, and so on. but also in the detail that both Aqiba and Eliezer began poor but through their master of Torah ended rich.

We note that The Fathers According to Rabbi Nathan Text A contains a sizable share of sayings not used in The Fathers, but only one name introduced only in the later document, Elisha b. Abbuyah, produces resonance. That is because of the famous stories about his apostasy, which we should expect to have discouraged inclusion of his wise sayings. That does not seem to me an indicative shift, only an interesting one. But I do not know what to make of it.

If I had to state in a single sentence the principal point of programmatic difference between The Fathers and The Fathers According to Rabbi Nathan, I should therefore conclude as follows:

The Fathers presents an ideal of the sage as model for the everyday life of the individual, who must study the Torah and also work, and through the good life prepare now for life after death, while The Fathers According to Rabbi Nathan

Text A has a different conception of the sage, of the value and meaning of the study of the Torah, and of the center of interest—and also has selected a new medium for the expression of its distinctive conception.

To spell this out: (1) the sage is now—in The Fathers According to Rabbi Nathan Text A—not a judge and teacher alone but also a supernatural figure. (2) Study of the Torah in preference to making a living promises freedom from the conditions of natural life. (3) Israel as the holy people seen as a supernatural social entity takes center-stage. And these innovative points—commonplaces in the Bavli but where the topics surface at all unfamiliar in the Mishnah-Tosefta—are conveyed not only in sayings but in stories about sages. What follows is that the medium not only carries a new message but forms a component of that new message. The sage as a supernatural figure now presents Torah-teachings through what he does, not only through what he says. Therefore telling stories about what sages did and the circumstances in which they formed their sayings forms part of the Torah, in a way in which, in the earlier document, it clearly did not. The interest in stories about sages proves therefore not merely literary or formal; it is more than a new way of conveying an old message. Stories about the sages are told because sages stand for a message that can emerge only in stories and not in sayings alone.

To conclude: the stories about sages portray a burden of values distinct from those expressed in the sayings of The Fathers. Those stories commonly are attached to portions of The Fathers According to Rabbi Nathan Text A that serve as exegeses of sayings in The Fathers, on the one side, or in Scripture, on the other. The framers of The Fathers According to Rabbi Nathan Text A in this way imputed to The Fathers (as well as to Scripture) the messages that, in fact, they themselves proposed to deliver. We take up the task of analyzing in their own terms the stories of The Fathers According to Rabbi Nathan.

V. *An Inductive Taxonomy of the Story in* The Fathers According to Rabbi Nathan. *(i) Indicative Traits of the Scripture-Story*

The narratives of The Fathers According to Rabbi Nathan Text A break down in a number of ways. One division, which further analysis justifies, separates stories about scriptural topics from those about sages. The former I earlier called simply scripture-stories, the latter, sage-stories. The one kind of story concerns the topic of biblical heroes or themes, the other, sages and their doings.

I see four definitive traits of the scriptural story. The first, and the paramount, trait is the profligate use of verses of Scripture. These predominate and govern, and—more to the point than mere quantity—the amplification of the sense of those verses proves a dominant interest. Indeed, more often than not, in a scriptural story, the point of the story is to clarify the scriptural verse or its broader narrative. When we come to stories about sages, by contrast, we shall locate few proof-texts and slight concern for the exposition of the meaning of verses of Scripture. The sage-story never takes as its point of tension and departure the clarification of the meaning of a verse of Scripture, and, it follows, citation of verses of Scripture will be economical and tangential to the sequence of action and thrust of narrative.

A second indicative trait is the invariably dominant role of the narrator (unseen, unidentified). The story is told not through dialogue alone or principally, but through the narrator's constant intervention. It is he who tells us what the snake was thinking as well as what he did. The interest in describing action is not paramount, rather, in ascertaining motivation and the consequence of improper deed resulting from inappropriate motivation.

A third trait, characteristic of the story in relationship to Scripture, is the redactor's insistence upon including along with a story other important exegeses of a verse of Scripture cited in the story. The redactor's point of interest becomes clear: the verse, with focus on its exposition—whether through concrete narrative or through abstract paraphrase and amplification. Stories about sages do not ordinarily bear the freight of (to us intruded) exegeses of verses cited in those stories. They run their course, beginning to end.

A fourth trait is the striking absence of movement. The Scripture-story rarely sets forth a coherent tale with beginning, middle, end, of tension and resolution, not to mention sustained interest in the characterization of the figures at hand. These ordinarily serve in the Scripture-story as card-board characters, serving to compose a tableau, which, frozen and at rest, in the aggregate makes its point. Stories about sages, by contrast, make their point not through a fixed and stationary tableau but through the unfolding of action, whether "he said to him..., he said to him...," or the tale of what actually is done.

What we have, in the aggregate before us, hardly constitutes a fully-realized story at all. The ultimate interest of the redactor predominates not only in the selection and arrangement of what is before us, but also in the substance of the narrative. In fact, the narrative tells no story at all but the purpose of presenting a setting for an exposition which is not a narrative at all. We may then distinguish both in subject-matter and in narrative technique the story based on Scripture and the story based on the sage, that is, the story within the setting of the written Torah, as read by sages, and the story within that of the oral Torah, as read by the same authorities.

VI. *An Inductive Taxonomy of the Story in The Fathers According to Rabbi Nathan. (ii) Indicative Traits of the Sage-Story*

The authorship of The Fathers had presented the message of sages solely in aphoristic form. Apophthegms bore the entire weight of that authorship's propositions, and—quite consistently—what made one saying cogent with others fore and aft was solely the position of the authority behind that saying: here, not there. Among the four types of narrative we find in The Fathers According to Rabbi Nathan, precedent, precipitant, parable, and story (scriptural or sagacious), the authorship of The Fathers completely neglected three. The authorship of The Fathers fully acknowledged the importance of the past, referring to historical events of Scripture. But they did not retell and include in their composition the scriptural stories of what had happened long ago. They understood that their predecessors lived exemplary lives, but they did not narrate stories about sages. They had every reason to appreciate the power of parable. But they did not think it necessary to harness that power for delivering their particular message, or even for stating in colorful ways the propositions they wished to impart. To be sure, in the compilation as we know it, the framers of The Fathers resorted to narrative, but only to serve as a precipitant, with great economy to describe the setting in which a stunning saying was set forth. They did not cite narratives in the form of precedents.

The authorship of The Fathers According to Rabbi Nathan clearly found inadequate the mode of intelligible discourse and the medium of expression selected by the framers of the document they chose to extend. The later writers possessed a message they deemed integral to that unfolding Torah of Moses at Sinai. They resorted to a mode of intelligible discourse, narrative, that conveyed propositions with great clarity, deeming the medium—again, narrative—a uniquely affective vehicle for conveying propositions from heart to heart. Not only so, but among the narratives utilized in their composition, they selected one for closest attention and narrative development. The sage-story took pride of place in its paramount position in The Fathers According to Rabbi Nathan, and that same sub-classification of narrative bore messages conveyed, in the document before us, in no other medium. A sustained reading of the sage-stories in our composition will show us how the framers made ample use of formerly neglected matters of intellect, aesthetics, and theology, specifically, to compose their ideas through a mode of thought and cogent thought, so as to construct intelligible discourse through a medium, meant to speak with immediacy and power to convey a message of critical urgency.

We start by demonstrating that the sage-story is fundamentally to be distinguished from the Scripture-story. To do so, I simply set side-by-side stories about a scriptural hero and a sage, as the authorship of The Fathers According to Rabbi Nathan presents both sorts of stories. The difference is not merely that one speaks of a hero that appears in Scripture, the other of one that derives from the chain of tradition of the Oral Torah. Much to the contrary! The contrast will show us right at the outset that quite different narrative conventions apply to the two distinct topics, the hero of Scripture, the hero of sagacity. Stories about the archetypal sage, Moses, "our lord" turn out not very different from stories on other scriptural topics. The striking contrast in the narrative qualities of the story about Hanina's and Abraham's beasts, given in what follows, tells the whole tale. Our example deals with a hero of the written Torah, Abraham, and one of the oral Torah, Hanina b. Dosa. The same point is made with reference to both figures. So the important point of difference will occur solely in the distinctive modes of telling the two stories. The narrative conventions do differ substantially:

VIII:VI.1   A.   Just as the righteous men in ancient times were pious, so their cattle were pious.

        B.   They say that the cattle of Abraham, our father, never went into a house which contained an idol,

C.　as it is said, "For I have cleared the house and made room for the camels" (Gen. 24:31), meaning, I have cleared the house of teraphim.

D.　And on what account does Scripture say, "And made room for the camels"?

E.　This teaches that they would not enter Laban the Aramaean's house until they had cleared away all the idols from before them.

VIII:VI.2　A.　There was the case of the ass of R. Hanina b. Dosa, which bandits stole and tied up in the courtyard. They set before it straw, barley and water, but it would not eat or drink.

B.　They said, "Why should we leave it here to die and make a stink for us in the courtyard? They went and opened the gate and sent it out, and it went along, braying, until it came to the house of R. Hanina b. Dosa.

C.　When it got near the house, [Hanina's] son heard its braying.

D.　He said to him, "Father, it appears to me that the braying is like the braying of our beast."

E.　He said to him, "My son, open the gate for it, for it must be nearly dying of starvation."

F.　He went and opened the gate for it, and put before it straw, barley and water, and it ate and drank.

G.　Therefore they say: Just as the righteous men in ancient times were pious, so their cattle were pious.

The contrast between the two stories could not be drawn more sharply. In the story about the biblical hero, we have proof-text after proof-text. In fact we have nothing like a narrative. "They say" that such and such did or did not do so and so hardly tells an engaging story. Then comes a lesson, E. By contrast, making the same point, the case involving Hanina's ass does involve a fully expounded narrative. The hero is the animal, not the authority. The story works out its message without the need for G, since the point is made within the limits and discipline of the story itself, with its point of tension—the stolen beast that finds its way home, that is released because of its own pious behavior—and the resolution thereof. The juxtaposed stories indicate that, where the written Torah supplies the materials for a narrative, the consequent tale hardly qualifies as a story at all.

This brings us back to those questions that define our reading of stories on sages. First, we wish to find out whether the subject-matter—sages' lives and deeds—imposes narrative literary conventions that differ from those that guide writers of stories about Scriptural figures. On the surface we come across numerous obvious differences in narrative convention. Three seem to me definitive:

(1)   The story about a sage has a beginning, middle, and end, and the story about a sage also rests not only on verbal exchanges ("he said to him..., he said to him..."), but on (described) action.

(2)   The story about a sage unfolds from a point of tension and conflict to a clear resolution and remission of the conflict.

(3)   The story about a sage rarely invokes a verse of Scripture and never serves to prove a proposition concerning the meaning of a verse of Scripture.

What about Scripture-stories? The traits of stories about scriptural figures and themes in retrospect prove opposite:

(1)   In the story about a scriptural hero there is no beginning, middle, and end, and little action. The burden of the narrative is carried by "he said to him..., he said to him...." Described action is rare and plays slight role in the unfolding of the narrative. Often the narrative consists of little more than a setting for a saying, and the point of the narrative is conveyed not through what is told but through the cited saying.

(2)   The story about a scriptural hero is worked out as a tableau, with description of the components of the stationary tableau placed at the center. There is little movement, no point of tension that is resolved.

(3)   The story about a scriptural hero always invokes verses from Scripture and makes the imputation of meaning to those verses the center of interest.

The sage-stories in The Fathers According to Rabbi Nathan do not cover a broad variety of topics but attend only to a few, selected subjects. Only certain aspects of the lives and doings of sages demanded attention, and then for highly particular purposes. The sage-stories attend to only four topics:

(1) the sage's beginning in Torah-study,

(2) his character and his deeds in relationship to the Torah,

(3) the role of the sage in important historical events,

(4) and at the end, the death of sages.

A list of the topics that are neglected, for example, the sage's childhood and wonderful precociousness in Torah-study, the sage's supernatural deeds, the sage's everyday administration of the community's affairs, the sage's life with other sages and with disciples— such a list could be extended over many pages. But it suffices to notice that our document has chosen a highly restricted list of topics, but then differentiated, within these topics, by telling quite diverse stories about different sages as to their origins, deaths, and the like. The upshot is that when the authorship of The Fathers According to Rabbi Nathan resorted to narrative in general and story-telling in particular, with special attention to sage-stories, those compositors had in mind a very particular purpose and message indeed. There was nothing random or episodic in their choices of topics, and the medium of story-telling served the message conveyed by the story set forth in our composition.

A. The Sage: (1) The Origins from Nowhere. Aqiba and Eliezer

The Fathers According to Rabbi Nathan contains stories of "the origins" of two sages, Aqiba and Eliezer. By "origins," the story-tellers mean the beginnings of the Torah-study of a famed authority. Life begins at birth into the natural family, but when we wish to tell sage-stories, beginnings are measured differently. The sage begins (supernatural) family life when he begins Torah-study. And the sages whose origins are found noteworthy both began in mature years, not in childhood (despite the repeated emphasis of The Fathers upon the unique value of beginning Torah-study in childhood). The proposition implicit in origins-stories then is that any male may start his Torah-study at any point in life and hope for true distinction in the Torah-community. But that does not account for the germ of the story, the critical tension that creates an event worthy of narrative, that poses a question demanding an answer, a problem requiring a solution through a tale with a beginning, middle, and end.

The critical tension of "origins" derives from the formation of supernatural, in contrast to natural, relationships. Life begins at the womb. But Torah-life begins at a supernatural birth, and there must be a tension between the natural beginning and the supernatural one. It is expressed through contrasting natural ties and relationships, to father and mother and brothers and sisters, or to one's wife, and supernatural ties to Torah-study. When a man undertakes to study the Torah, in the stories before us he abandons his natural relationships to his family, in the one case to his wife, in the other to his father. The point of origination of the sage marks the beginning of the wedding of the sage to the Torah, with the concomitant diminution of his relationship to his wife, who may be abandoned and indeed required to support the nascent sage's children as well as herself. The nascent sage furthermore gains a new father, the master or sage, and cuts his ties to the natural father, with the consequence that he loses his share in the estate to be provided by the father. These tensions generate the stories before us.

While told each in its own terms and subject to differentiation from the other, the stories make essentially the same point, which is that one can begin Torah-study in mature years and progress to the top, when one does so, one also goes from poverty to wealth through public recognition of one's mastery of the Torah, and a range of parallel propositions along the same lines. The supernatural relationship, which has superceded the natural ones to wife and father, generates glory and honor, riches and fame, for the sage, and, through reflection, for the natural family as well. That is the point of the stories of the origins of sages, which take up what is clearly a pressing question and answer it in a powerful way.

What of the redactional question? When the compositors of The Fathers According to Rabbi Nathan made up or selected the stories at hand (we do not know which), did they make up the stories, or revise them, so as to conform to the requirements of a larger setting, in which the planned to situate these stories? The answer— one which will be repeated for sage-stories of all kinds—is negative. The stories before us are attached to the saying of Yosé b. Yoezer, *"And wallow in the dust of their feet, and drink in their words with gusto."* The base-saying therefore introduces the desired theme, which is Torah-study that requires one's accepting with humility the reduced status of disciple before the master. But once the theme of sages' origins in the Torah are introduced, as we shall see, the entire composition moves in its own direction. Nothing in the redactional structure defined by The Fathers makes an impact upon the structure or unfolding of the stories at hand, which are autonomous. VI:IV.1 serves as a deftly constructed joining block, between the already-completed materials to follow on Aqiba, then Eliezer, and the rather pointed and germane exegesis of the statements of Avot. Clearly, the authorship has a powerful interest in including stories about sages' lives, and the structure of The Fathers served as a suitable framework—that alone.

VI:IV.1 A.   Another comment on the statement, "And wallow in the dust of their feet:"

       B.   This refers to R. Eliezer.

       C.   "... and drink in their words with gusto:"

       D.   This refers to R. Aqiba.

This pericope serves as a prologue to the vast stories to follow, first on Aqiba, then on Eliezer.

VI:V.1   A.   How did R. Aqiba begin [his Torah-study]?

B.   They say: He was forty years old and had never repeated a tradition. One time he was standing at the mouth of a well. He thought to himself, "Who carved out this stone?"

C.   They told him, "It is the water that is perpetually falling on it every day."

D.   They said to him, "Aqiba, do you not read Scripture? 'The water wears away stones' (Job. 4:19)?"

E.   On the spot R. Aqiba constructed in his own regard an argument a fortiori: now if something soft can [Goldin:] wear down something hard, words of Torah, which are as hard as iron, how much the more so should wear down my heart, which is made of flesh and blood."

F.   On the spot he repented [and undertook] to study the Torah.

G.   He and his son went into study session before a children's' teacher, saying to him, "My lord, teach me Torah."

H.   R. Aqiba took hold of one end of the tablet, and his son took hold of the other end. The teacher wrote out for him Alef Bet and he learned it, Alef Tav and he learned it, the Torah of the Priests [the books of Leviticus and Numbers] and he learned it. He went on learning until he had learned the entire Torah.

I.   He went and entered study-sessions before R. Eliezer and before R. Joshua. He said to them, "My lords, open up for me the reasoning of the Mishnah."

J.   When they had stated one passage of law, he went and sat by himself and said, "Why is this alef written? why is this bet written? Why is this statement made?" He went and asked them and, in point of fact, [Goldin:] reduced them to silence.

Clearly, our opening component in the *magnalia Aqibae* is a narrative. The tone and program establish the mood of narrative: he was... he had... he did.... But how shall we classify the narrative, and by what criteria? One important criterion is whether the narrative describes a situation or tells about something that happened, with a beginning, middle, and end. The one is at rest, the other in movement.

These constitute questions with objective answers. Do we have a tableau or a story, or, for that matter, a parable, or any of those other types of narratives we have already classified? By the simple criterion that a story has a beginning, middle, end, which dictate points of narrative tension, and a clearly delineated program of action, we have a story. The components do more than merely set up pieces in a static tableau. They flow from one to the next and yield movement—hence narrative action.

What about the parable? Aqiba's origins in no way form or appeal to a parable or serve for parabolic purposes there is a named authority, a specific hero. The passage also forms more than a "dramatization" of the (stated) proposition that one can start Torah-study late in life, or of an exegesis of Scripture, e.g., a setting that serves to precipitate a comment on a verse of Scripture. If we compare the materials at hand to, "One day he saw a skull floating on the water and said...," we realize the difference.

What about the Scripture-story? The blatant differences require slight amplification. We note that verses of Scripture scarcely intervene, and there is no focus on the exegesis of a verse of Scripture. At D, Aqiba and his interlocutors do not interpret the verse but simply draw upon its statement of fact.

An authentic, successful story,[4] as I stress, has a beginning, middle, and end: movement from tension to resolution. In the present story there is a beginning: he had not studied; a middle, he went and studied; and an end, following Goldin's persuasive rendering, "he reduced them to silence." True, the action takes place mainly in what Aqiba thought, rather than in what he did. But in the nature of things, the action of going to study the Torah forms the one genuinely dramatic deed that is possible with the present subject-matter. The beginning then works its way out at B-F. The middle is at G-H: Aqiba was so humble as to study with his own son. Then at I-J we have a climax and conclusion: Aqiba proved so profound in his question-asking that he reduced the great authorities to silence. That conclusion hardly flows from A-H, but it is absolutely necessary to make the entire sequence into a cogent story. Otherwise we have merely bits and pieces of an uncompleted narrative.

Let us proceed to what follows in the context of the telling of the story of Aqiba's origins.

VI:V.2 A.   R. Simeon b. Eleazar says, "I shall make a parable for you. To what is the matter comparable? To a stonecutter who was cutting stone in a quarry. One time he took his chisel and went and sat down on the mountain and started to chip away little shards from it. People came by and said to him, 'What are you doing?'

B.   "He said to them, 'Lo, I am going to uproot the mountain and move it into the Jordan River.'

---

[4] Terms defined in volume one of this exercise.

C.   "They said to him, 'You will never be able to uproot the entire mountain.'

D.   "He continued chipping away at the mountain until he came to a huge boulder. He quarried underneath it and unearthed it and uprooted it and tossed it into the Jordan."

E.   "He said to the boulder, 'This is not your place, but that is your place.'"

F.   "Likewise this is what R. Aqiba did to R. Eliezer and to R. Joshua."

The parable without F simply says that with patience one may move mountains. The parable by itself—not applied—amplifies or at least continues VI:V.1.E, the power of words of Torah to wear down the hard heart of a human being. But the parable proves particular to the preceding story, since the add-on, E, F, applies the parable to VI:V.1.J, the humiliation of Joshua and Eliezer. We may wonder whether, without the announcement at A that we have a parable, the parabolic character of the tale would have impressed us. The answer is that the general traits of a parable—an anonymous illustration in concrete and everyday terms of an abstract proposition—do occur in A-D, at which point the parable worked out its proposition: "he continued chipping away...." Even E, without F, can remain within the limits of the announced proposition of the parable, that is, the power of patience and persistence. So only F is jarring. It clearly serves the redactor's purpose. It does not transform the parable into a story (!), since it does not impose upon the prior narrative that particularity and concrete one-time-ness that form the indicative traits of the story alone. In all, we may dismiss from the evidence of the story the present complement to the foregoing.

VI:V.3 A.   Said R. Tarfon to him, "Aqiba, in your regard Scripture says, 'He stops up streams so that they do not trickle, and what is hidden he brings into the light' (Job 28:11).

B.   "Things that are kept as mysteries from ordinary people has R. Aqiba brought to light."

"He said to him" does not make a story, and what is said does not bear the marks of a story, whole or in part.

VI:V.4 A.   Every day he would bring a bundle of twigs [Goldin: straw], half of which he would sell in exchange for food, and half of which he would use for a garment.

B.   His neighbors said to him, "Aqiba, you are killing us with the smoke. Sell them to us, buy oil with the money, and by the light of a lamp do your studying."

C.   He said to them, "I fill many needs with that bundle, first, I repeat traditions [by the light of the fire I kindle with] them, second, I warm myself with them, third, I sleep on them."

VI:V.5 A.   In time to come R. Aqiba is going to impose guilt [for failing to study] on the poor [who use their poverty as an excuse not to study].

B.   For if they say to them, "Why did you not study the Torah," and they reply, "Because we were poor," they will say to them, "But was not R. Aqiba poorer and more poverty-stricken?"

C.   If they say, "Because of our children [whom we had to work to support]," they will say to them, "Did not R. Aqiba have sons and daughters?"

D.   So they will say to them, "Because Rachel, his wife, had the merit [of making it possible for him to study, and we have no equivalent helpmates; our wives do not have equivalent merit at their disposal]."

It is hard to classify VI:V.4 as other than a narrative setting for a conversation. But the conversation makes no point by itself. In fact the whole forms a prologue to VI:V.5, which does make a powerful point.

VI:V.6 A   It was at the age of forty that he went to study the Torah. Thirteen years later he taught the Torah in public.

B.   They say that he did not leave this world before there were silver and golden tables in his possession,

C.   and before he went up onto his bed on golden ladders.

D.   His wife went about in golden sandals and wore a golden tiara of the silhouette of the city [Jerusalem].

E.   His disciples said to him, "My lord, you have shamed us by what you have done for her [since we cannot do the same for our wives]."

F.   He said to them, "She bore a great deal of pain on my account for [the study of] the Torah."

This item completes the foregoing, the narrative of how Rachel's devotion to Aqiba's study of the Torah produced a rich reward. The "they said to him... he said to him..."-sequences do not comprise a story or even establish much of a narrative framework. The upshot is that for Aqiba we have a sequence of narratives but only one story, that at the beginning. The composite does not hang together very well, but it does make a few important points.

This brings us to the story of the origins, in the Torah, of Eliezer:

VI:VI.1 A.   How did R. Eliezer ben Hyrcanus begin [his Torah-study]?

B.   He had reached the age of twenty-two years and had not yet studied the Torah. One time he said, "I shall go and study the Torah before Rabban Yohanan ben Zakkai."

C.   His father Hyrcanus said to him, "You are not going to taste a bit of food until you have ploughed the entire furrow.":

D.   He got up in the morning and ploughed the entire furrow.

E.   They say that that day was Friday. He went and took a meal with his father in law.

F.   And some say that he tasted nothing from the sixth hour on Friday until the sixth hour on Sunday.

The narrative is rather strange, since none of the actions is given a motivation. That immediately-evident difference between Eliezer's and Aqiba's story will later on prove still more striking than it does now. But it suffices to note the points in which the two stories diverge in narrative technique. While in the case of Aqiba, we know why the great master originally determined to study the Torah, in the instance of Eliezer we do not. All we know is that at the mature age of twenty-two, he determined to study in the session of Yohanan ben Zakkai. My judgment is that the story-teller has in mind the task of explaining Eliezer's origins as Yohanan's disciple, not working out the inner motivation of the disciple. That accounts, also, for the random details, none of which fits together with the next. I see only a sequence of unintegrated details: he was twenty-two and decided to study the Torah. His father said, "Do not eat until you plough the furrow." He ploughed the furrow. Then he went and ate with his father in law. Some say he did not eat until Sunday. These details, scarcely connected, produce no effect either of a narrative or of a propositional character.

VI:VI.2 A.   On the way he saw a rock. He picked it up and too, it and put it into his mouth.

B.   And some say that what he picked up was cattle dung.

C.   He went and spent the night at his hostel.

Even if we read VI:VI.2 as part of VI:VI.1, all we have is more unintegrated details. Nothing in VI:VI.1-2 points to a cogent narrative, let alone a story. All we have are odd bits of information about what someone "said." The whole conglomerate does serve, however, to set the stage for VI:VI.3. The details necessary to understand what is coming have now made their appearance, and the climax is before us: he went and studied, and, because he had not eaten, produced bad breath. Yohanan recognized the bad breath and said, "Just as you suffered, so you will enjoy a reward."

VI:VI.3 A.   He went and entered study-session before Rabban Yohanan ben Zakkai in Jerusalem.

B.   Since a bad odor came out of his mouth, Rabban Yohanan ben Zakkai said to him, "Eliezer my son, have you taken a meal today?"

C.   He shut up.

D.   He asked him again, and he shut up again.

E.,   He sent word and inquired at his hostel, and asked, "Has Eliezer eaten anything with you?"

F.   They sent word to him, "We thought that he might be eating with my lord."

G.   He said, "For my part, I thought that he might be eating with you. Between me and you, we should have lost R. Eliezer in the middle."

H.   He said to him, "Just as the odor of your mouth has gone forth, so will a good name in the Torah go forth for you."

VI:VI.4 A.   Hyrcanus, his father, heard that he was studying the Torah with Rabban Yohanan ben Zakkai. He decided, "I shall go and impose on Eliezer my son a vow not to derive benefit from my property."

B.   They say that that day Rabban Yohanan ben Zakkai was in session and expounding [the Torah] in Jerusalem, and all the great men of Israel were in session before him. He heard that he was coming. He set up guards, saying to them, "If he comes to take a seat, do not let him."

C.   He came to take a seat and they did not let him.

D.   He kept stepping over people and moving forward until he came to Ben Sisit Hakkesset and Naqdimon b. Gurion and Ben Kalba Sabua. He sat among them, trembling.

E.   They say, On that day Rabban Yohanan ben Zakkai looked at R. Eliezer, indicating to him, "Cite an appropriate passage and give an exposition."

F.   He said to him, "I cannot cite an appropriate passage."

G.   He urged him, and the other disciples urged him.

H.   He went and cited an opening passage and expounded matters the like of which no ear had ever heard.

I.   And at every word that he said, Rabban Yohanan ben Zakkai arose and kissed him on his head and said, "My lord, Eliezer, my lord, you have taught us truth."

J.   As the time came to break up, Hyrcanus his father stood up and said, "My lords, I came here only to impose a vow on my son, Eliezer, not to derive benefit from my possession. Now all of my possessions are given over to Eliezer my son, and all my other sons are disinherited and will have no share in them."

We have a beginning: Hyrcanus plans to go and place Eliezer under a vow of ostracism. That not only begins the story, but it also creates an enormous tension. A dramatic setting is set up: do not let the father sit down at the back, so that the father will sit among the greatest men of Jerusalem (B-D). Yohanan then calls upon Eliezer to speak, and, after appropriate urging, he does. The tension is resolved at the climax, which also is the conclusion. I cannot think of a more perfect story, since every detail contributes to the whole, and the story-teller's intent—to underline the reward coming to the disciple, even though his family originally opposes his joining the sage—is fully realized. We note, therefore, that the conglomerate of narratives involving both Aqiba and Eliezer in fact rest in each case on a single story, and that story forms the redactional focus, permitting the aggregation of further materials, not all of them of a finished character, and some of them not stories at all.

Let us now stand back and review the whole composite involving both Aqiba and Eliezer, which, in the aggregate, makes the point that one can start Torah-study in mature years. VI:IV.1 serves only as a preface to the autonomous materials collected on the theme of how two famous masters began their studies late in life, having had no prior education. Both figures, moreover, started off poor but got rich when they became famous. These are Eliezer and Aqiba. There is no clear connection between the materials and the original saying. Perhaps the reference to wallowing in the dust of their feet in connection with Eliezer is meant to link up to the detail that he put a piece of dirt or cow dung in his mouth, but that seems to me far-fetched.

We refer first to Eliezer, then to Aqiba, but tell the stories in reverse order. The diverse stories on Aqiba are hardly harmonious, since one set knows nothing of his wife, while the other introduces her as the main figure. The first set, No. 2ff., emphasizes how slow and steady wins the race. The lesson is that if one persists, one may ultimately best one's masters. No. 3 goes over the same matter, now with a parable to make the point that if one persists, he can uproot mountains. This seems to me appropriately joined to the foregoing, with the notion that Joshua and Eliezer are the mountains, as is made explicit.. Tarfon then goes over the same matter in yet another way, No. 4. No. 5 then goes over the theme of studying in poverty. No. 5 seems to me a rather pointless story, but it leads to No. 6, which presents its own message explicitly. I treat No. 6 as distinct from No. 5 because it introduces the distinct theme of Aqiba's wife, and that has nothing to do with studying in poverty, but rather, the wife's toleration of the husband's long absences. No. 7 then carries forward the second theme of the foregoing, Aqiba's wealth later on and how he lavished it on Rachel. I find puzzling the failure of the story-teller to take an interest in the source of Aqiba's great wealth.

The sequence on Eliezer goes over a recurrent theme, but is as incoherent as the foregoing. No. 1 presents a number of problems of continuity, since 1.1-D are simply gibberish, there being no clear relationship between C and B. How E-F fit in I cannot say. One may make a good case for treating VI:VI.1 and VI:VI.2 as continuous. But because of the detail of 9.A, on the way he saw a rock, it seems to me that we are on good ground in treating the latter as a fragment of yet another story, rather than as a bridge. VI:VI.3 is on its own coherent and complete, a cogent and readily comprehended statement on its own. VI:VI.4 also works well, beginning to end. The details given in D then account for the appendix which follows, VI:VII-X.

B. The Sage: (2) Supernatural Patience as the Torah's Way of Life

The natural next question draws our attention to the consequence of rebirth in the supernatural realm defined by the Torah. Studying the Torah changes one's character and therefore also one's relationships with other people, just as it has redefined the disciple's relationships with his (natural) family. The supernatural character of the sage finds expression, for instance, in the sage's remarkable—and unnatural—patience. So we turn to the description of traits of personality and character exhibited by those who study the Torah as sages' disciples.

Patience and forbearance, necessary traits of the sage, serve to win people to the Torah and so to give them their share in eternal life. Sagacity attained through discipleship leads to eternal life. Learning not joined to discipleship yields death. The patience of the sage certifies his successful discipleship, his authentic learning of the Torah. The deeper issue—the traits of personality and character that Torah-learning is supposed to instill—is worked out through the stories before us. And that is the important point: it is specifically through telling stories about sages, not merely formulating abstract statements of their ideal, that the authorship of The Fathers According to Rabbi Nathan delivers the message at hand.

XV:IV.1A.   What characterized the patience of Hillel the Elder?

B.   They tell the following case, concerning two people, who went and made a bet with one another for four hundred zuz.

C. They stipulated, "Whoever can go and infuriate Hillel will get the four hundred zuz.

D. One of them went [to try]. That day was a Friday, toward nightfall, and Hillel was washing his hair. The man came and knocked on the door, saying, "Where is Hillel, where is Hillel?"

E. Hillel wrapped himself up in his cloak and came to meet him. He said to him, 'speak."

F. He said to him, "Why are the eyes of the people of Palmyra [Tadmor] bleary?"

G. He said to him, "Because they live in the sands of the desert and the winds blow and scatter the sand into their eyes. Therefore their eyes are bleary."

H. He went and waited a while and came back and knocked on the door.

I. He said, "Where is Hillel, where is Hillel?"

J. He wrapped himself up in his cloak and come out.

K. He said to him, "My son, what do you need?"

L. He said to him, "I need to ask a matter of law."

M. He said to him, "Go ahead."

N. He said to him, "Why are the feet of the Africans flat?"

O. He said to him, "Because they live by swamps, and every day walk in water, therefore their feet are flat."

P. The man went his way, waited a while, came back, and knocked on the door.

Q. He said, "Where is Hillel? where is Hillel?"

R. He wrapped himself in his cloak and went out.

S. He said to him, "What do you need to ask?"

T. He said to him, "I have to ask a matter of law."

U. He said to him, "Ask." He then wrapped himself in his garment and sat down before him.

V. He said to him, "What do you need to ask?"

W. He said to him, "Is this the way princes reply? May people like you not become many in Israel."

X. He said to him, "God forbid! Watch yourself. What do you want?"

Y, He said to him, "On what account are the heads of the Babylonians long?"

Z. He said to him, "My son, you have asked an important "law." It is because over there they do not have smart midwives. When the baby is born, the ones who deal with it are slave-boys and slave-girls. Therefore their heads are long. But here, where we have smart midwives, when a baby is born, they raise it in a cradle and rub its head. Therefore their heads are round."

AA. He said to him, "You have cost me four hundred zuz."

BB. He said to him, "Hillel is worth your losing four hundred zuz without Hillel's losing his temper."

XV:V.1 A. What characterized the impatience of Shammai the Elder?

B.   They say, there was the case of a man who stood before Shammai. He said to him, "My lord, how many Torahs do you have?"

C.   He said to him, "Two, one in writing, one memorized."

D.   He said to him, "As to the one in writing, I believe you. As to the memorized one, I do not believe you."

E.   He rebuked him and threw him out.

F.   He came before Hillel. He said to him, "My lord, how many Torahs were given?"

G.   He said to him, "Two, one in writing, one memorized."

H.   He said to him, "As to the one in writing, I believe you. As to the memorized one, I do not believe you."

I.   He said to him, "My son, sit."

J.   He wrote for him, Alef, bet.

K.   He said to him, "What is this?"

L.   He said to him, "An alef."

M.   He said to him, "This is not an alef but a bet."

N.   He said to him, "What is this?

O.   He said to him, "Bet."

P.   He said to him, "This is not a bet but a gimmel."

Q.   He said to him, "How do you know that this is an alef and this a bet and this a gimmel? But that is what our ancestors have handed over to us—the tradition that this is an alef, this a bet, this a gimmel. Just as you have accepted this teaching in good faith, so accept the other in good faith."

XV:V.2 A.   There was the case of a gentile who was passing behind a synagogue and heard a child reciting in Scripture: "This is the clothing which they shall make: a breast plate, ephod, and robe" (Ex. 28:4).

B.   He came before Shammai and said to him, "My lord, all this honor—for whom is it designated?"

C.   He said to him, "It is for the high priest who stands and carries out the service at the altar."

D.   He said to him, "Convert me on the stipulation that you make me high priest so that I may carry out the service at the altar."

E.   He said to him, "Is there no priesthood in Israel, and do we not have high priests to stand and carry out the acts of service at the altar assigned to the high priest, so that a mere convert who has come only with his staff and wallet may come and take up the service of the high priest?"

F.   He threw him out.

G.   He came before Hillel and said to him, "My lord, convert me, on the stipulation that you make me high priest so that I may carry out the service at the altar."

H.   He said to him, 'sit, and I shall tell you something [of the rules of the office you propose to enter]. For if someone proposes to greet a mortal king, is it not logical that he should learn the rules of going in and coming out?"

I.   He said to him, "Yes."

J. "You, who wish to greet the King of kings of kings, the Holy One, blessed be he, surely should learn how to enter the house of the Holy of Holies, how to set up the lamps, how to offer an offering on the altar, how to arrange the table, how to set out the wood."

K He said to him, "Do what you think appropriate."

L. He first wrote for him, "Alef, bet," and the man learned the letters.

M. Then he presented the Torah of the Priests [the books of Leviticus and Numbers], and the man went on learning the words until he came to the verse, "The non-priest who draws near [the altar] shall die" (Num. 1:51).

N. The proselyte constructed an argument a fortiori concerning himself: if an Israelite, who is called a son of the Omnipresent, and concerning whom the Presence of God has said, "And you shall be mine as a kingdom of priests and a holy people" (Ex. 19:6), nonetheless is subject to Scripture's admonition, 'The non-priest who draws near [the altar] shall die' (Num. 1:51), I, who am a mere proselyte, who has come only with my wallet, all the more so!"

O. The proselyte was reconciled on his own.

P. He came before Hillel the Elder and said to him, "May all the blessings that are in the Torah rest on your head, for if you had been like Shammai the Elder, you would have wiped me out of this world and of the world to come. Your humility has brought me into this world and the coming one."

Q. They say that to that proselyte two sons were born. One he called Hillel, and one he called Gamaliel, and they called them, Hillel's converts.

The stories on Hillel, and Shammai present in narrative and dramatic form a single proposition: patience should characterize the sage.

The narrator leaves no doubt concerning his aesthetic power. He begins in each case with a clear beginning, stating the issue at hand and establishing a tension, so XV:IV.1.C. Whoever can infuriate Hillel wins enough money to live for two years. Then there is a triad of action, D-G, H-O, P-Z, with the first two components closely matched, the third exhibiting points of difference so as to lead to the climax and resolution. Then we have a clear conclusion, AA-BB. The second story, XV:V.1 provides as its generative tension the story about the encounter with Shammai, yielding the meeting with Hillel. It is of course not a story about Shammai at all; that component serves only to establish the point of tension—the doctrine of the two Torahs—and its resolution in the encounter with Hillel. It yields in narrative form the conclusion and the lesson that people have to accept the teachings of the "tradition" in good faith. XV:V.2

matches the story in its narrative pattern, with a beginning supplied by Shammai, a middle and climactic conclusion produced by Hillel. Now the lesson is that one's own reasoning yields the correct reading of the Torah. The conclusion, XV:V.2P-Q, reverts back to the superscription, XV:IV.1, indicating that it is from a single hand that the whole composite has come to us in its final statement.

A further story that conveys the importance of patience as the expression of one's conforming to the personality required by the Torah follows:

XLI:III.1   A.   There is the case of R. Simeon b. Eleazar, who was coming from the house of his master in Migdal Eder, riding on an ass and making his way along the sea shore. He saw an unusually ugly man. He said to him, "Empty head! what a beast you are! Is it possible that everyone in your town is as ugly as you are?"

B.   He said to him, "And what can I do about it? Go to the craftsman who made me and tell him, 'How ugly is that utensil that you have made!'"

C.   When R. Simeon b. Eleazar realized that he had sinned, he got off his ass and prostrated himself before the man, saying to him, "I beg you to forgive me."

D.   He said to him, "I shall not forgive you until you go to the craftsman who made me and tell him, "How ugly is that utensil that you have made!"

E.   He ran after the man for three miles. The people of the town came out to meet him. They said toward him, "Peace be to you, my lord."

F.   He said to them, "Whom do you call, "my lord"?"

G.   They said to him, "To the one who is going along after you."

H.   He said to them, "If this is a "my lord," may there not be many more like him in Israel."

I.   They said to him, "God forbid! and what has he done to you?"

J.   He said to them, "Thus and so did he do to me."

K.   They said to him, "Nonetheless, forgive him."

L.   He said to them, "Lo, I forgive him, on the condition that he not make a habit of acting in that way."

M.   On that same day R. Simeon entered the great study-house that was his and gave an exposition: "One should always be as soft as a reed and not as tough as a cedar."

N.   "In the case of a reed, all the winds in the world can go on blowing against it but it sways with them, so that when the winds grow silent, it reverts and stands in its place. And what is the destiny of a reed? In the end a pen is cut from it with which to write a scroll of the Torah.

O.   "But in the case of a cedar it will not stand in place, but when the south wind blows against it, it uproots the cedar and turns it over. And what is the destiny of a cedar? Foresters come and cut it down and use it to roof houses, and the rest they toss into the fire.

P.   "On the basis of this fact they have said, "One should always be as soft as a reed and not as tough as a cedar."

This story opens with a striking encounter. There is a meeting and
the sage insults the ugly man, who responds appropriately: Go tell
God about it. Simeon realized his error. The narrative relies on
considerable action: the sage runs after the man, is met by the townsfolk who great him with honor, the insulted one realizes the state of
affairs and curses the sage. Then the sage gives an exposition which
makes the point that is required. The narrative that has preceded
hardly serves merely as a setting for the exposition. Quite to the
contrary, the exposition forms the climax and conclusion of a well-
told story, with a beginning and a critical event, a middle, a conclusion of considerable power and meaning. There are even elements
of characterization, movement within the story in the presentation
of the personalities of both sage, who learns something, and the
opposite party, who is given his just and rightful reward: a lesson
he precipitates.

C. The Sage: (3) Sagacity and History

The sage plays a public, not solely a private role. I have already
explained why, within the genealogical theory of Israel as one extended family, the sage as supernatural father forms the critical element in the history of the family, Israel. That history of course is
defined by the encounter with Rome in particular. Rome will be
represented by its persona, its family hero, counterpart to Abraham
or Jacob or Moses, just as is Israel, and that can only be the emper-
or. That is why, in addition to the theme of Torah-study, the sage-
story bears a second important burden, namely, that of history and
eschatology, this age and the age to come.

All sage-stories in The Fathers According to Rabbi Nathan that
deal not with the lives and deeds of sages concern the one large historical question facing Israel: its history in this world and destiny in
the world to come. History finds its definition in a single event: the
encounter with Rome, involving two aspects, first, the destruction
of the Temple and the sages' role in dealing with that matter; second, the (associated, consequent) repression of Torah-sages and their
study. Israel's history in this world works itself out in the encounter
with Rome, Israel's counterpart and opposite, and that history in
the world coming soon will see a reversal of roles. The centrality of

study of the Torah in securing Israel's future forms the leitmotiv of the stories at hand. We begin with the important story about the destruction of the Temple. That protracted story finds its setting in an exegesis of the saying in The Fathers that the world stands on deeds of loving kindness. These then are found by the exegete at Hos. 6:6, and the intrusion of that verse carries in its wake a narrative—not a story but a narrative-setting for a saying—about Yohanan ben Zakkai and his disciple, Joshua, in the ruins of the Temple. Only at the end of the matter do we find the major historical story of the destruction.

IV:V.1 A.   ... on deeds of loving kindness: how so?

B.   Lo, Scripture says, "For I desire mercy and not sacrifice, [and the knowledge of God rather than burnt offerings]" (Hos. 6:6).

C.   To begin with the world was created only on account of loving kindness.

D.   For so it is said, "For I have said, the world is built with loving kindness, in the very heavens you establish your faithfulness" (Ps. 89:3).

IV:V.2 A.   One time [after the destruction of the Temple] Rabban Yohanan ben Zakkai was going forth from Jerusalem, with R. Joshua following after him. He saw the house of the sanctuary lying in ruins.

B.   R. Joshua said, "Woe is us for this place which lies in ruins, the place in which the sins of Israel used to come to atonement."

C.   He said to him, "My son, do not be distressed. We have another mode of atonement, which is like [atonement through sacrifice], and what is that? It is deeds of loving kindness.

D.   "For so it is said, 'For I desire mercy and not sacrifice, [and the knowledge of God rather than burnt offerings]' (Hos. 6:6)."

IV:V.3 A.   So we find in the case of Daniel, that most desirable man, that he carried out deeds of loving kindness.

B.   And what are the deeds of loving kindness that Daniel did?

C.   If you say that he offering whole offerings and sacrifices, do people offer sacrifices in Babylonia?

D.   And has it not in fact been said, "Take heed that you not offer your whole offerings in any place which you see but in the place which the Lord will select in the territory of one of the tribes. There you will offer up your whole offerings" (Deut. 12:13-14).

E.   When then were the deeds of loving kindness that Daniel did?

F.   He would adorn the bride and make her happy, join a cortege for the deceased, give a penny to a pauper, pray three times every day,

G.   and his prayer was received with favor,

H.   for it is said, "And when Daniel knew that the writing was signed, he went into his house—his windows were open in his upper chamber toward Jerusalem—and he kneeled upon his knees three times a day and prayed and gave thanks before his God as he did aforetime" (Dan. 6:11).

This entire construction serves as a prologue to what will now follow, an account of the destruction of the Temple, which forms the background to IV:VI.1. We have not a story but a narrative that forms a setting for a saying, so IV:V.2. From "one time…," we are given the occasion on which the colloquy of B, C, took place. Still, there is a narrative side to matters that emerges from the implicit movement from B to C. But classifying the passage as a story seems to me not justified. The autonomy of the sage-story is shown once more, for the story that follows, utterly independent of the preceding, exhibits all of the indicative traits we have defined and demonstrates that the introductory materials have simply provided a proper setting for the stunning account before us.

IV:VI.1 A.   Now when Vespasian came to destroy Jerusalem, he said to [the inhabitants of the city,] "Idiots! why do you want to destroy this city and burn the house of the sanctuary? For what do I want of you, except that you send me a bow or an arrow [as marks of submission to my rule], and I shall go on my way."

B.   They said to him, "Just as we sallied out against the first two who came before you and killed them, so shall we sally out and kill you."

C.   When Rabban Yohanan ben Zakkai heard, he proclaimed to the men of Jerusalem, saying to them, "My sons, why do you want to destroy this city and burn the house of the sanctuary? For what does he want of you, except that you send him a bow or an arrow, and he will go on his way."

D.   They said to him, "Just as we sallied out against the first two who came before him and killed them, so shall we sally out and kill him."

E.   Vespasian had stationed men near the walls of the city, and whatever they heard, they would write on an arrow and shoot out over the wall. [They reported] that Rabban Yohanan ben Zakkai was a loyalist of Caesar's.

F.   After Rabban Yohanan ben Zakkai had spoken to them one day, a second, and a third, and the people did not accept his counsel, he sent and called his disciples, R. Eliezer and R. Joshua, saying to them, "My sons, go and get me out of here. Make me an ark and I shall go to sleep in it."

G.   R. Eliezer took the head and R. Joshua the feet, and toward sunset they carried him until they came to the gates of Jerusalem.

H.   The gate keepers said to them, "Who is this?"

I.   They said to him, "It is a corpse. Do you not know that a corpse is not kept overnight in Jerusalem."

J.   They said to them, "If it is a corpse, take him out," so they took him out and brought him out at sunset, until they came to Vespasian.

K.   They opened the ark and he stood before him.

L.   He said to him, "Are you Rabban Yohanan ben Zakkai? Indicate what I should give you."

M.   He said to him, "I ask from you only Yavneh, to which I shall go, and where I shall teach my disciples, establish prayer [Goldin: a prayer house], and carry out all of the religious duties."

N.   He said to him, "Go and do whatever you want."

O.   He said to him, "Would you mind if I said something to you."

P.   He said to him, "Go ahead."

Q.   He said to him, "Lo, you are going to be made sovereign."

R.   He said to him, "How do you know?

S.   He said to him, "It is a tradition of ours that the house of the sanctuary will be given over not into the power of a commoner but of a king, for it is said, 'And he shall cut down the thickets of the forest with iron, and Lebanon [which refers to the Temple] shall fall by a mighty one' (Is. 10:34)."

T.   People say that not a day, two or three passed before a delegation came to him from his city indicating that the [former[Caesar had died and they had voted for him to ascend the throne.

U.   They brought him a [Goldin:] catapult and drew it up against the wall of Jerusalem.

V.   They brought him cedar beams and put them into the catapult, and he struck them against the wall until a breach had been made in it. They brought the head of a pig and put it into the catapult and tossed it toward the limbs that were on the Temple altar.

W.   At that moment Jerusalem was captured.

X.   Rabban Yohanan ben Zakkai was in session and with trembling was looking outward, in the way that Eli had sat and waited: "Lo, Eli sat upon his seat by the wayside watching, for his heart trembled for the ark of God" (1 Sam. 4:13).

Y.   When Rabban Yohanan ben Zakkai heard that Jerusalem had been destroyed and the house of the sanctuary burned in flames, he tore his garments, and his disciples tore their garments, and they wept and cried and mourned.

IV:VI.2 A.   Scripture says, "Open your doors, O Lebanon, that the fire may devour your cedars" (Zech. 11:1).

B.   That verse refers to the high priests who were in the sanctuary [on the day it was burned].

C.   They took their keys in their hands and threw them upward, saying before the Holy One, blessed be he, "Lord of the world, here are your keys which you entrusted to us, for we have not been faithful custodians to carry out the work of the king and to receive support from the table of the king."

IV:VI.3 A.   Abraham, Isaac, and Jacob, and the twelve tribes were weeping, crying, and mourning.

IV:VI.4 A.   Scripture says, "Wail, O cypress tree, for the cedar is fallen, because the glorious ones are spoiled, wail, O you oaks of Bashan, for the strong forest is come down" (Zech. 11:2).

B.   "Wail, O cypress tree, for the cedar is fallen" refers to the house of the sanctuary.

C.   "... because the glorious ones are spoiled" refers to Abraham, Isaac, and Jacob, and the twelve tribes [who were weeping, crying, and mourning].

D.   "... wail, O you oaks of Bashan" refers to Moses, Aaron, and Miriam.

E.   "... for the strong forest is come down" refers to the house of the sanctuary.

F.   "Hark the wailing of the shepherds, for their glory is spoiled" (Zech. 11:3) refers to David and Solomon his son.

G.   "Hark the roaring of young lions, for the thickets of the Jordan are spoiled" (Zech. 11:3) speaks of Elijah and Elisha.

The story unfolds in a smooth way from beginning to end. It serves, overall, as an account of the power of the Torah to lead Israel through historical crises.

Specifically, the story-teller at three points—(1) the comparison of Vespasian and the Jewish troops and Yohanan and the Jewish troops, (2) Vespasian and Yohanan in their director encounter, then at the end, (3) with the destruction itself—places the sage into the scale against the emperor, Israel embodied by the sage against Rome realized in Vespasian. Then the Torah makes the difference, for, in the end, Israel will outweigh Rome. The story's themes all form part of the larger theme of Torah-learning. The centerpiece is Yohanan's knowledge that the Temple is going to be destroyed. This he acquired in two ways. First of all, his observation of the conduct of the Israelite army led him to that conclusion. But, second and more important, his knowledge of the Torah told him the deeper meaning of the event, which was in two parts. The one side had Rome get a new emperor. The other, and counterpart, side had Israel get its program for the period beyond the destruction.

The opening unit of the story, A-T, seems to me seamless. I can point to no element that can have been omitted without seriously damaging the integrity of the story. I see no intrusions of any kind. If that is a correct judgment, then the climax must come only at S, confirmed by T and what follows. That is to say, it is the power of the sage to know the future because of his knowledge of the Torah. Establishing a place for the teaching of disciples and the performance of other holy duties forms a substrate of the same central theme. And yet, deeper still, lies the theme of the counterpart and opposite: Israel and Rome, sage and emperor. That motif occurs, to begin with at A, C, which have Vespasian and Yohanan say precisely the same thing, with one difference. Vespasian calls the Jewish army "idiots," and Yohanan calls the troops, "my sons." Otherwise the statements are the same. And the replies, B, D, are also the same. So the first episode sets the emperor and the sage up as opposites and counterparts.

The second episode has the people unwilling to listen to the sage—the emperor has no role here—leading the sage to conclude that it is time to "make an ark and go to sleep in it." If I had to choose a point of reference, it would be not the sleep of death—then Yohanan would have wanted a bier—but the ark of Noah. Yohanan then forms the counterpart, in the story-teller's choice of the word at hand, to Noah, who will save the world beyond the coming deluge. I would then see F-G as a chapter in a complete story. E, on the one side, and H-J, on the other, link that cogent chapter to the larger context. E prepares us to understand why Vespasian recognizes Yohanan, an important detail, added precisely where it had to come, and H-J form the necessary bridge to what is coming.

The next component of the unitary story again places Vespasian in the balance against Yohanan. Now Yohanan tells Vespasian what is going to happen. Each party rises to power as a direct outcome of the destruction of the Temple: sage vs. emperor, one in the scale against the other. The colloquy with Vespasian, L-S, form the only part of the story to rely upon a narrative consisting of "he said to him... he said to him...." The point, of course, is clear as already stated. Then comes the necessary denouement, in two parts. First, the Temple actually was destroyed; we are told how, T-W, second, Yohanan responded in mourning, X-Y. Here too we have that same counterpart and opposite: Rome, then Israel, with Israel represented by the sage, Rome by the emperor. What follows of course is not narrative, let alone story. IV:VI.2 provides an exegesis A-B, followed by a colloquy. IV:VI.3 is a singleton, and IV:VI.4 joins the destruction of the Temple to the history of Israel and its heroes, all of whom wept as did Yohanan. But I do not see in the inclusion of IV:VI.4 an attempt to compare Yohanan to the named heroes. This is virtually certain, since the story itself at IV:VI.1.X invokes the figure of Eli, who is noteworthy for his omission in IV:VI.4.

What follows is another set of stories about the historical event of the destruction of the Temple. We deal with the victims in the aftermath of the war. These seem to me miscellaneous in character.

XVII:III.1   A.   One time Rabban Yohanan ben Zakkai was walking in the market place. He saw a young girl gathering barley from under the hooves of the cattle of Arabs. He said to her, "My daughter, who are you?"

B.   She kept silent.

C   Again he said to her, "My daughter, who are you?"

D.   She kept silent.

E.   She said to him, "Hold it a minute." Then she covered herself with her hair and sat down before him. She said to him, "My lord, I am the daughter of Naqdimon b. Gurion."

F.   He said to her, "My daughter, what ever became of the wealth of your father's house?"

G.   She said to him, "My lord, is it not an apophthegm in Jerusalem: "[Goldin:] "Money will keep if you don't keep it," and some say, "... if you give charity."

H.   He said to her, "What ever happened to your father-in-law's money?"

I.   She said to him, "My lord, this came and took the other along with it."

J.   At that moment said Rabban Yohanan ben Zakkai to his disciples, "For my entire life I have been reciting this verse of Scripture, 'If you do not know, O you fairest among women, go your way forth by the footsteps of the flock and feed your kids beside the shepherds' tents' (Song 1:8).

K.   "But I never learned what it meant until I came to this day and I have now learned what it means.

L.   "For the Israelites have fallen subject to the most despicable of all nations, and not only to that despicable nation alone, but even to the dung of their cattle."

M.   The girl further said to him, "My lord, do you remember when you inscribed your seal on my marriage-contract?"

N.   He said to her, "Yes I do," and he said to the disciples, "By the Temple service! I inscribed my seal on this girl's marriage-contract, and in it was written the sum of a thousand-thousand golden denars in Tyrian coinage.

O.   "In the time of this girl's father's household they never went from their houses to the house of the sanctuary before woolen rugs were spread out [for them to walk on]."

The appearance of the proof-text accounts for the inclusion of this story, which does not intersect in any direct way with the base-clause. This same theme continues in the sizable anthology on the theme of captive girls of rich families, and that makes it virtually certain that the anthological principle is pointed—the instability of money—and not merely topical—captive Israelite women.

VI:VI.1 A.   Why was he called Sisit Hakkesset?

B.   Because he reclined on a silver couch at the head of all the great men of Israel.

We have nothing more than a gloss of the preceding story, about who was present when Eliezer's father came to disinherit him. What follows glosses the rest.

VI:VIII.1   A.   They tell concerning the daughter of Naqdimon b. Gurion that she had a bed spread worth twelve thousand golden denars.

B.   She spent a Tyrian gold denar from Friday to Friday for [Goldin:] spice puddings.

C.   She was awaiting levirate marriage [and the levir was yet a minor].

No one has mentioned the daughter, but that does not stop the compiler from intruding whatever he has in hand on that uninvited theme.

VI:IX.1 A.   Why was he called Naqdimon ben Gurion?

B.   Because the sun's rays penetrated for his sake [a play on the root NQD which occurs in both the name and in the verb for penetrate through].

C.   [Explaining the reference to the sun's shining for his sake, the following story is told:] One time the Israelites went up to Jerusalem for a pilgrim festival, but they had no water to drink. [Naqdimon b. Gurion] went to an official and said to him, "Lend me twelve wells of water from now until such-and-such a day. If I do not pay you back twelve wells of water, I shall pay you twelve talents of silver," and they agreed on a due date.

D.   When the time came, the official sent word to him, 'send me twelve wells of water or twelve talents of silver."

E.   He said to him, "There is still time today."

F.   The official ridiculed him, saying, "This whole year it has not rained, and now is it going to rain?"

G.   The official went into the bath house, rejoicing.

H.   Naqdimon went to the study house.

I.   He wrapped himself in his cloak and arose to pray, saying before him, "Lord of the world, it is perfectly clear to you that I did not act in my own behalf or in behalf of the house of father. I acted only in your behalf, so that there would be water for the pilgrims."

J.   Forthwith the skies got thick with clouds, and it rained until the twelve wells were filled with water and overflowing.

K.   He sent word to the official, "Pay me the value that I have coming to me from you of the excess water [since I have now returned more water than I took]."

L. He said to him, "The sun has already set, and the excess water now has come into my possession."

M. [Naqdimon] went back into the study house, wrapped himself in his cloak and arose to pray, saying before him, "Lord of the world, do it again for me, just like before."

N. Forthwith the wind blew, the clouds scattered, and the sun shone.

O. He came out and the two met one another. He said, "I know perfectly well that the Holy One, blessed be he, has shaken his world only on your account."

The story on its own right is well composed and cogent, beginning to end. It makes its point through contrasts of details, e.g., G-H, and, in general, gives ample evidence of narrative care. No one has any interest in relating this story to the context of the earlier tales. The story is formed of these elements: C-G, the beginning, which introduces the point of tension: the risk taken by Naqdimon in behalf of the pilgrims. Then at the middle, H-L, the problem deepens. Naqdimon is able to provide the water, but there is more water than is needed, and this the official claims for free. The climax and conclusion produces a second miracle, greater than the first, at M-O. So the story develops in sequences of ascending action, with each point leading to the next and drawing our interest toward what is to come. The net effect is powerful, because every detail contributes to the main point of tension and conflict, and because each component deepens our engagement. There are no easy solutions, and the miracle is truly miraculous.

VI:X.1 A. Why was he called Ben Kalba Sabua [sated dog]?

B. Because whoever came into his house hungry as a dog went out of his house sated.

VI:X.2 A. When Caesar Vespasian came to destroy Jerusalem, the zealots wanted to burn up all of [Ben Kalba Sabua's] goods.

B. Kalba Sabua said to them, "Why do you want to destroy this city and seek to burn up all those goods? Hold up for me until I can go into the house and see what I have in the house."

C. He went in and found he had enough food to feed everybody in Jerusalem for twenty-two years.

D. He immediately gave orders: "Heap it up, sort out the grain, sift and knead and bake and prepare food for twenty-two years for everybody in Jerusalem."

E. But they paid no mind to him.

F. What did the men of Jerusalem do? They brought the loaves of bread and bricked them into the walls and plastered them over with plaster.

VI:X.3 A.   [But ultimately] what did the men of Jerusalem have to do? They boiled straw and ate it.

  B.   And all the Israelites stationed near the walls of Jerusalem said, "Would that someone would give me five dates—I would go down and cut off five heads."

  C.   They would gave him five dates, and he would go off and cut off five heads of Vespasian's troops.

  D.   Vespasian examined the excrement of the population and saw that there was not a trace of grain in it.

  E.   He said to his troops, "If these men, who are eating only straw can come out and kill off [our soldiers], if they had all the food that you are eating and drinking, how much the more so would they be wreaking havoc among you!"

The final gloss of the original story further enriches the materials on the third name on the list. The story, No. 2, is rather strange. It omits crucial details, e.g., an explanation for F. To the story teller, it would appear, the contrast between the action at D-E and the fact at F makes the important point. The story-teller assumes that we know that the zealots burned the stores so as to encourage the resistance, a detail not in hand here. No. 3 presents a secondary development of the story, which yields a very positive picture of the zealots. It seems to me that No. 3 forms a cogent statement, beginning to end. It surely can stand by itself. Still, the two elements—burning the stores, the courage of the starving soldiers—do explain one another, with the former accounting for the conditions of starvation, the latter accounting for the daring do of the Israelite army. It goes without saying that the entire appendix to the original story has no more bearing on the exposition of the saying of Avot than did the stories about Aqiba and Eliezer.

Since Israel's history took on shape and meaning in the conflict with Rome, the equal and opposite force on earth, and since, in that conflict, the sage weighed in against the emperor, events in the life of the sage formed the counterpart to happenings in the life of the emperor: history, so far as in Roman-Byzantine times, people such as Eusebius wrote history. When, therefore, we considered stories of the origins of sages, we took up the counterpart to tales of the origins and rise to power of emperors. And as we turn to death-stories of sages, we take up the sages' counterpart to stories of the great deeds of emperors.

D. The Sage: (4) How the Sage Dies

Two moments in the life of the sage formed the center of interest: origins, meaning, beginnings as a Torah-disciple, and death. The death-stories are told under the aspect of the Torah and serve to show the supernatural power of the Torah to transform even the moment of death into an occasion of Torah-learning. The two points, start and finish, served to define and delineate the middle. How a sage coped with the death of a loved one had to draw into alignment with how a sage studied the Torah; the Torah obviously provided the model of the correct confrontation. How a sage died— the death-scene, with its quiet lessons—likewise presented a model for others. The encounter with death took narrative shape in the account of how the sage accepted comfort:

XIV:IV.1   A.   When the son of Rabban Yohanan ben Zakkai died, his disciples came in to bring him comfort.

B.   R. Eliezer came in and took a seat before him and said to him, "My lord, with your permission, may I say something before you."

C.   He said to him, 'speak."

D.   He said to him, "The first Man had a son who died, and he accepted comfort in his regard. And how do we know that he accepted comfort in his regard?

E.   "As it is said, 'And Adam knew his wife again' (Gen. 4:25). You, too, be comforted."

F.   Said he to him, "Is it not enough for me that I am distressed on my own account, that you should mention to me the distress of the first Man?"

G.   R. Joshua came in and said to him, "My lord, with your permission, may I say something before you."

H.   He said to him, "Speak."

I.   He said to him, "Job had sons and daughters who died, and he accepted comfort in their regard. And how do we know that he accepted comfort in their regard?

J.   "As it is said, 'The Lord gave and the Lord has taken away, blessed be the name of the Lord' (Job 1:21). You too, be comforted."

K.   Said he to him, "Is it not enough for me that I am distressed on my own account, that you should mention to me the distress of the Job?"

L.   R. Yosé came in and took a seat before him and said to him, "My lord, with your permission, may I say something before you."

M.   He said to him, 'speak."

N.   He said to him, "Aaron had two grown-up sons who died on the same day, and he accepted comfort in their regard.

O.   "For it is said, 'And Aaron held his peace' (Lev. 10:3),. and silence means only comfort. You too, be comforted."

P   Said he to him, "Is it not enough for me that I am distressed on my own account, that you should mention to me the distress of Aaron?"

Q.   R. Simeon came in and said to him, "My lord, with your permission, may I say something before you."

R.   He said to him, 'speak."

S.   He said to him, "King David had a son who died, and he accepted comfort in his regard. You too, be comforted. And how do we know that he accepted comfort in his regard?

T.   "As it is said, 'And David comforted Bath Sheba his wife and went in unto her and lay with her and she bore a son and called his name Solomon' (2 Sam. 12:24).. You too, be comforted."

U.   Said he to him, "Is it not enough for me that I am distressed on my own account, that you should mention to me the distress of King David?"

V.   R. Eleazar b. Arakh came in. When he saw him, he said to his servant, "Take my clothes and follow me to the bathhouse [so that I can prepare to accept consolation], for he is a great man and I shall not be able to resist his arguments."

W.   He came in and took a seat before him and said to him, "I shall draw a parable for you. To what may the matter be compared? To the case of a man with whom the king entrusted a treasure. Every day he would weep and cry saying, 'Woe is me, when shall I get complete and final relief from this treasure that has been entrusted to me.'

X.   "You too, my lord, had a son, he recited from the Torah, Prophets and Writings, Mishnah, laws, lore, and has departed from this world without sin. You have reason, therefore, to accept consolation for yourself that you have returned your treasure, entrusted to you, whole and complete."

Y.   He said to him, "R. Eleazar b. Arakh, my son, you have given comfort to me in the right way in which people console one another."

The structure of the story, focussed on the superiority of Eleazar b. Arakh (counterpart to the constructions in The Fathers 2:2ff. built along the same lines), should not obscure its larger sense. The first four disciples, Eliezer, Joshua, Yosé, and Simeon, all invoke biblical models. Scripture is insufficient. Eleazar then presents an argument resting on the Oral Torah: the son had studied the Torah, inclusive of the Mishnah, laws and lore. He departed from this world without sin, so "you have returned the treasure entrusted to you." The written Torah presents a mere set of examples. The oral Torah, by contrast, provides not only the model but also the measure and the meaning. The sequence of names, to which our attention is first attracted, allows the message to be stated with great force, and the climactic statement underlines the power of the Oral Torah to define the appropriate response to the death of the child. The polemic is clear, and, we find, consistent with that of Hillel.

We come now to the stories about the death of a sage, with special reference to Yohanan ben Zakkai and his disciple, Eliezer, the only two death scenes (other than those of martyrs, below) presented in The Fathers According to Rabbi Nathan. Both death-scenes respond to lists of omens pertinent to one's condition at death. In the first, Yohanan's, there is no correspondence at all, since Yohanan is not represented as dying with a serene mind:

XXV:I.1   A.   Ben Azzai says, "Whoever has a serene mind on account of his learning has a good omen for himself, and who does not have a serene mind on account of his learning has a bad omen for himself.

B.   "Whoever has a serene mind on account of his impulse, has a good omen for himself, but [Goldin:] if his mind is distressed because of his impulse, it is a bad sign for him.

C.   "For him with whom the sages are satisfied at the hour of death it is a good sign, and for him with whom sages are not satisfied at the hour of death it is a bad sign.

D.   "For whoever has his face turned upward [at death] it is a good sign, and for whoever has his face turned toward the bed it is a bad sign.

E.   "If one is looking at people, it is a good sign, at the wall, a bad sign.

F.   "If one's face is glistening, it is a good sign, glowering, a bad one."

XXV:II.1   A.   At the time that Rabban Yohanan ben Zakkai was departing from this life, he raised up his voice and wept. His disciples said to him, "Lord, tall pillar, eternal light, mighty hammer, why are you weeping?"

B.   He said to them, "Now am I going to appear before a mortal king, who, should he be angry with me, is angry only in this world, and if he should imprison me, imposes imprisonment only in this world, and if he should put me to death, imposes death only in this world, and not only so, but whom I can appease with words and bribe with money?

C.   "Lo, I am going to appear before the King of kings of kings, the Holy One, blessed be he, who, should he be angry with me, is angry both in this world and in the world to come, whom I cannot appease with words or bribe with me.

D.   "And furthermore, before me are two paths, one to the Garden of Eden, the other to Gehenna, and I do not know on which road, whether I shall be drawn down to Gehenna or whether I shall be brought into the Garden of Eden."

E.   And in this regard it is said, "Before him shall be sentenced all those who go down to the dust, even he who cannot keep his soul alive" (Ps. 22:30).

XXV:II.2   A.   In regard to Moses Scripture says, "And I will take away my hand and you shall see my back, but my face shall not be seen" (Ex. 33:23).

B.   And further, "And he spread it before me and it was written on its face and on its back" (Ez. 2:10).

C.   Its face refers to this world, its back, to the world to come.

D.   Another interpretation: its face refers to the distress of the righteous in this world and the prosperity of the wicked in this world, its back, to the reward given to the righteous in the world to come, and the punishment inflicted on the wicked in Gehenna.

XXV:II.3   A.   "And there was written therein lamentations and jubilant sound and woe" (Ez. 2:10):

B.   Lamentations refers to the penalty inflicted on the wicked in this world, as it is said, "This is the lamentation with which they shall lament, the daughters of the nations shall lament with it" (Ez. 32:16).

C.   "... and jubilant sound and woe refers to the reward of the righteous in the world to come, as it is said, With an instrument of ten strings and with the psaltery, with a jubilant sound on the harp" (Ps. 92:4).

D.   "... and woe": refers to the punishment that is coming to the wicked in the world to come, as it is said, "Calamity shall come upon calamity, and rumor upon rumor" (Ez. 7:26).

XXV:II.4   A.   [Yohanan ben Zakkai] would say, "Clear the house on account of uncleanness and prepare a throne for King Hezekiah of Judah."

The narrative of XXV:II.1 hardly qualifies as a story, since we have little more than a tableau: the setting of the stage, the giving of a speech. Yohanan is dying and "he said to him... he said to him...." The message is very powerful. Yohanan reminds the disciples that the judgment at hand is inexorable and incorruptible, and he does not know the way in which he will now go. The colloquy hardly qualifies as a story, and, when we come to Eliezer's, we see the possibilities for action as a vehicle for the unfolding of the narrative, characterization as a mode of making its point(s), and sustained sequences of exchange—whether word or deed—as the deep structure of the story. The essentially stationary character of the present death-scene is shown at XXV:II.2 3, which form little more than exegeses of Scripture. At XV:II.4, then, we have a further "would say" for Yohanan. These snippets scarcely qualify as a story by any definition.

XXV:III.1   A.   [Ben Azzai] would say, "If one dies in a serene mind, it is a good omen from him, in derangement, it is a bad omen.

B.   "... while speaking, it is a good omen, in silence, a bad omen.

C.   "... in repeating words of the Torah, it is a good omen for him, in the midst of discussing business, it is a bad omen.

D.   "... while doing a religious duty, it is a good omen, while involved with a trivial matter, it is a bad omen.

E.   "... while happy, it is a good omen, while sad, a bad omen.

F.   "... while laughing, a good omen, while weeping, a bad omen.

G.   "... on the eve of the Sabbath, a good omen, at the end of the Sabbath, a bad omen.

H.   "... on the eve of the Day of Atonement a bad omen, at the end of the Day of Atonement a good omen.

After the sizable interruption illustrating the first unit of the sayings, we revert to the completion of Ben Azzai's statement on this theme. A mark of the end of a systematic list is the change in the established pattern, as at H.

XXV:IV.1   A.   When R. Eliezer was dying—they say it was the eve of the Sabbath [Friday afternoon toward dusk]—R. Aqiba and his colleagues came in to see him, and he was dozing in the room, sitting back [Goldin:] on a canopied couch. They took seats in the waiting room. Hyrcanus his son came in to remove his phylacteries [which are worn on week days but not on the Sabbath, about to begin]. But he did not let him do so, and he was weeping.

B.   Hyrcanus went out and said to the sages, "My lords, it appears to me that my father is deranged."

C   [Eliezer] said to him, "My son, I am not the one who is deranged, but you are the one who is deranged. For you have neglected to light the lamp for the Sabbath, on which account you may become liable to death penalty inflicted by heaven, but busied yourself with the matter of the phylacteries, on account of which liability is incurred, at worst, merely on the matter of violating the rules of Sabbath rest."

D.   Since sages saw that he was in full command of his faculties, they came in and took up seats before him, but at a distance of four cubits [as was required, because Eliezer was in a state of ostracism on account of his rejection of the decision of the majority in a disputed case]. [Bringing up the case subject to dispute, so to determine whether he had finally receded to the decision of the majority,] they said to him, "My lord, as to a round cushion, a ball, [a shoe when placed on] a shoe maker's last, an amulet, and phylacteries that have been torn, what is the law as to their being susceptible to uncleanness? [Are they regarded as completed and useful objects, therefore susceptible, or as useless or incomplete and therefore not susceptible?]"

E.   [Maintaining his earlier position,] he said to them, "They remain susceptible to uncleanness, and should they become unclean, immerse them as is [without undoing them, e.g., exposing their contents to the water], and take great pains in these matters, for these represent important laws that were stated to Moses at Sinai."

F.   They persisted in addressed to him questions concerning matters of insusceptibility and susceptibility to uncleanness as well as concerning immersion-pools, saying to him, "My lord, what is the rule on this matter?"

G.   He would say to them, "Clean."

H.   And so he went, giving the answer of susceptible to uncleanness to an object that could become unclean, and insusceptible to one that could not become unclean.

I.   After a while R. Eliezer said to sages, "I am amazed at the disciples of the generation, perhaps they may are liable to the death penalty at the hand of Heaven."

J.   They said to him, "My lord, on what account?"

K.   He said to them, "Because you never came and performed the work of apprenticeship to me."

L.   Then he said to Aqiba b. Joseph, "Aqiba, on what account did you not come before me and serve as apprentice to me?"

M.   He said to him, "My lord, I had no time."

N.   He said to him, "I shall be surprised for you if you die a natural death."

O.   And some say, He said nothing to him, but when R. Eliezer spoke as he did to his disciples, forthwith [Aqiba's] [Goldin:] heart melted within him.

P.   Said to him R. Aqiba, "My lord, how will I die?"

Q.   He said to him, "Aqiba, yours will be the worst."

XXV:IV.2   A.   R. Aqiba entered and took a seat before him and said to him, "My lord, now repeat traditions for me."

B.   He opened a subject and repeated for him three hundred rules concerning the bright spot [to which Lev. 13:1ff. refers in connection with the skin ailment translated as leprosy].

C.   Then R. Eliezer raised his two arms and folded them on his breast and said, "Woe is me for these two arms, which are like two scrolls of Torahs, which now are departing from the world.

D.   "For were all the oceans ink, all the reeds quills, all men scribes, they could not write down what I have learned in Scripture and repeated in Mishnah-traditions, and derived as lessons from my apprenticeship to sages in the session.

E.   "Yet I have taken away from my masters only as much as does a person who dips his finger into the ocean, and I have taken away for my disciples only so much as a paintbrush takes from a paint tube.

F.   "And furthermore, I can repeat three hundred laws on the rule: You shall not permit a sorceress to live."

G.   Some say, "Three thousand."

XXV:IV.3   A.   "But no one ever asked me anything about it, except for Aqiba b. Joseph.

B.   "For one time he said to me, "My lord, teach me how people plant cucumbers and how they pull them up."

C.   "I said something and the entire field was filled with cucumbers."

D.   "He said to me, "My lord, you have taught me how they are planted. Teach me how they are pulled up."

E.   "I said something, and all of the cucumbers assembled in a single place."

XXV:IV.4   A.   Said R. Eleazar b. Azariah to him, "My lord, as to a shoe that is on the shoemaker's list, what is the law? [Is it susceptible to uncleanness, as a useful object, or insusceptible, since it is not fully manufactured and so finished as a useful object?]"

B.   He said to him, "It is insusceptible to uncleanness."

C.   And so he continued giving answers to questions, ruling of an object susceptible to uncleanness that it is susceptible, and of one insusceptible to uncleanness that it is permanently clean, until his soul went forth as he said the word, "Clean."

D.   Then R. Eleazar b. Azariah tore his clothes and wept, going forth and announcing to sages, "My lords, come and see R. Eliezer, for he is not in a state of purity as to the world to come, since his soul went forth with the word pure on his lips."

XXV:IV.5   A.   After the Sabbath R. Aqiba came and found [Eliezer's corpse being conveyed for burial] on the road from Caesarea to Lud. Then he tore his clothes and ripped his hair, and his blood flowed, and he fell to the earth, crying out and weeping, saying, "Woe is me for you, my lord, woe is me, my master, for you have left the entire generation orphaned."

B.   At the row of mourners he commenced [the lament,] saying, "My father, my father, chariot of Israel and its horsemen! I have coins but no expert money-changer to sort them out."

The snippets of death-scenes of Eliezer are sewn together, but the distinct components are fairly easy to recognize, through the repetitions, on the one side, and the shifts in setting and premise as to the location of authorities, on the other. Nonetheless, the flow is smooth, beginning to end, a credit to the compiler. The detail of No. 1 becomes a main point later on, that is, the ruling on objects Eliezer had held subject to uncleanness, sages taking the opposite view. No. 1 moves along to the complaint of Eliezer that the disciples had kept their distance from him. No. 2 picks up at this point, but by introducing Aqiba, suggests that the tale is distinct from the foregoing, which already has him on the scene. The same happens later with Eleazar b. Azariah's paragraph. No. 3 then goes back over the matter of No. 2—the distance of the disciples—and goes over its own point. No. 4 does not appear to know anything about much that has gone before, as I said, and No. 5 is independent as well, since up to now we have had Aqiba at the death scene, while here Aqiba finds out about the death only after the Sabbath and on a different set.

The story serves as a good illustration for three of the positive omens Ben Azzai has listed, while speaking, while repeating words of the Torah, and on the eve of the Sabbath. But he clearly is not represented as happy or cheerful or laughing, so, in the aggregate, I think that an illustration of the omens of Ben Azzai formed a negligible consideration in the mind of the story-tellers. The center of interest of the story is Eliezer's complaint against the disciples, who did not study Torah through service to him. The interplay of Eliezer and Aqiba then forms the centerpiece, with Nos. 1, 2, 3, and 5 placing Aqiba at the heart of matters; Eleazar b. Azariah dominates at No. 4.

The materials form a nuanced and powerful story on their own. Each detail points toward the next, each sequence of action, the one to follow. The master, very much an individual and not a type, leaves a legacy of reproach, a distinctive and particular message. We have slight experience in dealing with sages as distinctive individuals, since stories over all represent them as either symbols on their own—e.g., the sage as against the emperor—or as models of virtues for the many to emulate, e.g., Hillel's patience, Yohanan b. Zakkai's resort to the Torah to cope with the destruction of the Temple. The following is a brief reprise of the same materials:

XIX:II.1   A.   When R. Eliezer fell ill, his disciples came in to see him and took seats before him. They said to him, "Our lord, teach us something."

B.   He said to them, "This is what I shall teach you: go forth and let each take responsibility for the honor owing to his fellow.

C.   "And when you say your prayers, know before whom you are standing up to pray.

D.   "And on account of this teaching, you will gain the merit to enter the world to come."

XIX:III.1   A.   Said R. Eleazar b. Azariah, "There are five things that we learned from R. Eliezer [on that occasion], and we got more pleasure from them than we got from them when he was alive.

B.   "And these are the topics: the rule, as to uncleanness, covering a round cushion, ball, shoe last, amulet, and phylactery that was torn.

C.   [We said to him,] "In these matters concerning which you gave rules for us, what is the law?"

D.   "He said to us, "They are subject to uncleanness, and [should they contract uncleanness] be careful in their regard to immerse them just as is, for these are absolutely firm rulings that were stated to Moses at Mount Sinai."

This seems to me a mere reprise of the foregoing. A different sort of death-scene describes the martyrdom of sages. We have already encountered the following story:

XXXVIII:V.1   A.   A sword comes into the world because of the delaying of justice and perversion of justice, and because of those who teach the Torah not in accord with the law.

XXXVIII:V.2   A.   When they seized Rabban Simeon b. Gamaliel and R. Ishmael on the count of death, Rabban Simeon b. Gamaliel was in session and was perplexed, saying, "Woe is us! For we are put to death like those who profane the Sabbath and worship idols and practice fornication and kill."

C.   Said to him R. Ishmael b. Elisha, "Would it please you if I said something before you?"

D.   He said to him, "Go ahead."

E.   He said to him, "Is it possible that when you were sitting at a banquet, poor folk came and stood at your door, and you did not let them come in and eat?"

F.   He said to him, "By heaven [may I be cursed] if I ever did such a thing! Rather, I set up guards at the gate. When poor folk came along, they would bring them in to me and eat and drink with me and say a blessing for the sake of Heaven."

G.   He said to him, "Is it possible that when you were in session and expounding [the Torah] on the Temple mount and the vast populations of Israelites were in session before you, you took pride in yourself?"

H.   He said to him, "Ishmael my brother, one has to be ready to accept his failing. [That is why I am being put to death, the pride that I felt on such an occasion.]"

I.   They went on appealing to the executioner for grace. This one {Ishmael] said to him, "I am a priest, son of a high priest, kill me first, so that I do not have to witness the death of my companion."

J.   And the other [Simeon] said, "I am the patriarch, son of the patriarch, kill me first, so that I do not have to witness the death of my companion."

K.   He said to him, "Cast lots." They cast lots, and the lot fell on Rabban Simeon b. Gamaliel.

L.   The executioner took the sword and cut off his head.

M.   R. Ishmael b. Elisha took it and held it in his breast and wept and cried out: "Oh holy mouth, oh faithful mouth, oh mouth that brought forth beautiful gems, precious stones and pearls! Who has laid you in the dust, who has filled your mouth with dirt and dust.

N.   "Concerning you Scripture says, 'Awake, O sword, against my shepherd and against the man who is near to me' (Zech. 13:7)."

O.   He had not finished speaking before the executioner took the sword and cut off his head.

P.   Concerning them Scripture says, "My wrath shall wax hot, and I will kill you with the sword, and your wives shall be widows, and your children fatherless" (Ex. 22:23).

The story establishes the tension at the outset: why do we die as do sinners? This question is resolved in the colloquy at C-H, at which act I concludes. The second act has the sages appeal to the executioner to spare the one the sight of the martyrdom of the other, I-L. The third and final component has Ishmael's lament: the mouth that taught the Torah will be avenged. The sage who dies in peace addresses his lessons to the Torah-community: the decline of the great tradition because of the failure of the sages and their disciples. The sage who dies as a martyr teaches a lesson of hope to Israel at large: God will ultimately exact justice of those who sin by persecuting Israel, just as God exacts strict justice even for the peccadillo of pride.

To conclude: the materials we have reviewed, with their beginnings, middles, and endings, their actions whether described or merely implied within verbal exchanges, their tensions and resolutions, follow the pattern familiar within the earlier categories. That positive trait is joined to a negative one. Just as before, so here too, the story about a sage never serves to prove a proposition concerning the meaning of a verse of Scripture. The subject-matter—the sage, hero of the oral Torah, as distinct from the hero of the written Torah—does generate its own narrative literary conventions, that differ from those that guide writers of stories about scriptural figures, and a few remarkably cogent propositions do emerge from stories on sages. To these we now turn.

E. The Propositions of Sage-Stories

We want to know what, if any, points emerge from stories about sages themes and how these propositions (if any) relate to those of stories about scriptural heroes. These are the propositions that emerge in the stories:

1.   VI:V.1: Great Torah-authorities began their study of the Torah in their mature years.
2.   VI:V.1: Patience and persistence in the study of the Torah will guarantee progress in learning.
3.   VI:V.1: Words of the Torah will wear down the heart and produce repentance. It follows that the purpose of study of the Torah is to purify the heart and produce repentance.
4.   VI:V.1: Study of the Torah requires systematic analytical inquiry, explanation of detail in terms of a whole, not merely repetition of what is written down. Aqiba is the model of the analytical mode.
5.   VI:V.2: This is not a story, and its point is already made by the story at hand: patience and persistence wear down the rock.

6.   VI:V.3: This is not a story and it contains no point.

7.   VI:V.4-5+6: People should study even though they are poor. Wives who make it possible for their husbands to study the Torah will be richly rewarded.

8.   VI:VI.1-3: One may begin study of the Torah in mature years.

9.   VI:VI.1-3: A person who gains a bad odor because of devotion to study of the Torah will become famous in the study of the Torah.

10.   VI:VI.4: One who cuts his ties to his family because of devotion to study of the Torah will in the end win out over his siblings and inherit his family's property. More generally: sacrifice in the study of the Torah produces a reward.

Stories on a common theme yield a single message: people may begin study of the Torah at any point in life, and, if they work hard, they will achieve success, riches and fame. If they cut off their ties from their family, they will end up inheriting their family's estate, and if their wives tolerate their long absences and support them and their family, their wives will share in their success, riches, and fame. It follows that the stories on the common theme of the origins of great masters, as preserved in The Fathers According to Rabbi Nathan, address the question of the breakup of the families of mature men who choose to study the Torah and respond by promising success, riches, and fame, for those who in mature years do convert to study of the Torah. The lesson of the origins of the great masters is to give up home and family in favor of the Torah. In conclusion, let me answer the questions with which I began. First, does the subject-matter—sages—generate its own narrative literary conventions, that differ from those that guide writers of stories about scriptural figures? Do we find propositions emerging from stories on sages? The answers to both questions decidedly favor the affirmative. The distinctive narrative conventions make one cogent and critical point.

The next set of stories yield these propositions on how the knowledge of the Torah affects the personality and character of the sage, and so make their own, cogent point:

1.   XV:IV.1 One should be patient even when put to the test. Extraordinary patience is the mark of the great sage.

2.   XV:V.1 The Oral Torah comes down from the ancestors and has to be accepted in good faith, since it is only by tradition that the Torah, written or oral, is to be received and understood.

3.   XV:V.2 The great sage is patient, and through patience and reason wins people to the Torah. The sage who is impatient drives people away from the Torah and deprives them of eternal life.

4.   XII:XIII.1 One who reads the Torah but does not serve as a disciple of the sages does not understand the requirements of the Torah and makes errors which will cost him his life.

5.   XLI:II.1 If one does not spend his time studying the Torah, he is punished by sickness.

6.   XLI:III.1 A sage must treat other people with unfailing respect: one should always be as soft as a reed and not as tough as a cedar.

We may state the point of these stories in a simple sentence. *The sage learns through study of the Torah, which is accomplished solely by service of the master, to be patient and affable and forbearing.*

The stories before us follow diverse patterns, but overall the literary conventions we outlined earlier apply here as well: the story about a sage has a beginning, middle, and end, and the story about a sage also rests not only on verbal exchanges ("he said to him..., he said to him..."), but on (described or implicit) action; the story about a sage unfolds from a point of tension and conflict to a clear resolution and remission of the conflict; the story about a sage rarely invokes a verse of Scripture. These traits assuredly characterize the stories we have reviewed. That means that where a distinct subject comes into view, the narrator of stories about sages will nonetheless follow a fixed set of everywhere applicable narrative conventions. The point of differentiation among stories derives from the contrast between the topic, sage, and the topic, Scripture and its heroes and other topics. Stories are told in one way for the one topical category, in another for the other.

The stories we have reviewed establish the following propositions:

1.   IV:VI.1 The sage had the foresight that would have prevented the destruction of the Temple. All that was required was to give the gentile monarch a sign of submission.

2.   IV:VI.1 The sage had the foresight to know that Vespasian would be made emperor. This he learned through his deep knowledge of the Torah.

3.   VI:IV.1 The sage had the foresight to plan even before the destruction of Jerusalem for the life of Israel afterward. That life would involve study of the Torah by master and disciples, the saying of prayer, and the fulfillment of religious duties.

4.   VI:IV.1 Israel and Rome weigh in the balance against one another, the emperor and the sage.

5.   XVII:III.1 The destruction of the Temple placed Israel under the rule of despicable nations.

6.   VI:IX.1 Divine grace will produce a miracle for someone who takes risks in behalf of the community at large. This is not a Torah-study story and it is not told about a sage.

7. VI:X.2-3: This story is not told about a sage, but it makes a point cogent with sages-stories. The rich man had foresight and showed generosity, but the zealots ruined things.

These propositions yield a simple point: through knowledge of the Torah the sage leads Israel to the age to come, when Israel will supplant Rome. The leadership of zealots on the battlefield led to the destruction of the Temple, the senseless destruction of the food supply of Jerusalem, the calamity that had overtaken Israel. The leadership of the sages, armed with foresight and backed by God, will show the right way. The fresh topic—the sages and history—does not require the invention of modes of narrative different from those that served to deal with the sages' origins, on the one side, and their correct personality and sagacity, on the other. As before, we find the same narrative conventions: the story about a sage has a beginning, middle, and end, and the story about a sage also rests not only on verbal exchanges ("he said to him..., he said to him..."), but on (described or implicit) action; the story about a sage unfolds from a point of tension and conflict to a clear resolution and remission of the conflict; the story about a sage never serves to prove a proposition concerning the meaning of a verse of Scripture.

The lessons imparted by the stories of the next group are these:

1. XIV:IV.1 The oral Torah is the true source of comfort.
2. XXV:II.1 When a sage dies, he appears before an incorruptible judge, and, moreover, he does not know for sure what his fate will be.
3. XXV:III.1-XXV:IV.1-5 The sage dies in full command of his faculties, giving rulings on questions of the Torah, teaching disciples, assured of knowledge of the future by reason of his mastery of the Torah. The sage at death underlines his place in a chain of tradition, having learned from his teachers and handed on to his students knowledge of the Torah. But the tradition progressively diminishes, as the failure of each generation to acquire mastery of the Torah equivalent to that of its predecessor exacts a cost through neglect and forgetfulness of the Torah. The disciples have therefore to bear a heavy burden of guilt for neglect of the Torah that they should acquire from their master, just as he bears that same burden of guilt for not learning what he should have learned from his.
4. XXXVIII:V.2 Sages suffer the death penalty for the sin of pride.
5. XXXVIII:V.2 Sages are martyred but know that, in due course, God will punish those who have sinned against them.

The death-scenes yield a variety of lessons, since they present nuanced, and not merely conventional, portraits, with a measure of action and not merely set-piece speeches. If I had to single out the main point sages wished through the topic at hand to underline, it is God's perfect justice. This emerges at No. 2, 4, and 5, but cannot be excluded even from the story of Eliezer's death, No. 3. The historical events represented by sages' deaths, therefore, are so portrayed as to bring that comfort that is contained within the conviction of divine vengeance for injustice and divine faithfulness in exacting justice on sinners and evil-doers, Israelite and gentile alike. For if the sage is punished for mere pride, there can be no limit to the matter—just as Yohanan b. Zakkai says.

To repeat at the end our standard conclusion: does the subject-matter—sages—generate its own narrative literary conventions, that differ from those that guide writers of stories about scriptural figures? Indeed so. But these conventions apply to all types of stories about sages. Do we find cogent propositions emerging from stories on sages? Yes, we do, and these propositions intersect, whether the story concerns the origin of the sage, his particular sagacity, or his role in the history of Israel.

VII. *The Sage-Story: The Unique Medium of The Fathers According to Rabbi Nathan Text A*

People told stories because they wanted to think about history, and, in their setting, history emerged in an account of what happened, with an implicit message of the meaning of events conveyed in the story as well. They further conceived of the social entity, Israel, as an extended family, children of a single progenitor, Abraham, with his sons, Isaac and Jacob. Consequently, when they told stories, they centered on family history. The sage in the system of The Fathers According to Rabbi Nathan Text A constituted the supernatural father, who replaced the natural one; events in the life of the sage constituted happenings in the history of the family-nation, Israel. History blended with family, and family with Torah-study. So the history of the family, Israel, took place in such events as the origins of the sage, meaning, his beginnings in Torah-study; the sagacity of the sage, the counterpart to what we should call social history; the doings of the sage in great turnings in the family's history, including, especially, the destruction of the Temple, now (presumably after the fiasco of the emperor Julian's aborted plan, in ca. 361, to rebuild the Jerusalem Temple) perceived as final and decisive; and the death of the sage, while engaged in Torah-study. And these form the four classifications of story in our document.

A particular kind of story in The Fathers According to Rabbi Nathan Text A, the sage-story, served a particular purpose, conveying a message that that authorship found best expressed in that medium. Not all narratives, or even all stories, in the document come under that generalization. But all sage-stories that are unique to The Fathers According to Rabbi Nathan Text A in rhetoric and logic, but not in proposition, turn out to carry out a very clear-cut purpose. What that means is simple. Since we may definitively differentiate sage-stories unique to The Fathers According to Rabbi Nathan Text A from sage-stories (and all other narrative) that are not unique to that document, we may say that the set of unique stories locate themselves where they do because they make the statement that authorship wanted to present in just the way that they do.

So the limits of the document do delineate boundaries between one kind of sage-story and another kind, and that result tells us that the documentary statement represents choices concerning the system that the authorship of that document wished to set forth. The authorship of The Fathers According to Rabbi Nathan Text A stood apart from other authorships, certainly not in every detail—they did, after all, adopt for themselves the structure and contents of The Fathers!—but in important aspects of their work, seen all together and all at once. It follows that our authorship has materially participated in the framing of narratives of a particular species and sub-species. If, then, there was a pre-existing corpus of stories, from which our authorship chose some but not others, then one of two conclusions must follow. Either that pre-existing corpus of stories (if there was one) did not encompass the sage-stories unique to The Fathers According to Rabbi Nathan Text A (and that makes us wonder how sizable a pre-existing corpus can have been). Or the other (not-necessarily prior) authorships had access, within that common corpus, to, but did not choose, these particular stories, and only our authorship did. There is, of course, no way of knowing which of these two conclusions is correct. But it hardly matters, for the upshot, either way, is the same. That is, whether the stories were made up by our authorship, or whether they were available but only (in the extant canon) our authorship chose them, the fact is that these particular stories, with their distinctive narrative conventions, represent the taste and judgment of a singular authorship, even though they do not necessarily derive *ab origine* from that authorship. That we cannot show, so do not know.

What then does it mean to know, as we now do know, that a given authorship has made particular choices about how to tell stories of a distinctive narrative character in order to convey a message of a well-crafted quality?

We cannot differentiate the messages of the unique stories from the messages of the shared ones in The Fathers According to Rabbi Nathan. The stories unique to our document bear distinctive traits of intellect and narrative convention but I see no message in them that will have amazed those story-tellers whose work occurs both in The Fathers According to Rabbi Nathan Text A and a variety of other documents. So what is special to our authorship and what is shared among various authorships? The answer yields the positive point. Setting The Fathers According to Rabbi Nathan Text A side by side with The Fathers, we find that our authorship makes a number of important points that the authorship of The Fathers does not make—or even accommodate. And those very same points, fresh to our document, play an important role in those other documents with which our authorship shares striking affinities in its interest in narrative in general, the story in particular: the Yerushalmi and the Bavli and their closest friends. So, over all, there is a correlation between extensive use of narrative, on the one side, and an interest in history, biography, eschatology, the holy society, and related matters.

VIII. *The Narrative as a Documentary Indicator*

If that is the fact, then there is a dimension at which a number of distinct documents, seen whole as well as examined as they may prove differentiated by their large-scale constituents, do intersect. The measure of that dimension is taken in a simple way. I state it as a question: do we perceive commonalities of topic and proposition that link together diverse documents and distinguish one set of writings from another that lacks those same commonalities? If we do, then we may point to those shared propositions and topics as a system of thought that encompasses several documents and draws them together into a single common statement. Certainly we may point to premises common to Yerushalmi, Bavli, The Fathers According to Rabbi Nathan, and related writings, but not explicitly affirmed or implicitly stated in The Mishnah, The Fathers, Tosefta, and associated writings. And the contrary of course is the case. Both sets of premises are accessible of systematic description, and each—I state as a matter of hypothesis—will have required its quite distinctive medium of expression, perhaps also a particularly appropriate mode of cogent discourse as well. The preceding chapter suffices to show out of the materials of Lamentations Rabbah the plausibility of that hypothesis.

The upshot is that as indicated by their narrative preferences as much as by their distinctive traits of rhetoric, topic, and logic of coherent discourse, documents form components of encompassing religious systems, Judaisms (in the terminology I have invented to cope with data such as those under discussion here). Stories make their entry into a Judaism because, along with other genres of writing, they serve an important purpose, one that, in the view of authorships of important writings, cannot have been accomplished so well in any other way. The advent of stories therefore attests, in its own way, to the character of the (complete) system to which the stories give (partial) expression. It is no accident that the authorship of The Fathers did not include narratives in general, and sage-stories in particular, even while that authorship was composing its picture of the formation and transmission of the Torah revealed to Moses at Sinai. And it also is not adventitious that the authorship of The Fathers According to Rabbi Nathan Text A reached a different view of narrative and its power to present its detail of that larger statement that that authorship wished to make.

In so stating, we move across the frontier that separates one document from another and towards that common ground that is shared by two or more authorships: the Judaic system that animates them all. And that is the difference that our improved understanding of the place of the story in the documents before us makes, specifically for the Fathers According to Rabbi Nathan, Lamentations Rabbah, and Song of Songs Rabbah. In seeing each document as in some ways different from, but in others congruent to other documents, we reach that point at which the documentary focus has allowed us to see whatever we are going to perceive within the limits of one piece of writing.

INDEX OF SUBJECTS

INDEX OF ANCIENT SOURCES

THE BRILL REFERENCE LIBRARY

OF

JUDAISM

The Brill Reference Library of Ancient Judaism *presents research on fundamental problems in the study of the authoritative texts, beliefs and practices, events and ideas, of the Judaic religious world from the sixth century B.C.E. to the sixth century C.E. Systematic accounts of principal phenomena, characteristics of Judaic life, works of a theoretical character, accounts of movements and trends, diverse expressions of the faith, new translations and commentaries of classical texts – all will find a place in the* Library.

1. Neusner, Jacob, *The Halakhah. An Encyclopaedia of the Law of Judaism.* 5 Vols. 2000. ISBN 90 04 11617 6 (*set*)
   Vol. I. Between Israel and God. Part A. ISBN 90 04 11611 7
   Vol. II. Between Israel and God. Part B. Transcendent Transactions: Where Heaven and Earth Intersect. ISBN 90 04 11612 5
   Vol. III. Within Israel's Social Order. ISBN 90 04 11613 3
   Vol. IV. Inside the Walls of the Israelite Household. Part A. At the Meeting of Time and Space. ISBN 90 04 11614 1
   Vol. V. Inside the Walls of the Israelite Household. Part B. The Desacralization of the Household. ISBN 90 04 11616 8
2. Basser, Herbert W., *Studies in Exegesis.* Christian Critiques of Jewish Law and Rabbinic Responses 70-300 C.E. 2000. ISBN 90 04 11848 9
3. Neusner, Jacob, *Judaism's Story of Creation.* Scripture, Halakhah, Aggadah. 2000. ISBN 90 04 11899 3
4. Aaron, David H., *Biblical Ambiguities.* Metaphor, Semantics and Divine Imagery. 2001. ISBN 90 04 12032 7
5. Neusner, Jacob, *The Reader's Guide to the Talmud.* 2001. ISBN 90 04 1287 0.
6. Neusner, Jacob, *The Theology of the Halakhah.* 2001. ISBN 90 04 12291 5.
7. Schwartz, Dov, *Faith at the Crossroads.* A Theological Profile of Religious Zionism. Translated by Batya Stein. 2002. ISBN 90 04 12461 6
8. Neusner, Jacob, *The Halakhah: Historical and Religious Perspectives.* 2002. ISBN 90 04 12219 2
9. Neusner, Jacob, *How the Talmud Works.* 2002. ISBN 90 04 12796 8
10. Gruenwald, Ithamar, *Rituals and Ritual Theory in Ancient Israel.* 2003. ISBN 90 04 12627 9
11. Boyarin, Daniel, *Cultural Rabbinic Essays.* 2003. ISBN 90 04 12628 7
12. Strange, James F., (*in preparation for 2003*). ISBN 90 04 12626 0
13. Neusner, Jacob, *The Perfect Torah.* 2003. ISBN 90 04 13033 0
14. Neusner, Jacob, *Rabbinic Narrative. A Documentary Perspective.* Volume One: Forms, Types and Distribution of Narratives in the Mishnah, Tractate Abot and the Tosefta. 2003. ISBN 90 04 13023 3

15. Neusner, Jacob, *Rabbinic Narrative. A Documentary Perspective*. Volume Two: Forms, Types and Distribution of Narratives in Sifra, Sifré to Numbers, and Sifré to Deuteronomy. 2003. ISBN 90 04 13034 9

16. Neusner, Jacob, *Rabbinic Narrative. A Documentary Perspective*. Volume Three: Forms, Types and Distribution of Narratives in Song of Songs Rabbah and Lamentations Rabbah and a Reprise of Fathers According to Rabbi Nathan Text A. 2003. ISBN 90 04 13035 7

17. Neusner, Jacob, *Rabbinic Narrative. A Documentary Perspective*. Volume Four, The Precedent and the Parable in Diachronic View. 2003. ISBN 90 04 13036 5

ISSN 1566-1237